W9-CHD-044

WITHDRAWN

Between History & Poetry

Edited by Donna Krolik Hollenberg

The Letters of H.D. *&* Norman Holmes Pearson

Between History & Poetry

University of Iowa Press ⊔ Iowa City

PS
3507
.O726
Z494
1997

University of Iowa Press, Iowa City 52242
Copyright © 1997 by the University of Iowa Press
All rights reserved
Printed in the United States of America
Design by Richard Hendel
http://www.uiowa.edu/~uipress

No part of this book may be reproduced or used in any form or by any means, electronic
or mechanical, including photocopying and recording, without permission in writing
from the publisher. All reasonable steps have been taken to contact copyright holders of
material used in this book. The publisher would be pleased to make suitable
arrangements with any whom it has not been possible to reach.
Printed on acid-free paper

Library of Congress Cataloging-in-Publication Data
H.D. (Hilda Doolittle), 1886–1961.
Between history and poetry: the letters of H.D. and Norman Holmes
Pearson / edited by Donna Krolik Hollenberg.
p.   cm.
Includes bibliographical references and index.
ISBN 0-87745-595-3
1. H.D. (Hilda Doolittle), 1886–1961—Correspondence.   2. Women
poets, American—20th century—Correspondence.   3. Editors—United
States—Correspondence.   I. Pearson, Norman Holmes, 1909–1975.
II. Hollenberg, Donna Krolik.   III. Title.
PS3507.O726Z494   1997
811'.52—dc21
[B]   97-6855

02 01 00 99 98 97   C   5   4   3   2   1

Page ii, left to right: H.D., Norman Holmes Pearson, and Bryher at Yale, 1956. Courtesy of
the Beinecke Rare Book and Manuscript Library, Yale University.

14300

TO LOUIS H. SILVERSTEIN

CONTENTS

ACKNOWLEDGMENTS

I have had generous support in the editing of this book. Louis H. Silverstein, to whom it is dedicated, worked with me at the beginning, provided moral support throughout, and read a draft of the completed manuscript. He and Monty Montee opened their home to me during many pleasurable visits to the Beinecke Library. My work in progress also benefited greatly from several valuable discussions with Louis L. Martz, a colleague and close friend of Norman Holmes Pearson, and from a long interview with Perdita Schaffner, H.D.'s daughter. Further, I wish to thank Pearson's stepdaughter, Susan Addiss, and his niece, Elizabeth Rice-Smith, for generously granting me interviews, as well as his associates Donald Gallup and Wilda Hammerman. Others who provided valuable information and help include Leo Dolenski, George Heywood, Steve Jones, Jan Miel, Gilbert Li, Robert Spoo, Patricia Willis, Tom Wolfe, and Robin Winks.

I am also very grateful to Adalaide Morris for her careful critique of the whole manuscript in an earlier, longer draft. Special thanks to John Gatta for release time from teaching at a crucial stage, to Ann Charters for help with the preparation of the manuscript, and to my excellent research assistants, Joey Monaco and Allison Hild.

My research was enabled by an H.D. Fellowship at the Beinecke Library and several small grants from the University of Connecticut Research Foundation. An earlier version of one chapter appeared in *Sagetrieb* (Fall 1995). I wish to thank Burton Hatlen for his careful proofing of that material.

Unless otherwise indicated in the notes, the unpublished letters of H.D., Pearson, and others are at the Beinecke Library. Special acknowledgment is made to the Yale Collection of American Literature, Beinecke Rare Book and Manuscript Library, Yale University. I wish also to acknowledge assistance from the Bryn Mawr Library, the Rosenbach Memorial Library, and the Lilly Library of Indiana University.

Publication of Pearson's letters is by permission of Yale University. Previously unpublished letters by H.D. are copyright ©1997 by Perdita Schaffner. Grateful acknowledgment is given to New Directions Publishing Corporation for permission to quote from previously unpublished letters by Ezra Pound, copyright © 1997 by Mary de Rachewiltz and Omar S. Pound, and to Perdita Schaffner for permission to quote from previously unpublished letters by

Bryher, copyright © 1997 by Perdita Schaffner. Grateful acknowledgment is also given to New Directions Publishing Corporation for permission to quote from the following copyrighted works of H.D.: *Trilogy* (copyright © 1973 by Norman Holmes Pearson) and *End to Torment: A Memoir of Ezra Pound* (copyright © 1979 by New Directions Publishing Corporation).

Finally, my deepest gratitude is to my husband, Leonard M. Rubin. For his listening and commenting and proofing and caring, I am more thankful than I can say.

H.D. and Norman Holmes Pearson engaged in a prolonged and wide-ranging relationship that was vital to her development as a writer. Beginning in 1937, when they met, until H.D.'s death, in 1961, they exchanged more than a thousand letters: they wrote about their work in progress, their reading, other writers, friends in the worlds of psychoanalysis and publishing, their travels, their families and personal friends. Their complete letters would fill several volumes. In this selection I have given the highest priority to letters about H.D.'s creative process, her reading, and the publication of her work within the context of their developing friendship. In addition to annotating the selected letters, I have provided commentary summarizing or quoting germane portions of unselected letters to preserve the coherence of the correspondence. Further, because they were often both writing to other members of H.D.'s circle about her manuscripts, I have referred in the commentary and notes to important ancillary correspondences (for example, those between H.D. and Bryher, Marianne Moore, Ezra Pound, and Richard Aldington and between Pearson and Bryher) that elaborate materials touched on in the H.D./Pearson letters. Taken in its entirety, then, this edition documents the dynamic between H.D. and Pearson and anchors it in a broader literary milieu.

Other editorial decisions concern the integrity of the correspondence and the text. I have included all chosen letters by H.D. in their entirety, but have elided passages from Pearson's letters if they are not germane to the focus stated above. These elisions, often more than one paragraph, are indicated by [. . .] at the places in his letters where they occur. I have refrained from correcting the authors' grammar, punctuation, or paragraphing, despite the disparity between their correspondence styles. (I have, however, silently corrected typographical and common spelling errors, leaving only those that are characteristic.) While Pearson's letters usually conform to stylistic conventions, H.D.'s often do not. They give the impression of having been dashed off in medias res. Her use of the comma, in particular, reflects her breathing pattern, and she took short cuts, omitting words and using ampersands and abbreviations. Also, perhaps as a lingering effect of the paper shortage during the war, she often didn't bother to indent paragraphs. Instead, she sometimes indicated a change of subject by leaving a space in her line of type. Since these spaces vary in size they are difficult to reproduce consistently, so I have silently closed them and have indented only when she did.

Other decisions regarding the text are as follows: I have indicated whether a letter (or part of a letter) is typewritten or handwritten by the signs "TS" or "MS." I have standardized the placement of the date and return address, enclosing uncertain dates (and other uncertain words) in square brackets. I have silently deleted words that are crossed out. I have filled in the names of people whose names have been abbreviated the first time these names appear in each letter.

Between History & Poetry

"A Whole Deracinated Epoch"

Hilda Doolittle (H.D.) met Norman Holmes Pearson in 1937 when she visited New York City, during one of the few trips to America she made after going abroad in 1911. Then fifty-one, H.D. was a glamorous expatriate, who divided her life largely between a home in Vevey, Switzerland, built by Bryher,[1] her close woman friend, and a rented flat in Lowndes Square, London. An established writer, she had published five volumes of poetry, including *Collected Poems* (1925), a verse drama, and several works of prose fiction. Pearson, a Yale graduate student, twenty-three years younger, was sent to interview her about the sources of her poetry, by William Rose Benét,[2] a childhood acquaintance of hers who had become influential in American literary circles. H.D.'s beauty and cosmopolitan allure in the mid-thirties are captured by the poet Horace Gregory:[3]

> I remember her most clearly, standing in the lobby of a Shaftesbury Avenue theater, waving me a greeting, with a cigarette in her hand. She was, so I thought, an American Aphrodite, taller and less sensuous than her Greek

ancestress, but with the same powers to attract and charm: she moved with an ease and brilliance that outshone all those who surrounded our small company. . . . In contrast to her, how middle-class, how drab other people looked — how cumbersome and ill at ease they seemed in evening dress: how hopelessly *English*. H.D.'s talk was like her verse, angular and swift, with small rushes of words. Her accent, like Ezra Pound's, was British-American-on-the-Riviera.[4]

Pearson was interested in the sources of H.D.'s poetry in connection with the *Oxford Anthology of American Literature*, which he was coediting with Benét. It was to be a pioneering anthology, one that showcased the work of contemporary American writers as "a second great period of literary creation"[5] for an academic community thus far unenlightened.[6] Perhaps because she was absent from the American scene, H.D. was eager for more contact with American writing, in which she felt a "drive and push" that was missing in Britain.[7] She was pleased to be included. Clearly she was also charmed by Pearson, whose family's roots in colonial New England she shared on her father's side.[8] Her letters show that they discussed these roots at their first meeting, as well as Pearson's poetry and his interest in Cotton Mather[9] and American cultural history.[10] Certainly she appreciated his offer to sort out problems she was having with the publication of her books,[11] for she invited him to return to Kenneth Macpherson's[12] apartment, where she and Bryher were staying, to chat further.

H.D. and Pearson were drawn together by more than their common ancestry, however. They shared the experience of having lived in central Europe in the early thirties. After graduating from Yale in 1932, Pearson had studied at Oxford, England, and in Berlin in 1933,[13] the same year that H.D. began her analysis with Freud in Vienna. Indeed, both recognized the growing threat of Nazism and anticipated a second world war. Pearson had actually heard Hitler speak at a rally. Later, in a letter to William Carlos Williams,[14] he connected his desire to do counterespionage work with that experience:

I had the satisfaction of seeing tangible results to the work that I did; that I had the chance to do something about a situation that I had hated almost from the first time I heard Hitler speak or saw him smugly at a Wagnerian opera. It was on all counts something that I had to do, and therefore I was lucky to be able to do it.[15]

Similarly, H.D. later described "shadows . . . lengthening" and swastikas painted in chalk on the sidewalks, conveying the sense of foreboding that impinged upon her psychoanalytic sessions. "No one brushed these swastikas out," she wrote. "It is not so easy to scrub death-head chalk-marks from a pavement."[16] In a letter to Pearson in 1938, she worried about friends in Vienna, commenting, "Things are much worse than people realise, on the whole."[17]

During World War II, Pearson was based in London with the Office of Strategic Services (OSS), and he and H.D. endured the Blitz together. As their friendship grew, Pearson came to represent "home" to H.D., not only because he was American but because he understood the particular quality of her imaginative response to the repeated disasters in Europe. H.D. began to entrust him with manuscripts in progress (particularly those of *The Gift* and *Trilogy*), and he responded to drafts of her work with great sensitivity and tact. After the war, when Pearson returned home to teach at Yale, his efforts on her behalf expanded. H.D. had suffered an emotional breakdown, was recuperating in Switzerland, and was becoming increasingly isolated. Following her cues, Pearson took a more active role in her work; his signature "C" or "Chevalier," prevalent from this time on, dramatizes his intervention. Gratefully, H.D. often addressed him this way as well, so that the nickname became a repeated gesture of mutual affection.

It is important to distinguish the romantic role-playing between H.D. and Pearson, encoded in the name "Chevalier," from her "romantic thralldom" to other male mentors, a self-destructive psychological dynamic that has been analyzed by many feminist critics.[18] H.D. herself reflects upon the painful ironies of this dynamic in an unpublished journal, "Compassionate Friendship" (1955), in which she lists seven men she calls her "initiators."[19] These include Ezra Pound,[20] Richard Aldington,[21] John Cournos,[22] D. H. Lawrence,[23] Cecil Gray,[24] Kenneth Macpherson, Walter Schmideberg,[25] and Erich Heydt.[26] Most were former friends or lovers, and themselves artists or, in the cases of Schmideberg and Heydt, they were psychoanalysts who, like Freud, helped H.D. understand her relationships with these intimates. Most of these men were also "agents of destruction," as she says of Cournos — that is, her feelings about them were charged with ambivalence. That H.D. omitted Pearson from this list is telling and indicates her appreciation of his championing of her work.

However, the name "chevalier" is not without its own ironies, when viewed as an acknowledgment of a tie between a relatively unnoticed woman poet and an influential male critic in the forties and fifties. It playfully stylizes (and thus subtly distances) the increasingly important part that Pearson played in

H.D.'s life and work. For, as the years passed, Pearson became the only person H.D. consistently allowed into the workshop of her creative process.

After the war, Pearson arranged the publication of *By Avon River*, and he influenced the direction of the cycle of romances that reflected H.D.'s war experience and its parallels in history. When H.D. had difficulty concluding the second of these, "The White Rose and the Red," with the death of its heroine, Elizabeth Siddal Rossetti, Pearson guided her out of the painful European scene and the Pre-Raphaelite period. He suggested that she write a novel about her Moravian ancestors in the eighteenth century, which would bring her back spiritually to America. Most significantly, Pearson enabled H.D.'s return to poetry. It is unlikely that she would have written *Helen in Egypt* without the "mystery" of their attachment. Nor would she have been as informed of the activities of Ezra Pound and of his new works, to which she reacted in *End to Torment* and her late poetry. Also, Pearson positioned H.D. to receive a medal, at the end of her life, from the American Academy of Arts and Letters,[27] the first bestowed upon a woman poet.

H.D. and Pearson exchanged more than a thousand letters. In them H.D. confided details about her work in progress, commented on her reading, and gossiped about members of her literary circle. Pearson's responses sparked the conception of specific works and contributed to the form of others. He often shepherded her work through the publication process, protecting her from the potential sting of rejection and guiding its reception by reviewers and critics. Always alert to what would benefit readers, he elicited various autobiographical notes from her and prompted her to write the retrospective commentary *H.D. by Delia Alton*, in which she explained the purposes, goals, and underlying themes of her work. Indeed, the H.D. archive at Yale, which Pearson established, ensured her manuscripts and letters a future audience.[28] Thus he helped H.D. to engage in a process of literary consolidation that complemented the psychological integration she had sought earlier in her analysis with Freud. Under Pearson's aegis, H.D. came to regard her self and her life as a single emblematic text, a "Legend" that coincided with and transcended the devastation of her war-torn epoch.

In fact, the experience of trauma and recovery was at the root of their friendship from the beginning. For despite her sophistication and accomplishments, in the mid-thirties H.D. felt a lingering sense of vulnerability, a residue of World War I, when she had suffered extensive personal losses. Up until that point, her life had been comfortable, even privileged. She grew up in Bethlehem and Philadelphia, Pennsylvania, in an atmosphere of intellectual and

artistic accomplishment, the daughter of Charles Leander Doolittle, a profes-
sor of astronomy from an old New England family, and Helen Eugenia Wolle
Doolittle, to whose Moravian pietist background she later attributed her spiri-
tual and artistic gifts.[29] She was her father's favorite, the only girl in a family
with five sons.[30] When she entered Bryn Mawr College in 1905, however, the
possibility of female achievement conflicted with inhibiting social conven-
tions. After little more than a year, she dropped out in a turmoil of nervous
exhaustion and academic failure. An engagement to Ezra Pound, who was
instrumental in kindling her desire to be a poet, had occurred at the same
time. Later, a competing attachment to Frances Gregg,[31] another fledgling
woman writer, led her to go abroad with Frances and her mother, to escape
the conflicts around her literary ambition.[32] As H.D. put it later, "I could not
have reached artistic maturity in the America of that day. We had no signposts,
at that time."[33]

In England, after Frances Gregg married, H.D. married Richard Aldington,
and they embarked on a literary life together. The year was 1913. Then came
World War I and the series of losses that destroyed this plan. Between 1915 and
1919, H.D.'s first child was stillborn, her husband enlisted in the army, her
brother Gilbert was killed in battle, and her father died of grief. Her marriage
failed, and she almost died, during her second pregnancy, of the influenza that
reached epidemic proportions at the end of the war.[34] As she wrote later, ex-
plaining the sadness in her early poetry,

> I was married in England in 1913 and then the — the — I call it the Iron
> curtain, a term we all understand. That iron-curtain fell between me and
> my somewhat — well — not hot-house, but in a way, very comfortable
> surroundings — I mean, I had in a way, a very petted and spoiled American
> life — one girl with brothers — [35]

Although she and her second child survived with the help of Bryher, to whom
she was grateful forever, H.D. continued to feel shattered. "Perhaps dispersion
is the key word," she wrote, describing the psychological state of herself and
the members of her artistic community between the wars. "We were dispersed
and scattered after War I."[36]

Despite his relative youth, Pearson had experienced his own share of trauma.
The middle child of Chester Page and Fanny Kittredge Pearson, prominent
citizens of Gardner, Massachusetts,[37] he had been raised in an atmosphere of
love, comfort, and deep-rooted security. However, this ended when he was
seven. During a boisterous romp with his friends, he fell and injured his hip.

The open wound did not heal, but its full import did not become clear until several years later, after he had become increasingly ill. The doctor's diagnosis revealed a crippling and life-threatening bone disease, osteomyelitis. In the pre-antibiotic era, cure was difficult and involved repeated surgery. The only palliatives were fresh air, sunshine, and special care.

Pearson was fortunate in having parents with the resources to provide these. His mother, Fanny, a teacher who loved reading, took Norman and his younger sister, Eleanor, out of school, to Florida for a year, where she tutored them herself. Eleanor remembers endless hours of Norman and Fanny reading all of Dickens's works while she swam and played on the beach.[38] When they returned to Massachusetts, Fanny and Norman continued their reading together. In fact, Norman spent a good deal of his time at home, after school, reading. Literature became his lifeline, as indicated in a favorite anecdote about his childhood. One day, as he sat in a wheelchair at the window in his bedroom, wistfully watching boys outside engaged in vigorous play, his mother came into the room, turned the chair around, and put a book in his hands.[39] Indeed, his affinity with H.D. appeared to replicate that profound emotional nexus, an echo that he acknowledged obliquely in an early letter to her:

> I have felt so often the beauty of our times together and how much they have meant to me. I suppose that it would [be] impossible for anyone else to understand precisely the depth of feeling I mean by this, but for me it was a very rare and beautiful experience touched ever so gently, but electrically, and then the finger brushed away. You asked in one of your letters to me why I did things for H.D. I did them for H.D. in part, and I did them also for H[ilda] in part.[40]

And many years later, Pearson described the way in which his childhood injury and brush with death dramatically altered the course of his life and affected his priorities, including his lifelong commitment to H.D.

> When I was seven years old, when I was fourteen, when I was twenty-one, and when I was twenty-eight I knew in the hospitals that I might easily die on the operating tables. I knew it from the eyes of people about me, I knew it sometimes from what they said to each other or to me. And I was definitively told that each time I became sick in the future it would be more difficult to recover. Life became very precious to me, and increasingly I became aware of how difficult it was for others. I wanted to make life hap-

pier for those others, but on their terms rather than my own, so that by their becoming free I could be all the freer.[41]

In this letter he also mentions his decisions to study literature and history, to join the OSS, and then to return to Yale to teach. Most crucially, he mentions his decision to mentor living writers at the expense of more traditional kinds of scholarship. In fact, the thousands of personal letters he wrote to H.D., Bryher, and others delayed the completion of his edition of Hawthorne's correspondence and also his promotion to full professor.[42]

H.D. was clearly moved and inspired by Pearson's example of prodigious energy and surpassing courage. During the war, in response to a gift from a college friend of Katharine Hathaway's *The Little Locksmith* (1943), the spiritual autobiography of a woman who had been a crippled child, she commented:

> Perhaps a little personal feeling creeps in as our friend Norman Pearson is one of those broken creatures — not nearly like the L-smith, no, *not at all* — but one has that inexpressable feeling of awe and pity at the same time, always aware that one must not SHOW any of one's sympathy. Pearson spent a year about seven years ago — having his bones re-broken and re-set or something of that sort and then he had to learn to walk, etc. all over again.[43] He has a brilliant mind and of course is a strange mixture of super-human courage and . . . well, what? Not pathos — that is too patronizing a word. But all this crept back into my feelings about the L[ocksmith], so am hardly detached from it.[44]

Indeed, H.D. interpreted the exigencies of history increasingly with the help of this man who became her literary adviser, agent, executor, confidant, close friend, and "chevalier." As the years passed, Pearson's mediation enabled her to maintain a psychological equilibrium crucial to her integrity and artistic development.

At the beginning, H.D. expresses gratitude for Pearson's offer of help in a language of emotional fragmentation and drift that she knows he will understand. Referring to her books as "my strange scattered little volumes," she writes, "I have my islands, that kingdom, and no protection for it."[45] And a year later, "it's important to fit in psychic bits of lost continuity."[46] In her first letter, her passionate avowal of the inviolability of the imagination in the face of "the dreary, tragic spectacle of our times" *assumes* his empathy and appreciation. In order to understand the aims of her poetry, she writes, one must "drag in a whole deracinated epoch." One must understand her need to integrate the embattled island of England with the classical islands of Greece and those off the coast of Maine, the lost islands of childhood and memory. Pearson will edit this letter and title it "A Note on Poetry"[47] in his anthology. It begins their correspondence.

———————— 1. TS ————————

French Line
S.S. Normandie[48]
December 12 [1937]
New York City[49]

Dear Norman Pearson.

Glancing at random, over the sheaf of poems you handed me, I fall on "Lethe" and "Song."[50] Those, I know, I wrote in Cornwall, spring-summer, 1918. I turn next to "Fragment Thirty-Six" and "The Islands." Those, definitely, were written at Corfe Castle, Dorset, the year conscription came in, in England — was that 1917?[51] The season was indefinite, rain beat against a high, dormer window in a picturesque cobbled street, under the famous ruins of a castle where a young king — you remember? — was done to death while actually reaching, I believe, for the ceremonial stirrup-cup.[52] I recalled my own Corfe Castle of that period, on seeing listed recently all the Edwards, in a volume dealing with the last. Anyhow, that town was reputably haunted, as was the actual house I stayed in, in Cornwall the following ("Lethe," "Song") year.[53]

Poetry? you ask. I am to say, why I wrote, when I wrote and how I wrote these fragments. I am to state this simply, for people who may not be altogether in sympathy with my own sort of work. I wish I could do that. I am so afraid I can not. But the inner world of imagination, the ivory tower, where poets presumably do live, in memory, does stand stark with the sun-lit isles around it, while battle and din of battle and the whole dreary, tragic spectacle of our times, seems blurred and sodden and not to be recalled, save in moments of repudiation, historical necessity. I had not the power to repudiate, at that time nor to explain. But I do so well remember one shock, a letter from Miss Monroe,[54] timed, nicely to arrive [and] greet me, when I had staggered home, exhausted and half asphyxiated. (I and my companion had been shoved off the pavements, protesting to a special policeman that we would rather be killed on the pavement than suffocated in the underground.)[55] Miss Monroe was one of the first to print and recognize my talent. But how strangely, farcically blind to our predicament! The letter suggested with really staggeringly inept solicitude that H.D. would do so well, maybe, and finally, if she could get into "life," into the rhythm of our time, in touch with events and so on and so on and so on. I don't know what else she said. I was laughing too much.

Ivory Tower?

That was and is still, I believe with many, the final indictment of this sort of poetry.[56]

We don't live. We don't see life. And so on.

In order to speak adequately of my poetry and its aims, I must, you see, drag in a whole deracinated epoc[h]. Perhaps specifically, I might say that the house next door was struck another night. We came home and simply waded through glass, which wind from now unshuttered windows, made the house a barn, an unprotected dug-out. What does that sort of shock do to the mind, the imagination — not solely of myself, but of an epoc[h]? One of the group found some pleasure in the sight of the tilted shelves and the books tumbled on the floor. He gave a decisive football kick with his army boot to the fattest volume.[57] It happened actually to be Browning. He demanded dramatically, "what is the use of all this — now?" To me, *Fortu*[58] and the *yellow melon flower* answered by existing. They were in other space, other dimension, never so clear as at that very moment. The *unexpected isle in the far seas*[59] remained. Remains.

Life?

Poetry?

Times and places?

"Leda" was done at the same time as "Lethe." Lotus-land, all this. It is nostalgia for a lost land. I call it Hellas. I might, psychologically just as well, have listed the Casco Bay islands off the coast of Maine[60] but I called my islands Rhodes, Samos and Cos. They are symbols. And symbolically, the first island of memory was dredged away or lost, like a miniature Atlantis. It was a thickly wooded island in the Lehigh River and believe it or not, was named actually, Calypso's island.

I don't know whether I finally shaped "Lais," "Helen" and "Fragment 113" in London or in Vaud.[61] I was back and forth those years, usually tempering my dash across the continent with a day or so in Paris. There, I saw a few people, picked up a few threads. Those poems belong to 1923–24, roughly. As to the song from the play "Hippolytus Temporizes," that is more difficult. I had made a few rough notes and jotted down a few metres in 1920 in the Ionian island of Corfu. I didn't get the play underway or shaped to my satisfaction till many years later. I think I made a rough outline in Vaud and finally in London (I remember it was a particularly stuffy dank, damp summer) I got the play finished. So the actual song might be dated Corfu, spring 1920 or London summer, 1926. The times of publication of this and the others was naturally different.

This leaves the early group, "O, wind," "Orchard," "Sea Gods," "Oread," "The Pool." I let my pencil run riot, in those early days of my apprenticeship, in an old-fashioned school copy-book — when I could get one. Then I would select from any pages of automatic or pseudo-automatic writing, the few lines that satisfied me. I was doing this anywhere, my first days in a dark London, autumn 1912,[62] then in Italy where I spent that winter, Capri especially, where I had some time and space and found the actual geographical Greece for the first time, Syren isle of the Odyssey. I can not give actual dates to these early finished fragments, but they would be just pre-war and at latest, early-war period. Finished fragments? Yes, I suppose they are that, stylistic slashings, definitely self-conscious, though, as I say, impelled by some inner conflict.

The "lost" world of the classics and the neo-classics is the world of child-hood. "What are the islands to me?"[63] This, I suppose — an inner region of defence, escape, these are the poems of escapism — if there is any such word. And of memory, suppressed memory, maybe. (And what about the mother of the Muses? Mnemosene, if I remember.) Actual memory, repressed memory, desire to escape, desire to create (music), intellectual curiosity, a wish to make real to myself what is most real, the fragrant pages of the early Greek poets, to tear, if it be even the barest fragment of vibrant electric parchment from hands not always worthy to touch, fingers whose sterile "intellectuality" is so often an inverted curse of Midas — these are some of the ingredients of my poetry. Times, places, dates don't seem so much to matter. Yet there are the times and places of these fragments, as well as I can time and place them.

And most dramatically, last Sunday I was called to the telephone. "Your island[s] were on the air," I was informed "and read beautifully." "Where?" I asked. "Radio City, just a few minutes ago," was the answer, "didn't you hear your poem?" No. I did not. I should have liked, in time, in actuality to have heard my "islands on the air," here in this island, to have made that link with those other islands,[64] Calypso's island or catalpa island as some have called it, vanished Atlantis in a river in Pennsylvania, sea-islands off the coast of Maine, Aegean islands sensed in passing and the actual Ionian island of Corfu, the early Capri, Syren island of Magna Graeca, and specifically, that island, noted in Phoenician days for its tin (a track ran past the house where I stayed in

Cornwall, reputedly first used by the mules carrying tin from the mines to the Phoenician galleys) — England. I should like to have heard my "islands on the air," here in this island, the latest in my phantasy of islands, final link and perhaps "clasp of the white necklace."

[no signature]

[MS note in margin] N.B.: Fragment 113-L[ife] and L[etters] [65]

Lais-swarm

NOTES

1. Bryher (Winifred Ellerman, 1894–1983), British historical novelist and philanthropist, met and fell in love with H.D. in 1918, supported her through the trauma of World War I, and later adopted her daughter, Perdita. While both later developed intimate relationships with other people, they remained close friends until H.D.'s death. In 1930–31, Bryher built Kenwin, a Bauhaus-style home in Switzerland, named after herself and Kenneth Macpherson, her husband in name and H.D.'s lover. The three lived together there in a ménage à trois.

2. William Rose Benét (1886–1950), American poet and associate editor of the *Saturday Review of Literature*, which he helped found; author of eight books of poetry, including *The Dust Which Is God*, winner of the Pulitzer Prize in 1942. As children he and H.D. attended the Friends Central School in Philadelphia. He had included her poem "The Islands" in his earlier anthology *Fifty Poets* (Duffield and Green, 1933).

3. Horace Gregory (1898–1982), American poet, professor, translator, biographer, and consulting editor at Grove Press. He first met H.D. in the mid-thirties and became devoted to her work. A friend of Pearson's as well, he was instrumental in the publication of *Bid Me to Live* (1960) and *Helen in Egypt* (1961).

4. Horace Gregory, *The House on Jefferson Street: A Cycle of Memories* (New York: Holt, Rinehart, and Winston, 1971), 226.

5. *The Oxford Anthology of American Literature*, vol. 2, ed. William Rose Benét and Norman Holmes Pearson (New York: Oxford University Press, 1938), 753. The publisher's announcement asserted that it "contains not only the prose and poetry of classic Americans, but also exceptionally generous selections from today's literary leaders. Thus, for the first time, the emphasis has shifted closer to the present."

6. In a letter to Bryher dated 19 December 1938, Pearson wrote that "the present is America's greatest period," because American writers were influencing writers of other nations, an influence denied in academic circles.

7. H.D., quoted by Barbara Guest in *Herself Defined: The Poet H.D. and Her World* (New York: Doubleday, 1984), 236.

8. H.D. traced her father's family back to Abraham Doolittle (1620), whose gravestone in Connecticut she mentions to Pearson in a letter dated 5 February [1938]. Both sides of Pearson's family settled in New England in the late seventeenth century. The family of his mother, Fanny Kittredge Pearson, was particularly distinguished. She was a seventh-

generation descendant of Captain John Kittredge of Lowestoft, England, who settled in Massachusetts in 1660, and the daughter of Russell Herbert Kittredge and Laura Holmes. Her older brother, Alfred Beard Kittredge, was a U.S. senator from South Dakota, and George Lyman Kittredge, the Shakespeare scholar, was a cousin.

9. On 5 February [1938], H.D. mentions the tombstone of her ancestor Abraham Doolittle, which she says is "very (your) Cotton Mather." She also asks about Pearson's poetry, exclaiming, "You never let me see a scrap!"

10. Interested in the connections between literature and cultural history, Pearson studied in the history, arts, and literature program at Yale. A protégé of Stanley Williams, he wrote a long paper in 1935 on Cotton Mather, in which he asserted that Mather's ornamental style needed to be read in relation to his Puritan ethos. Although his dissertation, completed in 1941, was a scholarly edition of *The French and Italian Notebooks* of Nathaniel Hawthorne, which led him to edit Hawthorne's correspondence, he remained interested in Mather. In 1940, he gave a paper on Mather's style at the Modern Language Association meeting.

11. On 14 December [1937], H.D. mentions a problem she had with poems first published by Jonathan Cape (*Heliodora*, 1924) and then reprinted in *Collected Poems* (1925), by Boni and Liveright. Apparently Cape did not send her proofs to correct, as promised in her contract, and the errors were simply reproduced in the later edition. She took the matter to the Society of Authors in London, but after a flurry of letters accomplished nothing, she decided to drop the case.

12. Kenneth Macpherson (1903?–1971), Scottish novelist, editor, and film critic, copublisher of *Close-up*. He was H.D.'s lover and Bryher's husband in name in the twenties and early thirties, when the three lived together in Switzerland. Although he and the two women remained friends, that living arrangement ended in the late thirties. Macpherson rented an apartment on East Sixty-fourth Street in New York, where he lived during World War II.

13. In an early résumé, composed in 1936, Pearson lists the following educational background: Gardner High School, 1927; Philips Academy, 1928; A.B. Yale, 1932; B.A. Oxford, 1934; two semesters at the Institut für Auslander, Berlin, 1933; one concurrent semester at Kaiser Friedrich University, Berlin.

14. William Carlos Williams (1883–1963), American poet and college friend of H.D. and Pound. Pearson began corresponding with Williams in 1937 in connection with the *Oxford Anthology*, and he became the prime mover behind the acquisition of a substantial portion of the poet's papers by the Beinecke Library (hereafter BL).

15. Pearson to William Carlos Williams, 9 January 1946, unpublished letter.

16. H.D., *Tribute to Freud* (New York: Godine, 1974), 59.

17. H.D. to Pearson, 14 April 1938.

18. Rachel Blau DuPlessis described this dynamic first in her essay "Romantic Thralldom in H.D.," *Contemporary Literature* 20, no. 2 (1978).

19. H.D., "Compassionate Friendship," unpublished typescript, BL, 35.

20. Ezra Loomis Pound (1885–1972), American expatriate poet. H.D. first met Pound in 1901 at a Halloween party in suburban Philadelphia, when she was fifteen and he was a freshman at the University of Pennsylvania. Their relationship grew in 1905, when she was a day student at Bryn Mawr. H.D. describes their early romance as well as Pound's continuing importance to her in her diary/memoir *End to Torment*.

21. Richard Aldington (1892–1962), British writer and H.D.'s husband. Their marriage failed during World War I, but despite living separate lives, they did not divorce until 1938. H.D. fictionalized her early relationship with Aldington in several novels, including *Asphodel* and *Bid Me to Live*. A selection of their correspondence has been edited by Caroline Zilboorg, in *Richard Aldington and H.D.: The Early Years in Letters* (1992) and *Richard Aldington and H.D.: The Later Years in Letters* (1995).

22. John Cournos (1881–1966), Russian-born American novelist and translator. He was H.D.'s confidant in London, where he worked for the British Ministry of Intelligence during World War I. Cournos's fiancée, Dorothy Yorke, had an affair with Richard Aldington, an act that contributed to the failure of H.D.'s marriage. For H.D.'s letters to Cournos, see Donna K. Hollenberg, ed., "Art and Ardor in World War One: Selected Letters from H.D. to John Cournos," *Iowa Review* 16, no. 3 (Fall 1986): 126–55.

23. David Herbert (D. H.) Lawrence (1885–1930), poet and novelist, met H.D. and Richard Aldington in 1914 in London through Amy Lowell. In the early years he and H.D. shared their work with each other. Their friendship lapsed after 1918, however, and remained unresolved at Lawrence's death. She described their relationship in several texts, most notably *Bid Me to Live*.

24. Cecil Gray (1895–1951), English composer and music critic. A member of H.D.'s London circle, he was the father of her daughter, Perdita. H.D. fictionalizes him as Vane in *Bid Me to Live*.

25. Walter Schmideberg (1890–1954), Austrian-born psychoanalyst and follower of Freud; married fellow analyst Melitta Klein, the daughter of British analyst Melanie Klein, and moved to London in 1932. With Freud's permission, H.D. underwent further analysis with Schmideberg between 1935 and 1937.

26. Erich Heydt (1920–), resident psychiatrist at Klinik Brunner in Switzerland, where H.D. recuperated from surgery in 1953. He remained a devoted friend until H.D.'s death.

27. When she married Richard Aldington, in 1913, H.D. became a British subject. Pearson was instrumental in her repossession of American citizenship, a prerequisite to this award, in 1958.

28. Susan Stanford Friedman has compared the function of the archive to the private publication of Emily Dickinson's poems in letters and handmade books. *Penelope's Web: Gender, Modernity, H.D.'s Fiction* (Cambridge: Cambridge University Press, 1990), 22.

29. H.D. describes the influence of her parents in *Tribute to Freud* (Boston: Godine, 1974), 31–35, and in her memoir of her Moravian childhood, *The Gift* (New York: New Directions, 1982).

30. H.D.'s mother, Helen, was the second wife of Charles Doolittle. The first, Martha Farrand, died in childbirth, leaving two sons, Alfred and Eric, who were H.D.'s half brothers. Between 1884 and 1894, the Doolittles had four children: Gilbert, Hilda, Harold, and Charles Melvin.

31. Frances Gregg (1885–1941), American expatriate poet and novelist, attended the Philadelphia College of Art. Her poems and early stories were published in *The Dial* and other little magazines in the United States. Later she married Louis Wilkinson and lived in England.

32. H.D. fictionalizes her conflicts during these years in her novel *HERmione* (New York: New Directions, 1981).

33. "Compassionate Friendship," 12.

34. H.D.'s losses during World War I have been documented in many books and articles, and in her own prose fiction, particularly *Asphodel* and *Bid Me to Live*.

35. "Compassionate Friendship," 12.

36. "H.D. by Delia Alton," *Iowa Review* 16, no. 3 (1986): 184.

37. Pearson had an older brother, Alfred, and a younger sister, Eleanor. His father, Chester, was a partner in the Goodnow Pearson Company, a chain of department stores in New England, one of which was located in Gardner, Massachusetts. He was very active in civic affairs and became the first mayor of Gardner in 1922. In 1950, Pearson Boulevard was named in recognition of his contributions to the community.

38. I am grateful to Elizabeth Rice-Smith, Pearson's niece, for giving me this and other helpful information about Norman's early years.

39. I am grateful to Susan Addiss, Pearson's daughter, for telling me this anecdote.

40. Pearson to H.D., 15 November 1938.

41. Pearson to Bryher, 16 October 1961.

42. Pearson's correspondence files at the Beinecke Library are vast. They include large numbers of letters to William Carlos Williams, Ezra Pound, Eugene O'Neill, and many others. In an interview with the author, Professor Louis Martz described Pearson typing these letters as like "someone playing the piano." Under Martz's chairmanship, the Yale Department of English finally recognized the value of this aspect of Pearson's contribution, promoting him to full professor in 1961. In addition to this activity, Pearson did have a distinguished academic career at Yale. He edited the letters of Nathaniel Hawthorne, championed the then fledgling field of American studies, directing Yale's program at the undergraduate and graduate levels, and was faculty adviser to the collection of American literature at the Beinecke Library. (For his activities at the Beinecke, see Donald Gallup, *Pigeons on the Granite* [1988]). He was also a popular teacher. In a vivid eulogy to Pearson, the novelist Tom Wolfe (Yale Ph.D., 1957) compared his graduate seminar in twentieth-century literature to a "journey of exploration," during which students felt the living presence of the writers studied, many of whom Norman knew personally (unpublished MS, possession of Susan Addiss).

43. In a letter to Bryher, 30 October 1938, Pearson described a bone graft operation that had incapacitated him for several months.

44. H.D. to Mary Herr, 8 April [1944], unpublished letter, Bryn Mawr Library (hereafter BML).

45. H.D. to Pearson, 14 December [1937].

46. Ibid., 5 February [1938].

47. For the changes Pearson made, see Diana Collecott, "Memory and Desire: H.D.'s 'A Note on Poetry,'" *Agenda* 25, no. 3/4 (1987/88): 64–70.

48. Although she is writing in New York, H.D. uses ship's stationery.

49. In the typescript the date, mistaken as 1927, and the place appeared at the end of the letter.

50. The second volume of *The Oxford Anthology of American Literature* includes the following poems by H.D.: "Garden," "Orchard," "Sea Gods," "Oread," "The Pool," "Leda," "The Islands," "Sapphic Fragments 36, 113," "Song," "Lethe," "Lais," "Helen," and "Hippolytus Temporizes."

51. The Compulsory Military Service Act received royal assent on 27 January 1916.

52. King Edward the Martyr was murdered at Corfe Geat in 987, and Edward II was imprisoned at Corfe Castle in 1326 but murdered in Berkeley Castle, Gloucestershire.

53. H.D. lived with Cecil Gray at his house in Cornwall (Bosigran) in the spring and summer of 1918. In the houses of Cornwall there were frequent "knockers." The local explanation was that they came from the ghosts of miners long ago trapped in the tin mines below.

54. Harriet Monroe (1860–1936), poet, founded *Poetry: A Magazine of Verse* in 1912 and edited it for twenty-four years. Ezra Pound became the magazine's foreign correspondent with the second issue, and he placed H.D.'s first published poems there in 1913.

55. During both world wars, the stations of the London Underground Railway were used as air-raid shelters. In 1917 Special Policemen were posted to keep order.

56. In his influential *Mythology and the Romantic Imagination* (1937), Douglas Bush comments on H.D.'s debt to the Victorian Hellenists, writing that, unlike them, "H.D. . . . has been mainly content to inhabit the ivory tower which those Hellenists were always breaking out of" (505).

57. H.D. fictionalizes this scene in *Bid Me to Live*, her *roman à clef* about her life during World War I. There, Rafe (Richard Aldington), home on leave, shows off in front of Bella (Dorothy Yorke) at a party during an air raid, by kicking the books across the floor.

58. "Fortu, fortu, my beloved one" is the first line of Robert Browning's "The Englishman in Italy." His "Home-Thoughts, from Abroad" ends: "The buttercups, the little children's dower / — Far brighter than this gaudy melon-flower." Both poems are from his *Dramatic Romances and Lyrics* (1845).

59. Cf. Robert Browning, "Some unsuspected isle in the far seas!" in *Pippa Passes*, part 2.

60. H.D.'s family vacationed there in the summer.

61. During the 1920s H.D. divided her time between London and Montreux, in the Swiss canton of Vaud.

62. Actually, 1911. Her "Autobiographical Notes" indicate that she spent the next winter (1912–13) in Italy — Christmas with her parents in Rome and early spring with Richard Aldington in Capri.

63. From "The Islands," 1290.

64. Here H.D. engages in a linkage of names and places, indicative of her desire, in poetry, to restore a shattered integrity.

65. Though H.D. seems to indicate that "Fragment 113" appeared in *Life and Letters Today*, it was first published in *Hymen* (London: Egoist Press, 1921).

CHAPTER ONE

"New Puritans" in a Civilian War

1941-1946

H.D. was at Kenwin in Switzerland on 3 September 1939, when Britain and France declared war on Germany. Her letters to Silvia Dobson,[1] the young English writer whose farm in Kent would provide sanctuary later in the war, reveal that she had been following the political situation closely. She shared the British people's sense of betrayal when Chamberlain's "peace with honour," promised at Munich, turned out to provide, in her words, "neither peace nor honour."[2] Although urged by Bryher to rejoin her family in America, where she would be safe, she chose to return to London as soon as she could, out of loyalty to her adopted country and its people, who were the first to read her poetry, and out of a sense of conscience and principle that Bryher has called "the Puritan element," an attitude also held by Pearson, who was to use the code name "Puritan" in his OSS activities.[3] H.D. could not leave Switzerland immediately, however, because the trains were full and it was considered "more patriotic" to give travel priority to younger people involved in war work. She did manage to cross in November and remained in her flat in Lowndes Square, where Bryher joined her the following September, for the duration of the war, with only intermittent trips to the English countryside.

In her memoir, *Days of Mars*, Bryher writes that despite the bombing, she found World War II easier to bear than World War I, because the whole citizenry was involved: "there was not the dreadful gap between soldiers and civilians that had caused so much stress in 1914."[4] H.D.'s letters to Marianne Moore[5] and Silvia Dobson indicate that she shared this sentiment, particularly poignant in her case in view of her profound losses during World War I, which she tended to construe as punishment for her personal sins. As Barbara Guest has pointed out, H.D. felt comparatively "morally free" during World War II.[6] In fact, as the Luftwaffe began its air attack on Britain in August 1940 and bombs rained down on London, setting the city aflame, her letters reveal relief and even exhilaration at being able to withstand the "constant hammering."[7] In September 1940, she writes to Marianne Moore: "Every new morning is like a return from a bout of fever . . . and strangely I, personally, and others who have been able to stick it, seem to feel more alive and physically stronger than for years." She admires the "heroic power here and wonderful miraculous courage, in simple people, the 'unknown warrior' that Mr. Churchill speaks of."[8]

Later letters, however, also convey the strain under which she was living, and the resulting emotional roller coaster. H.D.'s exhilaration at being alive alternates with overt fear of death, exacerbated by worry about the safety of her daughter, Perdita, who drove a volunteer food canteen amid the bombing. In October 1940, she writes to Moore, who promoted her literary interests in America: "Death becomes the one important idea — and that idea is so familiar — I just didn't want to leave things untidy."[9] Moreover, as the bombing continued into winter, she felt the cumulative effect of inevitable deprivations and restrictions. In an undated letter to Silvia Dobson, deduced to have been written during 1940–41, she complained of "terrible face-aches," which she attributed to "neuralgia or nerves from the blitz," writing: "I was (I am) so cold — numb and can't seem to manage pen or machine."[10]

Yet despite these shocks and deprivations, H.D. continued to write; indeed, the effect of the war years was cathartic. Not only did she complete her Moravian memoir, a group of short stories, the poems collected in "What Do I

Love?", and her tributes to Freud and Shakespeare, but she also achieved a breakthrough in poetic form with the composition of the three long poems that Pearson would later title *Trilogy*. The cumulative stress and accomplishment are reflected in a letter to Mary Herr,[11] a former classmate from Bryn Mawr, with whom H.D. kept in touch sporadically. On 8 February [1944], H.D. writes: "I have never worked so hard as in the past few years — a terrific creative urge that, I suppose, is a sort of 'escapism' but a cerebral drug, too that has kept me sane and alive — the writing is crazy, if you will — but has acted as a sort of safety valve."[12]

While H.D. endured the shock of collapsing buildings and the nightly roar of anti-aircraft gunfire at the beginning of the war, Pearson was finishing his doctoral dissertation and preparing to get married. (He received his Ph.D. from Yale University in 1941 and married the same year.) Although his career as a scholar and teacher seemed promising — he had already edited two books and taught at the University of Colorado and Yale — the war cast its shadow on him as well. Uncertainty about America's role affected college enrollments, and it was unclear whether junior faculty would be rehired. When America did enter the war in 1942, Pearson wanted very much to serve, but he was prevented from enlisting by his physical handicap. Anxious to participate, in the fall of 1942, Pearson wrote a series of letters to English departments around the country to find out what they were doing to assist in the war effort. According to Robin Winks, such interventionist activity brought him to the attention of others at Yale and on the outside who were engaged in the OSS. With his Yale pedigree and Oxford connections, he seemed the perfect candidate for overseas service.[13]

For Pearson the invitation to join the OSS in a research/administrative capacity offered a perfect opportunity to see action in the war, thus preventing him from being sidelined. As he wrote to his mother, he had "felt the inevitability of war ever since [he] lived abroad," and this was "the only kind of draft" to which he could respond. Now he could help get "the boil over with so that peace might be established" by doing a job "of very real importance."[14] Moreover, the years abroad with the OSS provided a personal turning point. He excelled at his assignments, becoming the head of X-2, the cryptonym for the counter-intelligence branch in London. There was no question in his mind, then, that he could succeed in life outside of academe, despite his physical disability, should he so choose. As he told an interviewer at Yale in 1950, after he had returned to teaching: "I had to do this because I wanted to find out if I could really make a décision between teaching and the outside world. Had I gone into teaching to escape life?"[15]

<hr>

2. TS

Nov. 19 [1941]

Dear Norman,

So much has happened since we met, so long ago, in Kenneth's rooms. I feel 20 years older and about 50 years younger, old values return . . . there is NOTHING to say about what we have been through. Mercifully, we are all right. My daughter[16] is in the country, using her languages on war-work, fortunately as I was weak with worry during the blitz and fires when she was driving a mobile canteen for firemen and pioneer workers. I do hope you will all be spared anything of "our" sort of thing, during 1942. I was greatly touched to hear of your marriage[17] and I know you must realize, though I did not write, how happy I am, not only for you but for Mrs. Pearson and the two children who are so blessed in having a young father and a big brother, combined. I know it must be difficult for you to write, but a line would be so appreciated. Forgive this silly card! We are rather run out here in suitable greeting cards, as you can see! However the busy-bee is always seasonable. Bryher frets sometimes, as she spent so much of her time on the continent, but she is very good and adaptable and spends a full day in shopping and helping with the house; even a small place like mine is a one time job now. What are you writing? Forgive all the mistakes, I always wanted to write you fully and tell you how happy I am about your life, and here is this last-minute greeting — post to USA must go out by November 20th. Please remember me to Wm. B[enét] if you see him. I WILL hope to write you sometime. This with all thoughts to you and your 3, from

Hilda (Aldington)

From Pearson's arrival in London on 12 May 1943, until his return to America in the summer of 1945, he and H.D. experienced a particularly intense phase of their relationship. In addition to seeing each other regularly for Sunday dinner, they attended poetry readings, lectures, and parties together, and exchanged fifty letters. In the midst of the stress and frustration of dingy, bombed-out London, when mutual support was necessary for psychological survival, Pearson quickly became one of the "Lowndes Square group," according to Bryher, who pays special tribute in her war memoir to his energy and fortitude. Other members of the group included Bryher, Perdita, the Sitwells, Silvia Dobson and her family, the Hendersons, Robert Herring, and George Plank, names that occur frequently in the letters.

"New Puritans" in a Civilian War, 1941–1946

In her essay "Running," Perdita remembers Pearson's role in their lives during the war as intermediary between H.D. and Bryher, who felt trapped because they were thrown together in close quarters for the first time, with no escape except separate vacations to the countryside.[18] In a sense Pearson took over this role from Kenneth Macpherson, who had emigrated to America, breaking up the earlier family unit. In addition to helping Perdita find work in the London office of the OSS, which brought her closer to her two mothers, Pearson became the confidant and catalyst of both H.D. and Bryher, giving them focus and someone to write for who was both interested and responsive. With his encouragement, Bryher began her major work as a historical novelist, writing one novel after another, and H.D., whose work in the thirties was largely unpublished, began a process of revision and renewal that was significantly enhanced by Pearson's interest in collecting her early drafts for a future "shelf" at Yale, which was itself an implicit testament to her poetry's lasting importance.

It is clear from these letters in 1943 and 1944, that H.D. and Pearson, both far from home in a time of crisis, were drawn together as much by their sense of a shared colonial American background as by a love of literature: there are several references to a joint "'racial' heritage" in the letters. Perhaps this sense of common roots gave H.D. the courage to show Pearson her unpublished work, as well as to confide in him specific literary interests and concerns. For example, H.D. must have discussed with him a concern about the dearth of women poets in literary history who could serve as role models. For, in an unselected letter, dated 23 May 1943, Pearson describes an old review by Charles Kingsley of Shelley and Byron he has just read, and comments that it was full "of masculine Christianity and how the great poets were all GENTLEMEN."

Most important, as H.D. began to trust Pearson's responses to the manuscripts she showed him, especially to her Moravian memoir, *The Gift*, and to her watershed poem, *The Walls Do Not Fall*, she came to rely on his judgment, feeling that he could understand the philosophical underpinning of her work better than most people. Pearson's correspondence with his mother during 1943 provides insight into the basis of this affinity. He describes the semireligious zeal he feels about the American role in the war, a viewpoint that dovetails with H.D.'s vision of the redemptive role of the artist in *The Walls Do Not Fall*. Describing a Thanksgiving church service at Westminster Abbey that "opened with the clergy and choir marching down the church with an American flag at their head," Pearson muses on what "our Pilgrim fathers" would have thought, concluding that they would not have been very surprised: "They used to feel they were a chosen race, whose strength and example could save England. We're not saving England now; she has saved herself; but it's a joint affair, and I doubt if either one could have done the job alone."[19]

So great was H.D.'s confidence in Pearson's reading of her work that she would ask him to write the jacket copy for *The Walls Do Not Fall*, for its publication by Oxford University

Press. She was also guided by his response to *Tribute to the Angels* to the extent that she wrote a third poem, *The Flowering of the Rod*, at his suggestion, to complete what they both came to think of as her "war trilogy," which he thought was an important contribution to "civilian war literature" that also included works by Edith Sitwell, Eugene O'Neill, Joyce, Eliot, and Thornton Wilder. Indeed, although the relationship between the characters Mary and the mage Kaspar in this last poem is based on H.D.'s therapeutic relationship with Freud, about which she had just written in the memoir *Writing on the Wall*, the poem's dedication to Pearson acknowledges his important supplementary role in the speaker's resurrection.

Not mentioned in the letters to Pearson, however, except for an offhanded reference to having invited Arthur [Bhaduri] for a drink in a note in October 1943, is H.D.'s growing fascination with spiritualism. H.D. had met Bhaduri in 1941 and participated in regular séances with him and his mother, May Bhaduri, during the war years. Although Pearson probably knew about H.D.'s activities, as well as about her fixation on Lord Hugh Dowding, the British air force commander who believed that he could communicate through mediums with dead airmen, the omission of any substantial references to these people and activities suggests that he was dismissive of them. Later, however, when H.D. was trying to publish her "occult" fiction based on these experiences (*The Sword Went Out to Sea*), he was supportive.

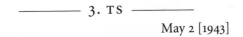

3. TS

May 2 [1943]

Dear Norman,

I would have come flying around to "sit" with you the other day over your lunch, but was nursing the tooth which I had taken out the day after — and like Bill Benét, I now feel vastly rejuvenated though for a very different reason. We have a tiny room downstairs where we could put you up, if at any time, you were at a loose end. We have kept it rather secret, just for a few pals — Mrs. Compton Mackenzie[20] was so happy there that we had (much as we liked her) more or less to prod her out, as we have another friend from the country to whom we had promised it . . . but there is no one now and as I say, just I F it happened that you were at a loose end, there is bed and breakfast for you. I wish you had been here if only for a minute, so that you could visualize a home from home, right here and now, and for all time in the heart of London. We are on the 4th floor — USA 5th floor — and weathered the Blitz in a miraculous manner. We had such fun at the Reading of "Famous Poets"[21] (I ask you) that we forgot the war for a whole week and now I have got into a happy frame of mind and want to go on forgetting it — four years is too long! However, actually, we have been miraculously preserved — Bryher has been a wonder with her good deeds and constant care; she knows all the people in the neighbourhood and when I go out with her, it is positively embarrassing as her progress is one triumphal procession. Someone's teeth here, someone's gout there, someone's baby there, someone's son in the near-east somewhere else — we have shaken down into a cozy small-town and I do so look forward to your joining our village group. Which wife is this — of Benét's?[22] I was sorry not to have met the brother and grieved when I heard over the radio of his death[23] — so soon following that of Laurence Binyon[24] whose death left a strange gap in our reading. I look forward to introducing you or presenting you to some of our friends — they have heard of you of course, already. Robert Herring,[25] the Sitwells,[26] two delightful dames, called Ivy Compton-Burnet[t] and Margaret Jourdain,[27] Elizabeth Bowen,[28] the novelist of whom we are very fond, and so on. I am glad you are working in a garden — I must get away now soon for a short time, as have been here without even a weekend since September. We have such a haven in Cornwall,[29] a great farm or manor house, where you too would be welcome, but the trip is now impossible.

[MS] Well, God bless you — and let us know how you are — with love from Bryher and

Hilda

———— 4. TS ————

c/o American Embassy
Grosvenor Square
14 May 1943

Dear Hilda:

I still purr like a cat with its contented tongue in a bowl of cream, when I remember my pleasure in at last seeing you and Bryher again. It was a good noontime! We shall extend them.

My list of your books, which I enclose, is I am afraid really of not very much help. I jotted down the titles of those I had on one of those hectic last nights in New Haven, when I expected each evening to be leaving the next day. It was done simply to remind me of what I had, and therefore what I should like to get. I shall write Susan to take off from the book I mentioned the more complete list — though one or two of the items I have he had not seen. It will take months to get back here on this side, but it should be of some help. Actually you ought to note down where each poem first appeared, and when. It's most important in terms of copyrights etc., and if one hasn't done it a devil rises in every later situation of permissions. Perhaps we can dabble at it together. I hope you won't mind this pawing over your literary body. It's only pride and admiration of all you've achieved that makes me anxious to see a full knowledge of it preserved.

Ah, these new warm days have brought a new life to me! The may is in full flower, and their white sprinkled over the countryside green gives a bridal effect to the world. Maybe it's a marriage to hope we can now celebrate, after the splendid mutual effort in Tunisia.[30] Shall we all join hands — we sluga-beds, and go a-maying?

The sheep have gone from the park outside our gate, and I miss cocking my elbows on the rail to watch them. Do you recall Hulme's "The moon leaned over the fence like a ruddy-faced farmer, and the stars twinkled in the skies like the pale faces of city children?"[31] I've got it wrong, trusting to a bad memory; but I'm beginning to be a moon instead of a star, I think in these un-warlike beginnings of the year.

Since moons exist only on reflected light, you and Bryher must be my suns.

Love,

Norman

Hippolytus Temporizes (Boston)

Hedgehog (London)

Palimpsest (Boston)

Choruses from Iphigenia (London) Another edition: Cleveland

Collected Poems (6th edition, N.Y.)

Heliodora (London)

Kora (London)

The Usual Star (London)

The Tribute and Circe (Cleveland)

Red Roses from [sic] *Bronze* (N.Y.)

Hymen (N.Y.)

Ion (Boston)

Sea Garden (London)[32]

─────── 5. TS ───────

May 15 [1943]

Dear Norman,

I who don't write letters much (unlike Br[yher]) must write you because there is a sort of "brook and river meet" feeling and I am afraid to let it lapse — I mean I really AM, for the first time in my long life (56 remember)

trying to READ my own books, at least make a list of them — and started to put book plates in my own books, then had to read them, so your list coming with that of Buffalo library have made me turn over a new leaf. I am afraid I have been very slack in the past about answering these University letters — must now make an effort, in fact I feel that my own mad effort to bridge the gap in years and oceans is probably a symbol of what is going on in a big way with the "english-speaking." Have been doing "home work" as I call it to Br, with anthologies. . . . Well, your list. You have left out HEDYLUS,[33] we may have an odd copy somewhere — There was American Caravan II.[34] I had copy in Switzerland but not here — a rather long prose bit and there are American Miscellany bits, 1923, 1925 and 1927.[35] I am really deeply grateful to you for your "this pawing over your literary body" and will be glad for the list that Susan (lovely name) may copy out, but don't nag her with it. I have a strange feeling that I may be going to USA as soon as possible, once war is over — am making a sort of amateurish effort to collect letters from publishers etc. that might be of value, myself being a sort of literary liaison officer of English-speaking people — in a vague general way, but between ourselves strictly CON-FIDENTIAL, there are people sent over from time to time, semi-officially, in that sort of capacity, really not half as useful nor knowledgeable (spell.) as H.D. I mention this, as a note from you, no matter how informal (and of course in no way binding) might possibly be helpful — that is IF. Osbert Sit-well was extremely interested and thought my idea very purposeful from both sides of English-speaking world. However . . . more of this later, we have so much to say to one another. I will jot down the Doolittles just for a joke for you, on separate page — the amount of hunting I had, to find it . . . as I say by way of a joke and also to show that you and I must have, racially much in common . . . the temperamental, emotional, I take for granted. I wish for one year, I could watch the seasons come and go — this is not a very bad begin-ning to a bad poem — I mean, just in their order — that alone would make a year in the USA worth everything to me. I mean Robert Frost WINTER[36] . . . *and* the other seasons in tidy rotation! I do feel we are working together — and more of all this later and much love

from

Hilda

Abraham Doolittle		1620	Abigale Moss
Samuel	"	1665	Mary Cornwall
Jonathan	"	1689	Rebecca Ranny
Samuel	"	1729	Elizabeth Hubbard

"New Puritans" in a Civilian War, 1941–1946

Samuel	"	1752	Anne Arnold
Willard	"	1782	Piany Roberts
Charles	"	1813	Celia Sanger
Charles	"	1843	Helen Wolle
H.D. – 1886			

──────── 6. TS ────────

Flat 10

49 Lowndes Square

London S.W. 1

August 9, Monday [1943]

Dear Norman,

I am posting you *Times* — I do not want it again. Also, a MSS copy of THE GIFT, which might amuse you to pick over while I am away. I am sorry it is such an untidy copy, have one clean copy here but had not time to correct it. Houghton Mifflin have copy in Boston but as Chapter 4 and Chapter 7 were badly cut about by censor, and the point of the whole story lost, I asked them to hold it with a book of poems they have, till later.[37] I do not think they are any too keen, anyhow — but I had to get it off my chest so sent over, air-mail, single chapters . . . so there is that copy anyhow. I usually destroy originals but find I have my first rough typed copy (I work direct on machine) and would be glad to hand it over to you for your collection, later, if you want it. *The Gift* is a thing I have worked at, off and on, for 20 years — but it only finally snapped into shape after I had scrapped all early efforts, during the bad raids, when I began this final copy, and it had to be worked out through the minds of the children or the child. I am sorry the paper is so bad and the copy so dim — don't bother with it, I will do the fresh one if you bring me this on my return, but it occurred to me this morning that you might understand a few things in it, as hardly anyone can or will. I will write you but may not have type-writer — but will let you know how things are. One of the Dobsons is due up early to-morrow morning and she is going to get my few bags to the station for me. @ Miss Silvia Dobson

Woodhall

Shipbourne

Kent

is the address — have I already given it to you?

It is difficult to write you to thank you for coming in on Saturday. Yes, I did rest much better. I suppose there has been a deep unconscious strain, all the time, really, being in a "foreign" country. I feel much happier already about Bryher and I need not repeat my feelings about Perdita. Please don't over-do things. I wish I had talked more about YOU the other night. But we will meet again before very long. You will take care of yourself? This is only to explain the MSS and is not really a letter — not the letter, I mean, that I would have it. Please, please do keep well.

Love
from
Hilda

———— 7. TS ————

25 August 1943

Dear Hilda:

Willy-nilly, get to the office or not this morning, I *must* write you the letter I've begun at least six times since you left. I occasionally pride myself that I've become orderly in this civil service life of mine, but this is all ostentation. The truth is that I run from one thing to another like a frantic mouse. I leave safe cheese only nibbled at to run to trapped cheese for another toothful. I slip from the spring catch with only a hair from my nostril lost, scurry back down my hole, and sleep long enough to begin the whole mad circuit over again. The scraps of paper bearing the rubric of a letter to you are to be found all over London.

I'm happy that our evening leaves a satisfying memory with you. It was an act of brutality on my part. I was sure it was right; but then I was not sure. You know how such things are. One acts forthrightly enough, but the reminiscence: then comes the question, should I have, was it too violent?

The Gift was a gift which I shall cherish and am cherishing. I am in it now, and hugely satisfied with it. Of course I should like the first rough draft if you still have it. Is it queer, greedy, like a small boy at Lord's waiting outside the tea pavilion with his autograph book for the square-leg to come out?

I know a young man in America who lives and breathes your poetry. I've seen and taught numberless starved schoolteachers from the middle-west to whom your work means bread and wine. I simply want there to be in America the materials for those who someday will want to write about a fellow-American. I want to be able to give access to the tiny things, out-of-the-way things for those who want and need tiny and out of the way things. Perhaps it isn't really necessary that they should have these at all; but, in analogy, I think the first thing *I'd* give to the starving people of Europe would be sweets and wine; *then* food. Isn't America still a little on the starved side. This is all rather clumsy, but you will catch its attempt.

Perdita is working in splendidly.[38] The girls are hugely fond of her, and I admire the ease with which she has stepped into a new situation and caught up a new kind of work. Now she proceeds like an old hand. I do not hover over her, like a clucking hen over its chickens. She may miss the cluck, but she's better without it. And really she doesn't need it. I hope she'll like the work. I, certainly, feel lucky to have her with us.

Monday I saw two of the old Mysteries performed in the ruins of St. Dunstan's, in Idol Lane, off Great Tower Street. Incendiaries stripped the church bare, left it like an empty tomb. I was reminded of Fountains Abbey or Tintern, . . . the green fields surrounding the Cistercian ruins being replaced by city lanes and smoked stone business blocks. The altar was the stage, the plays "The Creation" from the Towneley Cycle, and "The Deluge" from the Chester Cycle. A deluge for us too; will there also be a new creation?

London is full of surprises like this noontime performance. I saw "Mrs. Noah" scuttling up the street after the show. I called out congratulations to her. "Thanks," she said. "Forgive me, I've got to get back to the office."

So have I.

> Love,
> Norman

———— 8. MS ————

> Woodhall
> Shipbourne
> Kent
> Thurs., Aug. 26 [1943]

Dearest Norman:

Just to thank you for your good letter. I am sorry about the other six. Perhaps it is as well I did not get them. One seems to shed a skin or husk, once in so often — a biological process — in fact, the whole race has got to slough-off, out of it — the past, I mean — and this "new creation" is already on us — here one, here another, glued to their rocks, isolated or "insulated," as I said of myself the other evening. If two such transitional beings meet and can not clutch at each other across the abyss, then life ends, all life! I suppose the thing is with Bryher, for instance, that she *knows*; she sympathizes with the "latter-day twice-born" (as I call them or us, in one of my new poems) but is

"New Puritans" in a Civilian War, 1941–1946

frightened as *my* going-on, means that she must slide back, stay stuck or go on herself. It is easier to stay stuck, and in her unconscious cosmic terror, she drags me back out of my element — that element depends on such really simple things, space, quiet, not too many outside impinging personalities! But *that* I was not allowed . . . maybe, a "test," a trial of endurance — such as is put on dedicated novices in any vocation. Well! "Brutality" is hardly the word is it? There is no brutality in a star-fish, though perhaps there is brutality in the over-whelming forces of the element it comes from.

I am due back early in the week & will give you a ring — there is a veritable plague of birthdays, Bryher's, Edith Sitwell's (she is coming to town, too) mine! Things will settle & much has been settled by your exquisite gesture to Perdita. We will meet & there will be much to say. Till then

love

from

Hilda

P.S. About the "out-of-the-way things" — I will do my best. "Nights" by John Helforth that you saw on the shelf was never circulated.[39] It represented a rather, lost, sad period (maybe about 1932) & I did not want to look back — later, I will hope to be more casual and tough altogether!

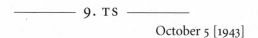 9. TS

October 5 [1943]

Dear Norman,

The old string and paper returns with some new sealing-wax, it need not be opened, it is the first very untidy script of *The Gift* — I have left it as it was — do not seem to be able to get on with the Notes and Appendix until this is out of the house. Br[yher] has come back and I am sure we are going to be less claustra-phobic this winter, no matter what happens outside or inside . . . things ARE so much better. Br says she hopes to be at the Belge place in good time for the talks, 2, is it? Anyhow, if you miss (though I may be there late) Hesther[40] will be on the prowl.

This in untidy haste —

[MS] with love

H.

Office of Strategic Services
United States of America
American Embassy
London
Wednesday morning
[6 October 1943]

Dear Hilda:

I feel oh so very righteous (PURITAN), having got up early, finished my breakfast, and done a spot of work, even before time for the office. You're right of course in saying I'M all Puritan. As for yourself I think you're *part* Puritan. And a lot more besides. But that part which is Puritan affects everything else, is never quite shaken off, is a strength to you as well as . . . a frustration if one imagines it never exists. I suppose we all have it somehow or other, regardless of birthplace. You, I, Bryher, and George Plank.[41] I'm sorry about him. Would he like a letter from me, if "home" means so much to him now?

I fear I won't be able to attend L'Institut Belge, tho my curiosity drives me to see how such things are managed, and my personal pleasure urges me to take any opportunity of seeing you and Bryher. However, this has been a hectic week, and I am slipping off to Cambridge this weekend to pay my long-postponed visit to the Trevelyans at Trinity.[42] Will it seem odd to be back in a university milieu again I wonder?

Were you ever wrong about where quotations came from? You have a memory. I possess only a sense of reminiscence.

Tell Bryher that if anyone was to beat me to Huxley's copy of Sachy Sitwell's little book on Dr. Donne,[43] I'm glad it was she.

Love,
Norman

[undated]

Dear Norman,

Thank you so much for your letter. I will send you this to-day, or start this to-day and if "continued," will send on more to-morrow. But I want first to thank you for coming along yesterday. We had not been going to the Grill for some time, but went there again yesterday and we like it again — our poor little Speranza is now on the down-grade, they all have their ups and downs. So won't you, just as soon as you can, just dash in and have lunch with us at

Grill or with me alone, if Br[yher] is busy at office? *It is a thing you do not think of* — I mean the fact that YOU give US so much — just the sound of your voice brings back so much. It's difficult to talk of this — and maybe I am a bit shy, as my bed-side talks with George were rather sad and forced — and weren't from my angle, REAL. But you do not know how terribly home-sick one is — YOU can not know. Well, now here we come to the poems [44] — and this is not a bad point. There is here this desperate cry for "home." This "home" does not exist we all know, except in imagination yet it DOES exist. The "rivers" are bridged over and cursed at, but they are "my" rivers and "sweet Thames flow softly" [45] too is mine and yours — and all the English-speaking's or the world's. ("Shakespeare is not our poet but the world's"). [46] And was it Goethe said, "another language is another soul?" Anyhow, another river is — but we must find our own river first — rivers of paradise or what you will. And here we have in XXIII, a "gem," in Japanese or early H.D. manner — but exact. I do not want to pick out gems or be a "clear-cut crystal". That catch-phrase is easy for journalists. A seed is not a crystal — and if my mustard-seed has grown too high and spread too many branches, that is a pity for the critic, that is a pity for H.D. fans (few and far between though they are — but you wrote me, for instance, of some boy in the west). But that is it, for the boy in the west, you said, we must give candy and sweets, rather than bread — wine rather than water. Yes. Yes. I agree there. But for us, starved, suffocated — flung from our raft on the beleaguered rock — "this England" — or the rock of latter-day falsity and laisser-aller, the between-wars, I mean — for us, clinging maybe still to our raft or lost in the desert — for us, water and "baked fish" — you will find the "baked fish" in XXIX. [47] That is how it is — and too, in the very midst of the "fifty thousand incidents" of the actual Blitz, there is that last desperate re-valuation or final valuation. I mean, here "long ago," two years ago, we do not know if we live to tell the tale, but we still cling to our standards — to this, I mean, our PROFESSION. Now here it is, very stark and written at the last — a sort of vindication of the writer, of the "scribe" — as VIII for instance, that was really "tapped out" in a sort of exhilaration of rage at the stupidity of someone who had written me from USA — and I do not blame them at all — someone who did not know and could not, what we were doing, how we had moreover been waiting for this to happen for years and years before it happened — some nice and kind and perceptive person, who remarked, apropos of a not-very-good poet and of some not-very-good-poems, that after all, it did seem strange to think of anyone troubling to try to express world-issues now, it was really so "pathetic." It was the word "pathetic," the sort of patting-on-the-head, the suave patronizing manner — that got me. Pathetic? O, yes, and now here, the serpent rears its head and it's a nice fanged little head with plenty of venom concealed . . . and it is hissing and coiling about, I think stirred to hiss a few words, a "few last words," maybe in defense of its "brood." Writers? Pathetic? "Yes — of course," it hisses but do you know that the "writer" is the original rune-maker, the majic-maker [sic], his words are sacred — that is what it is. You speak of a second-rate writer — but you just be careful — the second-rate may become first-rate — and anyhow — well, it is there in VIII, hissing its way to the end and its terse statement that the scribe "stands second only to the Pharoah" or what it really means, "stands second only to God" — the Pharoah actually being imbued with god-attributes.

———

But it was an English girl who made me still madder — with a letter to B[ryher] at *L[ife] and L[etters]* questioning the status of the poet, the writer in the future world-reconstruction — that is the "non-utilitarian" touch in the same VIII. (I am sorry to make this so long — I had to write you this way. This is Monday and I was called away from my desk. Where are we?) The parallel between ancient Egypt and "ancient" London is obvious — in I, one, the "fallen roof leaves the sealed room open to the air" is of course true of our own house of life — outer violence touching the deepest hidden sub-conscious terrors etc. and we see so much of our past "on show," as it were "another sliced wall where poor utensils show like rare objects in a museum." Egypt? London? Mystery, majic — that I have found in London! The mystery of death, first and last — stressed in XL, XLI, XLII, Osiris being the spirit of the under-world, the sun under the world, the setting-sun, the end — implicit there always the idea of the sun-rise — and above all the ever-startling miracle of the breath of life —

> where heat breaks and cracks
> the sand-waste,
> you are a mist
> of snow: white, little flowers.

Then the end XLIII.

Osbert seemed to like the way they were written, he wrote Br. to the effect that H.D. had neatly set traps, that snapped shut with the inevitable and unexpected idea or *mot* at the end. (Those are not his exact words.) But I liked O. liking them and I think he really did — he it was, who wrote Sir H[umphrey] M[ilford],[48] I told you.

I think IX is very neat, on re-reading.

XXX, XXXI, XXXXI may seem rather long — but oddly, XXXI, XXXII actually did tap-off all in one — rather startled me to just write all that in one fell swoop and made no changes, save for ordinary tidying-up — it rather startled me, so I let the thing stand — it is a bit larger "trap," I suppose, for a larger, bulkier animal — but it does snap-shut neatly — with (XXXII) "you find all this?"

Well, Norman — this long letter is too bad — I suppose this book is "philosophy." Now I start, I could go on . . . but please realize that I appreciate your interest. "Protection for the scribe" seems to be the leit-motif. And the feeling of assurance back of it of the presence of the God of the Scribe, — Thoth, Hermes, Ancient-of-Days, Ancient Wisdom, *AMEN*. And exactly the explicit place of the scribe in the mysteries of all-time — his "job" as "householder," XXXVI, his exact place in the sequence, in the pattern, again his "job," the keeping-track of the "treasures" which contain *for every scribe who is instructed, things new and old*.

I am sorry this is an un-even copy, but all the pages are there. O. still has a copy and Sir H., and one is in Boston and I have just a very-rough one.

———

I note this too on re-reading. I like the "winged head-dress" touch — it links Egypt with Aztec and with our own Indians. Do come and talk about rivers! I find the Delaware was first called Zuydt, South River by the Dutch, then Swenska, Swedes River by Swedes — then Lord de la Ware forced his claim and the river and the Lenape "roaming along its course" were named Delaware.[49] The Delaware, the river of the Lenape, was the *Lenape-wihittuck* & its branch, the Lehigh (where I was born) was *where there are forks* or *Lechauweeki*, shortened into *Lecha*, corrupted into *Lehigh*. And so on. There is endless exciting discovery to be made along these lines — don't you think? [50] Anyhow, thank you again so much. I will post this and send on the MSS later, as I must tidy-up my old pages for your more-or-less straight copy.

[MS] Much love (and greetings too from Br.)

Hilda

———— 12. MS ————

November 23, 1943

Hilda, my dear:

You will have thought I had forgotten the words for the new book. Never, never! What do you think of the attached. It is less than 150 words counted one way — more, or just about, if you reckon the necessary space for quoting. I like quotation; I like to let poetry speak for itself — once the way has been indicated, the introduction given.

I cannot find myself writing "H.D.'s is one of the rare voices of our time," "Admirers of H.D. will welcome . . . ," — these things are all true. Let the readers have the joy of re-discovering for themselves. For this *is* a book. You and Edith have it — the poetry of this war in England I mean.[51] The only really fine war play I've read (not published yet) is by another civilian, Eugene O'Neill.[52] But this civilian war literature is no paradox. Perhaps one must have the leisure for agony — not "leisure" as we think of it in terms of a quiet evening, a fire, a glass of wine, *but the leisure for activity in resolving the unresolved equations, of shaping* the base, for baking the bread to eat, of blending the tarragon with the vinegar.

At any rate will these lines suffice?[53] I shall not feel hurt if they are too late, or too brief, or on the wrong track. I think, if you like them, Sir Humphrey can space the words on the flap properly.

Love, Norman

———— 13. TS ————

February 24 [1944]

Dear Norman,

I hear from Sir H[umphrey] this morning. He says the New York Branch would like to bring out an American edition of the WALLS. He suggests 10% royalty on the American price. I think this must be all right — I will write him at any rate, to go ahead, unless you telephone to the contrary. I can't thank you enough for your help and the blurb is wonderful — faces me now on my desk!

————

Was interrupted here — and I wish I had not been as it has been bomb-bomb-bomb story all morning. I feel so dreadfully — but can't do very much. THAT one went into a row of houses or work-men's flats in Chelsea in the King's Road, really not so very far away. However tomorrow is another day — I don't quite yet know what to-day is. I do want to thank you for the blurb again — it does look wonderful. Please give us a ring if you have a moment. The sun is so beautiful and we must hope for a little calm to-night — but I was glad to show you our Christmas tree stars! They were blue and white the last time, it may be the atmosphere or they may string on different bulbs just to keep the party going. Please remember that an isolated pop or two after the "big show" is a few left-overs being emptied from guns before re-loading. It happens sometime in the day-time, it does not mean there is a waif-or-stray overhead — but of course, we don't know from time to time what may be happening. This is not the letter I started to write you but maybe I will have time for another when the atmosphere clears. We did so love having you here last night!

[MS] Ever

H.

———— 14. TS ————

May 21 [1944]

[no salutation]

Sunday — no Whit Monday. It seems like Sunday, dear N[orman], but Perdita's arrival just after lunch has excited and upset the usual programme. She IS so happy and I can never thank you enough for all you did for her and for us. She wanted news of you at once. We hear marvelous accounts of the T.S. E[liot] lecture — you must ring us up or ring her or both. She will be spending the days here and sleeping across the way, I expect. We will expect you Sunday as usual, if not sooner.

I have got the MSS stuffed into an envelope and will hope to register it to you tomorrow. I had quote from O[liver] W[endell] Holmes and could not verify it — it is page 55, I think.[54] Will you, if you get time to read the MSS, let me know of anything that should be altered or omitted. I believe *Life and Letters* is setting up some of it.[55] I do thank you, dear Norman for your help and interest. This is in a terrific rush between bouts of making ice-cream and hearing all about ALL.

Love

H.

In *Days of Mars*, Bryher describes 1944 as a year of "problems and disasters," in that although the preparations for the Allied invasion of Normandy, on 6 June, filled the English with hope, they also had to endure the "buzz bombs" and "doodlebugs" (rockets) that fell on London shortly after. Those who could headed for the countryside, as did Bryher and H.D., who writes to Pearson from Cornwall during the summer of 1944, in the following exchange. Getting H.D. to leave the city was not easy, however. Bryher reports that she refused to go until 20 July, out of loyalty to the city dwellers who had to stick it out. When they finally did get to Cornwall, Bryher wrote to Pearson, both women were "glued to the radio," and H.D. "fretted constantly about London in general."[56] H.D. was very elated when Paris was liberated in August, as her letter to Pearson on 20 August indicates. In an ancillary letter to Silvia Dobson, she adds: "the LIBERATION means so much to me and to Br[yher] — though to me especially, as it was to France I first went from USA before I saw England."[57] In the following exchange (cf. 31 August), Pearson responds to the strain as well as to the elation associated with the anticipation and aftermath of D-Day, when, in responding to the manuscript of "Tribute to the Angels," which was composed in the latter half of May, he cautions H.D. that what she has characterized as "victory or peace" poems are really "relief" poems, advising her to write "a third set." Her grateful response, asking if he has "any inspirational ideas" for the third part, indicates their closeness, and the degree to which she has admitted him into the workshop of her creative process.

———— 15. TS ————

24 July 1944

Dear Hilda:

I enclose a letter from the Oxford Press in the States confirming the fact that they are bringing out an edition of your book there — in fact it is probably already out by the time we've had the news. I hope you understand the reference to the additional poems. You will remember we discussed whether or not the volume might not be too thin for an American publisher who isn't too worried about paper, or at least not so worried as we are here. You suggested that they might use the additional poems in the series, but I put it as though I might persuade you, in order to give you a chance to change your mind if you wished to. I also enclose an original draft of a letter back, from which they might quote if they wished to. You'll see it follows the line of the blurb here. If three days for the public was a week less than the fact it won't worry anyone there. Three is such a good round number.

I walked by Lowndes Square tonight on my way home and found everything in order, at least when I looked at it from the James Russell Lowell side: Things are much as usual here. The queen's rooster cackles, the hens cluck of a morning, and with every dawn the birds sing in the tree at the end of the mews. I think often of you both. Do you milk cows, stroke ponies on the back, and pick berries? Do you lie in the sun and chew blades of grass? Ah me, yours are the fresh salad days!

Love,

Norman

Trenoweth

St. Keverne

Cornwall

July 27 [1944]

Dear Norman:

Thank you for *all*! I am asking Br[yher] to add a line to this as I feel so doped & light-headed with fresh air, wind-in-trees, red-admiral butterflies, honey (literally) in the honey-comb, oats-and-wheat in a field that sent me crazy in the wind yesterday, making patterns & circles, never to be recorded, like wind racing across golden snow-drifts; *hard* paths, defined originally *on dit* by the mules from the Phoenician ships, taking tin from the hills . . . well, that feeling of *certainty* when a path runs into & cuts through a grain field, that one can assuredly set foot on it — it is like the Red Sea parting with the grain-oats & wheat or *corn* mixing & making a music . . . notes . . . those little stalks whispering & cluttering . . . ? — do I mean that? I have been sick at heart at leaving "me palz" in bomb-alley: Mr. Goodhand, the superintendant, wrote that one was a "near-miss" . . . I must forget it for a little while. I know you would love it here. Now Br brings an envelope, so I will push this off at once with hers —

Again, *thank* you & I leave the matter to you; you have been so helpful & it is better, I think that the peace poem (not yet christened) has a hearing later.[58]

More later

and best love

from,

Hilda

Trenoweth

St. Keverne

Cornwall

July 31 [1944]

Dear Norman:

Again, in more normal mood, thank you for your letter and help re *The Walls*. Do you think a line as from you to Sir H[umphrey] M[ilford] indicated? I will write saying I have heard indirectly that Mr. Pearson has been in direct touch with them and has kept me posted. If indicated, drop him a line that I will keep it vague so you need not be bothered if too busy. You know his address — but to be certain: Sir H. M.

> Ox[ford] U[niversity] Press
> Southfield House
> Hill Top Road
> Oxford.

The weather has been shy — at least, the sun is only out for glimpses. But I am still wallowing in the *quiet*. I have my "Puritan" conscience out of its cupboard & it is making me feel wretched & "guilty" at leaving you all there in bomb-alley. But my hostess might come from another planet & I swallow and rage when she says "don't such a *very* small proportion get to London." So I am pretending to myself — a new charade — that I do not know what doodle-bug means! Perhaps it is better to cultivate a bland detachment . . . because 2 and 2 does *not*, (however you may focus it) make 4 in this island!

I am posting you 2 *Times Litts.* later. I have hidden Br[yher]'s cigarettes for her until she gets down to the dregs of her old lot. It is a gargantuan supply . . . writing at my dressing-table and still start alert at nothing-out-of-the-window, wondering what the QUIET is concealing! It lies like a green blanket soaked in some anodine . . . I feel I may be "coming out" of it at any moment now!

We get lurid and beautiful P.C.s from Perdita (Cezanne and Van Gogh) so I judge the Medici book-&-picture shop is O.K.

I have broken off to write Sir H. M. — I mentioned you as intermediary between N[ew] Y[ork] and H.D. — said I had asked you to write if indicated . . . to H. M., I mean! Said you had been so "kind and helpful" re blurb etc.

Now, this must be off. . . . I presume we stay a month all told — possibly, the week-end extra. We arrived here July 20th. Br. goes Eckington[59] for a bit often . . . but I can't plan so far ahead. In any case, we will hope to see you between trips.

Thanks again and love

> from
> Hilda

Trenoweth
St. Keverne
Cornwall
August 6 [1944]

Dear Norman,

Thank you for paper which will be enjoyed and posted on later to someone also appreciative. I am amused to get down to the bed-rock of the matter of "The jewel in the Lotus" folder! At least, old Merrill[60] brought that back to us . . . and now here is another, please do NOT return! It is quite good in its obvious way; he sent the paper marked. I sent you a "Cornish Litany"; I trust it keeps away the "things." Good Lord, indeed, deliver us! I was walking along alone to meet the others at Godrivy, the rocky low-tide sand crag, where we bathe, the other morning. There were tall hedges growing along the top of the irregular stone-wall either side and as I went through this with no one and nothing in sight, along the twisting narrow road, there was SUCH a THING as never could have been imagined. If it had been night, I could have sworn in a law court that I had at last encountered one of the true-blue Cornish Ghoulies, at long last. As it was, I SAW with my eyes what could scarcely be believed . . . the THING was yowling and howling, and it flew across the high hedge and down the stone wall and the yowl and the howl got worse as it landed at me feet. There was a clanking of chains . . . all this in day-light. . . . Good Lord deliver us. Or rather Good Lord deliver IT . . . for it was a long-legged beastie, a CAT that had caught its hind-leg in some sort of elaborate trap with maws and jaws and trailing odds and ends and the long chain clattering . . . Gosh! What to do now. My whole day — not to mention my whole life would have been ruined if I had let the cat go, howling as it was with pain and mental — yes, mental — agony. Well, I knew I could not touch it, it would scratch like a panther — so I, fortunately being a long-legged beastie myself, chased it up the narrow lane, called and coaxed and when it crouched in the wayside grass for a minute to take a final howling leap, I stepped on the length of chain . . . there we were. I knew I must stand there until someone came . . . and at last a child came on a bike but she was not able to help with any suggestion but like a darling, said she would go off and get "help." Well, while she was gone along comes a larger child on another bike, a girl of about 16, I should think, complete with post-man cap and jacket — so I accosted her. She hopped off her bike and in a most professional manner set her heel on a spring somewhere and off went the poor beastie, on ALL its legs . . . so I have felt better ever since. But it does go to show what a "ghost-story" can grow up out of (grow up out of? That sounds suspiciously Pennsylvania Dutch to me.) Well, thank you. Do for the Good Lord's sake and ours, take care of yourself. Greet old P[erdita] if indicated. I sent her a Litany — would one help Ezra?[61]

———

We are still having a heavenly time. I know you would love it here. I think all the time of my poor old pals . . . I feel your Alice is one of them, we get so very mate-y over the telephone.

Much love,

Hilda

[MS] Thank you so much for writing Sir H[umphrey] M[ilford] — & for all that!

——————— 19. TS ———————

Trenoweth

St. Keverne

Cornwall

Aug. 20 [1944]

Norman dear,

I thought the enclosed might amuse, via Chatto.[62] Will you keep it and return it IN PERSON and advise me, re said same. Br[yher] and I now start to make plans. We say we will hope to be back in from 7 to 10 days but having made that clear to ourselves, we may stay on the extra week. I got very home-sick and frustrated, but feel better now — it comes and goes — I think the news in France is more than I can sanely bear — here, it is just part of the war, a "good show" . . . but to me it is the liberating of something very, very personal — it may be our old deep-rooted Lafayette-complex that has over-taken me. I am sure, actually, that the USA part of London, is far more deeply moved and excited than the true-blue Anglo-Britains.

I am reading a marvelous book, *The American War of Independence* — can you believe it? It is written by Lt. Gen. Sir George Macmunn KCB DSO and is a revelation . . . it is a throw-out from review books sent to *L[ife]* and *L[etters]* way back in '39.[63] I can not tell you how much I enjoyed this history of the "American Rebellion." He claims that it was a hang-over of the British Civil Wars "come to roost" in New England. That it was really one of the 7 wars with France, with the tea-party used by agitators, as the greased cartridges were in India. I was so dumb that I had to ask Br[yher] about the cartridges . . .

well, it is anyhow a refresher and what I don't know about the "thirteen fortunate children" who would do nothing to aid "the parent country" won't be worth knowing!

I can't tell you how dreadfully I have worried about you all there . . . the contrast here is almost too great at times, to be endured. But I am soaking up sun and meeting more cats — a white one with a Persian ancestor followed up to, and from the beach where we bathe, yesterday. If it had been dark, he would certainly have been a "beastie"; as it was, he had stepped daintily out of a Madame Perriot (or who was she?) French fairy-tale[64] . . . he ran ahead or ran back occasionally to do a ballet-leap at a butterfly — otherwise, his pace was most demure.

This is not to remind you that you owe me a letter. I have just written Marya G[regory][65] saying that no matter HOW many letters N.P. owed them, it is THEY who should write him . . . so for once you see, I practice what I preach.

> [MS] Love
> from
> Hilda

———— 20. TS ————

31 August 1944

Dear Hilda:

I can't let this no-letter-writing on my part go on any longer, and though I came back to the office again tonight to work as usual, I won't begin until I've at least started my long-overdue letter to you. So long is it overdue that I blush. I blush with all the crimson of a late-summer rose; I blush because of my discourtesy; I blush for chagrin at the letters from you I've missed because there were none from me to answer.

But it does me, has done me, wonderful good to know that you and Bryher have been basking in the sun, and now Perdita with you. She slipped away from the office before I knew she had gone — Bryher's letter to me was the first notice I had. Which is a kind of proof, if proof you need, that I have been busy.

As to the letter from your admirer [it] is a little naive and the writer doesn't have much to hint that he'd be amusing. But he might be refreshing, or at any rate you would be refreshing to him. Would you like me to drop him a note and say that you're in the country and won't be back for some time, but that I'll let him know when you do. Then you can either have him to tea, or see him at my place if you don't want him actually to know your address. Personally I do think it's rather nice to find these admiring strangers popping into view. It's good to know that there are distant sensibilities which vibrate.

I'm pleased to see copies of the new printing of the WALLS in the bookstores, though doubt if they will be there long. I had a note from the Oxford Press in New York saying that they liked my blurb for their ads, and no doubt it will appear. Have you had notice of its publication yet?

Did I tell you that I sent a copy of the WALLS to John Gould Fletcher,[66] whose several letters to me during the past year or so I haven't answered except in this way. He seemed most keen about your "new style and point of view," and found the poem on pages 13–15 "important and very fine in its own way." I was pleased he liked it. Poor John has the move-on again, has leased out his house in Little Rock, and is fleeing back to New York for the winter. No doubt it will be a good thing for him. He hopes to earn some money by doing reviewing. I hope they let him have a chance.

I've been reading the new mss with terrific enthusiasm and do think you've hit a very fine stride. The tone is right and the feeling is as sure as ever. I wonder if I'm correct however in feeling glad that they came after the WALLS and that they now had probably better wait until a third set can complete what is so very much a war trilogy. These are "relief" poems, not quite either victory or peace poems. What I should suggest is waiting until your final part of the trilogy is ready, then perhaps reprinting the WALLS with these two extra parts added to it. Or is that too much like the *Quartets* of Eliot[67] or Ezra's *Cantos*,[68] as far as scope goes. I don't think so. I feel that's the way poetry goes now, inevitably and rightly. But, my dear H.D., what real warmth of pleasure it gives me to feel this new burst of poetry. I am writing this from the office or I should comment in more detail. I rather like, however, this bringing back of general impression.

The noise has come and gone, but it may come again, and I shall not at all feel happy until I know they are all finished with; and I do not want you to come back until that time. I hope you'll be good and mind me.

Tell Perdita that her boss is now officially a father to a son, and has passed out the cigars he's been hoarding for so long. Perdita would have enjoyed his completely out-going and contagious happiness. He was like a small boy who'd scored a goal at football.

Love,

Norman

Alas, *no* one can subscribe to *Yank*.[69] At least no civilian.

49 Lowndes Square
London, S.W.I
September 11 [1944]

Norman dear,

Man does not live by bread alone — nor by WORK either. You are working too hard. I am writing to scold you and to thank you, too in the same breath. Thank you for your last letter — and for having read the Angel series. I want myself to "do" something about it — either write a slight introduction or as you say leave it, and do a third to the trilogy. I suppose in all decency the Angels should be "dedicated" to Sir Osbert![70] Not Angels but Angels [sic]! They the Sitwells are rather separate — or by implication perhaps it would be more subtle to dedicate the Tribute to the Angels to Edith. Then if I do a third, it should be dedicated to Norman Holmes Pearson, don't you think ????[71] But as I haven't the foggiest of what the 3rd is to be about and am rather harassed and wrote the 2nd under compulsion — I don't know where I am. Have you any inspirational ideas????? One of my critics said I ought to slam out the Tribute as soon as possible as I had really "almost been forgotten" in the years between. I never was a one for slamming out things in professional sequence — and I don't like to approach Sir Humphrey — do you think USA would be indicated or do you think it better to "wait?"??? Br[yher] did not approve of a "protestant" making a gesture toward Our Lady but I thought I had made it clear tht she was "Our Lady universally," a Spirit — from the days of Numa and what-not.[72] Anyhow, the sequence happened like that and the dream conveniently arranged itself for me, or my own sub-conscious took over.

So now I have munched a figge — most delicious . . . old Uncle Norman[73] once said to me in Florence, "you are like the Italians, you eat with your eyes," so having fed my fill or almost satisfacto — what word do I seek — satisfactorly — spelling? — gorged the light on the dark green through the green-green glass on the brown-green and Nile green texture of the same said figges, I swallowed one — will gorge eyes and sense and the last will follow shortly. In the meantime, there is the texture and the smooth-cool look and feel and scent of the grapes — all very Eleusinian, Ceres and Iris and Our Lady of field and vineyard — our Calendar — a wonderful concoction sent me by R[obert] Herring, gives festivals and days, ancient and modern, Pagan and Christian, all mixed up and we have Sept. 2–10 to Ceres and the Greater Eleusinian Mysteries — and the 10th itself to Arthur, King of Britain and the

Round Table as Last Supper symbol and zodiac — enough to make you dizzy! Well, there is all that, the cycle of events — and now the pretty lady France flaunting her poppies and cornflowers in our faces . . . and St. Joan triumphant — a sword and fleur-de-lis . . . well! Did you know that she was ennobled by the title de Lis — funny, I found that in the Enc[yclopedia] Britt[annica] in Cornwall — but she never used it. I supposed then she WAS Lady Jeanne de Lis or whatever the French is for me-lady . . . so she is My Lady — we may get Br[yher] to see in time that we MUST have a LADY somewhere . . . now you must really come in here more often. It was good of you to cook the corn for us — real Eleusinian . . . I hope Br did not raise your hair too much with her horrors — she is wonderful, I am half the time, shivering with goose-flesh, a wonderful ghost-story feeling she gives me, she is usually right but her [doses?] are very strong! Come in and we will talk over all these things. I am on the point of writing S[usan] P[earson] but Br is sending her note at the same time so I am not delaying it as Br is out — and note would not go off, so this to you!

———

[MS] Now again thank you for flower-fruit and fruit-flowers (I almost ended by eating the purple-blue & blue-lavender & grape-hyacinth orchids last year). Love

from
Hilda

——————— 22. TS ———————

Flat 10
49 Lowndes Square
S.W.I.
Dec. 5 [1944]

Dear Norman:

I want to get this to you and don't know quite what to say. I enclose O[sbert] S[itwell] May review, as a refresher.[74] He sent me the rough proof — I took a bus to Putney — the trees etc. as per enclosed. I wrote the poems at odd moments, as a poet should — started the first, on the top of the bus brushing through those chestnut-trees. They link on to the first — I purposely tried to keep the link, but carry on from the black tunnel of darkness or "initiation," at least toward the tunnel entrance. I really DID feel that a new heaven and a new earth were about to materialize. It lasted as you know, for a few weeks — then D-day! And the "re-gathering, thundering storm." The Angel names are more or less traditional O[ld] T[estament], though I use the Mohammedan name for the planet Saturn, ruler of time and death, Azrael. The Venus name, I believe is Anael but I spelt it ANNAEL; it didn't seem to "work" until I did — it links on too with Anna, Hannah or Grace, so has an authentic old-testament angel ring. The italic-quotes are mostly from Revelations — one is from O[ld] T[estament] (XXIII). The one, XXVII, "angels unawares" I think is Hebrews. I think the others are all Revelations. The Latin in the last, *Vas spirituale* and *Rosa Mystica* are from the Laurentinian Litany to the Virgin, B.C. missel[75] — I think Br[yher] is wrong to say there is R[oman] C[atholic] implication — I distinctly link the LADY up with Venus-Annael, with the Moon, with the pre-Christian Roman Bona Dea, with the Byzantine Greek church Santa Sophia and the SS of the Sanctus Spiritus. I say she is NOT even

> *vas spirituale*
> *rosa mystica* — which is lovely poetry;
> *ora pro nobis.*[76]

Old *Zadkiel* is really our old *Amen* again — now, having an angel-name; there is a traditional Zadkiel but do not know if mentioned in Writ — but there is Uriel, I believe and some are named in Aph.[*sic*] Book of Enoch which I can never place, though see quoted. I dedicated the book to O[sbert], as I told you, with the last lines of *Walls* . . . possibly we will reach haven, heaven. I believe there is a list of Angels in Mr. Eliot's Milton.[77] If you come on it, let me know.

This just to get to you. We look forward to Sunday. The two contracts signed and sealed are in order and Sir H[umphrey] M[ilford] said as soon as he could get the paper — I asked to have the format like WALLS — he would have Angels set up. I imagine spring — but spring will soon be here — D[eo] V[olente] we will be here to see it. We did enjoy Sunday last. Give us a ring if indicated — in any case thanks and thanks —

H.

As the war came to an end, H.D. was in high spirits about her work. In addition to her Freud memoir in *Life and Letters Today*, her war "trilogy" was being published by Oxford University Press in both England and America as it was being written, and reviewers were comparing her to the major writers of the day. In April 1945, with peace in Europe around the corner, H.D., Bryher, and Robert Herring went to Stratford-upon-Avon to celebrate Shakespeare's birthday, an experience that brought them close to others of their countrymen who were deeply grateful to have survived the war. In *Days of Mars*, Bryher describes the procession to the gravestone, an English cultural shrine, as a profound "religious experience": the English connected their survival with their greatest poet, and came in love and homage to him and to their country. After the German surrender, in July and August H.D. returned alone to Stratford, and probably she wrote the poem *Good Frend* [*sic*] there. In addition, she read G. Wilson Knight's *The Olive and the Sword*, which she particularly enjoyed, because it "shows *war* also used as background for even the light comedies — and comedy/tragedy!" [78]

--------- 23. MS ---------

Noel Arms
Chipping Campden
Gloucestershire
July 29 [1945]

Dear Norman,

I have so many things to thank you for. The *review* [79] first! I had, as I told you, only glanced at it *subrosa*. It is much more complete and all-encompassing when read at leisure & in print. I treasure it & will do so. I love the juxtapositions — Eliot, Joyce & our Thornton Wilder! [80] Actually, too, it seems to include or predict the *Flowering of the Rod*. I thank you for that, too. Only here, have I had time and real space in which to grouse and brood. I shall brood a bit longer on our *Rod* — feel I do not want it or them to leave the nest. Actually, I have not shown the series as yet, to anyone except N[orman] P[earson] . . .

My Lady-doctor [81] arrived at this moment and took me for a most wonderful trip, by way of Stow-on-the-Wold, Bourton-on-the-water, Fosse Bridge to *Biberg*, a national trust town (as is our Chipping) ridiculously Walt Disney! I bet *you've* never been there, for all your Copenhagens and Venices-of-the-North! (Now I am back home at *Noel Arms* and this town is perfect — a Christmas card town; plenty of fruit-picking gypsies cluster at corners and one would never be surprised to meet a herald-camel — and the caravan would not be out-of-the-picture! Well — *how are you*? What happened to you over election? [82] Our distinguished little pub was a Lion's Den of roars. Now it is strangely quiet . . . rather sinister; perhaps it's all right . . . Bryher writes me sustaining letters from Cornwall.

And the chocolates! I brought them along wrapped in their stork paper . . . *have* I enjoyed them??

The Lucy place is not yet in order, for the public, I am told. But here is the young poacher, complete with stag!

I return, alas on Wednesday, as from Aug. 1–15 to:

> c/o Mrs. Denny
> 19 Old Town
> Stratford-on-Avon
> Warwickshire

Please do send me a line!

This is the briefest thank you, Norman.

> With love
> from
> Hilda

──────── 24. TS ────────

Sept. 1 [1945]

Dear Norman,

Just a line to say that I do hope you found your wife better.[83] I am sure your being there, at any rate, has cheered her enormously. I hope the children are well, too. We have been simply dragging along — I feel much happier since coming back — what with all that fresh air and the garden and so on — but we all get so tired. Perdita however, seems full of beans and is looking forward to her new work. I think she will be very popular, already several friends have been nibbling, as to future travel plans. I wonder if we ever WILL get away? I envy you the trip across and the beans and corn. I have enjoyed the Emily Dickinson so much.[84] I took the volume out to the park yesterday — but keep it under lock and key, so to speak. I am sorry you will not be here for the Sitwell parties. Well — really, this is the briefest greeting to you both, as Bryher wants the letter to get out at once. Unwin does not want the Freud memoir, but I am sure someone will in time. I had another second-rate publisher ask for it — but I won't let it go, except for the best. It comes up well, I feel in *L[ife]* and *L[etters]*.

Again thank you for helping Perdita and for cheering us up so much. I will not repeat in detail thanks for the parcels — they give us hope and comfort as well as material sustenance. God bless you both —

> Hilda

The mixture of relief and longing, in H.D.'s letter above, was not lost on Pearson. He recognized that the duress she suffered during the war threatened her health and that her need to get out of England was more serious than she acknowledged. While he was in America during the summer of 1945, visiting his family and preparing to conclude his own war duties in Europe, he contacted the English Department at Bryn Mawr, asking them to extend an invitation to H.D. to lecture to the student body. While underscoring the appropriateness of the invitation, given her growing reputation as "one of the most distinguished contemporary American poets," he also stressed her need for a respite in America. "As a British citizen, by marriage, it is impossible for her to leave England without an official sponsoring and invitation," he explained, adding that the "experience of five war-shattering years . . . has made her particularly anxious to visit her own country and her relatives again."[85] As an added inducement, he offered his personal papers and expertise, should the college library wish to mount an exhibition of her work during her stay.

To H.D.'s delight, Bryn Mawr responded quickly, inviting her to give "a course of lectures or conferences in the second semester."[86] Her immediate reply, to Bryn Mawr's president, is full of excitement and challenge at the offer. In addition to asking practical questions, about the size of the student groups and the length of the sessions, she wonders if they would like her to "stress specially modern trends" or to talk about her personal contact with prominent writers of the day with whom she shared literary anecdotes: Yeats, Ford Madox Ford, Walter de la Mare, the Sitwells. "Would the students want criticism on their own poems," she asks, because she "would like to feel that [she] was bringing something to them" for she is "sure they would help and stimulate [her] immensely."[87] On December 10, intent on going, she wrote a letter to Pearson for legal purposes, authorizing him to look after her literary affairs in the United States until she is able to cross, which will be "in the near future." In the three letters that follow, from late December 1945 to January 1946, we see H.D.'s excitement at the prospect of lecturing at Bryn Mawr. In addition to reporting on commonplace details of her upcoming visit, she presses Pearson to join the other lovers of poetry whom she has queried by sending her a list of twelve favorite poems on which to meditate.

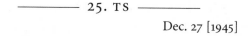

25. TS

Dec. 27 [1945]

Dear Norman,

Please forgive me for not having written sooner, but Bryher wrote and we sent greeting and I did post you an American copy of the Angels on December 17, as for your Christmas. Now this morning I have word from Bryn Mawr; "please cable if we can help in arrangements for trip. Katharine E. McBride."[88] It came fortunately just now, as we are all three due at rendez-vous chez Miss Windsor[89] at 11 this morning. She says one of the Ministries is vetting my papers. I may have to have some interviews etc. I have asked Miss W[indsor] to try to get me off late February or early March. In the meantime, I am waiting for a letter from Bryn Mawr about room etc. We spoke of that. I wrote Miss McBride on November 8, asking about this, but have had no answer. This worries me more than anything else. I have written friends in and near Philadelphia and they say things are as bad as New York and Washington. I have had several invitations from people in Pennsylvania — but I feel that I should be near the college if I am really going to lecture, as I am pretty breathed out and even a short train trip might tire me for talk afterwards. On the other hand, I may feel so much stronger there . . . but to begin, at least, I would like to have place near the college and naturally, I don't want to LIVE with people, if possible; want to be private and at least partially alone; at least a "room of my own." I am not a-social or anti-social, just have to reserve strength, at least until I get my bearings. I will expect and hope to go about a bit, of course.

I have had lovely letters from people about the lists, Walter de la Mare[90] is most co-operative and the old Pearsall Smith[91] people, and Osbert and so on. I think that is going to help. Will you please get your own list ready for me — but it is not a list from you as "critic"; this, I will explain in each case. I spoke of this when you were here. You must not let me down about this. Think it out; it takes some thinking or feeling rather. What would you take across Lethe if you were RATIONED as to memory, about 12 short poems or sections or lines from dramatists, Latin tag if you want or French — well, I leave it to you. I will want more lists from people over there. I did write at length to one rather "representative" old lady, for her list — as for her generation, though I did not say that. She wrote back, just the WRONG thing, "I haven't my reference books and poetry, at hand." I don't want things looked up and selected from BOOKS. Its what is there and what you want to stay there. I think this is a good attitude; poetry in general, through the minds or hearts of the more modern writers. Don't you think so? Anything can be dragged in.

I can not begin to thank you for all you did for us all these years. We have had a hectic Christmas as Edith turned up and a friend of hers from Paris, a Madame Weil — pronounced VEAL — English married to Norway, long separated and through ALL of the war there. She is rather elderly and very intelligent and just pleasantly mate-y and shabby — the Edith dressed her up in her own clothes, bracelets, hats and so on. It has been a great trial to us, as Madame W. was just cozy and slummy (to use Bryher's word of us) and then suddenly "Madame" (and she is in appearance rather like one) became so to speak, La Duchesse de Wiel! They will be here another week, then a bit of rest for us — in the social way, at least. The parties get bigger and more mixed. Mrs. Sachie[92] got in very wrong by being rude to one of their pet publishers — and I got in wrong by not remembering the head of an important committee that I (I ask you) belong to, one of the Author's[93] sub committees, but very recherche, I can tell you. Georgia had a magnificent hat that had been given to her, she told us all about it, and Edith of course, was hat-ed and Madame la Duchesse de Wiel, but all very confusing, as there were just three hats, so to speak, and two were Edith's. Beryl is as usual with her rings and castanets: Arthur, whimsical and charming and looking rather frail[94] . . . Here, I was interrupted but must finish though I seem hardly to have begun. I had a nice letter from S[arah] Lawrence, and Marya wrote me such a delightful letter. I will try to answer both soon. I do not think S[arah] L[awrence] is indicated, as I don't know if I can manage B[ryn] M[awr] even — but it was good of them to write and good of you all to help, and I am taking the letter along as it may add weight to my "bag," chez Miss W[indsor] and the ministry vetting department.

Bryher joins me in all the very best to you there, you, meaning you 4 and as well all who may remember us. We will hope to get our affairs settled this end soon, and then over the hills and far away. Perdita joins me too, and thanks you again for all you did for her. We have spoken much of you and of last Christmas-es.

Ever gratefully,
Hilda

--------- 26. TS ---------

Thirty-Nine Goodrich Street
New Haven, Connecticut
23 January 1946

Dear Hilda:

Why is it that you and Bryher get my last minute letters, the ones dashed off at top speed? I think it must be because I always save what should be best for last, and then like the punished Puritan suffer for the vanity of my wishes. Susan and I are off to Mexico tomorrow morning, driving as best we can southwards via, Richmond, the Carolinas, New Orleans, Laredo, down the Pan-American highway to Mexico City. Then at one time or another to Acapulco, Oaxaca and such places in Mexico proper, and finally to Yucatan by plane where I want more than anything else to see the Mayan ruins. I want to see ruins made by something other than bombs, and a civilization which has simply disintegrated, not blasted to hell. It may restore balance. But of the trip you will be hearing, for I shall flood you both with picture postcards, inscribed with the glowing rhetoric of tourist flyers: "bathed in the limpid light of the soft southern skies, the tourist will learn the gentle art of living in a land that time forgot." "With a startled cry of colour the bougainvillea leaps to welcome the stranger from the north." Bear with me! And the timing of the trip is perfect, for I should be back at home early in March just as you and Bryher reach the States. My trip was almost spoiled by the thought that I might miss a month of Bryher had she come in February as first planned.

But now for the list, which I promised you and which I never forgot even though dilatory. It is made according to specification, as they first come to my mind in any meaningful sense. There are so many reasons for choosing poetry, and in truth not the least would be the semantic aura of the particular poem in terms of the reader, his accidental association as well as his critical perception. The former seems as valid to me in terms of a reader as the latter. Like the friend of mine who could never say "My Father who art in Heaven" because the word "father" to her meant a drunkard who came slobbering home. But that sort of thing, although legitimate, I have not included in my list, as also even on the highest critical grounds I exclude anything of yours, for its inclusion would be unuseful or at least embarrassing. Without ranking them, my list would be as follows:

Shakespeare: the description of Cleopatra on the barge.
"Full fathoms five"
Yeats: "Byzantium" (not "Sailing to Byzantium," altho I like that too, and usually pair the two).
Wordsworth: "Ode: Intimations of Immortality."
Keats: "Ode to a Grecian Urn"
Milton: "Samson Agonistes" (altho this is pure cheating, but you know my weakness. There is no such thing as a "part" of it).
Whitman: "When Lilacs Last". . . .
Spenser: From the "Shepherd's Calendar" the lines from the April(?) Eclogue, beginning: "Bring hether the Pinke and the purple Cullumbine" (this is the only catalogue in poetry I approve of, and I like to mouthe it. Cf in contradistinction such MacLeish and Sandburgian efforts as those lists of states, rivers, and geographical phenomena as sound like a train announcement or the index to an atlas. In nature like a seed catalogue!)

Herrick: "Corninna's Going A-Maying"

Marlowe: final speech in Dr. Faustus, that contains the equivocal "O
Lente, lente curite noctis equi" and the (or as) greatest cry of poetic
drama. (Stop it with the stroke of twelve).

Dryden: "A Song for St. Cecilia"

Anon: that ballad beginning: "O Western wind when wilt thou blow"
Anon has so many fine poems that perhaps I shouldn't choose).

Well, that's the dozen, and I'm so generous a baker that were I to make the
dozen of my trade I'd go on and on. These all represent something very defi-
nite to me. I can't say I have them by heart, as I do such gems of my childhood
as "Up and down the beach we fly / one little sandpiper and I." Perhaps be-
cause I don't have them by heart is the main reason I want to take their text
with me. But if I did have these they would help. They would touch off the
spark of my memory and echo the note of my experience. They would be like
the pitch-pipe to set the tone of my own song.

Now for a last moment news of myself. Washington wanted me to take my
holiday as quickly as possible in order to come back for a series of consulta-
tions in March. How much longer I'll have to stay I don't know but I hope not
long. As yet I haven't much idea what I'll be doing in the autumn, but Yale (or
at least some of it) is trying to negotiate for my appointment as Director of
Undergraduate Studies for a new department of American Studies.[95] It's a little
chauvinistic, but not unimportant in a time when America has responsibilities
which its citizens must assume. I'll know definitely whether the offer will be
satisfactory. Other things brew too, but we'll see. There is no other news!

The copy of TRIBUTE TO THE ANGELS arrived in time for New Year's
and delighted my heart. I always like true friends in a new dress. What damned
fine poems they are! You know how I feel about the trilogy. You'll be embar-
rassed at my H.D. shelf, but I look at it with love and pride. As for the Freud,
I'm sorry that Jock couldn't take it, and what I want you to do is to send me
the typescript so that on my return I can take it to Pantheon Press so that I
can recommend it to them. You know how I feel about it too. As for my failure
to see him in London, you are clairvoyant. My appointment was for the day
before I left. And I did go to the wrong Warwick Square with no time to
correct it after. I plan to write him, but will you give him a ring on the phone
and tell him how much I regret?

I had an extremely nice note from Pup, and will you tell her that altho I
don't know the address I've forwarded the letter to some one who will know.

Tell her that I saw Gerstle Mack[96] in N.Y., and he is off to California for the month of Feb, but is looking forward to seeing her when she returns.

Come quickly, all three of you. My love, equitably distributed.

As ever,

Norman

Hope my first letter reached you . . .

——— 27. TS ———

Jan. 29. [1946]

Please note: Flat 10, in addressing. Your letter wandered up the street but came home in the end!

Dear Norman,

I am so excited about your trip. Yucatan is just the ONE place that I have always thought about. I am sending this just to thank you for the list. It is excellent, personal and "professional" at the same time. It will be a great help. I feel yours is the best "starter" I have had. I had "Full Fathom Five" too — otherwise our lists are quite different. I expected more "Full Fathoms" — so far, only us, I think — the chief repeater here is Nashe, "Adieu, farewell . . ." I think I have had 4, counting myself. I suppose it suits our mood, full circle again. Everyone has had — I was going to write plague — but flu or grippe is what I mean. I had two dreadful days, then a wonderful week's convalescence. At least, that is my excuse for consuming Bryher's mother's excellent Veuve Cliquot Ponsardin, 1926. I am glad you have a Herrick. I have "Fair Daffodils" and "Bid me to Live" — rather Valentin-ish but then he is. That latter is mere sentiment. Also, "Go Lovely Rose" . . . another valentine. My list isn't very high-brow. It would be fun if you would come to Bryn Mawr and do your own shouting. Don't you think so?

I hear now direct that I am to go into the Deanery. I have word from Miss Windsor that she hopes to get me a place March 1 or 2 — but rap on wood or something, I am afraid to speak lest it all vanish into thin air. We are all on our toes waiting for Perdita who is due to go off Sunday, then Br[yher] follows the 20th, I believe.

Writing on the Wall

Will you note corrections in pencil. There was difficulty about Schmide-berg[97] as he never qualified wholly in England, though got his Doctor abroad — one of those things. This correction is indicated on Page 100 of the type-script; it is correct in the *L[ife] and L[etters]* copy. There are only, as far as I find, two mistakes in *L. and L.*. Hans should be HANNS, toward the end of 78 and top of 79. It is correctly spelt through later pages. On page 84 of the L[ife] and L[etters] under XV, *should* is spelt wrong; 9 lines from page end.

Two sections of the type-script were deleted by Robert Herring and I think on the whole, I agree with him in this. You will see them crossed out on Pages 113–114, and 140–141. I note throughout, that the Editor has put in single quotes instead of double-quotes, " ". I think it preferable in the print. I did not indicate this in the MSS but if there is re-print made in USA, perhaps you will make this clear. I think the printed L[ife] and L[etters] can be followed as a whole but I send the MSS as I know sometimes they want the typed pages for setting.

Note that page 145 of the MSS, I have deleted the whole line-reference to E[zra]. Just left "my first live poet, E." — this was thanks to your suggestion, while here. You will note other slight changes, in the MSS, but Robert Herring has indicated in the printed pages. At the very end, could a little space be given to the date and place? That is important. It is all right in L[ife] and L[etters] as it comes at page-end.

I think it would be "polite" to make some reference to the fact that the Writing has appeared in *L. and L.*. I do not think this is absolutely legally necessary but perhaps a note to that effect would be indicated. I leave it to you. And can I have proofs IF it comes out over there? I don't want you to go out of your way about it. I suppose I will be, D[eo] V[olente], by that time at the Deanery.

I think this is about all. I will write again if anything more occurs to me. I do appreciate this so much. I have not got in touch with Jock as everyone has been so ill — some offices quite closed down. I am sure he himself WANTED to do it. Bryher says the older people here still have some odd feeling about the Professor.

> Again thank you
>
> H.

Sadly, despite her preparations, H.D. never made the trip to America. As the letters that follow indicate, she returned to Switzerland instead, having suffered the physical and psychological breakdown that Pearson had feared. Suffering from "acute malnutrition and shock,"[98] she was psychologically dazed and depleted by the strain of the war to the point of extreme agitation and flight from reality. At the end of February, Bryher and Walter Schmideberg arranged for her to be flown by private plane to Seehof, Privat Klinik Brunner, Küsnacht, near Zurich, where she was to remain under treatment until mid-November.

In March, Bryher broke the "grave news" of H.D.'s illness to Pearson, who was "heartbroken" to hear of it. H.D. was terribly anxious about going to America, Bryher wrote. She kept saying, "'you see, I have a Puritan spirit and I want to be there by March 1 at latest.'" [99] She was a "war casualty if there ever was one." Indeed, H.D.'s emotional lability is evident in her side of the following correspondence, where she swings from exhilaration at the beauty of her surroundings at the Klinik Brunner to rage and helplessness at the thought of being kept there against her will to remorse at the trouble she has caused everyone. The worst was over by mid-October, when Bryher reported to Pearson that "with a bang dear Hilda came to herself." [100] It is noteworthy that H.D. wrote "The Guest" section of *By Avon River*, her tribute to Shakespeare, during this troubled interval. [101] Having recovered, she was able to leave the Klinik Brunner in mid-November and to take up residence in Lausanne and Lugano, where she was to write some of her most powerful poems.

Like H.D.'s, Pearson's health also interfered with his postwar plans, increasing the empathy between them and putting the awards he had won into perspective. (For his wartime services Pearson was awarded the U.S. Medal of Freedom, the Medaille de la Reconnaissance Française, a rosette as a chevalier of the Legion d'Honneur, and the Knight's Cross first class of the Norwegian Order of St. Olaf.) In the autumn of 1945, he helped to close the OSS branches in England, Germany, and Austria. In January 1946, unsure about his status at Yale, he negotiated with a number of other universities for a position and took a long recuperative trip to Mexico with his wife, hoping to return to Yale in the fall as an assistant professor. Although he did receive the offer from Yale, his plans were delayed by an unexpected hospitalization. Having gone to Chicago in August for what he thought was a routine checkup, he was placed in the hospital for several weeks while the bone of his hip was scraped and treated with penicillin, a treatment that ultimately proved effective. From his hospital bed, probably thinking of the many who had died, or who had not survived the war so successfully, Pearson responded to H.D.'s having dedicated *The Flowering of the Rod* to him, with the heartfelt statement that her poem's dedicatory words, ". . . pause to give thanks . . . ," meant more to him than any other tribute to his war efforts.

Norman Pearson Esq.
c/o The American Embassy
1 Grosvenor Square
London w.1
England
June 11, 1946

Dear Norman,

I have just received your *Zapotec Urn from Monte Albán, Oaxaca* fascinating card, from Mexico. What a time you must have had. I didn't get to Bryn Mawr, after all, but I brought my notes with me, and am continuing the work here. I am in a fabulously romantic 18th Century Manor House, with a garden to match; the roses are especially beautiful and most of them have been brought from *Versailles*; I have a bowl of them on my table now; the exquisite *Gloire de Dijon* is a special favorite of mine, with its in-curved gold petals.

I do hope you will write again and don't forget that "stack of cards" you promised me.

I am staying on here, as the change is re-making me, altogether. I *was* disappointed about Bryn Mawr, but was cheered up by receiving *The Flowering of the Rod*; I am so glad that you suggested the title to me, & I hope the copy I asked the *Oxford Press* to send, reached you?

With love again and gratitude and thanks,

ever affectionately,
H.D.

28 August 1946

Dear Hilda:

[. . .]

There is so much to say, but first of all there is THE FLOWERING OF THE ROD. It finally reached me four or five days before I left for Chicago, and I brought it with me here. Dear Hilda, how can [I] thank you? It is my greatest honor from the war. No medal, nothing can compare to the pride I feel in seeing my name in it. I cherish it as I cherish life itself. And I have a particular gratitude because on the morning of my operation, when time always goes slower than seconds become minutes, and this time when hours went by before they wheeled me up, I had your book with me and read it again.

". . . pause to give thanks. . . ." Naturally I have a particular affection for the book, but for me it gains even a new height in your poetry, so precise and meticulous, so beautifully controlled, so exquisitely and naturally formed. It has achieved the trilogy even more wonderfully than I had dared hope. Now I am only anxious to have the three parts appear together, as I am anxious too to be at home where I can take the separate thirds into a single reading. It is a great achievement, really, this easy use of great skill; and it comes like a single burst of strength. It was worth waiting a long long time for. Out of the war the "certain ecstasy" and the "hunger for Paradise;" and even more the "sense of direction," the "bee-line." What will, I think, to the true and eventual critic be so apparent is the delicate, inevitable and fruitful interweaving of motifs which bring these poems, the three thirds, into a transcendent unity. I said I was proud of the dedication. I am really humble; you are the one with the right to pride!

I shall not try to dissect it for you; I shall not even pretend to thank you adequately, but I shall be grateful always always with my heart.
[...]

I can't begin to tell you how relieved and happy I was to learn that at last you had gotten to Switzerland, and to hear from you of the charm of the manor house where you are. It seems to me that an 18th-century milieu is just what one needs these days, a kind of surrounding decorum. It shocks me only to see how long it has been since your letter of the 11th of June and this answer, but I have never stopped thinking of you, and I shall not now stop writing. Do let me hear from you as you feel the strength to write, and stay on for the winter at least. Everything seems worse in England these days so far as food is concerned, and you will be helping them by eating other rations. Love and again my gratitude for the *Flowering*.

> Affectionately,
> Norman

--------- 30. MS ---------

September 5 [1946]

Dear Norman,

It was so good to hear from you again. It is as lovely as ever here. The grape-vine and the virginia creeper that frame my windows, remind me of all the beautiful things we share together. The mountains are always a delight to me. The room becomes more familiar and I am so comfortable here. I think these surroundings are almost too beautiful and I am delighted with everything around [me?]. The little picture reminds me of the Prince and the Frog, the first story in the Grimm you sent that I love so much.[102] The book was a constant delight to me and I read over all the special favorites. Do let me hear again.

Love,

Hilda

———— 31. M S ————

Sept. 26, 1946

Dear Norman,

I want you to know that I am making every effort to get away from here. I want to hear from you but numberless letters, books & parcels were never delivered to me. I am trying to get back to London, with the idea of making that lecture tour, after all. I don't want to get stuck in Bryn Mawr. Perhaps later, you might have some further suggestion.

I was very ill for 2 months in London, cerebral meningitis that was precipitated by the fact that I came across Bryher, lying unconscious (or dead, for all I knew) in her bed, in that little bed-room. She had talked of suicide from the earliest days, when she came to see me, before Perdita was born. She tried it, Spring 1920 in Zermatt, where I was completely cut off and helpless with a stranger, a Miss Wallace, whom Bryher had asked along, to do some typing for us. I was always afraid she would make away with herself, during the Blitz. Then, one terrible night, she injected herself & lay moaning in the same bed. There is no doubt that we were both a little crazy but I do not yet fully know why I was brought to this place. I was here 4 or 5 months, enduring *shock treatment* of a most pernicious nature.[103] My papers were taken away, I was locked up without food or water & injected with — I don't know what. To-day, for the first time in 7 months, I saw Bryher with Walter Schmideberg. She seemed well & happy. I don't understand it at all. The flight alone, after 2 months in bed was enough to kill one. It was my first day up, & after a long motor-run, I was huddled into a curious plane by a Doctor whom I scarcely knew. It took us 10 hours to get here, instead of the usual 2. Fletcher wrote me. I answered, please tell him. Evidently, my letters were never sent out. I wrote Susan & yourself & Perdita, all the time. Could you send P[erdita] a wire & say I am all right, that I hope to get to London, then USA, *to see her*. I am sure Bryher meant it all for the best. Please do not disillusion her. I will soon write again, dear Norman. Ever gratefully,

H.D.

──────── 32. MS ────────

Norman Holmes Pearson
The University of Chicago
Chicago 37, Illinois

──────

Department of Surgery
Saturday September 29, 1946
Returning:
Flat 10
49 Lowndes Square
London S.W.1
England

Dearest Norman,

I should write you a separate & very long letter for each of the times you came to see me. We loved having you so. I am heart-broken to hear of your illness. I got the books; it was wonderful of you to send them — and letters — this last thanking me for "The Flowering" should be turned the other way round. It was your idea & your constant thoughtfulness and rare goodness that made "The Flowering" possible. Here, I have been very happy, but now that autumn has set in, I am very home-sick for old friends & old surroundings. Will you be coming back soon? I do hope and pray that you do. Susan was so very good to write and all the gifts from her meant so much to us all. Do thank her again. It has been a beautiful summer & wonderful to get away, after the war years. We have suffered so much together but our friends have been so good. I did so little — you did everything. I am grieved and sorry that I was such a trouble to everyone. Will you thank all who helped, with goodness & self-sacrifice. I will hope to thank you and them personally, in time. Now I am just recovering some health and sanity. I have been very ill indeed & suffering for years, before the final break came. Thank Horace and Marya again for writing me here. Mr. Tenney [104] was so kind — and how I enjoyed that evening & all our meetings with the Sitwells. What long years these have been — but there was much love — and now again, Love

from Hilda

1. Silvia Dobson (1908–1994), British writer, who met H.D. and traveled with her to Venice in 1934, lived on a farm in Kent with her family during the war, before traveling to Europe with the Joint Relief Organizations. She has published parts of her correspondence with H.D. in *Iowa Review* and *Conjunctions*.

2. H.D. to Silvia Dobson, 9 September 1939, in "'Shock Knit Within Terror': Living Through World War II," *Iowa Review* 16, no. 3 (1986): 233.

3. Bryher, *Days of Mars: A Memoir, 1940–1946* (London: Calder and Boyars, 1972), 115.

4. Ibid.

5. Marianne Moore (1887–1972), American poet and editor of *The Dial*, was a classmate of H.D.'s at Bryn Mawr in 1905. Although the two were not close friends in college, they admired each other's work later. They began a lifelong correspondence in 1915, when H.D. wrote to Moore from London in connection with the publication of her poems in *The Egoist*, which H.D. and Richard Aldington edited. The relationship deepened in 1920, when H.D. and Bryher visited New York and, during World War II, H.D. shared her concerns with Moore.

6. Barbara Guest, *Herself Defined: The Poet H.D. and Her World* (New York: Doubleday, 1984), 253.

7. H.D. to Marianne Moore, 30 October 1940, unpublished letter, Rosenbach Memorial Library (hereafter RML).

8. Ibid.

9. Ibid.; see also Cyrena Pondrom, "Marianne Moore and H.D.: Female Community and Poetic Achievement," in *Marianne Moore: Woman and Poet*, ed. Patricia C. Willis (Orono, Maine: National Poetry Foundation, 1990).

10. H.D. to Silvia Dobson, undated letter, *Iowa Review*, 236.

11. Mary Herr (1885–1960), a classmate of H.D.'s at Bryn Mawr, was a librarian in New York City and Chicago. A lifelong friend, she cultivated and maintained H.D.'s connection with the college.

12. H.D. to Mary Herr, February 1944, unpublished letter, Bryn Mawr Library (hereafter BML).

13. Robin Winks, *Cloak and Gown: Scholars in the Secret War, 1939–1961* (New York: Morrow, 1987), 251.

14. Norman Holmes Pearson to Fanny Kittredge Pearson, 12 December 1942. The correspondence between Pearson and Fanny Kittredge Pearson is at BL.

15. Peter Braestrup's interview with Pearson in the *Yale Daily News*, 8 March 1950.

16. Perdita (Macpherson) Schaffner (1919–), writer, the author of several introductory essays for the republished works of H.D., as well as memoirs of other members of H.D.'s literary circle. Perdita was raised by both Bryher and H.D., who was estranged from her husband, Richard Aldington, and, in 1928, she was adopted by Bryher and Kenneth Macpherson. She spent a substantial part of her childhood in Switzerland, where she learned German, French, and some Italian in addition to her native English. After the war, she lived and worked in New York City, marrying John Schaffner, a literary agent, in 1950.

17. Pearson married Susan Silliman Bennett on 21 February 1941. She had two daughters

from a previous marriage: Susan S. Tracy (later Susan S. Addiss) and Elizabeth B. Tracy.

18. Perdita Schaffner, "Running," *Iowa Review* 16, no. 3 (1986): 7–13.

19. Norman Holmes Pearson to Fanny Kittredge Pearson, 5 December 1943.

20. Née Faith Stone, wife of the British novelist Compton Mackenzie (1883–1972), who was separating from her husband at this time. She wrote three autobiographical memoirs of their life together: *As Much As I Dare* (1938), *More Than I Should* (1940), and *Always Afternoon* (1943). They cowrote *Calvary* (1942), a book of vignettes from World War II, the proceeds of which went to a war relief fund.

21. "The Poets' Reading," held in Aeolian Hall on 14 April 1943, was arranged by the Sitwells to benefit the Free French in England. H.D. had invited Pearson, but he was unable to attend. The poets who participated included Edmund Blunden, Gordon Bottomley, Hilda Doolittle, T. S. Eliot, Walter de la Mare, John Masefield, Vita Sackville-West, Edith and Osbert Sitwell, W. J. Turner, Arthur Waley. Members of the royal family were in attendance, including the two princesses. Perdita Schaffner gives an amusing account of it in her essay "A Day at the St. Regis with Dame Edith," in *American Scholar* 60, no. 1 (Winter 1991).

22. William Rose Benét was married four times: widowed twice and divorced once before he met and married Marjorie Flack, author and illustrator of children's books, in 1941.

23. Stephen Vincent Benét (1898–1943), American poet and younger brother of William Rose Benét, winner of a Pulitzer Prize for *John Brown's Body* (1928) and another, awarded posthumously, for *Western Star* (1944).

24. Laurence Binyon (1869–1943), English poet, art historian, critic; scholar of St. Paul's School and Trinity College, Oxford. Works include several scholarly books about art, a play, and *Collected Poems* (2 vols., 1931).

25. Robert Herring (1903–1975), English writer and editor, assistant editor, *London Mercury*, 1925–34; film critic on the *Manchester Guardian*, 1928–38; editor of *Life and Letters Today* (1935–50). Published works include poetry, a novel, travel writing.

26. Edith Sitwell (1887–1964) and her younger brothers, Osbert (1892–1969) and Sacheverell (1897–1987), the children of British aristocrats, were distinguished writers and patrons of the arts. Osbert and Edith waited out the war at Renishaw, the family estate in Derbyshire. Sacheverell, who joined the Home Guards, remained with his wife, Georgia, at Weston Hall in Northamptonshire.

27. Ivy Compton-Burnett (1884–1969), prolific British novelist, lived with Margaret Jourdain (1876–?), scholar of furniture and the decorative arts, beginning in 1919. They saw a great deal of H.D. and Bryher in London during World War II.

28. Elizabeth Bowen (1899–1973), distinguished Anglo-Irish novelist, worked for the Ministry of Information during the war and as an air-raid warden in London. Her novel *The Heat of the Day* (1949), which H.D. admired, was set in wartime London.

29. Trenoweth, a flower farm that Bryher co-owned with her friend Doris Banfield, who ran it with her husband, John. In her biography, Barbara Guest reports that on it was a "mini-manor," designed by Sir Edward Lutyens.

30. On 13 May 1943, the *New York Times* ran the headline "African War Over." The Allies captured the German general Von Arnim, along with seventeen other generals and 175,000 German and Italian troops.

31. T. E. Hulme (1883–1917), British philosopher, translator, critic, and poet. He helped conceptualize the Imagist movement and founded the Poet's Club in 1908. His poem "Autumn," which Pearson misquotes here, was published in the club's Christmas anthology. The original lines were "I walked abroad, / And saw the ruddy moon lean over a hedge / Like a red-faced farmer."

32. Publication data for these texts are available in Michael Boughn, *H.D.: A Bibliography, 1905–1990* (1993).

33. H.D.'s novel *Hedylus* was composed around 1924; a portion was published in 1924 and the whole in 1928.

34. H.D. refers to her short story "Narthex," in *The Second American Caravan*, ed. Alfred Kreymborg, Lewis Mumford, and Paul Rosenfeld (New York: Macaulay, 1928), 225–84.

35. *American Poetry: A Miscellany* (New York: Harcourt Brace, 1920, 1922, 1925, 1927), an anthology of contemporary poetry without a general editor, consisted of new poems by poets who came together by mutual accord. It was first published in 1920 and contained poems by H.D. in 1922, 1925, and 1927.

36. H.D. probably refers to Frost's poem "Winter Eden," from *West Running Brook* (1928). The poem describes the actions of wildlife in "A winter garden in an alder swamp" during "[a]n hour of winter day."

37. Unidentified.

38. Thanks to Pearson's OSS contacts, Perdita had been given a job in the office of James Angleton in London, where she was assigned to the Italian desk in Counter-Intelligence.

39. *Nights*, a novella in two parts, was composed over the years 1931–34 and was published in a limited edition by Pool, the press established by Bryher and Kenneth Macpherson.

40. In an earlier unselected letter (4 October), H.D. refers to Hesther Marsden-Smedley's stay at their flat and mentions that Pearson might like to meet her because her husband is important in government circles.

41. George Plank (1883–1965), American engraver and illustrator, moved to England in 1914 and painted posters for the Red Cross during World War I. During World War II, he joined the Home Guard and became ill from the physical exertion their activities required. He became a British citizen in 1945.

42. Humphrey Trevelyan, a Cambridge don who had spent some time at Yale, was in the British intelligence service. He and his wife, Mollie, often entertained Pearson at their home in Trumpington, near Cambridge.

43. Sacheverell Sitwell's poem "Dr. Donne and Gargantua" was published first in 1921 in a limited edition of 101 copies. It was later included in *The Hundred and One Harlequins* (London: Grant Richards, 1922). Pearson was an avid book collector, an interest he shared with Bryher.

44. H.D. refers to the MS "The Walls Do Not Fall."

45. H.D. is probably referring to the refrain "Sweet Thames, run softly till I end my song" from Edmund Spenser's "Prothalamion."

46. Walter Savage Landor to Robert Browning.

47. The references to phrases from *The Walls Do Not Fall* can be found in H.D.'s *Collected Poems 1912–1944*, ed. Louis Martz (New York: New Directions, 1983), 509–43.

48. Sir Humphrey S. Milford (1877–1952), director of Oxford University Press, 1913–45. The press published *The Walls Do Not Fall* in 1944.

49. H.D.'s allusion to the connection between the name of the Delaware River and the appropriation of Native American land and culture by the British shows her sensitivity to the political implications of names and naming. Her information corresponds with that in a book by C. A. Weslager, *The English on the Delaware, 1610–1682* (1967), who attributes the naming to Captain Samuel Argall, who dropped anchor in 1610 "in a great bay," which he later called "the De La Warre Bay" in honor of his superior, Sir Thomas West, the third Lord de la Warre, then lord governor of the Virginia Colony.

50. H.D. has shared with Pearson her love of wordplay and her awareness of the hidden history that etymology reveals.

51. Edith Sitwell's *Street Songs* (1943).

52. Eugene O'Neill (1888–1952), Nobel Prize–winning American playwright, was deeply depressed by concerns about the war. In the period from 1939 to 1943, he interrupted his work on *The Iceman Cometh* and *Long Day's Journey Into Night* to develop ideas for three antitotalitarian plays that remained unfinished, "The Visit of Malatesta," "The Last Conquest," and "Blind Alley Guy." Since Pearson was in contact with the dramatist, whose papers he also acquired for Yale, he would have been privy to these MSS.

53. Pearson's jacket copy read: "H.D. is well known to all lovers of verse as one of the earliest 'Imagists.' These, her latest poems, come from the very midst of the 'fifty thousand incidents' of the Blitz. The memorable poetry of these times is not likely to be military in the old sense. This is a civilian's war, and this is civilian war poetry.

> Pompeii has nothing to teach us,
> we know crack of volcanic fissure,
> slow flow of terrible lava,
> pressure on heart, lungs, the brain
> about to burst its brittle case
> (What the skull can endure!)

The outer violence of the scene touches the deepest hidden sub-conscious terrors. The past is on show. The house of life becomes 'another sliced wall where poor utensils show like rare objects in a museum'. The mystery of death invades; but above all is the ever-startling miracle of the breath of life."

54. In *Writing on the Wall*, H.D. refers to the "Chambered Nautilus" of Oliver Wendell Holmes as a favorite of hers when she was a schoolgirl. She incorporates the following lines from Holmes into her text: "Till thou at length are free," "Leaving thine outgrown shell by life's unresting sea!" and "Build thee more stately mansions, O my soul."

55. *Life and Letters Today* published *Writing on the Wall* in parts, throughout 1945 and 1946.

56. Bryher to Norman Holmes Pearson, 27 August 1944.

57. H.D. to Silvia Dobson, undated letter, *Iowa Review*, 238.

58. H.D. is referring to *Tribute to the Angels*.

59. Bryher and Robert Herring published *Life and Letters Today* out of Eckington during the war.

60. Merril Moore (1903–1957), American psychiatrist and poet, was a friend of H.D. and Bryher. He won a Bronze Star in 1944 for fighting in the South Pacific. In an unselected letter, Pearson refers to a mysterious flyer on Oriental porcelain that Moore had sent

to H.D. from New Zealand — the flyer was for an exhibition that had been held before the war and they seem puzzled about why it should surface now. Here H.D. refers to another clipping that Moore had sent, from the *Auckland Star* (30 March 1944), which describes his discovery that a good many American servicemen read and became interested in Hitler's *Mein Kampf*. Later, Moore wrote the foreword to the Pantheon Press edition of H.D.'s *Tribute to Freud* (1956).

61. H.D. is probably alluding to Pound's treasonous broadcasts from Italy during 1944.

62. This may have been a letter from an admirer, sent to H.D. from Chatto and Windus. See letter 20 above.

63. Sir George MacMunn (1869–1952), author of *The American War of Independence in Perspective* (London: G. Bell and Sons, 1939). His view appears to correspond with H.D.'s psychohistorical readings of the past.

64. H.D. probably refers to Charles Perrault (1628–1703), author of "Puss in Boots" and other Mother Goose stories.

65. Marya Zaturenska Gregory (1902–1982), Russian-born American poet, received a Pulitzer Prize for *Cold Morning Sky* (1938); wrote seven other volumes of poems and a biography of Christina Rossetti; edited six anthologies, some with her husband, the poet Horace Gregory.

66. John Gould Fletcher (1886–1950), American expatriate poet, whose work was published with H.D.'s in the early Imagist anthologies. He returned to the United States permanently in 1933 and settled in Little Rock, Arkansas. During World War II he spent much time alleviating the suffering of Japanese Americans who were interned in a relocation camp in Arkansas. He suffered from depression and drowned in a pond near his home, an apparent suicide.

67. Eliot's *Four Quartets*, which also contain a response to the war, appeared in 1943. The four poems ("Burnt Norton," "East Coker," "The Dry Salvages," and "Little Gidding") are named for places that have special significance to Eliot, and are linked thematically.

68. Ezra Pound began his Cantos around 1917 and continued adding to them until 1968, when the publication of *Drafts and Fragments of Cantos CX–CXVII* marked his realization that, at eighty-two years of age, he would never finish them.

69. *Yank* was a weekly newspaper published by the Special Services Branch of the U.S. Army. It was available to members of the services for five cents.

70. *Tribute to the Angels*, the second part of H.D.'s *Trilogy*, contained this dedication:

> To Osbert Sitwell
>
> . . . possibly we will reach haven,
>
> heaven

71. *The Flowering of the Rod*, the third part of H.D.'s *Trilogy*, contained this dedication:

> To Norman Holmes Pearson
>
> . . . pause to give
>
> thanks that we rise again from death and live.

72. *Trilogy* (New York: New Directions, 1973), 102.

73. Norman Douglas (1868–1952), writer; assistant editor, *English Review*, 1912–15; first gained recognition with *Siren Land* (1911); lived mainly in Italy, settling for long periods in Florence and Capri, where he died.

74. Osbert Sitwell reviewed *The Walls Do Not Fall* in *The Observer*, 28 May 1944. In the

review, he deplored the "persistent clamour" of that time, against which H.D.'s "pure, cool poetry . . . comes as an immense relief."

75. H.D. probably refers to the Litany of Loreto, which addresses the Virgin Mary with forty-nine titles that incorporate all of her roles in the faith. It was published in 1558 in Germany as "Litania Loretana."

76. The lines "not *vas spirituale* / not *rosa mystica* even" can be found in *Collected Poems*, 574. The phrase "*ora por nobis*" (pray for us) is from the Litany of Loreto.

77. T. S. Eliot's essay "Milton" focuses on the rhetorical quality of Milton's music; it does not contain a list of angels.

78. H.D. to Bryher, 18 July 1945. The correspondence between H.D. and Bryher is at BL.

79. Pearson reviewed *Tribute to the Angels* in *Life and Letters Today* 46, (July–September 1945). He sees the poem as a continuation of *The Walls Do Not Fall*, in that both books "are parts of the same single affirmation of the strength and endurance of the civilian in war, who through Apocalyptic fire gains integrity, and through integrity rebirth." He compares H.D.'s two books of war poetry with Eliot's poetry after "Ash Wednesday," with Joyce's *Finnegan's Wake*, and with Wilder's *Skin of Our Teeth* (a "cheerful adaptation" of *Wake*).

80. Thornton Wilder (1897–1975), novelist and dramatist, began giving his manuscripts to Yale in 1937. He was well known to both H.D. and Pearson.

81. Dr. Elizabeth Ashby, a psychiatrist whom H.D. had consulted earlier, shared H.D.'s interest in astrology.

82. In July 1945, in the general election in England, the Labour Party defeated the Tory Party, and Clement Atlee became prime minister.

83. Norman Pearson returned to the United States because Susan Pearson was hospitalized.

84. H.D. is probaby referring to *Bolts of Melody*, ed. Mabel Loomis Todd and Millicent Todd Bingham (New York: Harper, 1945). It was a groundbreaking book that introduced a large number of hitherto unpublished poems to the public.

85. Norman Holmes Pearson to J. Alister Cameron, 25 September 1945, unpublished letter, BML.

86. J. Alister Cameron to H.D., 1 November 1945, unpublished letter, BML.

87. H.D. to Katharine McBride, 8 November 1945, unpublished letter, BML.

88. Katharine E. McBride (1904–1976), American educator, author of books on psychology, and president of Bryn Mawr College.

89. Rita Windsor was Bryher's travel agent.

90. Walter de la Mare (1873–1956), English poet, novelist, and anthologist; works include *Behold This Dreamer* (1939) and *The Traveller* (1946).

91. Logan Pearsall Smith (1865–1946), American-born writer, whose sisters married Bernard Berenson and Bertrand Russell. Publications include *Words and Idioms* (1925), *All Trivia* (1933), and *Milton and His Modern Critics* (1940).

92. Georgia Doble, wife of Sacheverell Sitwell.

93. H.D. refers to the British Society of Authors, of which she was a member.

94. H.D. is probably referring to Arthur Waley and a quasi mistress of his, known as "Beryl the Peril." In an unpublished journal, Pearson reports meeting these two at an earlier gathering at the Sitwells'.

95. Norman Pearson returned to Yale as an assistant professor in 1946 and became the first director of undergraduate studies in American studies in 1947.

96. Gerstle Mack (1894–1983), architectural draftsman and art historian; works include several books on architecture, biographies of Paul Cézanne and Toulouse-Lautrec. He was active in the OSS and a friend of Pearson's.

97. In *Writing on the Wall*, H.D. refers to him as "the analyst Walter Schmideberg" and as "Mr. Schmideberg" (*Tribute to Freud* [1974], 76, 77). The difficulty about his credentials may be related to the battle between his wife and her famous mother over Melanie Klein's interpretation of some of Freud's ideas.

98. Bryher to Pearson, 6 June 1946.

99. Ibid., 7 March 1946.

100. Ibid., 16 October 1946.

101. In *H.D. by Delia Alton*, H.D. records having written "The Guest" between 19 September and 1 November 1946.

102. On 14 April [1945], H.D. thanked Susan Pearson for an edition of *Grimm's Fairy Tales*, illustrated by Josef Scharl. She writes: "It is entirely the book's fault that I have not written, as I open it on my desk and then become lost, drowned in it — and most lovely memories of having first had Grimm read to me with my two brothers before 'reading age' — most poignant and beautiful memories. I never found an edition that I could compare to my own first one — which was left behind when we moved from Bethlehem to Philadelphia when I was eight. I have the two volumes of the original Margaret Hunt translation which I am delighted to see has been used here" (unpublished letter, BL).

103. In an interview in August 1993, Perdita Schaffner informed the author that she was told that H.D. did not undergo shock therapy.

104. Calvin Tenney (1911–), also a Yale Ph.D. and OSS recruit, was Pearson's flatmate in London in 1944. After the war, he became a professor of Romance languages at Wesleyan University.

CHAPTER TWO

"Dear Norman, C.H.E.V.A.L.I.E.R."

1946-1951

After having recuperated at Klinik Brunner in Küsnacht, H.D. made the gradual transition from living in London or Burier-la-Tour with Bryher to living alone in a succession of residential hotels — in Lausanne in the winter or Lugano in the summer. For the most part, Bryher remained at Kenwin, a short train ride away, and the two resumed a more distanced relationship conducted partially through letters. By the end of 1946, H.D. was out of immediate physical and psychological danger and back to work, but she felt isolated from many of her friends and family, especially those in England and America. Having given up completely on "party politics," as she wrote Pearson, she had turned further inward to a more enduring "world of reality" she found in the English literary tradition (22 October 1946). At the end of the war she had paid tribute to this tradition in *Good Frend*, a sequence of poems published in *Life and Letters Today*, the title of which refers to Shakespeare. Consequently, her first literary task upon recovery was to complete her essay "The Guest," on Shakespeare and his contemporaries. Then, from 1947 to 1951, in a great outpouring, she wrote a sequence of long, experimental, historical romances — "The Sword Went Out to Sea," "The White Rose and the Red," and "The Mystery" — which reflected, respectively, her increased involvement in spiritualism during the war, her imaginative connection with the men and women of the Pre-Raphaelite circle, and her renewed recognition of the redemptive possibilities of the mysticism at the core of her Moravian heritage. Also, in this interval, after the first two of these romances, she assembled the journal "Advent," which became part of *Tribute to Freud*, and she completed *Bid Me to Live (A Madrigal)*, a roman à clef about her own literary circle in World War I, which was begun in 1939. In addition, between the two parts of "The Mystery," she wrote the journal-essay *H.D. by Delia Alton*, in which she explained the thematic core of her work thus far, an act of intellectual and emotional synthesis that was instrumental in her artistic development as well as helpful to her future readers.

Pearson celebrated and supported H.D.'s return to writing. He immediately offered to be her "literary *cavalier servante*," an enhanced version of his old relationship with her, in which he would assume more responsibility, negotiating with publishers as well as responding to work in progress (9 November 1946). Having withstood the devastation of the war himself, he understood H.D.'s need for a lifeline, and he recognized the spiritual depth and artistry of *Good Frend* and "The Guest." As he wrote to Bryher, he thought the poems of *Good Frend* continued "the fine work of trilogy" and that "when the proper perspective comes publicly to [H.D.'s] poetry it will be seen that she has never written better than in these last few years" (28 October 1947). His comments on "The Guest" in the same letter indicate that he understood the essay to be "not only criticism" but also a deeply felt "act of creation." He agreed with H.D. that the two pieces belonged together, suggested the title *By Avon River*, and arranged with Macmillan to publish the volume, supervising details of the editing and publication process.

Further, Pearson understood H.D.'s psychological vulnerability and sensed the potential danger of her isolation in central Europe. Comfortably ensconced in an assistant professorship at Yale,[1] he provided a restorative connection with her American home. He sent news of the activities of her writer friends,[2] reminded her of their common colonial heritage,[3] and acted as a surrogate parent for Perdita, who was now living in New York. Also, he kept her connected with the American literary tradition by sending new editions of books by canonized American writers and copies of his own essays, to which she sometimes responded with comments that linked her own writing to that of her American forebears. Most important, Pearson encouraged H.D. to keep writing, asking about the progress of her unfinished memoir of her Moravian childhood, *The Gift*, and affirming the value of her new experimental prose fiction despite its rejection by prospective publishers. In particular, his perceptive comments on the structure of "The White Rose and the Red" reveal his close attunement to H.D. They led her to write "The Mystery," set in eighteenth-century Prague, which took her back spiritually to her Moravian ancestors and then forward to the American heritage that she and Pearson shared. (He saw the latter novel as a companion piece to *The Gift*.) Moreover, he used his position at Yale, where he was now director of undergraduate American studies and faculty adviser to the Yale Collections of American Literature, to promise her (and Bryher) a "shelf" in that collection. In that capacity, in addition to arranging for the safekeeping of all of H.D.'s correspondence and published volumes, he encouraged her to prepare typescripts of all her manuscripts for publication, thereby assuring her unpublished work a future audience by securing it in a prestigious research university. His suggestion that she write an explanatory journal-essay about these works (*H.D. by Delia Alton*) was part of this process. Thus Pearson helped H.D. to lay the groundwork for a successful return to poetry.

In this interval the letters also contain allusions to H.D.'s renewed contact with Richard Aldington and Ezra Pound, relationships that Pearson mediated. Aldington was one of the first readers of H.D.'s novel "The Sword Went Out to Sea," which he thought "a remarkable piece of work" but one too difficult for commercial publishers to understand because of its experimental mixture of genres.[4] He urged H.D. to rewrite it as "straight fiction" of a more "objective" kind, a suggestion she refused.[5] Later, when an influential editor friend of Aldington's rejected the manuscript, it was Pearson who palliated H.D.'s keen disappointment, promising its publication in the future. Also, H.D.'s interest in the Pre-Raphaelites coincided with Aldington's preparation of an anthology of the English aesthetes.[6] He suggested books on this subject and encouraged H.D.'s fictional biography of Elizabeth Siddal, "The White Rose and the Red."

H.D.'s contact with Pound was more sporadic, partly because she deplored his political views and behavior during and after the war. (Pound had sent her a copy of *The Pisan Cantos* in 1948.)[7] Like Pearson and Aldington, H.D. deplored the fascist sympathies and activities that led to Pound's indictment for treason and his incarceration in a Washington mental hospital. In a letter to Bryher she connected these political sympathies with "confusion" about World War I, the decline of his reputation, and Oedipal rivalry with his father, an assayer at the United States Mint.[8] However, she stood by him on the basis of their earlier romantic relationship and his efforts on behalf of her poetry. In her letters to Pound from the late forties there is a sense of nostalgia for the prewar past and a wish to renew their connection as fellow artists. In this vein, she shared news of her new work, crediting him with having introduced her to William Morris.[9] Pearson encouraged H.D.'s loyalty to her old friend. He was an admirer of *The Cantos*, and his view of Pound's later poetry focused on Pound's mythmaking goals and innovative formal achievements, not on his politics.[10] Pearson began to teach graduate seminars on Pound's poetry at Yale as early as 1949, and he called on H.D. to help him and his students annotate *The Cantos*.[11]

The letters that follow, from 1947, show H.D. regaining strength. Although she occasionally feels isolated and immobilized in comparison to Bryher, who travels to England and the United States, she realizes her good fortune in being comfortable and well fed in Switzerland and not subject to the privations of postwar London, where food and other necessities were in short supply. She draws upon Pearson for news and books from America, exchanges literary gossip, and discusses her reading. In particular, she is excited to have rediscovered Henry James. She expresses a new feeling of kinship with the older expatriate and requests that Pearson send the latest American editions of his fiction. H.D. is also enthusiastically reading the poetry and fiction of Hermann Hesse[12] in 1947. Bryher reports this to Pearson, but H.D. does not, perhaps preferring to discuss literary interests she is more certain that they share.[13]

Probably because Pearson was extremely busy with professional activities in 1947, he wrote H.D. only four letters. (In addition to his teaching and administrative duties at Yale, which included directing the undergraduate American studies program, he was active in the English Institute, becoming chairman the following year.) His letters are long, however, and supplemented by gifts of books, journals, and other letters to Bryher, the gist of which he knew would be passed on. He tactfully expressed his desire to see H.D. again, as well as Bryher, but firmly insisted upon the benefit to her as a writer of remaining in Switzerland, assuring her that she can see both America and England better from her "mountain perspective."[14]

Jan. 14 [1947]
Monday

Dear Norman,

Thank you so much for the *Briarcliff Magazine*.[15] You said you had sent a Bryn Mawr edition on Williams![16] So you still think of me there! Well — more of that later. I heard from a girl, May Sarton,[17] from Cambridge, that she had arranged an H.D. reading at Harvard. I feel immensely flattered. I should really like to do it, I think, for I feel quite envious when people write that Edith [Sitwell] is on the air, all the time. I have not heard lately from them, except that they are tied at Renishaw and want to get to Italy. I have heard from Br[yher], in miraculously short time. I do hope you see her. I was so interested in the pictures in the magazine, I remember Williams' mother so well. We played Mozart (I think) together, there at their house, once when I went with E[zra] to see them. That is, we both played, treble, bass — a sort of informal duet. We both loved it, I think, anyhow, please congratulate W. W[illiams] on his work — how interesting the first article was, and I was glad to be remembered.[18] He was very popular with us all then, danced very well and was in great demand. He did a Polonius in the Mask and Wig — that is a skit Hamlet, he was in mixed purples and wore a beard. I dare say he remembers his "camel" speech. I also spent a short time with a party at Point Pleasant, with the Lambertons — we had great fun. I hear from the girl or woman I told you of, in New Jersey that Dorothy is near and that the other child, was being married to a Russian-Italian and seemed all right now.

I do thank you for your really grand suggestion and the Trilogy.[19] Will you christen it, as you did *The Flowering*? I must say, on the whole, that I am very pleased with those three — especially, the last. I have been boiling down some old notes and pages — I wrote far too much — but now after the Freud notes and the three volumes of poems, I feel happier and can calmly go over the past heap of MSS. — I will get to *The Gift* again, sometime. Yes — your book filled a gap.[20] Swiss friends were so happy, "but this is not America," one lady said, "these are O U R wedding-chests and these are S W I S S names — and you know of course, that Eisenhower is a Swiss?" I did not know that, did you? Well, the book is here with some other Christmas books — the print in England now is back to the old standards, I am glad to say — not up to USA, but very good. Bryher writes that Perdita may be coming back on a "flip" with her. I do hate that word, it terrifies me, the way she got off was too hair-raising, in a blizzard from London and gales, but she will have told you her happiness in the Azores and all the rest of it. I am glad you saw Francis.[21] He was a little hanger-on cousin, a friend of my younger brother — but I was always devoted to him, and he had a toy-theatre and insisted on playing out all of Romeo, and reading it aloud to us — rather an ordeal but even as a ten year old, he loved Shakespeare. They say *Antony and Cleopatra* in London, is too bewildering, done in Restoration costume, which as Herring pointed out, may have been "modern dress" at the time but doesn't help now. *Lear*, they say was good. I must get my *The Guest* copied for you. I just call it *The Guest* now. This is Bryher's machine. I am trying to hire one for myself, here. I am glad you got the funny photograph. I did have an amazingly interesting review of *Walls* in that *Poetry*. Do you remember? I think they did *Tribute* too.[22] I am allowed only this mean, flimsy little sheet, but will write again. I do thank you so for all your help and suggestions. Do write again soon.

With love,

Hilda

——— 34. TS ———

Minerva Hotel

LUGANO

May 8, 1947

Dear Norman,

I am all of a-dither with excitement over the three volumes that have arrived.[23] One was almost too much, *The American Novels and Stories* came first. Then just now, before lunch, the two others, *Great Short Novels* and *Writers and Artists*. I will follow this with one of my out-door pencil letters and try to tell you what this means to me here. I cannot tell you how snug and self-contained I feel, with this complete library. I brought hardly any books as I wanted to brush up, if you can brush up what isn't there, my lost Italian while continuing the polyglot French and German. I started on "Pandora" and was amazed again at the extreme felicity of those descriptions, outer as well as the intricate and intimate mind-reading that he gave himself up to. I feel there is something positively hair-raising like manifestations at a séance — though I have never been to one — in his conjuring up people out of the floor or the pavement, in USA as well as Europe. Though, oddly, I had thought the greater bulk of his stories were about people on the continent or in England. I can hardly wait to read *The Aspern Papers* again. Actually, I couldn't concentrate during those horrible years, though I started in 1940 to review Walter Pater, I got just so far — it wasn't that he didn't come up to my

expectations or that he had not worn well, as it were, it was simply TOO
BEAUTIFUL, one could not turn aside from the desert of one's predestined
journey, into the oasis; that was all. I could not even touch James. I remember
the discussion when he took over British papers during the last war — and his
supposed death-bed "civis Romanus sum." [24] Then I almost or even did meet
him at the Clover Club [in Philadelphia] when he lectured on Balzac when
I was, I think, 19. Again, I saw him in Rye standing on his door-step; Violet
Hunt [25] wanted me to meet him, but I felt too Daisy Miller-ish for that august
occasion. I have gone over the catalogue of May Sinclair's [26] books and claimed
all the imagists or near-imagists that I could find. I don't want them but it is
possible that you might like them sent over later, as they are gifts and auto-
graphed, I gather, and Br[yher] says they are difficult to get. I am positively
frightened by the three books, piled here at my elbow. I am afraid I don't want
to come to America now, as you have shipped it all to me here. A thousand
thanks and all blessings to you, dear Norman

> and love from
> Hilda

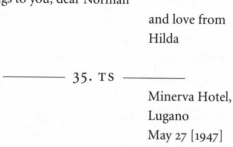

35. TS

> Minerva Hotel,
> Lugano
> May 27 [1947]

Dear Norman,

I have almost finished *Bostonians*. I am amazed at the modern post-war
atmosphere (post American Civil War) with those true-to-type Bloomsbury
intellectuals and mesmeric healers, all leading on to Mary Baker G.[*sic*] — As
I said before, one needs a vintage mind and a large understanding or long
view of the two continents. I find people I know, and people I have known,
from both continents. The descriptions of Marmion were true, in my day —
enough now to make my mouth water or my nose sniff huckleberry tangles,
sea-lavender and salt-weed. I knew that sort of derelict ship-building town in
Rhode Island and in Maine. I hear from the friends with whom I stayed as a
school-girl at Watch Hill, that their cottage and surroundings were swept away
in tornado. I have time here, really time, to concentrate on H[enry] J[ames],
and to realize many subtle points that I missed in early reading. The intro-
ductions and notes of the volumes you sent are most fascinating. Henry got
into trouble with William, for instance, as W. said Miss Birdseye of *Bostonians*
must be toned down — as everyone will know, dear James, that you are pok-

ing fun at dear Miss Peabody.[27] Henry remarks that Miss P. is not the only professional humanitarian who loses her specs — and anyway, dear William, there is such a thing as art for art's sake. There is another find, heart-breaking, did you realize that the old old lady in *Aspern Papers* is Shelley's wife's half sister, she who had the famous episode with Lord B[yron], and the poor child Allegra? I used to beat my poor brains over this, as H.J., always the perfect gentleman, had so arranged the story that the old, mysterious retired possessor of the poet's papers, had had an adventure with an AMERICAN. There was no one but Poe or possibly, just possibly Hawthorne, who could fit the part. What is my delight to find that H.J. so produced his story, to hide any trace of the original Miss Clairmont. Bryher sent me *The American Scene* with Auden introduction.[28] I am keeping that till later. I can not thank you enough for having sent these volumes, and here and now. It is hot — and we have loud purrings and chirpings from tree-toads and crickets, how I missed them! And I find that H.J. rediscovers them too, in one of his New England summer scenes, after some time absent in England. I am going now again, to MELISA (a bee?) to see about the Italian Eliot and the first O'Neill you asked for.[29] They promised them some days ago, but things were held up a bit over Whitsun here; they make a great festa [*sic*] of it. I heard that Eliot was holding forth on Milton-cum-Joyce (James J.), making cross-references, "Milton is almost as highly original and intellectual as" . . . etc. This is one of the usual pegs, the Milton peg, on which people hang or pin their Eliot phantasies, so maybe he is strictly academic and still wears the old school tie.[30] I hope at least, that he is as happy and well-fed as I am. I did hear, however, that he was upset over death of a brother. He was always rather uppish about talking about his family — or anything, for that matter. We have a wonderful polyglot crowd here — this pension is too, too delightful — the latest batch is or are from Belgium; they have just begun to get loose again, and a few Dutch, the latter, so far, VERY much the worse for wear; they look even more pallid and bedraggled than the English. However, they all make up for their past trials, by a look of childlike happiness, ecstasy really — they wander about (as I still do) in a dream. I do so look forward to hearing again. I want Bryher to come on here later — I think she will; in the meantime, I am fast rooted in this amazing oasis, of pine and palm.

Hilda

By the end of 1947, after having sent Pearson the two parts of her tribute to Shakespeare, H.D. was immersed in reading about the Pre-Raphaelites, the group of writers and painters whose legacy, she now felt, her own acquaintances and friends had inherited.[31] On July 11 [1948] she reports that her continuing interest in this group has led her to reread Dante's *Vita Nuova* in Italian. In her words, "Deep in my Pre-Raff notes and romance, I decided that I better know a bit more or a bit about Dante, re Gabriel's translations and so on; started boldly off; Dante Italian is not so very difficult, nearer the Latin; found a most fascinating three volume, illustrated edition, and had to re-read the *Vita Nuova*, and am now submerged and very happy, though it will hold up the Pre-Raff romance for some time." In this letter she also asks to be remembered to Thornton Wilder, whose novel *The Ides of March* (1948) she has particularly enjoyed.

After Pearson succeeded in securing the publication of *By Avon River*, H.D. confided increasingly in him about her experimental prose fiction, hoping that it would be published too. With this goal in mind, she considered giving Pearson power of attorney for her work so that he could act unimpeded on her behalf in America. Gratefully, in the following letters, H.D. calls Pearson's attention to his presence in "The Sword" as a helpful minor character, *H*oward *W*ilton *D*ean, the "perfect American," to whom she has playfully assigned an iconographic meaning that acknowledges both her own debt to him during the war and that of the Allies to America. Although she is elated at Pearson's interest in her new manuscripts, H.D. also expresses anxiety about the response of Air Chief Marshal Sir Hugh Dowding to her fictional portrayal of him in "The Sword," and she invites a critique of "The White Rose and the Red," which she finds difficult to finish.

────────── 36. TS ──────────

Hotel Minerva
LUGANO
July 31 [1948]

Dear Norman,

I do thank you for your long letter and the feeling of having you round again. I hope you are all happy there. I have heard of the library and its treasures.[32] I can not thank you and Horace enough for BY AVON RIVER.[33] I think that is the title as you first suggested it. I find one or two more mistakes but I better wait now, perhaps for proofs. Just one thing if it can be found; third to last page of "Guest"; "like the tiny pansy border in the illuminated book that Michael showed him, from his father's library." Will you ask Horace to add "illuminated," it is a long word and might break line if I did it in proof. I am trying to write H[orace], I am so very happy about this. It is really difficult to write letters so will you in the meantime, thank him. I have asked Bryher to write. I am at work on my very lovely book, *White Rose and the Red*, I think

I will call it. It is the Rossetti book. Marya wrote and asked Br if I could tell her the story of William Morris and Jane Morris, re Rossetti after the death of Elizabeth Siddal Rossetti.[34] I could not write, as I told Br to explain, as all that is in my story, or my story leads up to it; I will probably end with the death of Elizabeth Rossetti. I enjoy the book — what a treasure it has been — that you got for me, more than any of the other Morris volumes I had sent me or got from London Library. It is up to date, in psychology and insight — the story is hinted at in that volume if Marya wants to get it from Library. That heavenly picture of Morris as frontispiece! I have been so very happy with this "novel." I am writing it under a real *nom de plume*, I mean, one that fits me and fits the book, so it is not actually H.D. writing it. Not that it really matters. It started — the *nom de guerre* (literally), as I wrote a volume about the experience in this war and last war, myself and friends in London, and it is too near and too intimate for H.D.; anyhow, I could not have written it as H.D. All this in time, I call the first volume THE SWORD WENT OUT TO SEA (Synthesis of a Dream), a quote from W[illiam] Morris, THE SWORD, I mean. It has the old repercussion of war, war, WAR. I have a very nice little subsidiary character (not so very subsidiary in actual life) called Howard Wilton Dean, his wife in New England sends us pudding powders, her name is Mary Ann Dean. Do you not think those are good for you and Susan?[35] But THE SWORD is too near and too intimate, and the main character, Br says, might get mad;[36] anyhow, I don't want any publicity of that sort. I mean the main guy in the book is a certain Lord Howell and in "life," he was and still is an active acting real person — anyhow, that book can wait. But from that, I went back just 100 years to the Pre-Raffs — and my dear lovely beloved William Morris. It has made me so happy.[37] This is too much of ME. I will wait eagerly for more news of YOU. I do, do deeply feel how this Guggenheim prize must be a rest and stay to you.[38] It is being so courteously RECOGNIZED that means ALL, and that is what I felt when I got your letter with the letter copied from Macmillan and your telling me of Horace. You will explain why I did not write to Marya about the Morris-Gabriel tangle — or maybe illumination? They never referred to it at all, the people I knew. London people have the deepest loyalties — or had. By the way, please sign any papers for me, re AVON, please keep any fees, if any; all I ask and it is a lot, is the proofs! If in any difficulty, about anything legal, write my brother, he has power of attorney for me. He is: Harold Doolittle, 433 Glen Arden Drive, Pittsburgh.[39]

O — do not apologize for those POETS.[40] My only way to write, to continue writing, is to keep right out of any spot-light. You should know what I think, O dear Norman. I must stop now. All best to you and yours,

ever gratefully,

H.

———— 37. TS ————

Hotel Minerva
LUGANO
August 14 [1948]

Dear Norman:

I am writing in the cold light of dawn, after my excitement of hearing that you are interested in the MSS. I have just written to Robert Herring to post the copy that is housed in *L[ife] and L[etters]* out to you, at 39 Goodrich St., New Haven. That is the address? I asked Robert to confirm anyway, and to register the MSS, probably he will send in two envelopes. I am writing you a letter, sent ordinary, to your New Haven address, as it irks me to single-space and I have so much, so very much to say, re the MSS and the AVON and the Pre-Raff ROSE book. All that, I will simply pour out in torrents and post to New Haven.[41] In the meantime, thank you so very much for the most, most useful and valuable list of Morris treasures.[42] I am as a matter of fact, over- whelmed at the amount of work he did, and will keep this for reference. I have only his first poems and romances (the short early stories) with me, as I really did bite off a pretty large idea, and if I ALLOW myself to be intimidated, I just won't have the nerve to finish the ROSE book. But I think you will like it. And I am trying to finish it, well, it writes itself, and I just let it go on ad lib. But now, there is the usual, slight hectic end-summer feeling, particularly with us, as Br[yher] and my birthday come along and P[erdita] is due over and I be- lieve Faith Mackenzie is due at Gandria, a funny little nest of a village, near here, but only accessible by boat. I am not sure, but maybe Robert will be here for a week, too. Anyhow, it all heaves up and at one, the last of MY year, the end of our dear summer — and what a summer! Rain and floods — but here, I actually stuck to Dante those first rough-sea weeks and feel I did what I should, re Dante Gabriel Rossetti, who I do like too, that is, as character in my own ROSE book. I will send on the ROSE, as soon as it is shaped at all. There will be no trouble about that if, that is, they would like to do it as DELIA ALTON. And I have a lot of gossip about her and all — and Lord Howell, to come in my ordinary post letter or letters to you at N[ew] H[aven]. I am so touched in your interest, it IS a "story" — but first, let me repeat; my brother has Power of Attorney. Now, do you think it would be good if you had, as well? I mean, you, just for MSS and Anthology rights and so on? I wrote Harold D[oolittle] saying I was asking Br about it. Br seemed to think it might simplify things, but she said we would have to find out what law is in U.S., regarding having Power of Attorney for just one set of values. You see. You no doubt, know as much or more about it than the said Harold D., but do you think it would work? And would it, do you think, be amusing for the said Howard Wilton Dean, or would he, in the midst of his official duties find it too much? (H.W.D. always appears in the "little apartment off Hyde park" with an "imposing portfolio.") No, I do not like single-space and I make twice as many mistakes. I am also all a-dither at your real interest, and I do want your opinion, from all slants, on the great Lord Howell. The MSS has been read by only a few of "the few," that is, you will be number FIVE and I think the fate of it is in your excellent dean-ery.[43] I can not get over YOU doing the good typelist, and really you should not have, though it is most valuable and will get pasted in the back of my really lovely volume. O — yes — I would like a photograph of the miniature, if obtainable. I rather hope to stay on here all September and most of October, but it depends on the un-usual weather. I hope to get my room or one like it, again at the LA PAIX — but O — there is so much to say, and I want to rush this to you, air. Yes, all those things come back — you will see AND HOW from the MSS. I think H.W.D. is really quite a little gem of THE PERFECT AMERICAN, though I have not given him, in all, so much space — you remember Whistler? "You should not judge a work of art by its acre-age."

H.

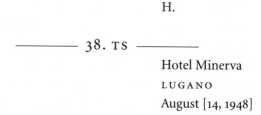

38. TS

Hotel Minerva
LUGANO
August [14, 1948]

Dear Norman,

I sent you to California, this morning, an air-letter. This is just to enclose two photographs, the pass-port one I sent you; I don't know that they will want one, but I would rather if they do, that they publish this, as it is the last one I had taken, and represents the H.D. of AVON. I have found a few more misprints in my AVON, and I will indicate them in this or will write you again. Yes — I will write you again. You may get several letters in a bunch, just gauge order by dates. I have much to say about s w o r d; I hope Robert sends it along at once. I asked him to make certain corrections, but I will probably indicate to you later, the chief ones, my poor typist is getting pretty old and was bombed; her eyes went rather weak, but she still writes asking for MSS, and I like her so much, an old Miss Woolford who was Havelock Ellis' typist, he sent her to us. I sent Book I to Rene Wormser,[44] to be held pending instructions, as I was at first rather keen to ventilate the MSS, I got so deep in it. Then I began on the r o s e, and Bryher thought that Howell might kick up a row. I don't see why he should, but I do feel that the whole volume is so very beautiful, if I do say so, and I do not want any "feeling," especially as it concerns the RAF and "messages." Howell was at first very interested, you will see all this in s w o r d. Then he turned rather funny, also see s w o r d.[45] Why? I don't know, unless he was already involved in some work having to do with the Russian situation, and thought he couldn't commit himself. In any case, it was a strange experience, the "high-water" mark, as old Delia Alton remarks. Bryher liked Book II, which I do think is *tour de force*, Bryher even said that the Elizabethan section had more of the spirit in its chapter than Edith in her whole book. Perhaps. I have also Greek, Roman and Normandy, all part of the "Synthesis of a Dream."

Herring seemed impressed but told Br confidentially that Dowding (Howell) was known to be rather persnickety just now, about write-ups, about the Battle of Britain. Actually, I did write Howell again, at Küsnacht and had a friendly letter from him,[46] but I got in wrong, as Robert had said before I was taken ill, that he would like to print something of his. I wrote rather late, suggesting this; Howell said R[obert] could have section from his first book, a book, by the way that the British Government had asked him politely but firmly to withdraw, just as it was about to appear — so I gather. Howell had two other books by very, very third-rate publisher, Rider or Ryder, of sort of psychic reputation, books badly printed; I managed to get them.[47] I have not them here, perfectly pedestrian and not very original, but some accounts of messages from a Mrs. Gascoigne and her daughter Mrs. Hill, of literacy and imagination. It was awkward as I had to write Howell that Herring had filled the paper for six months — I don't think Robert or Bryher wanted to print him. Howell gave me name of his agent, but I lost it, and sent him Christmas Greetings in 1946, did not hear again, though I sent him the synopsis of the chapters of the s w o r d; in themselves, the chapter-headings tell the story. The book had gone to USA. I said I wanted him to glance it over before final agreement. In the meantime, Br and Herring picked it over, and Br wrote to Wormser for BOOK I back. It has been at *L[ife] and L[etters]*. Actually, Robert read it after it came back from USA. I was not sending it to Viking, it was Aldington's idea. He by the way, I suppose, was rather relieved that John Geoffrey Alton turned out to be "in a small way, a hero." The later manifestation came up to scratch, Spencer (see page 4)[48] wrote me three air-mails all at once, from Le La Vandou, France, very keen and with the terrific news that William Morris called himself Hallblithe in *The Glittering Plain*.[49] The name as it was "given" by Bhaduri was Hal Brith. Well — with that, I went on with Book II, last summer, SUMMERDREAM it was and is.

I think Dowding is sincere in his psychic-research work, but it occurs that it is just possible, that he let himself in on the racket, as sort of espionage — this is of course, so very discreetly *entre nous*. There was that famous case about 1943, boats or a boat went down off Portsmouth, rumoured due to certain medium, giving away position. Lord D. has or had a brother, an admiral; I believe they live there. All this *entre nous*. He could be quite sincere, yet at the same time, make it an excuse to prowl round and see what mediums were up to, and who was phony. You may have some idea, when you read the story, I don't know; I don't in the least KNOW, but I believe he lost his only son in the war.[50] I will go on with this letter, but just enclose the list of PEOPLE OF THE PLAY. I think you know a number of them. They are not all listed.

I may repeat in later letters but it is, to me, so entirely fascinating — I mean the whole pattern. I don't know how many times I have read the MSS and I still find mistakes, will you correct, just by the way, any really crazy spelling. Robert's chief scream was that Lord Howell "stood out of the book like the Matterhorn among the hills"; but I cannot see how I could disguise him.[51] Robert says I did disguise Professor Freud and others; I didn't go out of my way to, I just wanted them like that in the texture of the cloth or the weave of the 'broidery. However, I shall be glad if you have any special comments, of any sort to make.

The lake is real *Glittering Plain* now, and I must get out or I will go a bit dotty. I am really so terribly excited that you are "in on this." I have some new comments buzzing but I must not go on. I do, do thank you for all of AVON, and more of that and more of THE SWORD WENT OUT TO SEA. SYNTHESIS OF A DREAM was my first title but R. A. commented, that that would be good sub-title, so I took above from William Morris.[52] No — I must stop — I am reminded of too much to tell you.

H.

Dramatis Personae are on last page.

THE FEW	GOLDWINGS
Gareth	Bryher
Howell	Dowding
Ben Manisi	Arthur Bhaduri
Mrs. Sinclair	Mrs. Dundas
Ada Manisi	May Bhaduri
Madge Burton	Dorothy Cole Henderson
Doris	Barbara
Philip Manning	Robert Herring
Frederik von Alten	Sigmund Freud
Jan Verstigen	J.J. van der Leeuw
Geoffrey Alton	Richard Aldington
Howard Wilton Dean	Norman Holmes Pearson
Mrs. Moss	Mrs. Ash
Allen Flint	Ezra Pound
Arthur Lovatt	Walter Rummel
Marjory Radcliffe	Dorothy Shakespeare [*sic*]
Randolph Spencer	Richard Aldington

This is roughly the order of appearance. I haven't put them all in. H[oward] W[ilton] D[ean] appears pages 45–46 Book I, and in Book II, pages 16–17. There is indication that he was there to help, "there is work, there is America," the message had come from Manisi. Geoffrey Alton is, in the story, killed in action, about 1917; R.A. is then the journalist friend from the far past, Spencer to whom Delia sends MSS, in Book II. He, by the way, the actual Aldington, thought the story should be lengthened, that is Book I and "something more made of it." He found Book II, which Bryher likes the better of the two, somewhat patchy.

H.

In October 1948 H.D. continues to mention William Morris in her letters to Pearson. She writes that she is reading Morris's "Jason," and treasures, in particular, a photograph of Morris Pearson has sent, commenting (on 19 October), that she carries it with her "with one of Sigmund Freud from which I am never parted." In this letter, she continues, "And I want to go on with Delia Alton; she looks into the future, in spite of all the darkness, there is hope in those pages, all of them, in the SWORD and in the ROSE."

In October and November, Pearson updates H.D. on his own work: book reviews and essays, the editing of Hawthorne's letters, an introduction to the Rinehart edition of Thoreau's *Walden*, which he will send her, and a projected four-volume anthology of English and American poetry with W. H. Auden. In addition to praising the "Rose," which he is enjoying, he also engages H.D. in a mild dispute over the birth and death dates of some of the Elizabethan poets included in *By Avon River.* On 10 November [1948], H.D. insists upon retaining some of the traditional dates, despite Pearson's suggestion that she comply with the findings of modern scholarship, because they reflect her state of mind during the composition of the essay. As she puts it, "I have made clear in the text that I was not a professed scholar but a very sick woman with a 'will and testament' to leave. It would alter the key, the tone, the rhythm, the meaning, the symbolism, the dedication, the devotion, the inspiration of the *Guest*, if I were now, to re-shape that amazing opening." She also insists upon placing her acknowledgment of his editorial role in the front of the manuscript, overriding his self-effacing objections.

In the exchange that follows, Pearson provides a critique of the structure of "The White Rose and the Red," suggesting that the last section seems like the beginning of a new volume.

—————— 39. TS ——————

39 Goodrich Street
New Haven 11, Connecticut
Sunday November 1948

Dear Hilda:

[...]

I haven't really spoken to you about the ROSE yet, and I could do it infinitely better now if I had the copy by me. I read it through once carefully, once hurriedly, so that some of my opinions might be altered if, after a rest, I came back to it again. First of all, as I did tell you, I was delighted with it, very much impressed both with the beauty of the imagination and with the beauty of the prose. It seems to me very fine indeed, and I was particularly taken with the formalizing concept of the book-within-a-book, which gave it depth and luminosity. One feels always going back towards pure desire and aspiration for understanding and creativity. Your central trio of Elizabeth, Rossetti, and Morris is absolutely right; and they blend into this common undefined central dream. No one has ever caught them quite as you have, and Elizabeth as the truly central focus is unsurpassed. I found the first two books almost exactly right; and when I qualify it is with little more in mind than the occasional sections, which I can elaborate if it interests you, such as the (to me) unduly lengthy and slightly confusing transition to Rossetti's conversation with the secretary to the medium, and possibly even his conversation with the medium himself; both of which seemed to me to distract slightly from the general composition. Generally speaking I should keep the focus as much as possible on Elizabeth (whose mixed beauty and vulgarity you have gotten superbly) even though she exists as much for the sake of (and in terms of) the others as in herself. This focal point being my bias (and it must be accepted by you when you read this, as explaining much of my point of view and my suggestions), I found the final book not so well integrated with the whole as the first ones had been. To me the holding point is this book-within-a-book, and I began to lose sight of it, thinking always of the advice I once heard as from George Moore, to "shape it like a vase, m'boy; shape it like a vase." Perhaps simply because you have her less concerned with her own aspiration for creativity, and remove her from the scene, the last book seems more like the beginning of a new volume than the end of another. Much more space is taken with Morris and Rossetti, without any culminating drawing back into Elizabeth again. And somehow the announcement of war at the end, perhaps again just because it does not seem to have been enough prepared for (or recently enough prepared for) to take on blood as a symbol. It seemed not really like an ending at all; as, I think, it must seem, if the book, even as a first part appears alone. If I had to hazard a guess as to what happened while you were writing this last section is that instead of looking back on what you had written before, and drawing it together, you were really starting your continuance of the story, of which you spoke to me when you wrote that the story could not be finished in this first book. The total result of the impression on me of this first section, is that the first two books of it are written with a delicacy of prose, imaginative power, and formalization which ranks it among the finest things you have done, and in some ways perhaps the best of the prose so far. It seems to me to be highly successful, and a sheer delight to read. I cannot praise it enough. I find the last book less successful, and if it is really the beginning of another section perhaps it should be clipped off of the first volume, and used to begin the next. Another way of putting it is that it is too leisurely for an ending; in an ending the pace must be quickened, the impact finally strengthened. In speaking this way, I assume a privilege that goes with my admiration and with the friendship which you cannot by this time question. If I seem to suggest changes rather than to concentrate on already-achieved excellences, it is because I so admire the book, and think it such a success that I believe you may want to do as almost always must be done with writing, to go back to it after a phase to give it the final perfections. [. . .]

Yrs. Norman

———— 40. TS ————

Hotel de la Paix
Lausanne
(Suisse)
Dec. 3 [1948]

My latest and greatest triumph: I had with your letter, one from LIFE, asking me to appear with the "important modern poets" in a photograph group with the Sitwells![53]

Dear Norman,

I do thank you for your letter. It is good that the ROSE has gone to Macmillan's. I appreciate your criticism and have been going over notes of ROSE. She kills herself, you remember, and I was rather subtly working up to it, with a sort of submerged war-phobia (rather than Rossetti's actual neglect) as being the reason for it. I agree, however, as to the apparent plot or lack of plot, I was trying to suggest a submerged or half-submerged PHOBIA. Many people in London dropped Rossetti after her suicide. This is not altogether a PLEA as for Gabriel, but simply another, more psychological and perhaps more authentic approach. However, I will wait till I hear from Macmillan before re-sorting or re-writing.

Thank you again for all your care of and for AVON. I did not send the form; I got stuck.[54] I had simply put in (or Br[yher] had) the dates of some of my opus-es, and you know those better than we do. Would you just make it out for me? I am so deeply grateful. Need they air-mail all those proofs? I simply wanted to [be] sure of my own poems and certain that my own (and your) corrections were seen to. I need not return the proofs, as you say, I can just air-mail you when or if I find any changes. I will of course, be glad to see the proofs.

I have not heard from Robert McAlmon.[55] I am rather grieved that ordinary, friendly little notes should be "for sale."[56] I am however, very, very touched that you should get them. I do, do thank you. I am deeply interested in all the Sitwell saga and so glad that you have them in charge, at Yale.[57] It is an ambassadorial bond between the four of us. I wish I were there, too. I have had news-cuttings from various sources; they seem to have survived "interviews" and been supremely tactful, all round. Perdita had a day with Edith. She wrote that E. was not well. I am grieved for that. But perhaps New Haven will be more of a rest and you yourself, "balm to the spirit."

This is my usual grumble, so much to say and so little time and space with which to say it. I do thank you again for all work on AVON and for AVON itself. You have written so beautifully and helpfully, too, about the ROSE. It is bitter cold here, a white fog. This, dear Norman, must go at once. I will try to write at length, surface, later.

Ever gratefully,

Hilda

In 1949 H.D. was happily along in the "sabbatical" year she had granted herself in order to tidy up old manuscripts. Pleased with having revised *Bid Me to Live* to her satisfaction,[58] she began to tackle other old notebooks.[59] Pearson encouraged this enterprise, urging her to throw nothing away, to send her old manuscripts to him for the archive at Yale, and later, to comment on them. They also discussed publication details regarding *By Avon River*, and his essays on topics in American literature.[60] In the letters that follow, H.D. comments on her old manuscripts.

———— 41. TS ————

Hotel de la Paix

Lausanne

Jan. 29 [1949]

Dear Norman,

Thank you for your letter of Jan. 24. It is good of you to suggest type work over there; for the moment my Miss Woolford seems able and wants the work; she writes the workmen have only just now got on to repairing her bombed little house at Wandsworth Common and she is glad to have something to do as she has a corner somewhere and feels she should be on hand. So I await some 8 to 10 sketches of 1940–1942 period and a rather delightful (I think) Bethlehem shortish sketch that I did winter 1943, called *The Death of Martin Presser*.[61] Now that would really make (I think) a beautiful little Christmas book or booklet or magazine contribution. *Martin* only went off a few days ago, but I will post these things, a few odd poems and what else I manage to scrape together out of the hay-stack, as soon as they come back from Wandsworth.

I look forward to the Sherwood Anderson article;[62] I will ask Bryher of it when she comes in this afternoon to take me out to our beautiful little tea-room down *rue petit chene*. I will ask her to write you of La Forgue.[63] He was a sort of vogue but I think local; I believe E[zra] rather suggested that Eliot was like LaF or Eliot himself fancied himself in the role; there was some sort of identification at that time. Eliot was doing a sort of mystery-clown act, appeared looking made-up but he may have been ill — great local discussions, "has he put on green paint?" I saw him at a picture show, looking like death. Osbert said he met a policeman on a bench outside the old Chelsea hall; policeman observed that the rather sensational dog he had on a string was the property of "the poet, T.S. Eliot": policeman (so Osbert said) would turn up at the house when he (O) was asked to dine there. "Was this a publicity stunt?" O. simply went on and on about it to me in London the last year or so — I really could not tell O. what! Well, this would be roughly the La F regime; I think T.S.E. snapped out of it.

I am so happy to "do a favor" regarding your seminar.[64] Do let me know of anything at all that you might want to know, that I might know. I do not think, Norman, that E.P. was even instructor at U[niversity] of P[ennsylvania]. He got in rather wrong as he would hold forth at the time, to our very dear saintly and blessed Felix Emmanuel Schelling[65] (of Elizabethan fame) on the fact that really Shaw was greater or at least as great as Shakespeare. This held up lectures, caused comment, did not make it easy for E. when he tried to get some sort of official recognition or travelling scholarship; he wanted me to "work" my family to throw in their weight but we were all devoted to Felix and anyhow, there were other things. E. got a job at Hamilton College (I am not sure just where Hamilton is). He was instructor there, in Romance Languages. He did not stay the course, was there less than a year, as I remember, and there was TALK. I can not write what my considered late opinion is of WHAT it WAS but I have my ideas and some recent clues. Anyhow, that must have been 1907, about. Marianne didn't come in to it till later. It was I who met her at Bryn Mawr. She sent some poems when R[ichard] A[ldington] and I were *Egoist*, 1913 or 1914. I jumped in, said yes, yes, E.P. liked them, a few were published;[66] E. and the others, I think then, met her in New York. W[illiam] C[arlos] Williams was brought to see us, by E.P.; I did not know Williams very well and only through Ezra. I hope these facts do not upset your programme, anyhow, please do write me if I can fill in any more gaps.

One of the very first worthies of Bethlehem married a Benézet of Philadelphia. Don't you think that was our Benét? I have read in some early Quaker romance of the Benéts of Philadelphia — but I do think Benézet might be the same. I could not swear in a law court, that our Master Benét was called Bill, it might as well have been Willie or my *cavalière servant* might have taunted him with the name. What more of Laura?

"Don't work too hard for me." [67] This has been the greatest help and I boast that I am being shelf-ed at Yale.

McAlmon sent me a very interesting shortish write-up of the "phoney war" and his escape via Spain. Bryher suggested it might be interesting to you, anyhow, I am asking her to write you of it.

Ever —

H.

Later in the winter of 1949, H.D. makes corrections in the galleys of *By Avon River*, and praises Pearson's essay "Anderson and the New Puritanism." [68] In response he describes a new lecture he is writing, "The American Poet and Science," in which he has referred to H.D. [69] H.D. also continues to comment on unpublished work she is sending for the archive: four poems omitted from "the Flowering of the Rod," "a Christmas poem," and several others from the 1930s that she finds "rather lifeless and dull and dead-wood," as well as several "sketches," done in London in 1940–41, which led to *The Gift*. On 6 February she thanks Pearson for urging her to "tidy up," saying she wouldn't have had the courage to go back to "that 1941 period" without this incentive. Her comments on *Bid Me to Live* are fuller: "I call it my Bloomsbury novel and I have written at it, for twenty years, before I got it. I did get it. It is the old last-war saga, but strangely tidied up, at long last. You may find it superficial, but it isn't. . . . The War I and War II, over-lap in some curious way, one of those pleats in time. . . . You have met some of this story before in *Synthesis of a Dream* and early work, but for once it is complete, rounded out; . . . I actually wrote FINIS to it, the summer in Vaud, before I crossed over to England, autumn 1939" (20 February). In the following letters, she continues to comment on her unpublished work.

——— 42. TS ———

Hotel de la Paix

Lausanne

March 16, [1949]

Dear Norman,

I am sending you two stories, AEGINA and HESPERIA. I have already sent you MSS of collection *The Moment*. I suggest that you please keep these last two with the five, already sent. I am sending later a title-page, *The Moment* and table of contents. I suggest that after the first story (called for the title or giving the title of the collection), that you follow with the two last sent, in their order. Every story in the collection, you may note, hinges on a decision taking place in, as it were, "a moment." That makes seven stories.

I am also sending later, the title-page for the war-sketches, and table of contents. I call the short war-sketch MSS, *Within the Walls*.

This is all comparatively simple. But now I have typed a series of poems. I do not "place" them, except as mile-stones on my own way. They follow, as a matter of fact, after Chatto and Windus, *Red Roses for Bronze*. They seem to follow *after* and yet are better technically, in many ways than the 1931 Chatto. Some of the poems or sections from the long-poems were published. I have noted that in the MS. I call this series, *A Dead Priestess Speaks*. That is the title of the first poem and rather described my own feelings. I do not want to publish this, nor in a way, many of the other things I have sent. Yes — some day, I want to see my Rossetti book and some day my other Delia Alton. But I am in no rush. But I do not want to feel that I have neglected these papers — any of them. You will file or place them on that famous "shelf," and someday, we can talk about their sequence and value. I have the carbon of each of these things I have sent you, and will keep them all together. I go over them in a way I have never done with my work. I can see, taken all in all, that there is a sequence, it is my COMMEDIA.

I hope you don't think I am wishing these things off on you. I sent *Madrigal*, too, and it really did take me twenty years to get that shaped.

Well, in time, you will read them or some of them. When I say I do not want to publish *Priestess*, I mean that it seems so far away and strange, after the published *Trilogy*. But there are some lovely shells and reflections in *Priestess*. I really don't think I have ever worked so hard — this bringing in the sheaves is more of a head-ache than the last books; *Rose* made me so happy and the *Sword*, too, as of complete fulfillment.

I should later, write a sort of history or geography of the where and when of these different styles; I must let that rest; I really have been at it, since I returned here from Lugano. I am thinking now of my summer; will you note: Hotel Croix Blanche, Lugano. I hope to get off end April, and I will have more MSS; it is all now out of my hands but I must wait the clear copies from London. This has been a most surprising Sabbatical!

Most of all, I return to my *Avon* proofs that I keep with these carbon MSS, after getting off top-copy to you. The *Avon* blesses them and you!

H.

March 17

A long letter from Bryher, just now, to tell me how happy she was with you and Susan, how beautiful your house is, the library and the sea.[70] I will be writing; I had to be firm with myself yesterday, to get this list of old and new MSS to you. I do feel rather abashed at the number of MSS, but it is an accumulation of two decades — plus. Thank you — inexpressible gratitude again from

Hilda

In March and April 1949, H.D. reiterates her gratitude to Pearson for creating the archive. On 27 March she comments on having just sent him "Advent," suggesting that he pin the following note to the manuscript: "This *Advent* is the notes I did on Sigmund Freud. It would follow or be prelude to the *L[ife] and L[etters]* writing. I explain this. It is not so very long. I repeat the incidents that I later bring into the child-story, *The Gift*, but I felt they should be assembled in their order as they first manifested with the dream-work with Freud in Vienna, in 1933." On 1 April, she writes that she has sent her old essays "Euripides, Pausanias, and a few Greek lyric poets," which she regards as "sort of high-flown school-girl essays," and she promises to send the manuscripts of *Pilate's Wife* and *The Gift*.

Pearson responds eagerly to having received these manuscripts. On 13 April, he mentions an H.D./Marianne Moore exhibition planned at Yale for the next spring and asks about H.D.'s earliest published works for a prospective bibliography.[71] He also encloses a copy of his lecture on science and poetry, mentions his new essay, "The Last Puritans," and suggests a possible visit to H.D. and Bryher at the beginning of August. Later in the spring and summer, Pearson updates H.D. on the planned exhibition, which has been delayed because Moore and her brother wish to wait until Moore's translation of La Fontaine is completed. He also congratulates H.D. profusely when *By Avon River* is published, promises to send reviews, and looks forward to seeing her in Lugano.

Besides visiting H.D. on his trip abroad, Pearson traveled with Bryher to Venice and Florence in search of Hawthorne memorabilia, while H.D. remained behind. In several letters in August, she replied to his cards from Italy, continuing a discussion of her novel "The White Rose and the Red," that probably occurred when they were together. On August 11, she expressed gratification at Pearson's "grasp of the Rossetti-Morris, Italian-English pattern — & how we came in." Also she commented on the connection between the "Sword" and the "Rose," calling the latter "a twin or companion piece" that provides the historical background of "the circle of Sir Galahad . . . founded at Oxford by William Morris." She imagined Pearson as "forwarding this tradition and this work."

The letters that follow occur after Pearson's return to New Haven. He has been reading Ezra Pound's letters to his parents in preparation for teaching his graduate seminar and has asked H.D. about the biographical sources of characters in Pound's poem, "Hugh Selwyn Mauberley." On 29 August he encloses a newspaper clipping describing the controversy following the award of the Bollingen Prize to Pound in 1949, with the following comment: "I suppose it's the only solution, but I'm rather sorry for Pound who, after all, did not ask for the prize."[72] H.D.'s response to this controversy is oblique and perfunctory. She prefers to focus upon her early memories of Pound and her own manuscripts.

─────── 43. TS ───────

> Croce Bianca
> Lugano
> September 5 [1949]

Dear Norman,

This is to thank you for your good letter of August 29; it arrived yesterday. Thank you for enclosed about the award; it is perhaps best that way but a pity that it should have had to be. I had the Martha Bacon[73] sent by Mrs. Patterson; I am so glad for the duplicate and am touched by her tribute. Bryher is writing you about the magazines. I remember Ezra speaking of Bill Shepherd (?),[74] I think. They contrived together to send me a valentine. How odd to think of letters of mine from that time, having been kept; do (I know you will) deal tactfully with them and the like. I met Lady Low.[75] I think they were Fabian, anyhow, I have impression that Sir Sydney Low was in the (then) socialist camp, but (then) a very different thing, linking on more almost to William Morris or even Bernard Shaw. I was taken to tea there, by Walter Rummel.[76] Lady Low was around, but not typically "smart," just very pleasant and open-minded, an aunt I think of Ivy Low who married the big Russian (Litvinov?). Lady Cunard I never met, but saw around. I met Nancy[77] from time to time, in Paris, at one time. Lady Low wouldn't, under any circumstances, be Lady Valentine. She was elderly, most respectable, almost, as I say, an inheritor of the good-works of the mid-Victorians. I did meet Victor Plarr[78] once or twice, I think at Yeats' rooms. He was, as I remember, rather small, dapper, like a lawyer or business-man. I think the music was at Wyncote, where the Pounds lived, the ladies clubs of that day, had group musicals; I assisted in a rather meagre way at one in which Katherine Proctor (an early friend of E) wanted to prove that — heavens, I have forgotten — Blake perhaps, could be sung to — was it? — Mendelssohn. I ran through some of the songs for her — in an amateurish manner, I was not up to the club standards, in any way. I did, after I left Bryn Mawr, join a class at one of the Philadelphia Musical academies. I was working at Beethoven Sonatas. I loved it, but felt I had not had sufficient early training. Julia Wells[79] was one of the three sisters, Matilda Wells was a schoolgirl with me at Miss Gordon's. Do ask any more questions. I have answered these in a rather sketchy way — as I remember the times and places. I am really writing to say thank you and more to follow — but I did want to send you the last section of the *Rose*. But my typist is away for her holiday, so I am sending you the rough copy that I did myself, just for you to glance at. I will send the other later, I have the carbon, with perhaps a page or two re-written and a list of corrections. You will see what I have tried to do. I don't think now, I can change it again. But I would like to say: "To Norman Holmes Pearson, in gratitude for his suggestion of continuing the story of the *Order of Sir Galahad.*" Do you think you would like the dedication? But read PART VI, the last section, before you decide. I am sending the copy with this, but ordinary mail. I have divided PART IV, but I indicate that on the dedication sheet that I enclose with PART VI. I am so happy to re-live Florence with you. Bryher suggests our going to Milan for my birthday. I have the lovely type-writer and will use it later. I can not yet thank you. Nor for all you did for us here, and my amazing satisfaction with *Avon* and the reviews that come in. We have been very rushed, happy but after a slight change, we have heat again, not such as we had, but with the three here and Sch[averell] and his wife and a contact now, with Bryher at Montagnola, things seem to hum. I would like to wave a magic-wand and have a proper village of my own here, where you could all come. Bryher was enchanted with H[ermann] H[esse]; it was her first visit, I had to go so carefully, as he is well entrenched. But next year, D[eo] V[olente], I will long to have you go there and to hear all your reactions. He is really a frail giant, the first person I have met that I can compare to Professor Freud, that is, in character, intellect, perception. He loves S[igmund] F[reud], corresponded but never met him. Br and P[erdita] go over and over, all details of your trip. And now I hear direct, and Bryher shared the first news with me, as I this, with her. This is one of my first typed letters in months, so you must forgive its slight pedestrian tone — and sense the winged heels that travel with you, in thought and spirit.

H.

Croce Bianca

Lugano

Sept. 22 [1949]

Dear Norman,

Thank you so much for the bewildering and lovely tapestry design. It is a delightful book and the short introduction is most illuminating. I must really get over to our "Upper-Rhenish region" again and see the birds, lovers, wildmen, kings and heroes for myself. The pictures are part and parcel of the *White Rose and the Red* motif, the "cards on the table," the designs that peeled off the walls at Pisa and Pre-R[aphaelite] idea of the School of Love altogether. Then, yesterday, there arrived the two Catlin volumes from Blackwell, Oxford.[80] I am afraid of getting involved in the print and pictures, if I do more than dip into them, before thanking you. I wonder more has not been made of Catlin, excerpts in anthologies and school-readers, besides that, the sketches are masterful and full of odd suggestion. I enjoyed the life, last winter. I will write more of this. I do not know why you have sent me the books, after your rare generosity with the typewriter. Is this my Christmas present? I have a calendar for you that I am posting in a few days, one of those book-folds with photographs, like the New England one we once had. But you must let me know of some "real" gift, I could send you.

Your Indians remind me of the G I F T. But I have not touched it since you left. I suppose you have by now, the surface chapter of R O S E that I sent you. I wonder if you will like the idea of the dedication and the final ending. I wanted to avoid the tragedy but I think it really does end the sequence and it is final, and I make Lizzie in a daze and forgetful, not rabidly self-destructive. I think, on the whole, the poor dear does not make such a bad end, after all, and L ' E N V O I with Allingham in the snow, I think perfect. Now, read it again and you will see the references back and forth and I will not quarrel with you over Florence N[ightingale?] or the Crimea. William Morris was as bored and distressed by Crimea as you are by atom-bomb.[81] It is a transference of symbols, merely. You M U S T see that. It is ultra-modern in all its implications, and I think that the motif or motive of the messages or the table has been clearly indicated, as a sequel or rather a fore-runner of the S W O R D. The villain of the piece is actually, one George Augustus Howell; I called him Manuel, he comes into all the later lives or the later-life of Rossetti. I could not use the name Howell, it was awkward as we have Lord Howell in S W O R D. But I think, on the whole, it is better to give the name Manuel as this fellow was a very odd card or weird card, as they say, was actually part of the Orsini plot to murder Nap[oleon] III, and was at one time in jail.[82] He it was, who was supposed to be the later Gabriel's bad angel, and it was after he came back from exile abroad, that the violation was made on Lizzie's grave in Highgate, to get at the sonnets, HOUSE OF LIFE. Anyway, Manuel gives the clue to nationality, he was half-Portugese. Charles Augustus must have had any number of names, in his day, I should imagine.

I have been reading Rebecca West, *Meaning of Treason*.[83] It is very good. By the way, I think in describing my memory of Low family, I got Sir Sydney — I can NOT remember, but another Sir Sydney (Webb?) mixed up with Low. But Lady Low was exactly as described, in black and Victorian old-world manners, good works and decorum. They lived simply — not "society" people. I have not heard from Ezra for some time; he must have stopped writing, after receiving AVON.

Perdita got off, standing all the way to Zurich. I have not heard, as from boat. She will be sure to let us know when she arrives. She was happy here and spent much time on the lake. I miss her and Bryher, but before so very long, I will be wending toward La Paix, about mid-October, I imagine.

I have your cat-card with some P. sent me, in my bag, and I think of you when I see the original Lizzie standing a-gog by my ink-bottle. All the very best to you all there; I do hope to hear soon.

H.

I am happy too, that ROSE succeeds in giving us the early Gabriel; though the final treachery is suggested in the last chapter, Lizzie sways the balance toward the VITA and DANTE.

In December 1949, H.D. mentions having carefully gone over the manuscript of *The Gift* for the last time. Referring to criticism Pearson offered in person, she says she cannot revise it now, because it is impossible to go back emotionally. On 23 December, she suggests that her story "The Death of Martin Presser," also on a Moravian theme, could serve "historically and emotionally . . . as a final statement of the child's search" and thus accomplish the same purpose as the revision he wanted.[84]

Pearson thanks HD for various Christmas gifts. The most important of these is the dedication of "The White Rose and the Red," which he claims, along with the dedication of *The Flowering of the Rod*," will be his "*passe-partout* to posterity" (23 December 1949).[85] In this letter he also updates H.D. on the latest phase of the Bollingen Prize controversy, which is manifesting itself in the pages of the *Saturday Review* and *The Nation* in a manner he finds distasteful.[86] He thanks H.D. again for sending to Yale her letters from Ezra and

Dorothy, which show Pound in a more "winning light," and continues to ask about the biographical sources of the Mauberley poems and about her own very early work for Presbyterian newspapers.

There is a gap in the correspondence in January and February of 1950. On 12 March [1950], H.D. refers to lost letters from Pearson that must have contained further questions about her early life and publications, for she continues to recount memories. "I don't suppose it was the fault of Bryn Mawr that I didn't like it," she writes. "My second year was broken into or across by my affair with Ezra Pound, who after all, at that time, proved a stimulus and was the scorpionic sting or urge that got me away — at that time it was essential — felt there, I had fallen between two stools, what with my mother's musical connection and my father's and half-brother's stars!"

On 24 March, H.D. reminds Pearson about the possibility of publishing "The Sword Went Out to Sea," a subject they had discussed in Lugano the previous summer. She has heard from Lord Dowding, who has withdrawn his earlier objections, and she hopes to discuss details with him on a prospective trip to London. Although we have no reply from Pearson on this subject, he writes a long letter on 21 June, in apology, announcing his relief at the completion of the poetry anthology with which he has been occupied all winter and spring. He then turns to Perdita's coming wedding, describing her fiancé, John Schaffner, and the wedding plans in detail, including his own role as surrogate father of the bride "in loco parentis." He mentions that H.D. and Bryher were "wise in not trying to come over for the wedding," since the young couple will be better able to receive them in the autumn when their household is established. In this letter, he also mentions the deaths of John Gould Fletcher and William Rose Benét, good friends whose widows he felt compelled to help with their literary estates, and the prospect of going to the American Institute in Oslo as a visiting professor in 1951–52. In her reply, dated 24 June 1950, "Midsummer Day, Wedding Day," H.D. expresses gratitude that both he and Susan Pearson are going to be at the wedding, regret at the reported deaths, and excitement at the prospect of having Pearson nearer at hand in the future.

In the following letter, H.D. refers to having received Pearson's most recent article, "Hawthorne's Usable Truth," which reminds her of her own cycle of romances.

———— 45. TS ————

Hotel de la Paix
Lausanne
July 26 [1950]

Dear Norman,

Thank you for the articles. I particularly liked your T R U T H. I am delighted with your "The Devil was only a definition." So many things are. Your coat of arms and the rose, as other comments in your TRUTH, take me back to my own RED ROSE. I did say something to you, to the effect that Crimea was only a definition of war, but I said it badly and you said, "who wants to read about the Crimea?" It was my attempt at focus and O — I do love that book! I had a wonderful proper copy made by Miss Christians who does Bryher's finals; I hope later to send you the carbon of it. I also had the SWORD done again, and cut out some weedy bits. They re-arranged conversations in clear, dramatic parallels. I will hope later, simply to have the Christians copied again by Miss Woolford, as there were a number of corrections that I wrote of. But that, later. Pup told me she could house any MSS, if you are overburdened. I have been enjoying, too, the *Peabody Sisters*.[87] Especially the chapter on Rome, and there I weave in again, in the last pages of TRUTH. I owe him a world, for my 7 year old introduction to Tanglewood.[88] How delightful to read of your Revere[89] and your Dr. Holmes; I had those Taylor (?) sentimental *Ladies Home Journal* illustrations, pinned round my wall, in my early school-days; "The Children's Hour," "the Chestnut," "Where the Brook and River Meet," "Home Staying Hearts" . . . can you believe it? How well you have presented this, and one realizes certain affinities with my own dear people (I call them especially my own) William Morris and his Saga translations, Rossetti with the Dante . . . yes, I remember another of the pictures on my wall, Hiawatha, of course! Your sending the folders with the signatures does weave in, under and around. I have so much. I am glad I stayed here this summer. I carry those lovely pictures always in my hand-bag. I have happy letters from Madame Schaffner and some more pictures they took there AND a tiny box of wedding-cake. I have not yet opened it. Bryher doled hers out, sacrificially, I mean ceremoniously or sanctified-ed-ly, crumb by crumb here and in London, Cornwall, Isles of Scilly where she now is. She should be back in about two weeks, she may take a tour on the return, with Rita, in France. I have seven letters from E[zra], I don't like to tear them up. I will try to post surface, also may enclose one from Olga and cards sent me by Mary or Maria; she has now two children. Please destroy any or all of these as you think best. My correspondence with E., this end, is by way of packets of post-cards that I select from my very old Greek cards, or I manage to find "masters" of sorts, well reproduced in cards here. I should write him, it is all so heart-breaking and impossible. I do hope you get some kind of happy holiday. Thank you for cheque that came for anthology poem or poems; I sent it to my brother to bank for me. You have been endless good to us all — how go on with it? I don't know if my N. Y. plans will be frustrated by the new "Crimea."[90] I don't know. Bryher writes that London was low and dull and horribly expensive and she wondered that a stone had been left standing, as she flew in, low over Westminster. No panic there — or anywhere, I don't think — but she said I must not worry, have apparently enough out here to last several years and I suppose I would stay put. I don't know. Will your Nordic plans be altered? This is such a scrappy letter but I have been visiting with you so lately in Salem and with TRUTH.

Ever,

H.

I hear from old Mrs. Russell[91] (wife of Bertie as she calls him or Lord Russell; Alys, you remember, is Pearsall Smith's sister, "Bertie's" first wife) that Bryn Mawr is after some MSS of H.D.; Alys R. is 83, in the first class there, I think. Anyway, she is most pressing but I told her that Professor Pearson of Yale had the pickings. If I find any extras, I might send later, I wrote, as I am so devoted to her.

In late August and September [1950], H.D. congratulates Pearson upon the publication of his anthology, *The Poets of the English Language*, and thanks him for sending her a copy. She also thanks him for placing her poems[92] and for his efforts on behalf of her Rossetti book. Once again she expresses the desire to publish "The Sword" first, reminding him of their earlier conversation in Lugano. She also praises Bryher's new novel, *The Fourteenth of October*, comparing it to a historical romance by William Morris. On 30 September Pearson asks for fresh copies of both "Sword" and "Rose," assuring her that someday both will be published: "I have pledged it. It has the seal of our fingers linked on the sword itself. Yours and mine." On 4 October H.D. rewards this devotion to her work by singling out the phrase "O my chevalier!," from Hopkins's "The Windhover," in Pearson's anthology, to describe his role in her life. She writes, "for there is your place, 'liaison' between my *Rose* people and others."

Later in October, Pearson updates H.D. on the status of various poems he has sent to *Wake*, *Poetry*, and the *Yale Review*, asking her for more. He also requests a copy of notes she wrote about Pound,[93] and promises to send a copy of the collection of Pound's letters that is to appear.[94] Congratulating H.D. on the publication of a poem in *Nine*, Pearson signs his letter of 23 October "your chevalier," a signature he will repeat frequently. In the following letter, H.D. expresses her pleasure and appreciation.

Hotel de la Paix

Lausanne

October 27 [1950]

Dear Norman, C.H.E.V.A.L.I.E.R.,

Bless you! It is so good of you to see about the poems, and I really do care and feel satisfied with a sort of *connaissance en participation*. You must do what you think about "May 1943"; title, as you think, though in a way, perhaps *What Do I Love* takes from the Xmas booklet surprise. Perhaps not. I do leave it to you, for not so many of my gift-booklets will have seen *Poetry*. Does it matter that "Georgius" and "Hymn" came out in *L[ife] and L[etters]*? I was under the impression that you had all the suitable poems, as I have only the carbon of the collection I made, entitled "A Dead Priestess Speaks." These are mostly long poems; "A Dead Priestess Speaks," "Electra-Orestes," "Callypso," "In Our Town," "Delphi," "Dodona," "Sigil," "Priest," "Master." These poems could be cut up into any number of fragments or segments. Is it possible that you never had the copy that I must have sent, about winter 1948? I was getting these scripts tidy before and after Xmas, that year. I will have fresh copies made if you never got the lot. By the way, "Georgius" is not dedicated to Bryher but to W.M., William Morris! You speak of the *Nine* poem, that was one of the Delphi sequence; they only wanted that one section out of four; these could be done separately. I only wrote the E[zra] P[ound] memories in a letter and have no copy, maybe Peter Russell [95] would let you have it, if he kept it. I am sorry that I did not post the little booklet sooner, will send it tomorrow but I told you of the poems in it. I will send you my carbon of Priestess poems, if I can find the very rough original, but I am sure I sent the top-copy to you. I did rather overwhelm you, at that time, with papers. There are quite beautiful segments in "Priest," which could be cut up. What an amusing sense of LIFE this gives me, to write you of these old poems. They come alive like crystals in sun-light. I really will try to go over every scrap now, as you have been so good about placing these. Dear Bryher — I am glad you thought W.M. was Bryher. It is perfect — and she IS! Now please — I leave everything to you, really, I do, titles, re-arrangement and so on. You do not even have to ask me. Someone, I suppose, reads the proofs carefully? That is all. This is all my own axe-to-grind but it isn't really, it is that spring feeling of *germination* . . . and I do thank you again for my little veg and for the lovely jars (Jars!) of maple-sugar that I have been so enjoying. I told you to watch my luck, what with those veg and all! I am so interested in all news and of your trips and your and Susan's feeling for dear Bryher's visit. I told you (did I not?) that she appeared at our Mutrux stylish tea-shop with a YALE football favour pinned on her jacket — or rather she pulled it out, like a magician and did I have a turn? I haven't seen anything of the sort for well over 40 years. All so interesting about the old uncle,[96] he is exactly like our Baron here, an old, old gentleman who has been (he says) in eight wars. The first when he was a child, the Paris commune — but that is a long story. He stopped me solemnly the other evening, most gallantly kissed my hand and said, "I have been waiting to wish you a very Happy New Year." Well, maybe it was symbolic for with the return of Bryher, with all good news of Perdita, of "all the Valentines" as she calls "them," I did and do feel so happy, so young and free from old worries and the clouds of the war-years. You changed the direction of all our lives . . . forgive, forgive all type-errors. I am rushing this out at once. And I will write again and send the poems if you let me know roughly what you have not-got. Peter Pan.[97] Yes, I saw Maude Adams myself and was shocked by a cruder edition of Peter Pan that May Sinclair took me to in London — maybe 1913!

Ever,

H.

In early November, after reassuring her that he does have her "Priestess Poems," Pearson asks H.D. to jot down which of her poems have appeared in *Life and Letters* and *Poetry*. H.D. responds to this request on 9 November [1950] and mentions sending him more manuscripts: her early "Notes on Thought and Vision" and "Responsibilities," a review of Yeats's poetry. In his reply, on 2 December 1950, Pearson mentions having sent proofs of her poem "Last Winter" to Ezra Pound, who responded enthusiastically. In the following letter, he continues to update H.D. about Pound's situation.

——— 47 · TS ———

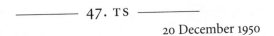

20 December 1950

Dearest Hilda:

[. . .]

I said in my last letter that I would pass on what I had learned of Ezra's life from the young man who came from him to me. He is a young man of rather stern convictions about the importance of integrity in life but with no very strong direction as to where the point of view should lie. He is a graduate student at the University of California who decided to do a biography of Ezra

"Dear Norman, C.H.E.V.A.L.I.E.R.," 1946–1951

for his dissertation. He says he is not yet ready to read the poems, and the incredible thing is that he is following just that course. He wants to live out a life which followed integrity, and he regards Ezra's as such tho he himself is probably more liberal than Ezra is. At any rate he has moved to Washington for six months, and every Monday he spends the afternoon with Ezra at the hospital, while he asks questions and Ezra gives him lists of good economic texts to read in order to be educated. Ezra has three such young persons to whom he devotes an afternoon a week each.[98] At precisely one o'clock they are at the gate of St. Elizabeth's [sic] and walk to where Ezra is sitting out of doors under the trees. Mrs. Pound is usually already there, for she goes every day of the week without fail from one to four during the visiting hours. She sits and listens while Ezra, presumably hears the lessons and gives out the next assignment. One of the students comes from the University of Maryland and is studying the classics. Another quit Hamilton College, and is reading economics under Ezra's tutelage: Douglas, Del Mar, Brooks Adams, and Frobenius to take it a little further. Penniless, this boy is sharing Mrs. Pound's single bedsitting room with her in a rooming house, and presumably they cook their meals together over the single jet gas stove from which she lives.

Most of the patients in the Hospital — in fact all but Ezra — have only an hour's exercise out of doors, and then they go to walk in a troop or sit in melancholy circles staring at each other. Ezra, however, has the three hours without supervision, except that he must stay within the extensive grounds. Whether it is fair or raining he walks and sits, and has another of those beach chairs in which he can recline throwing his head back to ease his neck.

Inside the hospital he has the unusual privilege of a tiny study to himself — really a closet, in which he has a table to write on and cases for his books. There he spends the mornings and evenings, but goes to sleep in the ward with other patients. His eyes are so bad that he no longer reads very much, he says, but spends his time typing out long letters with no address and no signature except for the cryptic "strictly anon," but he types hieroglyphics in a corner which Dorothy interprets when she gets back to her room. She addresses the envelopes and sends them out. For some reason I get a good many letters from them, all really kindly toward me ever since the one in which I blew him and his wife to hell and gone for their stupidity in misinterpreting me. Sometimes I get only an envelope with a clipping in it: one a tribute in an Italian paper to Fletcher; another an article on Schacht; one an offprint of an article on him in Italian.

Mrs. Pound says he is better than when he came, but cannot concentrate long enough to write any poetry, and it is not probable that the cantos will ever be finished. Sometimes, personally, I think they are finished; for I do not know whether he would have been able to reach a climax in a poem which says the same thing over and over (albeit sometimes most beautifully) if it had not been for the awful accident of history which led to the humility lines. Now anything else would be an anti-climax, and Pound cannot offer himself absolution even if he were willing to do so. Nor justification either, since the theme of his poem as a whole is not a personal issue but a condition to be proved by the facts of history as he would say they existed despite himself.

What strikes me more and more as I go on teaching him and reading him is how very much he comes out of the middle-western American "black republican" tradition. His concern with money is so very like the anguish of the farmers against Wall Street, like Bryan's "They shall not crucify man upon a cross of gold."[99] I understand that his grandfather, who was governor of Wisconsin, issued his own script once; his father helped in minting money; Ezra indulges in a kind of moral numismatics.

Did he ever think of money in the old days I wonder, or did he simply run an international literary exchange, in which the poetic coin of Provencal was shifted to Cavalcanti and the like, with no charges to the bourse?

I have been getting the graduate students to annotate the individual cantos, starting with the first fifteen. It is a way of making them read closely as well as widely. I shall have them mimeographed up as they are finished. Would it amuse you to see them? We did Mauberley together, you and I, so to speak, and I only wish we could talk over, or write over, these, so that I could be surer as to what Ezra intended them to be.

Yr

Chevalier

On 27 December H.D. responds that she doesn't have any "bright *trouvaille* as to Ezra and 'money in the old days.' There was never enough of it, and what there was he mostly gave away." She also mentions that Richard Aldington described the editors of *Nine* as Catholic fascists who use Pound as a political symbol. In the following letter, which anticipates H.D.'s visit to America upon the birth of her first grandchild, Pearson thanks her for sending the first part of the manuscript of her Moravian novel "The Mystery" along with the commentary on her work, which she has titled *H.D. by Delia Alton*. He is pleased with the way in which this novel concludes the cycle of romances, and he praises the clarification that her commentary provides.

15 January 1951

Dear Hilda:

My life is getting to be preposterous. Here a fortnight or more has gone by since *The Mystery* arrived, and with it Delia Alton's fine and sensitive study of H.D. — and none of my enthusiasm or gratitude sent back until now. The only way that I can seem to escape from the students is to borrow Susan's typewriter and at least begin the letter to you on the kitchen table which I hope you will be seeing, and eating from, before too long. But the chief thing is that the *Mystery* and its *ms*, and the H.D. arrived safely, and I have long since read them. I am delighted by the *Mystery*, so beautifully written and so haunting in its shifting scenes. The whole structure, without being obscure, adds immensely to the tone, is, shall I say, functional, certainly adroitly contributory. It lifts the leather curtain to silver and sevres. "The place is seething with overtones." This is one of the very best. Your chevalier bows low.

As for the H.D., Delia Alton has done well. It is like one of your needlepoints with the scene there in colors, a kind of small tapestry of history. It sets things right so that there can be no doubt. How many hands will finger the pages of its print some day, keep fingering them long after you and I no longer have the power to point the ruler like schoolmarms. I hope you are not sorry for having done it; I certainly am glad and grateful.

Norman

In February and March 1951, Pearson and H.D. discuss details of her coming trip to the United States, about which H.D. is anxious. They also discuss poems he has placed for her and his essays on topics in American literature. On 22 February he congratulates H.D. on becoming a grandmother, and expresses his pleasure at being the baby's godfather.[100] In the following note of gratitude, written from her hotel in New York after her arrival on 1 April, H.D. encloses a letter from Ezra Pound, whom she had written on 12 April canceling an earlier plan to visit him in Washington.

───── 49. MS ─────

Beekman Tower
N.Y. 17
April 16 [1951]

Dear Norman,

I have just written a letter to Susan — but I can not thank her — nor you. You gave a frame & stability to the whole structure — the tapestry stretched too loosely, on (as per *Sword*) what seemed too wide a frame. I am glad to be able to say, to feel, to know the *END* of a period — a life — a curtain. And after my 6 months at Küsnacht, to have been able to express it, to formalize it — & even well before I left, to have started *Sword*, after finishing *Avon*. And that is five years ago, May 13, that I was flown out from England, still during the wail of the sirens & the crash of bombs or guns in that lovely manor house on Lake Zurich. I am *glad* I had the time there. But you were part of that Last Trump of or in England & my loss of England has been balanced by my finding of the formula of it, of this world. Next time, I won't try to rest. Perhaps you can help me get in touch — you know — not so much that I want to talk literatuur (as E[zra] would say) but that I like, I love them, our poets. Enclosed was just brought in by Br[yher] — I should say you must help as well; keep me *out*, of touch.[101] So I am to "stimulate NHP's mind" — Golly! How he has stimulated mine. Drop the letter in your basket. I enclose my so-far favorite picture of *your* fellow! I will get another from them. How can I thank you for that — all that "name this child."[102] I will be with you in your 233 Hall.[103] I will be so happy again with MSS at La Paix, & I hope Lugano. This is really to send V[alentine] — I will write Mr. — (Dr.?) McG[ee][104] — you will send the address? P[erdita] rang last night — they are deeply grateful — all went well on return trip. I will write again, — C. —

from, H.

In a postscript to this letter, also dated 16 April 1951, H.D. encloses a letter from Marianne Moore, whom she has seen in New York. The letter contains a picture of H.D. circa 1917, which H.D. had long forgotten. Also, probably referring to a recent conversation with Pearson about her Moravian novel, she comments: "I am touched that the C[hevalier] in *Mystery* or *Miracle* is with you — and happy that you share Pennsylvania and the House of Köstnig with me. I was told (but perhaps legendary) that there was a thread with de Wattevilles. I went to school, along-of-Bill [Benét], with the real de Schweinitz children."

During the last two weeks in April, when H.D. is back in Switzerland, she and Pearson discuss the hope that Pascal Covici, an editor at Viking and a friend of Richard Aldington, will recommend "The Sword Went Out to Sea" for publication. Earlier letters from Aldington to H.D. indicate that she was very grateful to him for his receptive reading of that manuscript, and for offering to contact Covici.[105] In the following letter, in the course of commenting on old letters she is sending to Pearson for the archive, H.D. refers to her revised feelings about Aldington and to Pearson's role in mediating her relationship with him.

Ascension Day
Hotel de la Paix
Lausanne
May 3 [1951]

Dear Norman,

Thank you for your letters; I have written to Mr. Magee and sent surface, the RAF poem in LOVE,[106] saying it would say what I could not. The folder is most interesting and the poem beautiful. I also sent surface, the booklet to Mr. Covici. Thank you for the helmet too, symbolic.[107] I am back where [I was] before I left for New York, as Br[yher] sent me out nine envelopes of old letters etc. I am posting you surface, the first selected batch. The Sitwells are almost all undated and I did not even try to arrange them. Br said she dated hers as they came, but it did not occur to me to do this. I have not read them, you will use your usual discretion. They are all friendly and very kind and human; I think Edith felt our position there, in the Blitz, she wrote constantly. I have heard from none of them, since I left May 13, 1946. But I saw them here, passing through, spring 1947 and they were both most, most charming and affectionate. There is the first from Osbert, I think dated, 1939; he wrote it in answer to one of mine, asking as for Jean U[ntermayer],[108] if he could give me something for her refugees. I had met him a number of times but had not written. I only met Edith, up there, for the first time, as per that story, The Ghost. Their letters seem sort of impersonal, unlike the batch I send from Richard. Those were written 1929, 1930, 1931. I have noted this and R. dated every letter, but a few hasty casuals. I have never read these letters in a batch, and I must say they gave me a sense of that time and scene but I think better to let you have them. You can always say, if anything "comes up," that I sent the letters to you, to "store" for me. They are yours, for what they are worth. Richard's lot reads so much more vividly than any of his novels, it might be a little commedia dell'arte piece. The letters are not very discreet, but that is their charm. If you want to know who any of the dramatis personae are, just ask me. Egon who I took with me as a sort of buffer-state, is Eileen Macpherson, Kenneth's sister. I had a sort of authentic Rossetti feeling about that Paris and Italy lot of letters, almost "dear Liz, come back . . ." There is also a real, dynamic, perfectly English and inimitable Byronic feeling about the decor. I don't think Richard ever really knew what he was or what he did to people — there is Valentine in a taxi-smash (not the Lady V. of Ezra's canto) "pregnant but not by me." I think you will laugh. I did. There was apparently a great do, which I had forgotten about, getting that Imagist book together. I stopped writing completely, then a chance meeting in a bun-shop 1936, and the real divorce; then his book from USA but not a word except for that, during that terrible time. However, he more than made up by his part in the *Sword* and his recognition of Hallblithe. Now we write. But those letters are another story and rather more sedate. I am doing some more envelopes, a few letters of Lady Ellerman, one of John, Bryher's brother; letters of and about the Reading, letters that were sent when I asked for the Poet's selection of Poets, as for lectures, a few thanking me for the *Walls* or *Tribute*. Thank you too, for the Godspeed letter — it must have helped a lot, just over 12 hours crossing. There is much more to say. When I contrast the Aldington legend with your beautiful serenity and security there! I will write again of course. Now it is warmer, we had a bitter spell, and all heating off here in hotel. I saw Br for lunch yesterday, that made the frame four-square again. My thanks to Susan for everything . . . my thanks to you for making all that past "come true." I think sometimes Richard is almost the Joker, of the card-pack. At least, we and "they" had a pretty specific and valuable "card up our sleeve" and R. perceived its power — The Viking Ship and Hallblithe! It doesn't matter if the book is or is-not published. Just so it goes on living or vibrating and reaches a few people . . . I will think of EVERYTHING unsaid, the minute I seal this.

To C. gratitude

from *H.*

In May the two continue to discuss H.D.'s trip to America. When H.D. expresses excitement at having found *The Hedgehog* on the "shelf" in Pearson's New Haven office, he asks her to place that work in the "order" she described in *H.D. by Delia Alton*. He imagines both himself and H.D. to be part of a modern spiritual community (or "order") that rivals the earlier utopia of Aldington and Lawrence, and he shares her excitement at the possibility that Viking might want to publish "The Sword" (4 May 1951). H.D. responds enthusiastically to this notion of a mutually understood "order." She also updates Pearson on her correspondence with "Lord Howell," who now sanctions the publication of "The Sword" with his name changed, and she mentions her satisfaction with "The Mystery."

In June, Pearson tries to palliate the disappointment of Covici's rejection of "The Sword," and to support H.D.'s apparent refusal to do a journalistic type of autobiography, as Covici would like. Pearson argues that Covici, who discovered Steinbeck, is a proponent of naturalism in fiction, which prevents him from understanding H.D.'s experimentation in "The Sword." He assures her that it will be published and advises her not to change the name of Howell. H.D. accepts his reassurance. On 17 June [1951] she writes, "Yes — the

Sword is important. But simply again, as a record and a record I could not have done, if I had not persisted, even at Küsnacht, on REMEMBERING. For me, it was so important, my own LEGEND. Then, to get well and re-create it." [109] She also comments on a new chapter of "The Mystery" with its "swirl of 18c prophesy."

In August the two discuss the conclusion of "The Mystery." On 20 August H.D. writes that she has sent "perhaps the last of the book," despite an inconclusive ending, depending upon Pearson's advice. She adds that, although she is "devoted to the characters," she prefers not to continue the story "just now." On 29 August Pearson responds that the inconclusiveness is appropriate, given the theme of the book. He writes, "[W]hat you are doing is what you are describing, which is the life of this writing. Don't try to go on with it until you feel the pull of the grail again." In the exchange that follows, they continue to discuss the last section.

──────── 51. TS ────────

September 1 [1951]
Hotel de la Paix
Lausanne

Dear Norman,

I am posting you a book of Hermann Hesse, with some of his pictures. This book can not be bought, he was careful to state. He gave me and Br[yher] copies when we were up there, on Br's last visit. But I had already exchanged the translation of *Magister Ludi* that I had, and that he never had had, for one of these books — this in triumph, I gave to Br last birthday or one before last, 1949. So Br has two copies; I can borrow or take back one at any time. This is sort of toward Xmas. But please open it. I have much, much to say about visit here, intended to write a double letter but will try instead to write S[usan] direct, to thank for the wonderful set of albums. More, much more of this. I am anxious to get this off — your letter arrived this morning, another mystery, for how could S have got back in that time and you already seeing her? It is less than a week since she left Zurich. I have had only one card from the Valentines — the two — Br writes of the small one. I am so home-sick for him but Br is due here on the 7th and I return, D[eo] V[olente], with her to Kenwin on 17th, to stay there till Perdita and V[alentine] leave, very early October. But the above, as you know, always reaches me.

I sent more chapters, there were 9–19 in this second lot of *Mystery*. I meant, did you think it finished after 19? You will tell me. Yes, there is Ps-a and other things there,[110] some re-writing of *Gift* but clearer and in another setting. I am surprised that Miss Christian says she can type this for me in about two weeks, then, I can send you the proper last copy. There were a number of slight corrections in Chapters of first section, 1949; just two years later, I pick up the exact time, theme and thread, I think. Another section COULD do with Elizabeth de Watteville reading the letters after the Chevalier has left for Paris, and more of the Cathedral. But that will have to wait — and I will be so anxious to know if you really feel that it is finished . . . I am very happy about this and said in my *Notes* that the book was written, even if I did not transcribe it. I just want to collect and tidy-up what I have done — this was left unfinished before you came, 1949, to *Croce Bianca*. It looked so pretty when I took S[usan] to see it — but smaller of course than this and rather down in the hollow or half-hollow. I am sure you would be happy here; I had engaged first rooms before I left for N[ew] Y[ork]; so we will plan well ahead. Thank you for the lovely CAT; I carried it in my bag, with a list of boat-trips, time-tables and things to "do," but we had time really only for the one short *Giro* and the endless arcades. We thought and spoke of you constantly,

dear C

from *H.*

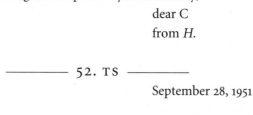

52. TS

September 28, 1951

Dearest Hilda,

[. . .]

The Hesse volume came safely, and I am quite mad about it. Except for you I should never have seen it, and yours and Bryher's signatures give it a kind of trilogy with Hesse's own. We intend to hang the Klingsor watercolor on another wall of our bedroom — the Tessin, Lowndes, the Middle Ages, all brought mysteriously together.

So, too have come the pages, 114–150. Most beautiful writing, and it is like soft gold, gold plate spun thin but perdurably strong all the same. And the three mss notebooks, for which my undying thanks. Don't throw such things away. They are a part of your shelf, now shelves. Your shelves and Bryher's shelves, and my own — again this trilogy; as though all things worked out in threes.

[. . .]

I sent you at Lugano, Bill Wms autobiography,[111] before I had read it. It has qualities, and it is Bill all right; but it could have been very much better, and it is sometimes a little too arch. As to the references connected with Bob [McAlmon], I suspect the whole tenor comes from some attempt on Bill's part to justify his enthusiasm for Bob's talent and why it never matured into anything of any real importance. He wants to make Bob a victim, whereas Bob was always his own Satan and his own victimizer. I shall take care of all that, and it is too silly to be very important. I am much more concerned with the accuracy of his remembrance of the Philadelphia days; and if it amused you, do set me right at whatever spots and points I should be. These things I ought to know, and would never know without your help.

[. . .]

Yr,

C

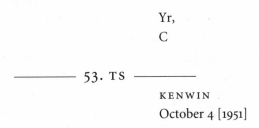

— 53. TS —

Dear Norman,

I am here until Bryher returns, in about ten days. Then, *La Paix*. Now, she will be about saying au-revoir to Perdita and Valentine, returning *La Grasse*. I will try to get some of the charming photographs of your god-son to send you. We were so very happy. Thank you for your good letter and the cat-book was madly appreciated — and the most illuminating N.H.P. folder. I think the fish is beautiful. I went over my books at Lugano but here, have had no time to revel in them. Two booklets[112] that I left out on my table had the pictures hopelessly gummed together. I just tell you. Not that you are likely to leave them simmering in the sun. But I had a grand time soaking them and re-sticking them and saved the day. Of course, my room had the full sun and it was foolish to leave them there on the table. But all the others are in order except for one that had no pictures. I don't know how that happened. I went over them and over them. This is album *S*. It is just possible as they are "religious" that one of the R.C. maids couldn't resist — but I don't think so. I have never had anything taken in all these almost-six years, except possibly some particular Culpepper lemon-cream from England that vanished mysteriously; one of the maids was horribly bitten by mostiks and asked me for something for her arm. I can't tell you what these picture-books mean — but, as I say, I have been in such a whirl, all the time, Br came the 7th, then we came back and they left here, the 1st of October. The reading-matter, information of these booklets is amazing. And arrangement — van Gogh a special revelation in sequence. I have a beautiful Hesse picture too, but have put it away — walls and some almond trees. I am glad you have *Mystery*. I wanted you to tell me if you feel it is finished? I do. And FINIS too, to a whole processus or life-time of experience. I am actually, thanks to you, now ensconced in a sort of ex cathedra arm-chair — can review the world from the elder's bench. I have not had the W.C. W[illiams]; I will tell you how it strikes me, later. I asked E[zra] P[ound] to sign a Fenellosa and send it to you, my second American Cheque. I said it was for your shelf — he wrote me the oddest letter. Then, Dorothy wrote, enclosing some iridescent feathers, pigeons? She said E. was happier, as these booklets, Square Dollar Series[113] or some-such, come out. I am interested in your Tibet encounter. I am glad Susan was happy in Lugano, we had great fun, parading the arcades. Much to say . . . much to say . . . I will really wind-off a dossier when I get back to *Paix*. I have not stayed here since 1939 and there are many memories connected with the place and environs. I came over, of course, for lunch now and again. But it is strange to be back, high-up here above the trees, really beautiful and grown of course in bush and bosk — *boscage* — since I last stayed here. I find your *Billy Budd* Nelson references, particularly revealing. Your *mystique* of innocence and Milton comments are all in line with my own Revelations.[114] I am reading the "Yarn" carefully again and will write you . . . "the world which was the ship in its passage out." I must not go on with this. By the way, our Howell writes now, that we may use name Howell, if we can not find a better — but I wrote him, that N.H.P[earson] had the MSS in hand and we both thought for the time, it was better to leave it — and do a limited edition perhaps later. I am in no hurry. You can see in *Mystery* that the Edenic (your word) serpent bites its own tail, at last. (Or did you say Adamic?) Anyhow, I do know the complete reward of having persisted and having recorded . . . now, you will let me know, one day, what will be best. How old and long ago does H.D. seem to me — and by some one of the many jokes of the Immortals, old Howell is H.D. too. He will be 70, the day after Shakespeare's and St. George's birthday — what effect did THAT have? I mean the St. George? Well — enough — you see it all, know and record. When will you [have] collected the "papers"? This is all *à tort à travers*, as they say in the back of the dictionary. Really — only to thank you — to thank you, dear C —

H.

In the remainder of 1951, H.D. and Pearson continued to discuss topics raised in the preceding letters: his essay on *Billy Budd*, their concern about Ezra Pound's imprisonment, and Williams's *Autobiography*. Pearson explains why he is on the board of editors for the Square Dollar series of booklets, which were masterminded by Pound.[115] He also expresses his growing belief that Pound has "suffered enough" and should be freed (8 October). On 3 November, besides mentioning her own cheque to the Square Dollar series, H.D. expresses distress at Williams's *Autobiography*: she comments that most of the parts "about the early H.D." are "pure invention." Also, H.D. asks Pearson to check on the progress of a manuscript sent to Yale University Press by Rachel Annand Taylor,[116] a personal friend of hers and Aldington's from the old London days. The year ends with the customary exchange of gifts and greetings.

1. Pearson was awarded tenure in 1951.

2. On 22 October 1946, H.D. asked specifically about Thornton Wilder, William Rose Benét, and Robert E. Sherwood, commenting that Sherwood's play, *There Shall Be No Night*, "helped us so, in London."

3. On 27 November 1946, Pearson sent H.D. a Doolittle engraving plate from an eighteenth-century geography book, suggesting that she use it as a bookplate. On 5 December [1946], H.D. accepted his suggestion gratefully, commenting that she "never felt quite 'at home' with the two [she] had." She continues, "I feel very important with such distinguished relatives. I am *sure* you must be a long-lost cousin." For reproductions of her two bookplates, see Michael King, ed., *H.D.: Woman and Poet* (1986), 25, 141.

4. Richard Aldington to H.D., 6 October 1947, unpublished letter. In a letter to Bryher, dated 1 July 1947, H.D. reports that she sent Aldington volume 1, "just to get an outside opinion. Much to my surprise and alarm, he said he had seen nothing like it, it was *so good* but — with all per humility — I should re-work, add here and there and make a BEST SELLER of it."

5. Richard Aldington to H.D., 6 November 1947, unpublished letter.

6. Richard Aldington, *The Religion of Beauty: Selections from the Aesthetes* (London: William Heinemann, 1950).

7. On 23 August 1948, in an unpublished letter to Pound, H.D. briefly describes her life during and after the war and thanks Pound for sending her "the Cantos," which she finds "full of suggestions and glimpses of old-time." She probably refers to *The Pisan Cantos* in this letter, but other letters to Pound and diary entries in "Compassionate Friendship" indicate that she also owned and referred to *The Cantos of Ezra Pound* (New York: New Directions, 1948), which was sent to her by Pearson.

8. On 13 October 1948, in a letter to Bryher, H.D. comments on the sources of Pound's political sympathies: "I wonder so much what DID HAPPEN. It may have been confusion about the last war, being there and not being in it, and E[zra] was made much of by many people; I know how they changed in tempo during the first war, and he may have felt they were no longer interested in the same way. He appears to me now, to have BEGUN the down-curve at the end of or just after World War I. . . . Anyway I feel there was some definite break or repercussion or even percussion in or at the end of War I, that sent him back to the old shock of being asked to leave Hamilton College." On 15 October 1948, she continues, "I have been going over the old American scene and 1914 pre-war Paris and a number of things now crop up, sign-posts that relate various phases of Ezra to certain things . . . and certainly the main factor was . . . his father being in Mint; E[zra] saw shelves of gold which to a child anyway, were in his father's hands, and he had no use of it; all so very, very obvious — his 'usury' (whatever that is) complex that crops up again and again in the Cantos."

9. H.D. to Ezra Pound, 22 September 1948, unpublished letter, Lilly Library, Indiana University (hereafter LL).

10. On 9 January 1946, Pearson wrote to William Carlos Williams: "I belittle him [Pound] on his own terms by still admiring much of what he did as a poet while distinguishing his poetics from his ideology and from him as a man. He started, as I once wrote, as

the Longfellow *de nos jours*; he ended up something much nastier" (unpublished letter).

11. Pearson supported the controversial award of the Bollingen Prize to Pound for *The Pisan Cantos*. (I wish to thank Donald Gallup and Louis Martz for this information.)

12. Hermann Hesse (1877–1962), German Nobel Prize–winning novelist and poet; moved to Switzerland in the 1920s; in the 1930s his Swiss citizenship became part of his stance against the Nazi government. Hesse and his wife, Ninon, lived in the vicinity. Hesse met both H.D. and Bryher and admired H.D.'s work. H.D. considered translating his early poetry.

13. On 29 June 1947, Bryher writes to Pearson that Hilda seems happy in Lugano, "and adores Hermann Hesse, the last year's Nobel prize man. I think his poetry good and some of his prose. But Hilda is much more excited over it than I am." Also, H.D.'s letters to Bryher from January through April 1947 contain specific references to Hesse's "Marchen" and other fiction.

14. On 20 January 1947, Pearson continues: "I see *The Gift* being a kind of U.S. Ausblick; and then will come a companion volume, a gift from England. But you could not do this from 10 Lowndes."

15. *Briarcliff Quarterly* was published out of Briarcliff Junior College. Volume 3, no. 11 (October 1946) was dedicated to work on or about William Carlos Williams. The prefatory note mentions H.D. in relation to Williams's years in Philadelphia.

16. On 31 December 1946, Pearson wrote that he had sent a copy of "the Bryn Mawr magazine which was devoted to Bill Williams."

17. May Sarton (1912–1995), prolific American poet, novelist, and diarist, taught at Harvard in the forties. Born in Belgium, she and her family moved to the United States as war refugees in 1916. Among her forty-seven published works are *Collected Poems, 1930–1973* (1974). She claimed H.D. as an inspiration; cf. Earl G. Ingersoll, ed., *Conversations with May Sarton* (Jackson: University Press of Mississippi, 1991).

18. On 20 January [1947], in his response to this letter, Pearson updates H.D. on the relationship between Pound and Williams. He writes: "[Williams] writes me that he had finally broken off with Ezra. Did I tell you?"

19. On 31 December 1946, Pearson wrote that he would ask Oxford University Press to print the three poems in one volume, and that he suggested that *Poetry* review the poems as a trilogy.

20. In the same letter, Pearson mentions sending H.D. a book about Pennsylvania that he hopes will be useful for *The Gift*.

21. Francis Wolle (1889–?), H.D.'s cousin and professor of English at the University of Colorado, Boulder. In his memoir *A Moravian Heritage* (1972), he devotes a chapter to H.D.

22. Cf. reviews of *The Walls Do Not Fall*, by Elizabeth Atkins, in *Poetry* 65 (March 1945), and *Tribute to the Angels*, by Jessica Nelson North, in *Poetry* 67 (March 1946).

23. On 19 March [1947], H.D. asked Pearson to send novels from James's "mid-period." She had already read his *Selected Stories*, ed. David Garnett, which was sent to her by Bryher. Pearson sent her *The American Novels and Stories of Henry James*, ed. and introduced by F. O. Matthiessen (New York: Alfred Knopf, 1947); *Stories of Writers and Artists*, ed. F. O. Matthiessen (New York: New Directions, 1946); and *Great Short Novels of Henry James*, ed. Philip Rahv (New York: Dial Press, 1945).

24. In *Henry James: A Literary Life* (1985), Leon Edel notes that James became a British citizen in 1915. Though the British seemed delighted, many Americans resented the implicit rejection in James's action.

25. Isobel Violet Hunt (1862–1942), British novelist, whose adulterous affair with Ford Madox Ford caused a scandal. H.D. had known both Hunt and Ford and was impressed by their family connections with the Pre-Raphaelite circle. She was to draw on Hunt's *The Wife of Rossetti* (1932) for her own fictional portrait of Elizabeth Siddal in "The White Rose and the Red."

26. May Sinclair (1863–1946), British suffragist, novelist, and poet. She was strongly influenced by the theories of Freud and became a pioneer in the "stream of consciousness" narrative technique, which she employed in *The Three Sisters* (1914) and *Mary Olivier* (1919). A mentor to many younger writers, her friends included Ezra Pound and Richard Aldington, as well as H.D. At her death she bequeathed a number of books to H.D. and Aldington.

27. In his introduction to this novel, F. O. Matthiessen mentions that William James initially thought the character of Miss Birdseye was too closely modeled on Elizabeth Peabody, Hawthorne's sister-in-law, who was still alive.

28. *The American Scene, Together with Three Essays from "Portraits of Places,"* ed. and introduced by W. H. Auden (1946).

29. On 11 May [1947], H.D. mentions that she has found Italian translations of O'Neill's *Strange Interlude* and Eliot's poetry at her favorite bookshop.

30. On 29 August 1947 Pearson responds to these comments, calling Eliot's reading at Yale the "success of the century." He continues, describing Eliot's lecture at the Frick Museum in New York: "There Eliot lectured on Milton, and assembled to meet him was a handpicked group of scholars, critics, and literary personages of a dignity quite beyond reproach and absolutely with éclat."

31. See "H.D. by Delia Alton," *Iowa Review* 16, no. 3 (Fall 1986): 174–221.

32. Pearson won a summer fellowship at the Henry E. Huntington Library in San Marino, California.

33. On 23 July 1948, Pearson wrote that he assumed that Macmillan agreed to publish H.D.'s book after consulting Horace Gregory, who endorsed it.

34. Marya Zaturenska to Bryher, 14 May 1948, unpublished letter. Zaturenska wrote that she wished H.D. would explain the "Rossetti–Mrs. Morris scandal."

35. On 8 August 1948, Pearson signs his response, "H. W. Dean." He writes: "You excite me very much at the knowledge of 'The Sword Went Out to Sea.' How can I be anything but pleased to be even a minor character in it, one of those aspects which like an antimacassar give a sense of homeliness to the scene. Must I wait until Lord Howell is dead before I too can read it."

36. H.D. refers to Lord Hugh Dowding (1882–1970), who was commander in chief of the Royal Air Force from 1936 to 1940 and led the squadron that repelled the German air attack on London in the summer of 1940. She heard him lecture on his spiritualist beliefs in 1943 and met with him later. In letters, he expressed displeasure at being in her book, even under another name.

37. On 5 August [1948], H.D. described this sequence to Pearson again: "I have THE SWORD and the Rossetti book, but they are under absolute hard-fast *nom de plume*,

DELIA ALTON, as it happens; it is the name of the dame in the book, and it just came out like that."

38. Pearson was awarded a Guggenheim Fellowship, during which he planned to finish his edition of Hawthorne's letters.

39. H.D. granted her brother power of attorney on 15 December 1934.

40. On 23 July 1948, Pearson objected to the autobiographical slant taken by *Poetry*, which featured pictures of the poets and autobiographical notes. He thought this diverted attention from the poem.

41. On 27 August [1948] H.D. writes: "I finish this ROSE with the meeting of William Morris and Jane Burden in Oxford; the time of the book, with all sorts of woven-in backward-glances, is the years 1855, 1856, 1857. I don't want to touch anything till after Christmas as I have been pretty tireless the last two years, with the AVON, SWORD and ROSE. But in due course, I would be grateful for a superficial opinion of ROSE, as it meant a great deal to me; I felt I had taken right over from Violet Hunt, whom I knew; she knew all of them and I give tribute to Violet in note, as I felt myself part and parcel of her own book *Wife of Rossetti* — the title of which I gave her, I think I told you." Pointing out the relationship between "Sword" and "Rose," she continues, "they all deal with the old mystical ideas of Round Table, brought into harmony or brought into step with the period; in SWORD, with the 'present-day England' of the last war; in *Rose*, with the England of just 100 years earlier; but the books are near-related. I could not have attempted ROSE without getting SWORD off my chest."

42. On 8 August [1949] Pearson sent H.D. a list of the Huntington Library's Morris holdings.

43. The manuscript had been read by Bryher, Richard Aldington, Robert Herring, and Eliza Butler.

44. Rene Wormser was Bryher's British lawyer.

45. In part 1, chapter 1 of "The Sword Went Out to Sea," the narrator describes her acquaintance with "Howell" (Dowding), with whom she shared an interest in paranormal phenomena during the war, including communication with dead RAF pilots. She alludes to a final letter from him, in February 1946, which "had or had not precipitated my illness" (p. 3) (MS at BL).

46. On 2 June 1945, H.D. thanked Dowding for his letter and explained that the "Viking motif" is important "in its wider application"; whether or not he is connected with the ship is "a minor consideration." She is concerned with "the weaving of threads from one pattern to another, from one state of being to another" (H.D. to Hugh Dowding, unpublished letter).

47. Hugh Dowding's books, *Many Mansions* (1943) and *Lynchgate* (1945), were published in London by Rider Press.

48. In "The Sword Went Out to Sea," both Geoffrey Alton, a war hero, and Randolph Spencer, a British journalist, are based on Richard Aldington.

49. Richard Aldington to H.D., 6 November 1947.

50. D. Bruce Ogilvie, a former RAF pilot, wrote that Dowding's son was not killed in combat but may have been permanently estranged from Dowding. See "H.D. and Hugh Dowding," *HD Newsletter* 1, no. 2 (Winter 1987): 9–17.

51. Robert Herring to H.D., 10 June 1948, unpublished letter.

52. H.D.'s title is from Morris's poem "The Sailing of the Sword."

53. On 6 December 1948, *Life* magazine ran a photo of a number of well-known poets gathered around the Sitwells (including Horace Gregory, Marya Zaturenska, and Marianne Moore), but the picture did not include H.D.

54. On 10 November [1948], H.D. mentioned sending Pearson a publicity questionnaire from Macmillan.

55. Robert Menzies McAlmon (1895–1956), American writer and publisher; Bryher married him in the twenties and enabled him to run Contact Press, which published works by American expatriates; cf. *Being Geniuses Together* (London: Seeker and Wamburg, 1938).

56. In an unselected portion of Pearson's letter, dated Sunday, November 1948, he mentioned receiving a letter from McAlmon saying that he had written H.D. for permission to sell to Pearson four letters from H.D. to himself.

57. In an unselected part of the preceding letter, Pearson described the visit to Yale of Edith and Osbert Sitwell.

58. On 18 November 1948, H.D. wrote to Bryher: "I have just sent off to Woolford, the last of my third 'Delia Alton,' the Bloomsbury that I had written so often but this time, I cut out all reference to you and Pup in Cornwall, brought in (I think) an unusual appreciation of Lawrence at the end — Frederico or Rico. It ended up on the genius of the place, Land's End and 'writing' and genius in general, dragging in Vincent van Gogh. It is not patchy, I simply took the first part from the old MSS you brought me, kept about one third, left out you and Pup and she, Julia this time, wrote at the end, a general appreciation as to Frederico or 'old Rico' whom she will not see again. It is really rather dynamic and like all the rest, I owe it to you, though it is sans dedication. That makes the third Delia Alton. It is a relief to have written FINIS to the whole Bloomsbury episode."

59. On 10 January [1949], H.D. reports having found "notes done *in situ*, 1940, 1941 which I never even re-read and they make my hair stand on end." She probably refers to *Within the Walls* (Iowa City: Windhover Press, 1993).

60. In the late forties Pearson published the following essays: "Anderson and the New Puritanism," *Newberry Library Bulletin* 2 (1948); "The American Poet in Relation to Science," *American Quarterly* 1, no. 2 (Summer 1949); and "The Last Puritans," and "Hawthorne's Usable Truth," in "Papers Presented at the Fiftieth Anniversary of New York Lambda Chapter, Phi Beta Kappa," Canton, New York, 1949. He also wrote an introduction to Thoreau's *Walden* (1948).

61. H.D.'s story "The Death of Martin Presser" was published by the *Quarterly Review of Literature* 12 (1965): 214–61.

62. On 24 January 1949, Pearson thanked H.D. for comments about his introduction to *Walden* and mentioned sending Bryher a copy of his essay on Anderson.

63. In his letter of 24 January 1949, Pearson informed H.D. that Ezra Pound translated the *Analects of Confucius* and was helping a friend of Pearson's who was working on La Forgue.

64. On 24 January 1949, Pearson asked H.D. to tell him how she, Pound, Williams, and Marianne Moore met, for a graduate seminar in American poetry.

65. Felix Emmanuel Schelling (1858–?), professor at the University of Pennsylvania, specialist in Elizabethan literature. His publications include *Literary and Verse Criticism of the Reign of Elizabeth* (1891) and *English Literature During the Lifetime of Shakespeare* (1910).

66. Moore's poems were published in *The Egoist*, May 1915.

67. On 24 January, Pearson wrote: "Don't work too hard for me. You deserve your sabbatical, and I am a swine to steal even a few hours from it."

68. On 8 February [1949], H.D. wrote: "I have so enjoyed the book-reviews of yours that Bryher brought and the Anderson article was informative and illuminating."

69. On 16 February 1949, Pearson wrote: "Will you be surprised to find yourself in it? Well, you are, and whether or not you know it, you have been influenced by science, though you proceed on a conceptual basis of intuition rather than inductive reason." In it Pearson compares the epistemological methods of scientists and poets: rational induction and intuitive metaphor-making, respectively. He argues that the prestige of science has forced poets to search out a revitalized manner of expression to match the scientific redefinition of physical reality, but that poetry surpasses science in its insistence upon engaging the spiritual as well as the physical world. He claims that in this atmosphere of change and redefinition, words can become dangerous tools for both, especially in the political sphere: "Tripped up in fog on the concrete rock of physical reality, the poet can smash his head as thoroughly as the scientist can. Like political witches, the poet can become a fog-maker for others." On 20 April [1949], H.D. responds to the last point in particular: "You steer a middle-course between very dangerous shoals. You keep to your formula though you allow for THAT fourth-dimension. I feel like one of your fog-makers in relation to one-track steel-rails to infinity; indeed, I have made 'fog-maker' my own."

70. Bryher visited the Pearsons at their summer home in Branford, Connecticut, on Long Island Sound.

71. On 20 April [1949], H.D. responds to his query with the following information: "I have asked Bryher to look for any old Presbyterian articles or stories. I have none nor has my brother. I may have given my only copies to Br years ago, instead of destroying them. I did some short stories, (I think) Edith Gray or Grey. I did a few child-story star-articles as Hilda Doolittle for the Sunday Pres[byterian] paper. I did some column-length newspaper stories for the MacLure Syndicate, Mary Marshall got those first published and she and her sister suggested trying Sunday School papers as they paid well. I think I had names given me for those, perhaps Edith G[ray] as well. I have asked Br to get list from *L[ife] and L[etters]* as I did a few things mid-thirties, as I remember, as D.A. Hill (Hil-D-A). . . . I did all those newspaper things, about 1910, before I left (1911) for my first trip 'abroad.'"

72. On 20 February 1949, the Library of Congress announced that Ezra Pound had won the Böllingen Prize for *The Pisan Cantos*. The award was immediately questioned as causing tension and estrangement among poets and publishers, and soon after a congressional committee was set up to study the situation. In early August some claimed they would seek reorganization of the Congressional Library of Fellows in American Letters. On 12 August, the Fellows defended their choice of Pound as the recipient of the prize.

73. In her review of *By Avon River*, in *Saturday Review of Literature* (29 August 1949, p. 29), Bacon claims that "nobody writing at the moment makes a more sensitive use of the image or can convey an idea by means of a symbol more deftly."

74. William Pierce Shepard taught Romance languages and literature at Hamilton College and introduced Pound to French Provençal texts.

75. Lady Low, daughter of General Robert Percy Douglas, fourth baronet. In 1885 she married Sir Hugh Low, who died in 1905. A close friend of Olivia Shakespear, she provided a distinguished drawing room for Pound's earliest readings in London. H.D. is confusing her with someone else.

76. Walter Morse Rummel (1887–1953), of the Morse telegraph fortune, was an American composer and pianist living in Paris. A friend of both Pound and H.D., he was involved in a love triangle comprising himself, Pound, and Margaret Cravens, whose suicide H.D. fictionalized in her novel *Fields of Asphodel*.

77. Nancy Cunard (1896–1965), journalist and publisher of the Hours Press, part of the Parisian circle also frequented by H.D., Bryher, and Robert McAlmon in the mid-twenties; author of *Black Man and White Ladyship* (1931).

78. Victor Plarr (1863–1929), librarian of the Royal College of Surgeons, was a member of the Rhymer's Club during the nineties, and met Pound in 1909. He wrote a memoir about Dowson titled *Ernest Dowson, 1888–1897*.

79. Julia R. Wells was a family friend of the Doolittles and H.D., who also knew Ezra Pound. H.D. stayed with her at Patchin Place, Greenwich Village, for a few months in 1911.

80. George Catlin (1796–1872), writer and illustrator, detailed his interactions with the Indians in books for children.

81. In his essay "To the Working Men of England," Morris opposes England's involvement in the Crimean War (1853–56). He thought it would detract from attention to domestic social problems.

82. The unsuccessful Orsini plot to murder Napoleon III (14 January 1858) was one of several attempts on Napoleon's life because of anger over the role he played in crushing the Roman Republic in 1849. Although Orsini was put to death, the case may have prompted Napoleon to move toward a more pro-Italian and anti-Austrian policy.

83. Rebecca West's *The Meaning of Treason* (1949) examines the trials of William Joyce, John Amery, and others in Great Britain after World War II.

84. H.D. repeats this wish on 13 October [1950], when she writes: "I thought that 'The Death of Martin Presser' would make a beautiful Xmas booklet, perhaps I will do that another year if the story is not published with *The Gift*. I prefer it to finish *The Gift*."

85. H.D. dedicated "The White Rose and the Red" as follows: "To Norman Holmes Pearson, in gratitude for his suggestion of continuing the story of *The Order of Sir Galahad*."

86. Pearson refused to add his name to a letter of protest signed by "a group of American writers" and sent to the editors of the *Saturday Review of Literature* regarding the publication of essays by Robert Hillyer (11 and 18 June) sharply critical of the award of the Bollingen Prize to Pound. In a letter to John Berryman (5 November 1949), he wrote that such a letter would "by its vehemence . . . make more people jump to the other side" (unpublished letter).

87. Louise Hall Tharpe, *The Peabody Sisters of Salem* (1950).

88. In her journal "Advent," H.D. notes that Hawthorne's *Tanglewood Tales* were her childhood "foundation or background" (*Tribute to Freud* [1974], 186).

89. H.D. refers to Pearson's essay "Both Longfellows," *University of Kansas City Review* 16, no. 4 (Summer 1950): 245–53, in which he reevaluates Longfellow's reputation. Pearson claims that Longfellow endowed such American heroes as Paul Revere with mythic power. In response to this comment, on 28 August Pearson wrote: "You caught the spirit of the Longfellow article absolutely; it was written for the American critics who have been belittling Longfellow until he is allowed no status whatsoever."

90. H.D. refers to the Korean War.

91. Alys Russell (1863?–1951), the daughter of Quaker preachers Hannah Whitall and Robert Pearsall Smith, devoted herself to good works at a young age and as an adult spent much of her life campaigning for temperance and women's suffrage. Although her marriage to Bertrand Russell was troubled and ended in divorce (1921), she remained devoted to him.

92. H.D.'s poem "Body and Soul" was published in the *Yale Review* 40 (December 1950): 220–22. It was retitled "Fire, Flood, and Olive-Tree" in *Selected Poems* (1957).

93. On 13 October, H.D. wrote that she "did some reminiscent notes, very human and touching I thought, of the early Ezra; but they were not 'suitable' for the book [*Nine*], Peter Russell wrote me."

94. *The Letters of Ezra Pound 1907–1941*, ed. D. D. Paige (1950).

95. Peter Russell (1921–), poet, translator, and Pound scholar, edited *Nine: A Magazine of Literature and the Arts*, from 1949 to 1956.

96. On 20 October 1950, Pearson described a visit to one of Susan's uncles, whose mind was beginning to slip.

97. On 23 October 1950, Pearson mentions having seen a production of *Peter Pan* in New York, which he enjoyed despite its being different from the one starring Maude Adams.

98. Pound's acolytes at St. Elizabeths in 1950 included Hugh Kenner, John Kaspar, Eustace Mullins, Michael Reck, and William Vasse. The last was a graduate student at the University of California who became associate editor of *The Pound Newsletter*.

99. William Jennings Bryan (1860–1928), U.S. politician and orator. During a depression in farming areas, he spoke against tariff protection and the gold standard and put forward an "easy money" policy based on the free and unlimited coinage of silver. He delivered a celebrated speech in 1896 at the Democratic National Convention, which contained the following passage: "You shall not press down upon the brow of labour this crown of thorns; you shall not crucify mankind upon a cross of gold."

100. Perdita's first child, Valentine, was born on February 21, 1951. On 2 March [1951], H.D. wrote to Pearson, "Yes, we really are related now — grand-mother and god-father!"

101. H.D. encloses an unpublished scrawled note from Pound, who is sorry she will not be able to visit him in Washington. After commenting that Valentine "sure does look like Chas. Leander — with a touch of Helen," Pound continues: "You can stimulate NHP's mind if you feel so inclined."

102. H.D. refers to the christening of Valentine, which took place in New Haven.

103. H.D. refers to Pearson's office in the Hall of Graduate Studies.

104. H.D. refers to the Reverend Magee, who officiated over the christening of Perdita's baby boy.

105. Richard Aldington to H.D., 6 and 18 November 1947.

106. H.D. refers to the poem "R.A.F." from *What Do I Love?*, a tiny book she sent as a Christmas greeting to friends. On 13 October [1950], she described the poem to Pearson as the middle in a series that includes "May 1943," and "Christmas 1944."

107. Pearson enclosed a Metropolitan Museum of Art sticker with a picture of an embossed helmet, Italian, ca. 1550.

108. Jean Starr Untermayer (1886–1970), American poet and former wife of Louis Untermayer, known for *Steep Ascent* (1927) and other volumes marked by a simple austerity that has been termed classically Hebraic.

109. On 23 June 1951 Pearson responds: "The important thing is remembering. Remembering and shaping (for shaping is understanding), since and before Küsnacht."

110. On 29 August 1951, Pearson speculated that her method in the novel was "linked up with the early P-A days, which is the effort to unravel, get at, get within the vistas of memories."

111. *The Autobiography of William Carlos Williams* (New York: Random House, 1951).

112. H.D. refers to the "Metropolitan Miniatures," color reproductions in postage-stamp size of outstanding masterpieces from the collection of the Metropolitan Museum of Art. Published from 1947 to 1959, these were produced in gummed sheets of twenty-four subjects each. Each sheet was accompanied by an album containing authoritative information about the objects reproduced.

113. The Square Dollar series began in 1951 under the editorship of John Kasper and David Horton. These two Pound acolytes began to publish essays that Pound believed every student should read. Sold for one dollar, the booklets included essays by Louis Agassiz, Fenollosa, Alexander Del Mar, and Pound's translation of the *Analects* of Confucius (1951). Pearson was on the editorial board.

114. In his essay "Billy Budd: 'The King's Yarn,'" in *American Quarterly* 3, no. 1 (Summer 1951): 99–114, Pearson claims that Melville's *Billy Budd* may fulfill the needs of today's reader more than *Moby Dick* and that *Billy Budd* shows the influence of the New Testament and Milton.

115. On 11 November 1951, Pearson wrote: "I gave them the use of my name, not really for any support of Ezra's particular views, but as a gesture of friendship to him. I feel a sort of relationship through you, which I cannot ignore. 'I can't go it alone,' Ezra said to a friend of mine; and he does so, paradoxically, want the support of the professors against whom he always, and frequently rightly, screams in protest."

116. Rachel Annand Taylor (1876–1960), British writer, specialist in Renaissance history. Her publications include *Aspects of the Italian Renaissance* (1923).

CHAPTER THREE

"Our Mystery"

1952-1954

The main creative event in this interval was the composition of H.D.'s long poem *Helen in Egypt* after a five-year hiatus during which she wrote no poetry. H.D. began the poem in the autumn of 1952, having been inspired in part by Pearson's importunement as well as by her reading.[1] Both H.D. and Pearson marveled at the mystery of its beginning. H.D. wrote that she was in a state of "eternal present" before she began to write, and Pearson repeatedly used the phrase "our mystery," alluding not only to H.D.'s unpublished novel "The Mystery" (which he had suggested) but also to her fulfillment of his wish for more poetry. For example, he remarked on the empathy between them, "that I should have wished for new poems, and find that you have begun them already, as though I read ectoplasmic waves from your vitality" (17 September 1953).

In addition, Pearson's allusions to "our mystery" refer more broadly to a mythopoeic view of history that the two shared. Both H.D. and Pearson regarded ancient myth as a repository of sacred revelation and substituted a metahistorical, spiritual definition of truth for an empirical one. Indeed, they practiced a method of interpretation related to this viewpoint: the tendency to see affinities and parallels in historical evidence, which then become the basis for claims of a formal identity that is interpreted to reflect universality. (This hermeneutic was standard practice in mythography and psychoanalysis, fields of inquiry that interested them both.) [2] Also, they shared an epistemological bias that favored intuition and emotion over empiricism and reason.[3] Evidence of this mythopoeic view of history is found not only in H.D.'s repeated admonition in the letters that she was telling the same story in each of her romances despite their different historical contexts, but also in her notes *H.D. by Delia Alton*, where she describes her attempts to synchronize historical time with "dream time" or "the gloire."[4] Pearson's appreciation of this view is evident in his role in the writing of "The Mystery" as well as in his urging her to write more "Delia Altons," in order to continue to convey the relationship of historical people and events to her mythical quest and legend.

Further, this tendency to transmute history into a drama of the soul was familiar to Pearson from his study of American literature, the history of which he conceptualized as being strongly marked by "the Puritan instinct of introspection," which had been vigorously revived in the nineteenth-century "New England Renaissance," particularly in the work of Nathaniel Hawthorne.[5] In fact, Pearson singles out the ability to extract the "innate spiritual significance" from the "outmoded historical data" of the past as Hawthorne's legacy.[6] It is significant that Pearson continued to send copies of his essays on American literature and editions of American writers to H.D., who read them and commented on her own relation to the writers in question. She also read widely in his (and W. H. Auden's) five-volume anthology, *Poets of the English Language* (1950), throughout the poem's composition.

Indeed, if Pearson's phrase "our mystery" exaggerated the intellectual and emotional affinity that set the poem in motion, H.D. did not correct him. Rather, she commented that it was his prodding that was responsible for "her embarcation on the good ship Helena for Egypt," and she adopted a strategy of sending him sections of the first part of the poem ("Pallinode") as they were completed in order to free herself to compose more (30 September 1952). She continued part 2 of the poem ("Leuké") in the summer of 1952, after being operated on for an intestinal occlusion, relying again on Pearson's responses for validation,[7] and she wrote part 3 ("Eidolon") during the first six months of 1954. As she had during the composition of *Trilogy*, H.D. asked Pearson for advice about the direction of part 3. This time, however, she did not follow his advice as fully as she had earlier, apparently because it implied a degree of emotional resolution that she could not achieve. After the success of her recording sessions and further consultation with Pearson, she added the prose captions in 1955.

Responding to H.D.'s excitement during its composition, Pearson regarded *Helen in Egypt* as the culmination of her career, comparable in scope and excellence to the poetic achievement of any of her contemporaries. Pointedly, he often called the poem her "cantos," a designation that reflected his own increasing involvement with Pound, whom he visited at St. Elizabeths Hospital and whose work he was reading, teaching, and promoting, despite the controversy that swirled around it.[8] His letters to H.D. in the early fifties update her on Pound's living situation, on the composition of his new poems, and on the study and annotation of his poetry. Beginning in 1953, H.D. was also reminded of Pound by Erich Heydt, the young psychiatrist who was to become a counterpart to Pearson in her emotional life and whose name begins to appear frequently in these letters. A broadly cultured man, interested in literature and music, Heydt immediately recognized H.D. as an important poet and encouraged her to discuss her connections with Pound and other male modernists. Heydt also respected H.D.'s work with Freud and regarded her more as a clinical colleague than as a patient.[9] Ancillary correspondence reveals that she was somewhat infatuated with him.[10]

In the following group of letters, in which he responds to H.D.'s disappointment at the publisher's rejection of "The Sword Went Out to Sea," Pearson encourages her to write by asking her to compose "Delia Altons" of the kind she did earlier, suggesting a subject that will become important later. Newspaper reports about the nationalist riots in Egypt remind Pearson of his visits to Cairo during World War II,[11] and he asks H.D. to recall her own earlier trip to Egypt in 1923.[12] When H.D. doesn't respond to this suggestion but rather continues to report on her reading and on old letters Bryher has sent from London,[13] Pearson continues to prod her to write about the past, this time about Norman Douglas, who has just died (10 February 1952). Unwilling to write more Delia Altons, as he suggests, H.D. comments informally on Douglas's last days instead and on the death of King George [6 February 1952], which seems to her to mark the end of an era.[14] The exchange between them throughout the winter continues to show Pearson trying to foster H.D.'s creativity.

──────── 54. TS ────────

Hotel de la Paix
Lausanne
March 3 [1952]

Dear Norman,

This is in immediate answer to yours, just in, of Feb. 29. Please believe me, I am so very sorry about all the sad illnesses and accidents — sad for them, and for you and Susan.[15] We did feel here, too, so very involved in things. Your remarks about the King and so on are most illuminating. Yes — one felt and feels, it is an end — then one asks, way, way down, IS it a beginning? Can England live on a fairy-tale? Perhaps. There is the CROWN, a reality, as I was saying to Kenneth and his friend who were here for nearly two weeks. They have gone on to Paris, then to Calais to pick up a car. Then, back here for another few days or a week. I wrote of them? I went down to their rooms every evening, or rather to one of the rooms, the "reception" room, they called it, most correct, formal, suitable — to lovely dec[oration]s — my dinner allowance before dinner. We talked and talked — but just that one hour daily — I must have told you. I am just a little rattled at their coming and their going. We talked of my London sketches and a little of *Sword* series. It is so strange to TALK at all, about these things. How clever of you to date the *Unitas Fratrum*.[16] It was a renewal or a survival, I think, of the original, prosecuted Church of Bohemia. The actual Bohemian Church was founded in the 8th century, but you must have read this in my *Mystery*. Yes — that is an idea for one or other volume. It is good of you to suggest D[elia] A[lton] doing "a few words," on this, on that. No, I am just holding on to what I have — and I will love having the new miniatures. It was just as I told you. I don't like to feel I am neglecting them. Like my squares of unfinished tapestry. The boxes are wonderful and as only a few came in last one, I am finding that I can stack some of the very early ones in box, that gives it a book-air and one feels they won't get bent or shabby. It is dim and dull. I want so much to say something . . . about your own worries.

Thank you for suggestion of Henry James. No, you never sent me the W[illiam] W[etmore] S[tory].[17] I am terribly sorry about the theft too — what a shock. It happened to me once, in a Sloane Street flat and to Bryher, at Lowndes Square. I am so glad you find a place for the letters, I didn't destroy many. I will go on sorting and maybe, find more of interest. You don't let me "let go." I have so much, am really excited about life, seem to find days too, too short. I seem to have found the "eternal present," *l'infini Sans Bornes*, the *Akasha* of the eastern mystics.[18] But I must trim my sails to it. It might be unknotting a bit of string was more important than — than what? It comes over me, sweeps over me — the miniatures for instance, take me so far. How much time have we? But Norman has all those papers, I say, I need worry about nothing . . . but somehow I am ON that *Viking Ship* still. It does not matter what became of the whole lot of mal-assorted war-masters and war-makers . . . O, I cannot get into such deep water. Isis? I never really answered about Isis.[19] It is Isis-iris, the heraldic iris and a game of chivalry as pitted against the game of power and power-passion voltage, all this set out neatly on a chess-board. But we are all pretty tired; I guess the old war-lords most of all. I hope to get into Kenwin to-morrow and will take your letter and talk of you and all of you there, with Bryher. Kenneth was wonderful this time . . . I had so completely lost him, during most of that N[ew] Y[ork] period and he simply seemed to disappear during *our* war. Now with talk of all sorts of Italian reactions, as for instance an intense loyalty to the *Crown* and tales of past communist activities, I feel more vivid interest, both sides. His friend is very charming too, and intelligent. The *Crown* and the *Chair* (pontifex maxima, Vaticana or what not) seem to be MONUMENTS in line with HISTORY and in the change-over and the flux and under-currents of our time, those two take on for better or worse, a new meaning. Look — I have finished this letter with much unsaid . . . would old post-cards mean anything to the collection? Thank you for all — and all, all sympathies to you both, dear C.

from H.

In the spring and summer, Pearson continues to help H.D. return to writing. Having pointed out that the copyright on her *Collected Poems* will expire soon, he proposes a new edition of her poetry, suggesting that she make him her authorized agent in the United States to facilitate this project (9 March and 3 April 1952). H.D. welcomes these suggestions but continues to express ambivalence. On 8 April she writes that she will be "greatly relieved to have the *Collected* in our hands," and that she "will sign any papers, gratefully, that you may think suitable," thanking Pearson for bringing into focus, as if "with a magnet," her "scattered" literary past. However, on 22 May she hints that she has "a beautiful script of *Madrigal*" on hand, but then disavows the idea "of any form of publication or publicity."

Their letters in June and July mention preliminary plans for the new edition of H.D.'s poems, as well as Pearson's other work. On 7 June H.D. thanks him for his essay on William Faulkner's novel *Light in August*.[20] His response, on 9 July, indicates that he also sent the novel itself to Bryher who, he hopes, will pass it on to H.D. On 18 July Pearson pressures H.D. for new poems to send to journals that have requested them, and then he comments, sympathetically, "But I suppose it is hopeless to ask. One can't turn them out like flapjacks." Happily, H.D. reports the beginning of new inspiration in the following letter.

─────── 55. TS ───────

Hotel Bristol

LUGANO

August 8 [1952]

Dear Norman,

I owe you two or more letters. I have been in a sort of electric coma — I must explain. Coma; you will get, our Lotus Land has been, like everywhere else, over-doing itself a bit. Into this shot like a thunder-bolt, a huge vol[ume] that Br[yher] sent me, *Lesbia Brandon*, an unpublished novel of A.C. Swinburne, complete with most exciting, exotic and erotic notes by one Randolph Hughes.[21] This got back for me my little Swinburne edition that I had left at Kenwin, mercifully found by Melitta[22] and addressed by Bear [Walter Schmideberg], as no, no book-shop here had a single line of his, except in some of those paper-backed anthologies.[23] I sent to London Library for more of R. Hughes, without much success, or rather they sent me an enormous tome of "19th Cent[ury]" bound up; there was one article of his, on the 1937 centenary. He also wrote something for *L[ife] and L[etters]*[24] which I remember dimly, but that was 1948 when I was deep in my own *Red Rose*. I had finally to stay in, mornings, as every time I went out, I had to change all over and wash-down, as in tropics. So now, I just go out, after lunch. I hear of you from Br; you can imagine how much this means to me, she said you spoke of the Boni rights; please take the matter in hand, as you see fit. It is so good of you. I thank you for offers of placing poetry — but I am true, I speak truth, when I say, I have written nothing, since that last poem to W[illiam] M[orris]; I think I sent you all the bits and pieces. I could write (I feel) anything — but now, I have done what [I] wanted. Isn't it time I rested? I was driven, compelled to get that "novel" right . . . I began really, after War I, as I said in those notes ["H.D. by Delia Alton"]. Apparently A[lgernon] C[harles] S[winburne] had some of the same sort of ideas and delays — O the book is really the turn of the tide. I mean I have waited for the "romantics" to come really back. You know what I mean? So now, I can just get caught up in the tide, no more swimming against the breakers. . . .

I do hope your heat has abated — we have had some storms, lately, but there were weeks and weeks of (what Bryher calls, in N. Y., now) "Jamaca [sic]." She has been so generous, a letter almost every day, news of M[arianne] M[oore] and through her, of Ezra; news of Gregories; the latest in, this morning, is full of you. How touching to think of that little Venus — and your birds.[25] Do hope Hawthorne is rewarding you . . . we all look forward to it. Dear Perdita — I had her for ten days here, all to myself, but I was in such a state, as she became vibrantly (in the heat) Amazonian, and went off, climbing mountains or being pulled up by antique mountain *funiculari* or swing-trolleys. I did go on some trips but I could not cope, entirely. I was always so afraid — Oh well — just identification of self with her and Miranda-Nicholas — I mean, her arriving or being-about-to-arrive at about the time of said M-N.[26] But it was all right. I took her myself, over to Locarno, saw her on the *Centovalle* train and she did get home — and was made so happy by Br telling her at station — farewell, that she (Br) was crossing soon after. All this has been a revelation to me, the new house, budget of letters even from Elsie.[27] Now, forgive this — it is too short. I must put it in the noon-box with my letter to Fido; she may still be there when this reaches you. If so, tell her that I have just written her *chez* Schaffner.

My very best to Susan, I do hope you are out of the worst of "Jamaca."

Ever,

H.

In late August, Pearson congratulates H.D. on the news of Perdita's second pregnancy and sends early birthday greetings. In response, H.D. assures him that the prospective new grandchild confirms her contentment in not publishing "Sword" and "Rose," and she thanks him again for his encouragement during a period when Bryher seemed doubtful.[28] In her next letter, 14 September, she reports the experiencing of "an intense inner life this summer, that is, after P[erdita] left, on July 14."[29] Then, she sends the very exciting beginning of a new poem, *Helen in Egypt*, in the following letter.

September 23 [1952]

H.D.

Helen in Egypt

I

Do not despair, the hosts
surging beneath the Walls,
(no more than I) are ghosts;

    do not bewail the Fall,
    the scene is empty and I am alone
    yet in this Amen-temple,

I hear their voices,
there is no veil between us,
only space and leisure

and long corridors of lotus-bud
furled on the pillars,
and the lotus-flower unfurled,

with reed of the papyrus;
Amen (or Zeus we called him)
brought me here;

fear nothing of the future or the past,
He, God will guide you,
bring you to this place,

as he brought me, his daughter,
twin-sister of twin-brothers
and Clytemnestra, shadow of us all;

the old enchantment holds,
here there is peace
for Helena, Helen hated of all Greece.

Dear Norman,

    You asked for some poems. I have written nothing for five years, but some-
how suddenly, this *Helen in Egypt* began; I have just finished 8 of these sections

in 3 days. I will send on the other 4. Then, I feel that I can go on and on, if the spirit moves, for this you will see, is again the old motive. Maybe a short note might be indicated. According to the old myth, Helen was never at Troy at all, Euripides wrote this play on the theme, *Helen in Egypt*. It is the "phantasmagora" or unreality of war as against the reality of the eternal and of Love.

II

The potion is not poison,
it is not Lethe and forgetfulness
but everlasting memory,

the glory and the beauty of the ships,
the wave that bore them onward
and the shock of hidden shoal,

the peril of the rocks,
the weary fall of sail,
the rope drawn taut,

the breathing and breath-taking
climb and fall, mountain and valley
challenging, the coast

drawn near, drawn far,
the helmsman's bitter oath
to see the goal receding

in the night; everlasting, everlasting
nothingness and lethargy of waiting;
O Helen, Helen, Daemon that thou art.

we will be done forever
with this charm, this evil philtre,
this curse of Aphrodite;

so they fought, forgetting women,
hero to hero, sworn brother and lover,
and cursing Helen through eternity.

This theme presents endless possibilities — and I have been really so happy. It is in a way, a synthesis of my *Walls* and the general theme of the "true tale" in *Sword* and *Rose*. I hope you will like this. I think Bryher and the little birth-day house-party was very good for me, and the long summer rest for I could not work in that heat. I bless it all now — and dear Perdita's visit. Thank you again for greetings and the little good-luck fish — you see what a charm it has proved? Bless you and thank you. I will type out the rest later.

Gratefully, dear C.

H.

——— 57. TS ———

233 HGS

Yale University

New Haven, Conn.

26 September 1952

Dearest Hilda:

IT IS SUPERB! KISSES ON BOTH CHEEKS, AND A DEEP BOW WITH A SWEEP OF THE PLUMED HAT. MAY I SEND IT OFF? [30]

Yr.

C.

——— 58. TS ———

Hotel Bristol

LUGANO

September 30 [1952]

Dearest Norman,

Thank you for your little letter-telegram, with sweep of plume. You will have had the rest of section I, eight poems in all. Then, yesterday, I sent you surface, without enclosing note, section II, again eight poems. The work has made me so very happy. I hope to go on with it, but must just wait till the spirit moves. You can of course, send them out, or it out. It was you asking me that is partly responsible for this embarcation on the good-ship Helena for Egypt. I suggested that a note might be indicated, re the *Helen in Egypt* myth or tradition that Euripides used in his play. I am sorry the last lot is rather badly typed, I was so anxious to get them to you, at least, to start them off, so as to leave my mind clear for another set, D[eo] V[olente], of *Helen*. Now, you can use the separate poems, ad lib, or not, as you think best. In part II (to come) will you note poem VIII, verse or section 8, I want *I ask not*, instead of *I care not*. I am not sure about "Simoan plain," II-5-V or II-V-5, but I have written Bryher to confirm or correct. In I-V-4, I want hyphen, *iron-casement*.

Proofs on that thick paper come very heavy to send back, by air, will you indicate if there are proofs, how much time, I can have and if I can send surface.

But again, re — note or notes, explaining the *Helen* phantom myth or the story of Achilles meeting her "among the shades," can be left entirely to you.[31] It is fascinating however, that there are these stories that so perfectly fit my legend.

It has turned cold but fortunately there is heating on now, and real comfort. Which being the case, I will hope to stay on here for another 3 weeks, anyway, perhaps longer, if I am working.

I do, do hope that you are well and not working too hard. Please forgive this rather scrappy note — I want to thank you so very much for plumed recognition of *Helena*.

> Ever, dear C.—
>
> H.

———— 59. TS ————

233 HGS
Yale University
New Haven, Conn.
2 October 1952

Dearest Hilda:

The birth of Helen in Egypt was so exciting that I could not resist sending the telegraphic note to record the arrival of the first canto. I knew it would be a day or two before I could write at more length; it has of course been longer, now, since the sequence of letters arrived with the stanzas in them. If I have not written, yet have I read — and that, several times. And as you know, although I think I do not need the repetition in order to recognize quality in verse; the fullness, the nuance, the suavity blossom with acquaintance. It is as you say the old motive — but, with a large but — . Which is only to say that there is a consistence; and if this is in a way a synthesis, it is a synthesis of a new richness on the old, and of what has developed in the way of sensibility and understanding. I need a little while longer and a rereading of the *Walls* and the *Claribel* to be quite sure of what is happening to the line. But nothing is lost, and there is a newness for the moment, and one of surety. It has been worth the five years for these to come out with the spirit. I shall be happy with these for a while, or happy in the sense of a larger cluster around the theme, if you are moved to sing that way. It is all very much of our time.

I suggested in my note the enthusiasm of sharing the canto. I mean it. I do not mean, however, doing it if you prefer to hold back for a little to watch the rest (if it be) come forth, so that one is not so to speak committed. At the moment I rather incline to not splitting the canto into sections, but if it is to be printed doing it altogether or not at all. But perhaps this will shift with time. At any rate, dear Hilda, you have made me very happy indeed, and I shall not quickly forget the excitement of the falling of the letters into my hand, each with their freight.

All love from

Yr. C

In October 1952, Pearson and H.D. discuss the appearance of a manuscript of poems by Pound,[32] which has been offered to Pearson by Peter Russell, the editor of *Nine*. Although H.D. was somewhat disturbed by Russell's discovery and by his attempt to sell the poems to Pearson, she offered an explanation of how they may have been preserved,[33] and left the matter in Pearson's hands, urging him to be tactful. On 13 October Pearson reports that the Pound manuscript was in the possession of "Mrs. Lewis Marlow," whom he recognizes as Frances Gregg. H.D. expresses surprise at this finding. On 17 October [1952] she sends Pearson the address of Andrew Gibson,[34] an old friend of Gregg's, should he want to know more about her life. In this letter she also notes that it must have been Frances who wrote "Hilda's Book" on the title page, and comments, "If I gave any Pound MSS or letters to F, it would have been before I left USA, the first time."

In the following letter, Pearson discusses the progress of *Helen in Egypt*, reiterates his plan to publish a new edition of H.D.'s poetry, and describes Pound's living situation at St. Elizabeths Hospital.

──────── 60. TS ────────

233 HGS
Yale University
New Haven, Conn.
22 December 1952

Dearest Hilda:

[. . .]

Your chevalier's plumed hat still sweeps in a deep bow of admiration for "Helen in Egypt."[35] It is shameful of me not to have written about them, but a series of impossible incidents intervened when total eclipses of time sense allowed. . . . But in any event, these are what mark my 1952! I asked for poems, and I got a masterpiece. This is really one of the finest things you have done. The diction is simply superb in its clarity. It is true classicism, what Ezra would call "making it new." The syntax is remarkable also for its sheer and sheenlike lucidity. Why do I start, will you ask, by matters which are not central. Because I suppose I do think them central to your achievement of the theme and conflict. The resolution, so to speak, is in the diction and syntax, with the calmness and certitude of the eternal and love. You triumph so wonderfully within the narrow verse limits you have set yourself, and when one sees emerging the longer imperial line of IV, and then suddenly the dancing measures of V, one feels the sense of masterliness. Perhaps you told me that it continues the Walls poems; at any rate it does, carrying it back in time in a mythopoeic sense that will permit it to go forward in time also. I see it also connected with the Mystery — sometimes I hope it is our Mystery.[36] Yes, dear Lady, I kiss your hand and bow in gratitude.

Bryher, I think, will have told you that I went to New York to see my lawyers about cleaning up this matter of the copyright on the collected poems, which Liveright now have. I want to get it out of their hands, where we have been denied really the chance to come forth again with a fresh group and collection. I am not sure just what shape it should take — not, I suspect at this moment, a complete collected work, but a fresh selection from the earlier poems, but getting into the books after that (after the Imagist label), and perhaps reprinting the Walls trilogy, so that it will be as it should be together; then the Avon poem, and then finally this. Bryher says you are writing again. This is splendid. The line develops nicely through them all; this will be a fresh H.D. which emerges, one known of course to some but not to the public. We must work this out carefully, shape it like a vase; when you catch your breath it will be something to mull over: the poems from the early days to be laid aside for the moment, in favor of this broader canvas. I do not look at this as rejection, but as a matter of emphasis, or of leading toward this present.

In this regard it is important that I should have from your brother all the statements he has had from Liveright. The lawyers insist on this, and I should at any rate like to do some checking as to what they have been doing in the matter of permissions. The English are so much more careful about this. All of the various matters which you have referred to me on the English side, or on this, I have taken care of, and have careful records in my files. But I do not know what Liveright has done when the matter has been referred to them. Could you drop a note to your brother and ask him to send them to me? I do not want to wait too long for them, because I must begin to move almost as soon as the New Year comes. I had been planning this collected works, with your permission; now I am so happy that it will have Helen in Egypt in it. And, by the way, if you want to indicate which ones you think could stand alone, do so and let me know. Otherwise I shall send them off and let one or two editors take a choice (not more; I do not want too much of it to get out before the whole is seen as a whole.)

. . . St. Elizabeths is an immense establishment, covering acres, with innumerable vine-covered brick institutional buildings in the massive manner, and lanes so long as so intercrossed that they carried street signs as in a small town. The main gate was a half mile from Ezra. But when I said to the keeper, as though I were enquiring the way to a five-star professor: would you know in what building we might find Mr Pound — he said at once, oh yes he's in . . . go down, turn, turn again; he'll be there. Ezra refers to St. Elizabeths always as "the campus." It fits a transfer of his old feelings about the Pound University at Rapallo; I had thought about it as a polite way of evading naming the true name of St. Elizabeths; but I see now that the grounds do look just like the campus of a hundred anonymous seats of learning.

When I wound my way to the proper building, only ten minutes remained before five. But for once the officials were kind, and a doctor suggested that since I came from away I might stay until supper was served, and have a half-hour at least, with him. I went out the back door of the building, and down the drive and came to a doorway leading into a dark narrow hallway, up from which went winding steps in a spiral, like the entrance to a haunted tower. Up, and then there was a printed sign above a bell: ring, please. I rang. There was complete silence in the darkened landing, until a key grated in the door and it was opened to lead me into Chestnut Ward. I went in, my eyes dividing to take in all sides at once.

I was in a long hallway, like a hospital corridor, but perhaps wider, off of which was room after room, two beds to each, all gray and colorless like the ashen faces of invalids, the patients themselves. In a near corner at my left was a television set, tuned in on a football game, with patients seated or standing about it, but forced to such volume of tone that a patient at the farthest end of the corridor could have followed the game by ear with ease, save for the blur and clamor of hoarse voiced announcers and cheering spectators at the game. Halfway down the corridor is an alcove. I should think it took the place of one of the bedrooms, and was intended for a general reception of the rare visitors who are likely to come to Chestnut Ward to visit relatives, not coming often because there is not much to say, and because the patients are, so to speak, "taken care of." Now it is reserved for Ezra's private use. He shares one of the bedrooms, but in this alcove, behind two screens which shut it more or less off from the hallway, he writes letters in the morning and receives guests in the afternoon.

There are many men in the ward; I should think perhaps fifty, of whom none are bedridden but who use the hallway as a clubroom. Some constantly pace back and forth along its length, looking straight ahead with eyes which see nothing, and dragging their feet as though these were loaded with chains. Chairs line the walls between the entrances to the bedrooms, and in them are more vacant stares, and the ends of cigarettes which smoke as though placed in an inhaling-exhaling machine. As I walked by, some of the men rose to stretch their hands to clasp me, wanting to be friendly in a demonical way. Calling to me, and I had to respond somehow. So, from me, was: "Hello, hello, hello! I'll be back. That's OK." It was a grim royal procession I made.

And at the very entrance to Ezra's alcove, just before the narrow opening between the screens and the wall, was a chair placed parallel to the wall; in it was an immobile face staring along the wall, its head wrapped in a skull bandage so that one saw no hair at all and he looked only like a faintly colored marble statue. He was one of the fates guarding the entrance to the corner of the underworld where I was to meet a Tiresias. And behind me was the noise from the television game, the shrieks and cries of football like the agonies of the damned. I could only think of the Cantos:

Who even dead, yet hath his mind entire!
This sound came in the dark
First must thou go the road
to hell
And to the bower of Ceres' daughter Proserpine,
Through overhanging dark, to see Tiresias,
Eyeless that was, shade, that is in hell
So full of knowing that the beefy men know less than he,
Ere thou come to thy road's end.[from Canto XLVII]

Pound's back to me, standing and talking to two young men who were about to leave, saying to one: this is for you and I will see you next Tuesday when you have worked on it; to the other: you know what you are to do. Later I learned they were translating some Chinese work on economics. One was

Chinese, the other earnestly nondescript. They were two of the graduate students from outside the "campus." They come regularly each week for instruction, mostly in economics. He is the Socrates with his flock of unorthodox wanderers who drift into his fold. They are the personification of the scores to whom he writes regularly in a correspondence course.

Dorothy Pound saw me. "You are Pearson?" "E.P. it's Pearson," tapping him on the shoulder. And then he turned, his face smiling, the wispy beard, the hair in loose shocks, a red shirt open at the neck, hanging outside over loosely fitting trousers, unchanged from the iconography established in the past. He introduced me and they went, D.P. with them.

It was an odd sort of an alcove: a great round oak table in the center, between it and the window which looked out on the leafless trees and the winter-turned grass was what I can only think of as one of the benches in a railroad station, with curved wooden seat and a high wooden back, so that if one sat there four in a row as there was room for, one felt on a school bench, or waiting for something (once a train and now the words of Kung).

Now I was there; he re-opened a folding aluminum garden chair in which one lounges. He lounged, and I sat bolt-upright in another chair. He had the perfect ease, the soft voice, the gentle manners which belong to his Chinese role as opposed to the persona of the ill-spelling phonetic-minded writer of letters. He talked and talked to put me at ease, always with the soft voice:

> Kung walked
>> by the dynastic temple
> and into the cedar grove
>> and then by the lower river, [from Canto XIII]

"I have a definition of usury for you. I sent it to Kenner.[37] I want you to have it." He took a pencil and wrote. "We need to study more in the discussions of the Church. You might set some students to work on it. . . . Well, the election. Stevenson: one always had the feeling that he might joke at the wrong time. I needn't say I didn't vote," and he smiled a little as though it were a delicious and secret joke between us. He told of the people who came: the couple who arrived each Friday afternoon with a thermos jug of tea. They were the political ones, who kept him in touch with that side of Washington. There was the editor of the Square Dollar series,[38] who seemed to have gotten onto his own style in some articles on Del Mar[39] in an obscure Iowa farm journal. There was the editor of some imitation *New Yorker* now published in Washington, whom he was influencing to include somewhat extraordinary material considering the nature of a chit-chat journal. "We've got to begin."

And always behind the softness of his words was the clamor from the television set, reminding one of the corridor in hell, and the noise seemed like the cries of the tormented demons. What I heard was a fugue between that clamor and his calm. Nothing, certainly, that he said was very important. But what was wonderful to me was to see him stretched out on his chair, hands folded under his head, talking as though the noise and his neighbors had no existence at all. It was wonderful because it was a way from madness; either he must develop this Confucian calm or he would be absolutely and raving insane. Perhaps he did after all say very good things; I could not listen, because I was hearing the situation rather than the words.

The time passed quickly. A little after five-thirty the attendant came. "I'm sorry, Mr Pound." You can be sure he mistered no one else in the ward. Ezra folded his chair, picked up a little folder of objects and a washcase, asked to be excused while he put them in his room, and then took me by the arm down the hallway to the door again. He was like a master of a house seeing one to the carriage. The servants did not exist; he talked as we walked, and when we reached the attendant standing by the exit, we shook hands. "You must write more often," he said; and I went out, the key turning in the lock behind me. Outside, I retraced the steps back along the building to the main office to call a cab. I was part way there when I heard a window open and a call. "Goodby, goodby," Ezra was calling to me; and then the window was closed suddenly. As though he were a schoolboy illicitly giving a last farewell.

· · · · ·

This is all rather windy on my part, and perhaps will have bored you. I went, however, partly because I thought it just possibly might be a little more specific than any other accounts you might have had.[40] I am told, otherwise, that he hopes the change in administration may mean that he can be released; but first of all of course he must be tried. I have no idea. Meanwhile he exists on these visitors in the afternoon and on the letters in the morning. Dorothy arrives punctually, seven days a week, at the moment when visitors are permitted. She sits there while he visits with his students, his colleagues, the visiting professors, who come to "the campus." Despite everything, Ezra has not had to give up the role of playing a role. Some of my graduate students want to visit him: he always receives them, then writes me about them, sometimes offers to enroll them as correspondents. Somehow he has added a chapter to the legend, which is not at all an anti-climax.

[. . .]

C

At the beginning of January 1953, Pearson writes that the *Atlantic Monthly* is interested in publishing part of H.D.'s new sequence of poems. On January 4, H.D. tells him to "choose what seems suitable" and asks if he would write "a few lines, giving the legend, as I have given it to you, of Helen, the phantom — and the meeting after his death, with Achilles — symbolical and mixed and mystical and all that, but clear enough" (9 January [1953]).[41] In this letter, she also mentions having heard from Olga Rudge,[42] who asked for "the usual aid to Ezra"[43] and that H.D. use her American connections to introduce Olga's daughter, Mary de Rachewiltz,[44] who is planning to visit Pound in the hospital.

In late January and the beginning of February 1953, Pearson responds sympathetically to news that H.D. has had an operation at the Clinique Cécil in Lausanne for an intestinal occlusion. He also congratulates her upon the birth of her second grandchild and reports his daughter Susan's wedding engagement, which he hopes will result in his being a grandparent himself soon. To comfort H.D., he writes frequently, sending offprints of his own essays and copies of editions of American writers he has introduced.[45] H.D. responds gratefully on 8 February, expressing her pleasure at the birth of Nicholas, who arrived "when [she] was 'on the table' — odd, symbolical accouchement." She continues that she has "done another 'Canto,'" and that she "hopes to go on forever, but slowly." Pearson's letters in mid-February continue with news of Pound, who, he reports, "is now working on the rest of the cantos" (12 February 1953). In the exchange that follows, H.D. responds to Pearson's edition of *The Pathfinder*, and Pearson discusses plans for the new edition of her *Selected Poems*.

─────────── 61. MS ───────────

March 2 [1953]

Dear C,

My Valentine is on the bed-table beside me, or rather over me, at the moment. And waiting on the bed-cover, is my *Pathfinder*. The introduction is excellent — & what a treat this is. I realize this time, 175- (as he writes it) is just my 1741 early Moravian period, & I read in some of the early records, just such accounts of canoe trips, canoes on Lehigh, Delaware & points west — just such descriptions, & you remember *Last of the Mohicans*, how Chingachgook was nursed by Moravians & buried in "our" old cemetery. I never realized that the dates over-lapped so exactly, in *Leatherstocking*.

Balzac summary is most, most interesting — with Hugo — also W. Irving, but the French estimate & *estime* is a revelation to me.[46] How they more than accepted, revered Poe, too. I have been reading your *Yale French Studies*, number 9;[47] Br[yher] brought me this as I had been having a go at Baudelaire; Adrienne[48] had sent Br a new short study, & in this book, I find quotation from Baudelaire himself, to the effect that every morning began with a prayer or invocation to his father, Marinette (whoever she is) *and Poe* — he made Poe almost a "familiar."

I am very comfortable, but now I am returning to getting dressed & having a whole 1/2 hr. walking in little park, just 5 mins. from door.

I must again thank you for letters & 2 beautiful miniature sets that I will enjoy later. Bless you — don't write. Br hears, right, left, center that *Pearson is over-working*! Do take care of yourself. So many, many thanks for our own *Pathfinder*.

H.

———— 62. TS ————

233 HGS
Yale University
New Haven, CT
8 March 1953

Dearest Hilda:

[. . .]

And I was happy that the Valentine arrived, and that the Cooper amused you. One must have for him, I think, the ability to play Indians in one's mind, except as — as you catch this easily — there are the landscapes. And Cooper did, you know, have an effect on landscape painters and painting here. The Hudson River school, those palisaded cliffs, the long stretches of woods: and interestingly enough, not just a matter of New York State, but also of the Susquehanna. So I have revelled in your picking this up and associating Leatherstocking tales with your Pennsylvanian memory. I had forgotten Chingachook and the Moravians. It all ties together. These landscapes in prose: a long span from Cooper's to Gertrude Stein's landscapes of Spain, but fun to travel along. Thank you for liking the little introduction.

[. . .]

Now I start to think about the new edition of your poems, all being in order except to notify Liveright to return the renewed copyright to me. The lawyers say this can be done, since you did not give formal permission or conveyance of the renewal to them. Knowing the crowd at Liveright, it will be sticky at first; and they will scream, but let them! We must have conferences about what should go in. My feeling, subject to your own, is that we ought not simply to add on to the earlier volume, but select from it, add some of the subsequent poems and perhaps translations, and then the longer ones. The Shakespeare

"Our Mystery," 1952–1954

poem; I would think the war trilogy and a few other war poems, and then the Helen sequence. This I mean only in the roughest sense of shape and area. I have not begun to think in detail. Perhaps if you do not come to see Nicholas, I might run over and we could make some tentative lists. The whole prospect is immensely exciting to me. Horace's advice and taste is always excellent and he says he will help.

[. . .]

All love and blessings to you from your

C

In her reply to the letter above, on 13 March H.D. writes that she "cannot concentrate on *Poems* now" and thanks Pearson and Horace Gregory for suggestions. In the next letter, H.D. describes her excitement at reading E. M. Butler's novel *Silver Wings*.

———— 63. TS ————

Hotel de la Paix
Lausanne
April 8 [1953]

Dear Norman,

Just a line to wish you very many Happy Returns of April 13. I had your Easter wire and gave it on to Bryher — thank you; also, for the Santayana volume — I presume it was you that sent it? This is only my 2nd typed letter, so I can not put myself into it, as I would like to do. I am all right, but bored and claustrophobic, as I have a mad desire to travel, to get right away. I am taking it out in re-reading some of Euripides and working toward a new phase of the *Helen*, in which, as I see it, she will leave Egypt; then, we have the whole Greek mythology to draw on. But I will not hurry this — it is my "travel," at the moment. I have a short novel, called *Silver Wings*, by E. M. Butler. We have all read it, Kenneth hated it, Br liked first part. I heard that E.M. Butler, the author, very learned, former Professor at Newton [sic][49] and also Manchester, much travelled etc. etc., had a sort of offer, via Leonard Woolf of Hogarth Press to have this set up in N.Y. or U.S.A. somewhere. Robert [Herring] was interested, but he is about the only one who thinks there is a lot in it. I will try to dig out an extra copy, it wouldn't take long to read. But I must wait to hear, via a friend, what Hogarth finally decided. I just wanted your opinion, as Robert and I both thought the little book simply simmered with under-currents, of one sort and another. While Br said it was my imagination and K[enneth] was downright hostile. It is not often that a little *novella* sets up such a scream. Yes — I think, I will send *Silver Wings* to you for your birthday; I will try to post it this afternoon. Perhaps it is the title, *Wings*, that got me. I really think that E.M. Butler — she is just about a year older than I am, Robert dug out this and other details in an old *Who's Who* — had and has something very poignant to say, and along the lines of my own *Sword* sequence. Now, I may be wrong, but will you "umpire" this contest. It was Br, of course, who got me the book; then, she rather turned-turtle on it; it may be that she feared that I might get too caught up in the occult side of E.M. Butler's other work; I am not so keen on her scholarly tomes, but am very impressed with the scholar and specialist (Faust, in particular and Saint-Simon.) Please do not loose [*sic*] *Silver Wings*; I wonder what Thornton Wilder would make of it? I mean, don't loose [*sic*] it, as if you don't like it or even hate it, like K., I will ask you to post it on to someone else for opinion. I am madly curious to know why it got me — though I do know. I think she had a *Wings* experience, but I can't discuss this outside.

Forgive this inadequate letter — to thank you for so much. I am reminded of the spur it gave me, last summer, to type out the *Helen* pages to send to you. I will let you know of any further canto. Anyway, this is to thank you — and again for the books and folders you sent me, which arrived while I was at *Cecil*. Blessings and greetings to yours — especial April 13 gratitude — always

dear C

from *H.*

I don't want you to pronounce on *Silver Wings*, from U.S. publication angle, so much as I want just your reaction. It is, in any case, an uncanny little book . . . bless you and thank you again and again. . . .

I have read *S.W.* five times . . .

In the following months, as H.D. gains strength, her letters return to the progress of *Helen in Egypt* and to others' interest in translating her work.[50] Pearson's letters show his efforts to publish *Tribute to Freud* and he responds delightedly to her news of progress. On 19 April he writes: "The chief thing is . . . the intense excitement of knowing you have done a final canto or section of *Helen in Egypt*. And I like the idea of leaving the door open. That is, partly because you can pick it up again if you wish; also, that the open door, the sails set, the new life or possibility of new life, is what a myth is as it tumbles down through time, even to your own creating of it in a new version." On 30 April he offers a more specific appreciation of "the seventh part," commenting that "with the choragus" she had achieved "a detached gentleness" of love, affection, pity, and hope. She responds gratefully, on 3 May, commenting that "the Helen sequence has given me a get-away, almost a new body — at least, after Dr. Perret sews me up,[51] I hope to feel that I have mentally & psychically built me a 'nobler mansion.' I am *so* glad that you think the *Choragus* a good idea — of course, she (they) or *Helen* can go on now forever, à la E.P.'s cantos. But I have that as idea & recreation. I don't want to get too Byronic."

In the following letter she describes re-reading Euripides for further inspiration.

──────── 64. MS ────────

May 11 [1953]

Dear C.,

Thank you so much for your last *Helen* letter. I am working on, or just reading the *Andromache* now, as Thetis comes in.[52] I find that she, like Proteus, could change her form, magically, so my *Choragus* might be Thetis, herself. It is refreshing to review my Greeks & the Euripides; it makes me happy, whether I do any more of the so-called Cantos, or not. Achilles "marries" Helen in the island of Leuké, according to one tradition. Leuké, as I make out, is in the Euxine or Black Sea,[53] hence pomegranate seeds to strike a note, or ring a bell, just off Attic Greek, Asiatic & exotic. Flowers! I don't know — but I won't force the blooms. Achilles' son married Helen's daughter, but Hermione was already promised to Orestes — & Orestes arrives in the *Andromache* to claim her; he eventually slays Neoptolimous at Delphi. I didn't realize this story — poor old Orestes certainly stopped at nothing. He & Hermione finally marry & are happy ever after. I never had such delight in tracing the family & the family skeletons! They seem so related & of course, Father Freud proved that they were. I am writing on a soft table-cloth at [Nyfffeneggrs?] — the table underneath is slippery, so this will probably look like Braille! I see F[?] tomorrow & just before I left the house, a book came from Pantheon, the "Boy," I presume. I will have my own copy now — F. lent me hers, a lovely, heart-rending book. I am so glad it is so suitably presented — the jacket & the lions, so perfect, for the moment. I thank you for Japanese prints & bronzes or ivories. I have only glanced at it, but it is a treasure, dreams reproduce in the black-and-white, adequately. Now, I must tell you what a treat the Santayana is.[54] I follow his trail, my own! I even found that he had stayed in our old Venice hotel, Danielli & I believe I had the very room he described, over the entrance. 8, I think. It was *the* room or the one next door. His sentiments, re England, are mine exactly & people came in that I knew, inevitably. We must have begun our Pilgrimage, about the same time. He says, I believe, 1912 was his settling-year, though he wandered as I did. Was he ever married — or "anything?" I have only read him, in the past, in articles & so on. He goes on, in the first chapter, about Spirit & renunciation, you know, & Plato, but this may be the conclusion of earlier revelations! I felt quite wistful, altogether, feeling that he had been so near — but he didn't like meetings much, & I was the same sort of Hermit. We expect Perdita now, in a week. I will talk much of you. Have our last letters crossed? This anyhow, to thank you for the books & the inspiration your last letter has proved.

Ever, H.

In June Pearson continues to send H.D. reports of his academic activities and news about her friends: Marianne Moore was awarded a gold medal in poetry from the National Institute of Arts and Letters, William Carlos Williams is shattered after his illness.[55] On 17 June he responds to E. M. Butler's *Silver Wings* with the following comment: "Only a creative intelligence could have done it. Butler, I thought, was particularly successful with the first section: really managed to get a feeling of a time we both recognize. I thought of Butts[56] and Crowley[57] and all the attempts, sensitive or brutal, to break through. You know them sensitively; you've done them in our Moravian cycle, in the Helen poem, in the *Sword*, everywhere."

In mid-July, their letters cross. While he has been tracking down data for his notes to the Hawthorne letters, she has been undergoing a second operation on her intestine. In the letter that follows she is postoperative and mentions meeting Dr. Erich Heydt for the first time. Pearson's response brings news of Ezra Pound and the projected publication of her Freud memoir, to which she replies gratefully. They continue to discuss Pound and Heydt throughout the summer.

——— 65. MS ———

July 15 [1953]

[no salutation]

Please forgive me — I have been here just a week, in Dr. Brunner's own house, *Am Strand*. I have had letters & wonderful book. I have had to put it aside, too exciting; Br[yher] has supplied me with novels. Your little Valentine is one of my book-marks, such a rare find. They are very kind here, *softer* than Vaud & all are anxious to practice their English; there was not *one* doctor or nurse with me at Cecil who would condescend to English — not that my funny French is not adequate, only it seemed odd to think one might *forget* one's French, in extremis — but it worked out, the Op[eration] was a great success but I am very weak. Br is due on 30th. She & Bear [Walter Schmideberg] brought me over in the car, that was a treat. Ezra has had a deluxe copy of *Callimaque* sent me, Greek with French trans[lation], this came from Italy. Why this?[58] I am deeply touched but wonder what struck him suddenly, a funny letter I can't read, "still trying to get you a KKKlimachus."[59] So interested in Susan's exploits with the poor pests — how clever of her — & you can't have your garden destroyed. A very nice doctor here, Dr. Heyd [*sic*] said, out of the blue, "do you know Ezra Pound??" It seems Heyd [*sic*] was at St. E[lizabeths] for a time, he said he never spoke to E. but admired him, holding forth to his students. This was uncanny, don't you think? They have a *literary circle* here & I am asked to read the principal part in [Oscar Wilde's] Lady W[indemere]'s fan. Can you beat it? Fortunately, I am, at present, excused from hectic social life. So *much* gratitude, dear C.

from H.

────────── 66. MS ──────────

Am Strand
July 25 [1953]

[no salutation]

Just had your good, cheering letter. Thank you about the *Freud*,[60] there is no hurry. I have written Br[yher] & I suggested that she & you make arrangements. I seem always to over-tax you both. I am deeply grateful. It was in 1946, when I was at *Seehof* that I had the correspondence & the let-down from N.Y. Oxford Press. You remember, they had practically accepted it, then decided that it was "neither biography nor autobiography." I suppose it did not fit in their files. Anyhow, I would like copies to give around. Thank you & don't rush things. I also had your handwritten letter. I know how you felt, "writing." I feel it now.

I had another very odd letter from poor E[zra]. I showed it to Dr. Heyd [*sic*] & he found it "interesting" & thought E. had some idea back of it.[61] Difficult to say. "I can not carry on alone." I will try to write him again. I now take my 4 o'clock tea (coffee) over in the main building; there is a lovely, long terrace & tables set out. But I prefer the open hall & even there, I am receiving "calls" & invitations. One very nice middle-aged bloke has his own *boat* & invites me out on lake. It is possible to decline, but this is one of the many courtesies. So much love to all, dear C.

from H.

August 4 [1953]

Dear C.,

Bless you & thank you for letter of July 31, & beautiful State House card. Now, I saw Bear twice, & Br[yher] for a long, lovely afternoon. You should be here, at length in chaise-lounge, watching our butterflies. I am so sorry about back — how I sympathize! I am so glad of your interest in *Dr. Heydt* — I have got his name right at last, & *Eric* [*sic*]. He is a rather exotic note here, & *sub rosa* among "us girls," my little sister says in confidence he is a German, half-Jew, who got away before the war. His culture is immense, he seemed to have read more of E[zra] than I had & discussed T.S. E[liot] — & almost everyone else, wants to know about my MSS & the "professor" who has charge of them. Yes — I must ask you, apropos MSS, did I send you a copy of the Freud, with fresh paragraphing? I mean, I wanted to cut up those long paragraphs — but perhaps you could do it, if I have not sent copy. I can not get at this, all is stored in La Paix. I have no copy here. But this can wait. I think I *did* write of this, but you will know how to thin out crowded space, not really weeding as you are doing, but levelling and spacing! Bless you again — & again — dear C. —

H.

Re Eric Heydt, this is in confidence; he is about your age, a subtly cultured man & brilliant analyst . . .

Throughout August, Pearson reports on the progress of the publication of *Tribute to Freud*, and H.D. sends news from Küsnacht. In response to his birthday greeting of 5 September, she reports the beginning of a second *Helen* series. The letters throughout the autumn focus on the progress of this sequence.

Sept. 9 [1953]

Dear C.,

Thank you for letter, letters & cards, & all Sept. 10 good wishes. I sent your Sept. 2 wire on to Kenwin, & the letter of yesterday. Br[yher] is due over to-morrow, then goes on, as for 12th to Hotel Bristol, Lugano. I felt best not to go but wait & move over to *Paix*, end Sept. or early Oct. I am very happy here & have begun a second *Helen* series. I call it *Leuké (l'isle blanche)*. It is supposed to be the Trojan side of the story; she gets to *Leuké* & meets *Paris* not Achilles. I should like: if I finish this, that the two sections come out together — when & if they are to be published, later. I do not want to hurry *Leuké*, it must "write itself." I am really so upset about that heat-wave — I mean with & for you. I wish I could share this temperate zone with you. It has been miraculous, after the early, midsummer sub-tropic or even tropic dank, steamy heat & devitalizing storms. Now summer & autumn are on the best of terms, a soft veil — late roses, with the fragrance of bursting plums, apricots, apples falling, quinces & pears. This garden is my *Leuké*. I mean *Leuké* means reality to me & return to life, & I want to get away from *war* obsessions — "and what is Achilles without war?" So I am trying to build up a balance, Paris the defeated (sic) for & by Love. The Paris image never appealed to me, but I see him, the early shepherd, the defender (as he was called), the wolf-slayer now, as the Imago or Eikon or Eidolon, compensating or balancing. Br[yher] seems interested, but I won't force or hurry this.[62] And thank you for *Freudbuch*. Don't hurry it. I want to catch up. I do wish I could *talk* to you — & how you would enjoy it & all the "funnies," & the fun.

> Devotion, gratitude
> love to all,
> *H.*

———— 69. TS ————

233 HGS
Yale University
New Haven, Conn.
17 September 1953

Dearest Hilda:

Your last letter almost made a birthday for me out of the day of its arrival. And I am enchanted — for it seems almost like another episode in our "Mystery" — that I should have wished for new poems, and find that you have begun them already, as though I read ectoplasmic waves from your vitality. We will have a volume of the two series; they belong together. Perhaps there will be a third, so that it will be a triangle (like the war poems) rather than parallel lines; enter more firmly into the world of myth. The thought excites me, but first you must think only of this one, carving it from the air

> as the sculptor sees the form in the air
>> before he sets hand to mallet,
> and as he sees the in, and the through,
>> the four sides
> not the one face to the painter
> As ivory uncorrupted: [from Canto XXV]

That is the way Ezra puts it. Yes, this one, and then (perhaps — we shall see) the third; so that there will be the two long unities which are passed into being through your hands. They will stand beside each other. It may be for this that you and I have been waiting. How do we know what we wait for, or how.

The cooler weather helped the days, last week, in New York, at the English Institute meeting. Before the first of the meetings on Pound's *Cantos* (there were four papers on them),[63] a very youthful looking boy came up to me. "You are Mr. Pearson, aren't you?" I nodded assent. "I'm Omar." It took me a moment to realize that he was Omar Pound.[64] We lunched together the next day, and I found him most attractive. His boyish looks are carried over into a boyish enthusiasm, tho it does not make him jejune. He leads his own life. "E.P." is like an "uncle." I had not realized that he had never lived at Rapallo but was brought up and educated by Dorothy's parents. Yet he does not seem, does not really talk, like an English boy. It is all somewhere between, as his life must have been. After the war he came to the States, did two years at Hamilton, and then quit. Now he is back to get his undergraduate degree, though he must be nearly thirty. Meanwhile, after his period in the army, he has been in Persia, and is devoted to Persian, wants to become the authority on the ancient travellers between the West and the Orient. "Not Chinese; I'll leave that to Dad." After Hamilton he thinks he can get a Canadian fellowship to work on Arabic. He talks freely about himself, and almost schizophrenically about E.P. He even volunteered that, paradoxically, perhaps the best thing for the *Cantos* was that Ezra had been taken out of his old life, and given the unimpeded chance to draw things together. He says Ezra's health is much improved, and that he notices the marked difference after his two-year absence. What is more re-markable is that E's powers of concentration and coherence of thought have markedly improved: he plays chess afternoons with E, who can now follow through an entire game, or even pick it up the next day. As for the Cantos, he says E will finish them (do his Paradiso) even if he is not released. He hopes for the latter of course, is more optimistic than perhaps I am, but agrees that even if released, whether by light sentence (counted as already served) or by vindication, it is not likely that he will be given a passport, and therefore cannot return to Rapallo. This, I think, would shatter E beyond even Confucian calm.

All love, as ever, from

Yr C

A new book just out, on Katherine Mansfield — by a New Zealander[65] — much on her early life there. Sounds interesting. Do you want me to send?

Sept. 23 [1953]

Dear C;

Thank you for letter of 17th. It means a great deal to me, as I am a little puzzled by this new turn of the *Helen* series. I have sent to you, surface, copy of the first two parts of *Leuké*. I have nearly finished part three and will try to type copy of that soon. Compared with the first series, the VII sections, each of VIII poems (I am checking this up, as a pattern for *Leuké*) this seems patchy. But it is a sort of tribute, or wants to be, to LIFE, the life after return from severe trial or near-death or seeming death. I want to do this and started off bravely, or rather blithely. Perhaps I will go on. It serves as a bridge between this period here (the summer of 1946 returned vividly, the writing of *Avon* here and beginning *Sword*) and the planning to leave. Br[yher] comes this weekend. I thought of returning with her but I think she wants me to stay on 10– 14 days longer. In any case perhaps Kenwin address is indicated. I will go there for a time. I am not sure where I will settle. Br thinks *Paix* is too full of associations. I feel so, in a way, too, though I have so many books, etc. stacked there and it is a convenient centre. Now books . . . thank you for the Stein. I find it most fascinating, picking up threads and associations and people.[66] Thank you and thank you. What an extraordinary contact with Omar. Mrs. Shakespear had charge of him and we gave him some of Perdita's old giraffes etc., I think he must be just a little younger than P, who was born 1919, as you no doubt know. I think T.S. E[liot] was sort of guardian for Omar. I only met him when he was a baby. Time . . . time . . . You see I am rather struggling with the type, but I want to get back to "serious" writing. I always feel the scribbled letters are a bit frivolous. Well . . . what a blessing, I repeat, is your letter of 17th. I will hope to go on with the poems — as you so strangely and mysteriously cherish "our Mystery," as you put it. So thank you again, again . . .

H.

Dr. Erich Heydt
Sanatorium Brunner
Küsnacht *bei* Zurich
Oct. 28 [1953]

Dear Norman,

I am now going to be a pest. I put Dr. Heydt's address at the top, so you can cut it out and hand to your book-shop, if you will. I want your five volumes of POETS sent him. Would you do this for me? Can you tell me if "The Way to Heaven" (God and Magog) by Martin Buber, would interest Bryher? I don't suppose you know, but there is so much talk of it here, and I can only get the German in Zurich.[67] I wrote to London Library for it, but they said their original copy had disappeared and they were unable to get another. So I suppose, it was read and probably appropriated. If you think this is quite impossible, do not get it, but I would be grateful if you would send it to ME @ Mrs. W. Bryher, Villa Kenwin etc., if you think it might do for one of Bryher's Xmas gifts. I can read it, in any case. I ask you to send there, as I can not pull myself away from here, though I consider Kenwin a center and Bryher has had all my things moved over there from La Paix. But she began to talk wildly of various trips, and I did not want to be there alone. I believe she is only, for the moment, going to London, next week. Then, returning to Kenwin. Then, poss[ibly] a trip after Xmas to USA. But I will wait till she IS there. I don't think though, that I will move over for the present. I am so busy, reading, reading; I finally seem to have almost time enough for your anthology. I never really got well into it. I read and read and read, and somehow in this mood, I think it best to stay-put, pro tem, anyhow, as I said. Another thing — your selections from Blake are so very satisfactory. Can you tell me if you know of an edition, that came out a few years ago, of the original script and drawings? I do not know which it was, Thel or The Marriage or what. I saw some illustrations of this in *Time*, I think. But this is prob[ably] very expensive, if edition has not sold out. Can you find out for me? I guess it is rather an awkward size, I could tell in a minute if I saw it, whether it would ring all those bells that your bit of Thel did.[68] The illustrations were coloured, some of them. It may be a very gaudy reproduction. I find your calendar[69] the greatest help, I follow Blake for instance, into my Mystery, Thel, 1789. Do not worry about the poems. I have done almost another section and it keeps my hand in, or my mind or/and Spirit. Do not trouble to comment, one can't really judge till it is all assembled. Tell me too — do you think there is any reference book on Litt. in general, better than the Benét?[70] I have that at Kenwin, now, may send for it, but just wonder, if any so-called "standard" book, deals adequately with short biographies of the authors, say those of your books? There is much to say. I have been going in to Zurich, a lot, many very good book-shops; E[zra] P[ound] in German, English parallel pages. By the way, the 30th is his birthday, if you send him a card. It is all I have done, find it almost imposs[ible] to write him. I enclose $30; I will send another check if necessary. I do appreciate your help — I hate to worry you in the midst of your busy, busy days but this is all "good work" in extremis. I will think of a thousand things to say, after I post this — well, I can write again. I appreciated your little *C* letter so much.

Ever *H*.

——————— 72. MS ———————

Nov. 11 [1953]

[Enclosed in this letter are MS copies of Leuké 5, sections 1–8, ending "Do I love war? Is this Helena?"]

Br[yher] is with you. I hope to see her soon; I am so eager for news. Please do not worry to comment on all this. I always feel that I can not go *on* to next section, until I get off the last to you. Ever thanks and gratitude

from

H.

——————— 73. TS ———————

233 HGS
Yale University
New Haven, Conn.
11 November 1953

Dearest Hilda:

[. . .]

But I have kept on reading and re-reading the Leuké, with devotion to the poem. I waited at first until I had some substance to go on: the poem has its significance of course in terms of the whole movement of the Canto-of-cantos. I do have four now; I presume there is something still to come for Leuké. Or am I wrong in thinking that, as it is, tho it has its fullness it lacks the complete turn which will parallel it to the first "Helen"? I look for the lyrical lift, and the passage up again at the end. My mind runs too to the third vision and version of our mystery in this form. It is the magical number three which gives it recurrence rather than simple repetition. One does not worry at the moment as to what form it takes. My mind goes back to the slice of Wall when the walls did not fall. Then it was spring for the metamorphosis. I see somewhere this coming into the ripeness of autumn; so that the poems (or the two groups of poems) — I cannot help feeling them together — and Avon too — progress as you have progressed; and this is your birth into Helen-Demeter. I do feel this, my lady. You will be at your most beautiful.

These are asides. The second, Leuké, movement, is a miraculous ascension, diaphanous but not nebulous, en route to the revelation — perhaps that is

"Our Mystery," 1952–1954

what I mean by the harvest of autumn. Here there is the whole sense of free-dom, such as you feel. And for that reason I like the difference in lengths of line, stanza form and the rest, which float or are a little jagged, swirling. 3, 4, 5 of I should not, I think, be changed; they are tentative, as the poetic vision is at that moment. It is not the moment for the epiphany or the fully revealed statue of her, the sculptured poem, the ultimate revelation. The re-emergence (do forgive the condition of my typewriter ribbon) of Helen, the metamor-phosis, as Ezra would call it, comes gradually. Must come so. That is why I wait for its fuller outline, even in Leuké! But the essence is always there; the accidence flutters, shifts, is gradually conceived and shaped. Yes, I am very happy with this, and it does add to the Helen. It stands better because of this; this because of it. My lady, I salute you! Like Helen you are always re-emerging to me.

Little points? How? Where? Perhaps I do not altogether like the line in III-4 "(they called his bark a caravel)." A little like filling? Let it simply be a caravel, and sharply so, without apology for diction, or rather the vision of diction. And of II-4 as repeated almost at once in III-3, that is, the final stanza. Again one is startled at the repetition, and not altogether is emphasis one's first reaction. I turned back to see. Yes it was there. All else came second. I am not sure it carries enough weight in itself to quite succeed. I am not sure of this; it is your poem; I was simply troubled at being troubled.

But how picayune! For I am infinitely happy at the achievement. I shall hug it to me. From you but not because of you: for it is something entirely in itself, with its own life. Yet it is our Mystery, as I said. That is an extra, an outside pleasure.

All of which is to send thanks and love from your

C

———— 74. MS ————

[undated]

[Enclosed in this letter is Leuké 6, sections 1 and 2.]

Dear C.,

I just posted air-letter to you — then typed out this, I and II of Section VI. I don't know *how* it is going on; I am surprised at each new "mystery."[71] I will send sections, as I finish . . . I do, do thank you!

H.

Possibly, I should be *all italics*?

Nov. 25 [1953]

Dear Norman,

Thank you for a good letter. About the books — I have got over idea of
Blake edition, so don't want that — and the *Gog and Magog* [Buber's *For the
Sake of Heaven*]. I just wanted to know if you thought it important enough to
get Bryher. But will you send another set of your *Poets* to George Plank, Mar-
vells, Five Ashes, Sussex, England. I would be so grateful. He has not seen the
edition and was so interested when I wrote him of it. Let me know if the check
is insufficient. Thank you so much for reading the poems that I sent. I had
7 sections, each with 8 poems, in the first *Helen*. This is part II or book II.
I had intended to carry this through for the 7 sections of 8 again. You have 5
of these, and I have begun 6. But I am writing this as I am living it, a sort
of poetic analysis, complete with couch and father-symbol. Theseus is more
William Morris, than Freud, however — what do you think? Now, I have been
so happy with this and would like to follow your suggestion, eventually, and
have three "books" of the *Helen*. I would be now, then, just about half way
through. But I depend on the MOOD entirely and can't force the sequence.
How happy you make me with your interest and enthusiasm! About the
"asides" you speak of, those can be worked over or worked at, in time. All criti-
cism is most helpful. I will look into "caravel;" I wanted to weave in the thread,
as to first *Helen*, and "caravel" is a "foreign" word, "foreign" to Greek —
Turkish, I think it is, Bryher knew it and implied it could be used poetically. It
means that to me, the shock of a new word; the ship or spirit-ship, must have
a "foreign" sound or look to it. I will re-read first *Helen* and see if this motif
is over-done or redundant. This is such fun.

I had your joint card, sent on by Bryher. But I missed her this time, as fog
delayed and then way-laid them, or might have, at Milan, though they finally
came down at Geneva. She says she will be over this coming Monday and I
will then hear direct of you all. She was so happy with you, and altogether in
USA. I do, do hope you have kept well after your flu attack — and all that
work. I am so lazy really and have been moved into a larger room with a huge
balcony, really a glassed-in outer room, if only you could see it.[72] I can not
sleep so well, however as the lights across the lake, through the trees, make
over-whelming demands on me; lying in bed, I just drift out into this fairy-
land, but not forlorn! I could draw the curtains, you may remark. But I can't.
Maybe, in a few days, I will get used to this. Now, I am here because I am
happy and find time to work. But I give my address generally, as Kenwin, as I

don't want people to get the idea that I am not well. I have never literally, been happier. I mean, in an all-round way. But if, if, if only you were nearer — and I miss Br so much, sometimes. I wish she would move to or near Zurich. She did talk of it at one time. There is much, much to say but I will stop here. Much to say . . . I will go back now, to re-reading the *Helen*. Bless you for it and all suggestions.

Ever, dear C.,
H.

Do you know of or/and can you get me a book of Wilder's, in which is a short play or sketch of Mary and the donkey on the flight to Egypt?[73] I think the donkey does all the talking. The book is called A Prolonged Xmas dinner or something of the sort. The only copy here known, was stolen from a library at Frankfort; not by Dr. H[eydt] but by a friend of his. Dr. H wanted this for possible, later Xmas plays — too late this year. I asked in shops in Z[urich], but they had not heard of it. Edition is out of print, anyway, I believe. I would be glad to buy a copy if Wilder had one, second-hand, but I don't suppose he has. . . .

I have just re-read your A[ntony] and C[leopatra] in the old script — wonderful![74] I have been finally roped-in to the reading-circle, am myself the Professor, taking them through and into *Midsummer* — if only you were here!

--------- 76. TS ---------

Dec. 2 [1953]

[Enclosed is Leuké, Part VI, Sections III and IV, beginning "Is there another stronger than his mother?"]

Dear C;

I have just copied these, as from yesterday's strophes. IV looks as if it would have to be re-set a bit. But I want to get this off at once, and leave way free for fresh "caravels" of inspiration. It IS a bit complicated, but I am explaining it to myself, as I go along. I have no idea where the "caravel" is taking us — but it is FUN.[75] I saw Br[yher] yesterday and I will write properly and thank you for the gifts. It was heaven to hear of everything . . . more later and THANKS.

H.

On 24 December H.D. thanks Pearson for being so receptive to her Helen sequence. She comments: "Thank you . . . for being my post-office and NOT a dead-letter office. They [her poems] live, as I send them and will live even if never published or read by anyone else — and you are, so far, my one reader." She also comments on how useful his anthology is to her and implies he needn't be jealous of Heydt. Heydt is "the other side of the medal," and "[t]o try to explain the unexplainable to him has opened up vistas."

In the first exchange between them in 1954, H.D. continues to mention Heydt's role in her inner life. On 6 January she comments that Heydt "is more 'jealous' of you than you could be of him," and she urges Pearson to send another set of his anthology for her to give Heydt. She claims that Heydt and his young friends help her to reclaim "our old days and back, still further in the late 20-s and Prague and Wien." In his response, on 9 January, in the course of other news, Pearson remarks. "Tell 'Papa 2' not to be jealous; I am not jealous of him, but only of his chance to be with my lady." In the letters that follow, H.D. continues to report on the progress of *Helen in Egypt*, and Pearson updates her on the activities and publications of Ezra Pound.[76]

——————— 77. TS ———————

[Jan. 17 1954]

Dear Norman,

I am sending these little scraps,[77] as to finish the last section, VI; I think I sent you all the poems. I must tell you now and forever, that the writing of the poems, this *Leuké* has given me "answers," a veritable *grimoire*. I can not judge the poems, but know the second canto or book has not the unique, concentrated drive of the original *Helen in Egypt*. But it is mysterious and really funny to me, to find the clues unravelling as I go along with the poems, rather scrappily, now and again. Treat this Leuké VI and all of it, in this manner. I just feel with Theseus that "myth, the one reality dwells here."

Thank you for the ten and six enclosed for (you will be glad to learn) Chorus from PORPHEUS. I will send it to Bank, it is good of you to trouble with these little things. Thank you so much for writing to the English publishers, for the *Poets*. I really am sorry to have bothered you. I will be relieved when Heydt gets his, as he has talked so much about the beautiful little books. They are wonderful to hold and read. I have just finished again, the whole of your Milton, what an excellent choice and I love the original script, it comes up absolutely new to me, the italics on the pages, the occasional halt to re-spell a lovely, funny word.[78] There is a sort of spell or charm about this and I am so grateful to you both. All your literary gossip is most interesting. No — Walter [Schmideberg] is rather fun here. I mean, I am glad to be able to visit him over at the House proper; pure Darby and Joan, rather a buffer-state between this wild, terrific, dynamic Heydt. He has embarked us now on Hofmannsthal, *Alkestis*[79] — always blackmailing me, "but I got it especially for *you*, Mrs. Aldington because you like the Greek." I suppose I will have to go on with the group. I tried to get out of the German, it is all so confusing, French, German at table and the Swiss-German! More later and infinite thanks, dear C.

from H.

────────── 78. TS ──────────

233 HGS

Yale University

New Haven, CONN

4 February 1954

Dearest Hilda,

[. . .]

One of the smaller national magazines had an interview in it this week with Ezra; and I am both quaking and waiting to hear his response.[80] Really it was quite disgraceful, poking fun at the people who go to see him: his "Wednesdays" and his "Thursdays," as he classifies them. What worries me a little more is that no interviews are supposed to be printed, and it is barely possible that if much of this sort happened they would tighten up on his visitors. That would be the death. A couple of his statements might interest you. When asked if he would return to Rapallo if released he said, No. "I hear there's a congenial group in England now. I think I'd go there." And when asked about Hemingway. "Oh, Hem. But there was a writer . . . who was a better writer than Hemingway. I mean Bob McAlmon. He wrote a better book than Hem. You can find some of his stuff in the Library of Congress. He wrote some fine stuff in Paris in the twenties. I think he stopped writing."

I had a letter from McA[lmon] a few weeks ago. He is still in Desert Hot Springs. I think he dabbles a little at writing, but not very intensively. However he manages to keep a kind of calm.

The new Eliot play made its first American appearance in New Haven a fortnight ago, and we went. The acting was poor, which rather shook the play to pieces. I am not quite sure what there was to shake, however; on the whole we were disappointed, and I literally went to sleep in the first act. . . . Since it was a cross fertilization between the Ion and The Importance of Being Earnest it might interest you to read. I daresay it reads better than we saw it acted. I shall give it a second try on the printed page. Signal me if you want me to send you a copy when it appears next month.[81]

I have sent you a copy of the most recent Hudson Review which contains a translation by Ezra of The Women of Trachis which I thought I'd like you to see.[82] Builds up Herakles rather effectively, and so balances the action some-what better than many translations of it. And there are some excellent cho-ruses. I shall be interested to know what you think of the langwidge [*sic*].

All love to you,

Yr

C

──────── 79. TS ────────

Feb. 9 [1954]

Dear Norman,

No; I never had the little reference book;[83] I should be so glad for it; I have been re-reading and checking off poems in the *Poets*. Almost all the small-fry are in the Benét, I think I have looked up almost all of the unfamiliar. Dr. Heydt is enchanted with his set; so is George [Plank]. I will write George and ask if bill came with his books, will want to pay it, of course. Did you have enough from me, as for the *Poets*; I have my note or checkbook but am rather vague about it. I went in especially to get the E[zra] P[ound] for you or him. I ordered a copy sent to you, from Kurt Staherli, the best English-Swiss shop, very good, here. I will send another copy if you like or other books. I asked them to look out the newspapers and send on to you, if they can get the old copies. They said both were Zurich papers. I finished the *Leuké* sequence, but it is as if written for me; I am getting it typed at any rate. It solved some problems for me — perhaps this is not "poetry" but it is my way of working. I may or may-not go on with it.[84] I leave the way open, as toward a general possible reconstruction of the hero-sage, Hercules, Osiris or Achilles in his course through the symbolic "Houses." I can play with this for years and may or may-not attempt it. Helen in the *Leuké* is satisfied, at peace with the Theseus-imago; anyhow, here, I am. I have been, it is true, battered at times, with the Bear — you call him Walter, I never did. He has black depressions, when he blames his being here on Bryher, and I cannot stand his blindness as to his own condition and to all that she has done. Well, never mind. I have half-hours with him, talking of the explorers and exchanging news, and won-dering what time it now is, in Lahore. Bryher writes of her being in her 10 year old Egypt, the same camels and so on, plus the Victorian.[85] I am so glad, so glad she got away. We do not know what will happen on her return, re Walter, but she must not be made to suffer.

I am posting the last of the *Leuké*, later. It is bitter cold, snow and the lake is frozen right out from the bank, probably from the other bank and we even think it might meet in the middle, and a whole Zurisee frozen is an event. My dear old Father Brunner (as he is called) is to be seen purveying lumps of bread to the swans; it is like a bird-sanctuary, so many birds and so near. Thank you for the cards; how very odd is the Saint![86] I had not heard of him before, had you? Please give my love to Ezra, I can NOT write, I don't know why, have had an envelope addressed for weeks. I heard the same about Eliot, as from London. Thank you for the *Hudson Review* to come. Also glad to look forward to your protégé's writing. There is much, much to say but I have got so behind with letters and try too, to write Br about every third day, difficult, as I am anxious that she should FORGET this worry here. And my days have been full of it. So good to see Bear, over at the House, but it is sad, sad, sad . . .

I hear from London of terrible cold and pipes frozen and all that. Here, we are really so ideally "Victorian," to use Fido's word. I can not even now realize my good fortune, only it has been in a way, threatened, by poor Bear's unhappiness. But this is all the same, a delight to me, because I feel that it has in a way, loosened the hold on poor Fido. It can not go on, they all say. I mean, she cannot be responsible; she writes it was a nightmare. I understand too, better, her problems, seeing Bear this way. And I really am glad that I can act as a buffer-state, of sorts. My love to Susan, please realize how difficult it is for me to write, she will understand. Fido does seem HAPPY. That, at the moment, is ALL that matters. She had been under a fearful strain. And how lovely is *Fabula*![87] All thanks again, again, dear C,

from

H.

In March H.D. complains of friction with Bryher over Walter Schmideberg, with whom Bryher has had a closer relationship than H.D. thought. Heydt has suggested that repressed knowledge of this relationship contributed to H.D.'s breakdown after the war. In April H.D. praises Pearson's essay and radio talk on Shakespeare[88] and asks his advice on a selection of her poems to be translated into German. In his response, on 31 May, Pearson offers to help with the selection and he praises the new stanzas of *Helen*, encouraging her to proceed to a final section of the poem so that it will comprise a volume by itself. He writes: "I liked the shift from the slower (but not languid) line of V to the sharp facets of characters and lights playing against each other in the last sections. It is as though these having been defined within the poem, as they must be, could bear their own naked weight at last. After all, this is an intention of poetry and a poem. Now, if and as you feel it, perhaps from the winter remembered in Lugano this summer, told to me this way, you must move on to the final section so that we can have the new volume. At the moment I feel there is so much here, of itself, that what is called for is a Helen volume by itself. Then we move back to the selected poems: with the war poems, 'Good Frend' and this reprinted, plus a choice from the early poems. The result: a shift in definition before the whole work gets reviewed as [if] the later poems were a tag to the earlier ones. Too much habit that way. It must be licked." In this letter Pearson also includes newspaper clippings about the Cheops dig in Egypt.[89]

On 4 June H.D. expresses interest in these clippings and responds to his suggestion of a final section. She writes: "I can almost think of doing a 3rd part or book or canto, when I get to Lugano — . . . . I think a *Helen* 'by itself,' is really indicated, but I must have time, like Marianne with her fables." She also expresses new concerns about the publication of "Sword" and her Freud memoir, because of a nasty letter she has received from Ezra Pound. The "abuse was virulent," she writes, "about me because of Freud" and she wonders how Pound got a copy.

On 5 June Pearson mentions acquiring, for the archive, early editions of H.D.'s books as well as ten of H.D.'s letters to Brigit Patmore. He also regrets having to postpone his trip to Switzerland until the fall and encloses another clipping about the Egyptian Spirit Ship, calling it "a version of our karabos (caravel), a metamorphosis and mystery." On 7 June he assures her that he did not mention her book on Freud to Pound and hopes that she will not stop its publication. In the letters that follow, the two continue their discussion of Ezra Pound's letter and a projected third part of H.D.'s *Helen in Egypt*.

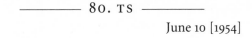

80. TS

June 10 [1954]

[no salutation]

Thank you for the beautiful Blake — and for the Venus earlier. I must leave Freud and anything else to you, but please WARN me, a bit beforehand; I feel FLAYED alive at the idea of reviews, good or bad. I must hang on to THE letter as it is being re-read, every word, the writing etc.; it is hand-written, envelope typed:

> 31 Maggio
>
> H.D.

I can't bbblow everybodies' noses for 'em. Have felt yr / vile Freud all bunk / but the silly Xristers bury all their good authors / they take up cures deguises like Maritain instead of sticking to reading list left by Dante / I admit I am slow getting back to it. And yu have / prob lost yr / latin (if yu ever had much) by hellenism. anyhow Richard St. Victor blew hell out of all modern psychology / all prot / post Calvin nastiness and all eurpo / philo-epistemology. And with 2 sentences. The human soul is not love but love flows FROM it. It does not delight* in itself but the love pouring *outward* from it. You got into the wrong pig-stye, ma chere. But not too late to climb out.

————

There is an ink-bracket as from "delight,"* with handwriting, "have a good time in dilept": this last word is so written but I can not decipher. The word "deguises," line three, is as written; I don't know what he means. The spacing is a little different, but punctuation and spelling are the same. Who is R[ichard] St. Victor? Anyhow, thank you, I will write again. Both psychiatrists here, think the letter is CLEVER; Heydt thinks it funny and exciting; Schmideberg sees in it (in best Wien tradition) affecation [*sic*] from the far past. Thank you for the check. I enclose or will send the Mary Herr list, as she sent it to me, for advice.[90] I told her to do as she thought best. If her own letter is overweight, I will send it surface, with some odds and ends of very old letters that turned up — destroy what you will.

I want to grow a new SKIN before I attempt the new *Helen*,[91] but I seem to see the way — perhaps toward EUPHORION, the son that is traditionally, the child of the marriage of Helen and Achilles in Leuké. But this is a symbol; I think this Euphorion is one-remove from Paris and I don't know how to bring this together, except as possible pre-vision or prophecy of Theseus, who was brought up, as you remember, by the Centaur, Cheiron, prophet and healer. Anyhow, everything is there — it is getting it human and divine together that I aim for. By the way, a star-note* to V-IV of H[elen] in E[gypt] — to the effect that Pylades did not marry Iphegenia, but Orestes other sister, Electra.

Thank you for B[rigit]'s letters — more of all this. I enjoyed your *Golden Apple*[92] with you. I am so excited about the "Caravel" findings.

Forgive this one page. I want to enclose Mary Herr, 1239 Wheatland Avenue, Lancaster, PA

Gratefully, C.

from *H.*

On 11 June Pearson reports a meeting with Kurt Wolff[93] in which they discussed H.D.'s manuscript "The Sword Went Out to Sea." He also describes the feuding between archaeologists and engineers that accompanied the discoveries at Giza, and encloses photos of the excavated ship from *Life* magazine.[94] On 12 June H.D. implies that talk about Pound at the sanatorium is prompting her to rethink her view of his poetry. In this letter she writes, "I met another young German chez Heydt; he says they read Ezra a great deal. 'Political?' I asked him; he said 'no.' I want to read *Cantos* more carefully but the manner is a bit 'catching.' I am sure E. would revile the *Helen* technique!" In this letter, she also asks, "You make me *feel* the new *Helen* — but where do we go from here?"

In response, Pearson refers to her past successes. On 24 June 1954 he writes: "As to Helen, the final section will grow in your womb. It is exciting to plant the seed there. Let the seed have its time. Perhaps what I was thinking of was some sudden twist for her metamorphosis and regeneration, not to *épater les bourgeois*, nor to *confuser les boches*, but by transposing her into our time (as in the other trilogy the rod blossomed for us,) to make people sit up and take notice. So dreams one, and then Helen comes, out of the morning mist. For surely we pursue her too; your poem, my interest, does that and proves the point. One sees her by the lake and in the hills while armor rumbles in the world. Put now in verse what Helen and the greeks mean to you, why you think of her, and put the landscape in and all your fears and love. I know them; let me have them now as verse. And it will be something quite new and startling as a poet; and differently concrete to make the tensions taut and then resolved. And while you do it, I will hold your hand, and keep my other arm about you."

H.D.'s reply, on 2 July from Lugano, is grateful but restrained. She writes: "The *Helen* suggestions . . . are inspiring, perhaps too much of an undertaking. I will dream over it all — I do thank you." Pearson does not give up, however. On 21 July he mentions planning to stop in Ephrata, Pennsylvania, en route to meeting a descendant of Hawthorne, "for you and for our Mystery." He will send cards from there, hoping that the landscape will "bring back at least corners of Zinzendorf's spirit." He asks, "Shall I meet Helen there?" In the letters that follow, H.D. reports on the progress of part 3 of *Helen in Egypt.*

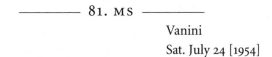

81. MS

Vanini
Sat. July 24 [1954]

[no salutation]

Thank you for New Ventures; it is exciting to see *Helen* in print.[95] I have just posted you, surface, "Canto" I & II of Book III. I feel it needs foot-notes, like my Portable Viking Dante,[96] but the enigmas will solve themselves, later, I hope. O — it is very, very hot & this little leaf of airmail paper glues itself to my hot hand. Do you know the "European?" A copy was sent me, Dec. 1953, of article 2, on Pisan Cantos, by one Alan Neame.[97] Viola J[ordan] had a copy sent her as well, she thought I had sent it, but I had not. She said it was the only criticism on the P[isan] C[antos] that had made them clear to her —

very dynamic writing & I was tempted to send for 1 & 3, but Br[yher] said the mag was notoriously faschistissimo & I would get on their "list." I will post this to you, as I am rather tempted to study the P[isan] C[anto] sections & I want to get on with *Helen*. Thank you for your letter of July 21 that I picked up, on the way out. I had a surprisingly affable note from E[zra], thanking me for Italian post-cards that I selected for him, from my collection, before I left Küsnacht. I will copy out & send you on a p.c. — Yes, I am so glad to be here. I go over the years, 1947 & 1948 at *Minerva*. 1949 with you at *Croce Bianca*. 1951 & 1952 at *Bristol*. For me, conditions are ideal for writing, as you know. I don't know the Janouski of E.'s cryptogram.[98] How fascinating about the Hawthornes — and that you may get to see the relative — & that you may contact a Z[inzendorf] *Mystery*. How much I owe you, for your sympathy & help. I am racing to catch the 16:45 post, so forgive this inadequate little note — with love & gratitude always, to

dear C from H.

Fido seems happy — no special news from Küsnacht, only an occasional card.

———— 82. MS ————

Vanini

July — no — no:

Aug. 3 [1954]

[no salutation]

Thank you, dear C, for first lot of charming art-cards. I have been so happy catching up with some of the miniature folders. Now, I have just had the Gnadenhutten card, following another, & in between, your letter, with a whole set.[99] I can not type, we are in a furious heat-wave. I did do the last *Helen*, which I love very much. I have sent you now, I think, I, II & III of "Canto" III. I just go on, as it happens, (one) I, I felt, was rather mixed. I started it at Küsnacht. Now, I have just scribbled a few lines, as toward [IV–I]. I don't know, if I can go on. As I say, the heat is positively volcanic. You write of heat, too . . . but I am glad you got hold of the H[awthorne] letters — & I find the Gnadenhutten *post-mark* positively uncanny. How you live with me & inspire me. It is unbelievable! Br[yher] writes of much rain there, but she seems happy with her writing & grateful for your help. You were here, at about this time, 1949, & we had then, heat, as I remember. We had a grand display, across the water, from Campione, on the Saturday; Sunday, the actual Day, was rather calm, though the drummers woke us at dawn and the children built their traditional beacon-fires on the mountains. Br is due out with Doris [Banfield] Long about the 10th. I hope we can take some trips, then; lately, I have just staggered into town, through the arcades, for morning-coffee & afternoon tea. I told you, Br wants me to go to Rome, mid-Sept., to meet my brother-&-wife, on a tour. P[erdita] may join us. I don't know, if I can manage. An occasional card from Bear; Melitta is there & Psycho-A[nalytical] congress is in full swing. Dr. Heydt seems to have deserted me, entirely — out of sight, out of mind, I guess. I sent you "European," surface, but have not got round to copy of E[zra]'s last letter. I will hope to write again — this is so inadequate, just to thank you. Ever, dear C.

H.

——————— 83. TS ———————

233 HGS
Yale University
New Haven, Conn.
21 August 1954

Dearest Hilda:

I am completely delighted with the final section of HELEN: Part III, and part iii of III. You have quite outdone yourself, and how you managed such concentration of your art amidst all the distractions, I cannot conceive. The whole thing blends together quite wonderfully. I have been reading and rereading it since the last section came, and with increasing delight. The sharp graphic detail of iii has tremendous power of imagery: the figurehead, the boat, the persons themselves. And because of what came before, all of the symbolic values are enforced here without the necessity for statement. I feel very happy indeed that you were willing to do III, for the musing over the past, the questions raised, and the twilight tone with a last burst of the evening sun finish the poem's day (its year). You have every reason to be happy about it, as I hope you are. I know that when a thing is done it is done, but at least you will continue to delight others.

You wrote several times that you thought some sort of foreword of explanation, rather of setting in myth and time, might be helpful; and what you wrote me was helpful, especially for the first reading of the trilogy. Wouldn't it be a good idea now, therefore, if you were to work over a page or two of prose, which I could use to precede the whole. Until the whole was done, you could hardly have written it. Now, while it is still fresh, and Lugano smiles at you, I think you could.

Do you intend at all to go over the early cantos, or, when I have the prose statement, shall I see what I can do with it? I can think of nothing particular that I think *needs* doing to the early sections. The only possibility might be the description of the fresh caravel in some detail in order to contrast with its final bleached form. There might be other contrasts of this sort, which could only be conceived by you as a result of having been through the path and known at last what would be found. But I do not stress this, as I say, nor do I think it a weakness of the early sections. I simply toss it in the air like a bubble, not knowing whether it will burst in the onslaught of tomorrow's eye.

Did I write you that Auden was using some sections from the war trilogy for a new anthology of modern American verse he is bringing out? I called them to his attention, and he was delighted with them. I am so glad to have a shift of emphasis from the earlier poems, good as they are. I have arranged all the business matters connected with it.

I have also just arranged contracts etc with the B.B.C., who are going to do your translation of the ION on their third program. At least a radio version; and I think that will be all right.

[. . .]

All love,
Yr.
C.

Many thanks for *The European*, which arrived this morning.

———— 84. TS ————

Sept. 7 [1954]

Dear Norman,

I have done *Helen*, VI, I–IV, but I seem to be stuck now. Actually, I have been greatly upset by news about Bear. Bryher is at Küsnacht and is due here, on the 9th and I will hear all news. She rang some days ago and said it was reported that Bear had cancer, of a fatal form and had only a few months to live. Now, she says there is hope of possible operation and six months at any rate. She says reports contradict each other; Melitta is there and I suppose, gives one version. It is so sad for Bryher. I had planned to go to Rome or to Venice to meet Perdita, but I have told Br that I will just wait here now, so that she can come here, at any time. It is not so far really, just the four hours on a good train, to Zurich. But we planned night-trip to Rome, as my brother is due there and P. flies directly there. I plan returning about end Oct. but I wrote Br that I would be ready to go earlier if my presence, near the clinic, would help in any way. It is unutterably tragic. I have been so happy here; Br came with Doris for about ten days, we had wonderful sun and still have, with plans going on here for enormous fete, as for the usual vendage. I wish you were here. Perhaps, I will suddenly over-take *Helen*; I think I did solve some of the "mysteries" in the last sections. Erich Heydt and a Hungarian friend were here for just two days and I am sure, if we needed him, he would come down again. I have not had any other visitors, but Br has been back and forth. I treasure all the folders and cards and was deeply touched at your visiting the various places. Now, I am happy with my *Miniatures*, they accumulated at one time and I have a lot to make up. I have written them for their list if they have one, as the folders went to *Paix*, for some time, some may have got lost. I do love them so, and am infinitely grateful for your arranging, — and to Susan for bringing that first lot. They grow on me, I feel I have such a treasure and look forward to my stack of them and old MSS, in my little room, at Küsnacht, later. I am happy feeding the deer in the *parco civico* and listening to their really charming "period" concerts, as from 11 A.M., strings, violins and harp sometimes add to the enchantment of those trees and majic [*sic*] lake. Kurt W[olff] of *Pantheon* was here, but he rang just as I was off to meet Br and Doris for a trip, so I postponed seeing him — then, he went to Munich. Tell him, if you see him, how I regret this. You will forgive this rushed note, I really do appreciate all the cards, the Greek ones, all the Moravian and allied "mysteries," the art selection. I have really been so deeply shocked about Bear, fearing reactions or repercussions on poor Fido. But I am better now, and look forward to her coming on Thursday.

I am sure the very things I most want to say have escaped me, but this is just to tell you why I have stopped working for the time; I will get back to it, I am sure. Please share all news with Susan, I think of her short visit here, in 1951 (was it?) and yours, in 1949.

Do you know, I have to look at a calendar when I write a cheque, now! Please forgive this again,

with all blessings,
dear C
from *H.*

Perhaps Fido has not told you of Bear — in which case, you do not "know" of it, till she writes, & this is confidential. . . .

233 HGS
Yale University
New Haven, Conn.
10 September 1954

Dearest Hilda:

[. . .]

Part IV arrived, (was it late last week or early this one), and I am enormously happy with it, realizing more than ever how this poem is a gathering together and a new formulation of so much that you have written about in your mature years. It is an essence of maturity, and a coming through with an understanding, in the fullest sense, of the intimate labyrinth of experience. Your experience, that is, and the experience of the past, in the sense that the experience of the past can only have meaning when it is absorbed into personality. And I sense the triumph of understanding through the distilled artistry of what you have written: the symbols of other poems — Writings and Wheels and the Mystery; the sea and almost, even, the Copenhagen mermaid in her absolute whiteness: the total pattern. And, then, the superb simplicity of the diction and the control of tone. It was as though you had made it my birthday when the poem arrived.

I had hoped that Ezra's new translation of the Confucian anthology of Chinese poems [100] would have been published soon enough to have had it in your hands on the 10th; but if not that, then it was by some lucky chance that it came today and I could send it to you. Think of it then as having passed from my hands toward you on your birthday. I have not had a chance to look at it, but what I have glanced at seems very fine indeed. If you like it, drop Ezra a note and say so. It would mean much to him, I know.

All love
from
your
C.

Sept. 22 [1954]

Dearest Norman,

Dr. Heydt rang this morning to say that the Bear had gone, about four this morning, he felt "peacefully." He had seen Bear yesterday and he said he seemed cheerful. They have wired Br[yher] of course, to Anticoli, and Heydt wants to bring her down here, in a few days, as from Zurich. Maybe Perdita will be in Z. or she will come direct here, from Rome. This is a shock but I am really very glad as Sch[mideberg] was suffering so, at the end.

I have written so many notes, about Sch. that I can hardly see, but I wrote Br that I was writing you at once.

I sent off the last *Helen*, surface, yesterday. Much can be changed, funny, it somehow ended itself right there. I have many things to say,[101] re your last long letter and the wonderful wire you and Susan sent. But you will forgive this

from Hilda —

——— 87. TS ———

233 HGS
Yale University
New Haven, Conn.
27 September 1954

Dearest Hilda:

[. . .]

I look forward to the last section of *Helen*. Odd that it should have ended itself almost at the moment [of Bear's death]; for there is much quite silently almost invisibly of the last months in the poem. Not overtly of course; it could not have been that. But there is always the touch of this Mystery; how does one explain it? To coincide thus. V of III arrived of course, and I have been over and over it, happily. It holds together beautifully. I am quite tempted by your suggestion of "Thetis Wings" for the section; but I want to see VI and then go over the whole together. I want the titles to hold dramatically together as a trilogy, and your introductory note may hold the phrases in itself. It is very exciting to think of your being so close to finishing this new work, and I shall be eager for each stage of the revision. I think of that only in terms of tidying here and there, as *you* see it; and perhaps the insistence of certain symbols here and there to bind it closer. Since symbols develop their own life as a long poem of this sort develops, and you know them now as you could not have known them at the beginning of your composition.

All love as always, from
Yr.
C.

October 1 [1954]

Dear Norman,

P[erdita] and Br[yher] are waiting for me to take a little trip to Morcote. I dash this off. The enclosed VI–VIII is corrected version of this last section that I sent with the rest of VI, surface. Then it seemed that this very last page would take the place of VII, as the other two have VII sections; but it seemed finished. I found this last page in my note-book, un-typed; it seems that if we put it in ITALICS, all of it and just call it EIDOLON, as the very last page of the whole of EIDOLON, that is Book III, it gives the clue, the final — that the figure-head OR the ship is this "dream" or mother-symbol OR Helen or what you will. I have much to say. Now, I will hope to get back to the beginning and go over the whole. I don't exactly know what you want me to do, in revision or explanation; I suppose some "notes" will come as I go along.

I find I can have five of these sheets now — sorry I stinted you before. I will try to write soon again. There has been so MUCH; my brother and wife, then Erich Heydt on the way to Venice, then he stopped here on the way back, just for dinner, last night. He was so wonderfully good and with Br, gave her sleeping-tablets and so on. Br seems all right, very tense, but we are all together and she seems to be working hard in her little room; everyone is so terribly kind. I have saved the last rough note-book of EIDOLON and will send it, later. You know I write straight through and then, at the end, just reverse and write on opposite page back to beginning, but I will number the rough pages. It is so worthless, but you seem to like to have the old books. Thank you for the Ezra, it looks a beautiful volume and I hope soon, to have the pleasure of reading it. Thank you so very, very much. You understand my hurry?

Gratefully, dear C —

H.

233 HGS
Yale University
New Haven, Conn.
10 October 1954

Dearest Hilda:

[. . .]

Part VI of Eidolon has been no exception. The little eidolon and the revised last verse of VI arrived a few days before the surface letter sauntered in. The post seems to have been slow lately. But I am completely happy with this ending. The lines and diction are wonderfully controlled, and like crystal; the images emerge sparkling and clear at the close. Bless you! This is altogether a true accomplishment.

As to any revisions of the whole, I mean only for you to look it over now that it is completed, thinking of its ending as you read the beginning, with (perhaps? just perhaps?) a stress or two of such elements as the figure-head when they first appear or rather re-appear.[102] This is the sort of the artefaking (making by art) that is only possible once one has unravelled it in progress, seen it through, dreamed it. Perhaps it will need nothing; only you can truly feel this.

I had thought that some of this you might have been able to do before I come. We could talk about it then. And thank you for saving the rough notebooks. I could bring them back with me.

Why not go with me someplace;[103] where we could even arrange after we were together. You will not find me otherwise than I have always been — that is, with love,

Yr

C

1. In particular, A. C. Swinburne's *Lesbia Brandon*, ed. Randolph Hughes and two books by E. M. Butler, *The Fortunes of Faust* (1952), a study of the Faust legend in literature, and a novel, *Silver Wings* (1953).

2. H.D.'s interest in psychoanalysis and mythography has been well documented. Pearson singles out his study with Malinowsky at Yale as an important early intellectual influence in a radio broadcast, "The Concept of American Studies," 25 May 1958, MS at BL.

3. In his essay "The American Poet in Relation to Science," Pearson argues that the poet's way of knowledge, through intuition, is a necessary corrective to the scientist's empiricism.

4. "*H.D. by Delia Alton*," *Iowa Review* 16, no. 3 (Fall 1986): 180–221.

5. See Pearson's essay "Anderson and the New Puritanism," *Newberry Library Bulletin* 2 (1948), and his entry "American Literature," in *Encyclopedia Americana*, 1960 edition.

6. See Pearson's essay "Hawthorne's Usable Truth" in *Hawthorne's Usable Truth . . . and Other Papers Presented at the Fiftieth Anniversary of New York Lambda Chapter, Phi Beta Kappa, Canton, New York, St. Lawrence University, Oct. 7, 1949.*

7. On 18 October 1953, H.D. wrote to Richard Aldington that she "sometimes wonder[s] if it [Leuké] makes sense, though Pearson seems to like it."

8. Pearson began teaching seminars on Pound's poetry in 1949, visited Pound at St. Elizabeths Hospital in the early fifties, wrote to him there, sent students to consult him, and helped to organize an exhibition of his work at Yale's Sterling Library in 1955.

9. He consulted her about the treatment of Joan Waluga and others.

10. On 22 August 1953, Bryher wrote to Pearson that H.D. "seemed so pleased to see me and is a little in love, I think, with the new doctor, a most intelligent man, and that again is good."

11. In January 1952, the *New York Times* reported the rising tensions between England and Egypt over control of the Suez Canal and Egyptian independence, with Egypt claiming the British were guilty of "imperialist aims" and the British claiming the Egyptians were guilty of "terrorist actions." On 26 January it reported that 1,500 British troops clashed with the Egyptian auxiliary police in Ismalia. On 27 January it reported rioting, and burning and looting of western properties, including Shepherd's Hotel.

12. On 28 January 1952, Pearson wrote: "But, oh, when I read in the papers about Egypt, and Shepherd's Hotel burned, and the riots etc., I think of how different it was when I was there — perhaps for me it centers more on Cairo because I never did really get along the Nile as you did. Do me a Delia Alton on Egypt and your trip there, and what Egypt is, etc. to you." H.D.'s trip to Egypt in 1923, with her mother and Bryher, included a visit to Luxor to see the newly excavated tomb of King Tutankhamen.

13. On 10 February 1952, H.D. says she has been enthralled by J. C. Furnas's *Voyage to Windward*, a biography of Robert Louis Stevenson, and that she has been rereading letters from Robert McAlmon.

14. On 25 February 1952, H.D. wrote: "I wish I could do a Delia Alton for him [Douglas], as you suggest. But I am trying to sort out papers, papers, papers. If I do this or

anything else, it will mean more MSS and pages. . . . This [death of King George] has upset us all in a strange way, I mean shaken us, as if some end of something — which indeed it is — and we may hope a beginning as well . . . I am a little up-rooted, disturbed by many letters to and from England — as if the King were one's personal — brother? Some relationship grew up during those black war-years."

15. On 29 February 1952 Pearson reported the death of his wife's uncle and an attempted robbery of his office.

16. On 29 February 1952 Pearson commented that the 500th anniversary of the Moravian Brethren (in five years) would be a good time to publish "The Mystery."

17. On 29 February 1952 Pearson mentioned that he sent James's *William Wetmore Story and His Friends* (1904), a biography of the expatriate American sculptor in which James continues to experiment with narrative point of view. Pearson explained: "[T]he opening section is a jewel of calling up the waves of memory and the sound of the surf of the past."

18. "Akasha" refers to "ether, the medium of sound" in *The Puranas*, according to John Garrett in *A Classical Dictionary of India* (1971). It is also defined as "all-pervading; space; vacuity" and as the chief and most subtle of the five elements with which Brahma is associated in *Harper's Dictionary of Hinduism: Its Mythology, Folklore, Philosophy, Literature, and History* (1977).

19. H.D. refers to an unselected letter from Pearson dated 28 January.

20. "Lena Grove," in *Shenandoah* 3, no. 1 (1952): 3–7.

21. A. C. Swinburne's novel *Lesbia Brandon* was denied publication until 1952, when it was published in an edition by Randolph Hughes, with notes and commentary. In the commentary, Hughes discusses the history of the novel's suppression, its relation to the literary tradition of the French novel, and the practice of flagellation in which Swinburne participated. In the foreword, Hughes declares the book to be particularly important in an age that "takes the American Mr. Ezra Pound and the American Mr. T.S. Eliot seriously . . . as literary artists" (xxx–xxxi), and a subsequent note calls Pound's *Pisan Cantos* "a barbaric something that is neither verse nor prose" (xxxi).

22. Melitta Schmideberg (1904–?), British psychoanalyst, wife of Walter Schmideberg and daughter of Melanie Klein, with whom she disagreed about key psychoanalytical concepts. She eventually moved to the United States and separated from her husband.

23. On 8 August 1952, H.D. writes to Bryher that she is still "deep in Swinburne, re-reading the *Golden Pine* blue books" that Bryher gave her in 1921. She continues: "I am weak with memories, it all comes back. Zermatt that time, all the visits here. It is the Swinburne partly, that has given me back the years, 'before the beginning of (time?) years.' That is, you and dear Perdita, always our July 17 meeting and Cornwall and the 1919 July trip to the Isles. Then the Isles of Greece. . . ."

24. Randolph Hughes, "Unpublished Swinburne," *Life and Letters and the London Mercury*, January 1948 (17–33).

25. On 18 July 1952, Pearson described a birdbath at his home on the seashore that consisted of a "bowl at the feet of Venus."

26. Nicholas Schaffner was born on 28 January 1953. H.D. refers here to Perdita's pregnancy.

27. H.D. refers to Elsie Volkart, Bryher's housekeeper.

28. On 26 August 1952 H.D. wrote: "Your encouragement meant so much to me, as

Br[yher] was, at one time, afraid in some way — that has gone now, and there is hardly a letter now, or hardly a week passes, without her referring to publication of *Sword*."

29. Perdita and her first child, Valentine, had visited earlier in the summer.

30. Pearson follows this letter with another "salute," of the same sort.

31. On 11 October 1952, H.D. writes Bryher, who was confused by the relationship between Zeus and Amen in the poem's opening: "I should have introduced the pages with a note, as I did with Norman. I think you know the myth, one of the 'readings' of the Troy legend; that is, that *Helen* on the walls was a 'double' or *eidolon*, made or sent by Zeus; he had rescued the original *Helen* and sent her to Egypt. It is, of course, difficult and metaphysical. I would preface the poems with story, and I asked N. to do so. When Achilles asks which was the dream, which the 'veil,' it is my own effort to re-adjust or get the two together yet separate. I am going on, but very slowly."

32. *Hilda's Book* consisted of poems written by Pound to H.D., between 1905 and 1907, as a private offering to a very close friend. Pearson later published them with H.D.'s *End to Torment: A Memoir of Ezra Pound* (1979), in a volume he coedited with Michael King.

33. On 10 October, H.D. wrote: "My sister-in-law, Sara [wife of her brother Eric], a difficult semi-invalid, was fond of Ezra. She may possibly have taken over something, as my mother told me in the move and general clean-up [after her father's retirement from the Flower Astronomical Observatory], that the papers and letters that I had left there, of Ezra's, had been burnt. This seemed best, anyhow; the letters were madly eccentric, as per usual."

34. Andrew Gibson, a British schoolmaster, was in love with Frances Gregg. However, Gregg married Louis Wilkinson, an English novelist who used the nom de plume Louis Marlow. She separated from him and later died in an air raid during World War II in Plymouth, England, where she lived with her mother and daughter.

35. On 28 December, H.D. responded: "I am glad you write of the *Helen*; I thought perhaps it did not wear so well. I am so happy about it, we will talk of all that, later. I really feel that pull and urge, having got a form or format and a region and much to go on with, if I want to or feel in the mood; there is Proteus, that 'character' who was King of Egypt, in the Euripides *Helen*; that could lead anywhere."

36. On 28 December, H.D. responded: "Yes, the *Helen* carries on the 'Mystery'; it is a miracle that it came clear like that. And a miracle that it waited until the end of the 'lustre' to manifest from the un-conscious to the conscious or to inspire or to what-not. Anyhow, I could not have written *Sword* and *Rose*, without the original old Adam to draw on or to draw. Then, the *nouvelle homme*, 'the new Mortal, shedding his glory. . . .'"

37. Hugh Kenner (1923–), Pound scholar and prolific critic of modern poetry, received his Ph.D. from Yale in 1950. His books include *The Poetry of Ezra Pound* (1951) and *The Pound Era* (1971).

38. Probably John Kasper.

39. Alexander del Mar (1836–1926), a nineteenth-century American economic historian, whose work prompted Pound to renew his work on the *Cantos*.

40. On 28 December, H.D. responded: "I am so glad of your documentation of the E[zra] P[ound] surroundings. I have heard chiefly from people who sat on that bench, Viola

and Olga who was over, taking Dorothy's place as 'attendant' for some weeks — O — O — how devastating for both of them. Olga wrote me the usual about people not working enough for E, etc. But I will write her, later, and not get involved this end. I think you people T H E R E are much better to judge and able to help and I know that you will do all that can possibly be done. I am G L A D that you got there, give love to them when you write, I write so seldom."

41. She refers to the legend that Helen was the bribe offered by Aphrodite to Paris in order to win the wager over who was the most beautiful. When Aphrodite won the bet, Hera was furious and substituted a phantom made of air in Helen's exact form to Paris as his prize. Thus, while Paris thought he had the real Helen, and Menelaus believed the same, Helen in actuality was brought to Egypt by Hermes and left there in exile. There she meets Achilles, with whom she conceives a child.

42. Olga Rudge (1894–1995), violinist, mistress of Ezra Pound from 1920 until his death.

43. H.D. seems ambivalent about doing more for Pound. In this letter she writes that she advised Marya Zaturenska to keep out of the efforts to obtain Pound's release and that she feels "that T.S. E[liot] has been in on this and should be, and you have done what you could." Eliot, Robert Frost, and Archibald MacLeish are generally the three poets credited with helping to obtain Pound's release from St. Elizabeths Hospital in 1958.

44. Mary de Rachewiltz (1925–), daughter of Olga Rudge and Ezra Pound, married Boris de Rachewiltz. They provided Pound with a place to live when he first returned to Italy, and she translated and edited his works.

45. On 31 January 1953, Pearson mentions sending H.D. *The Pathfinder* by James Fenimore Cooper, which he introduced, praising Cooper's mythopoeic powers: "Cooper's particular talents found their way through slapdash into their fullest expression in the mythical concept of the supremely skilled and deservedly lucky frontier hunter and guide, and in the depiction of the great expanses of unbroken American forests and the rolling waters within."

46. H.D. refers to Pearson's introduction, in which he quotes Henri Balzac and Victor Hugo, who both praised Cooper, Balzac comparing him to Walter Scott.

47. *Yale French Studies*, no. 9 (1953), titled *Symbol and Symbolism*, includes essays on Racine, Sartre, Valéry, Jacques Rivière, Rilke, and others, as well as "Four Unpublished Letters of Stephane Mallarmé to Stuart Merrill" and an essay by Neal Oxhandler, "The Balcony of Charles Baudelaire," that discusses Baudelaire's poem "Le Balcon" in relation to Baudelaire's life and his lover Jeanne Duval.

48. Adrienne Monnier (1892–1955), French writer and bookseller, was a leader in the Left Bank literary community, along with her companion Sylvia Beach. The two women were also friends of H.D. and Bryher, having translated into French the latter's book, *Paris 1900* (1929).

49. H.D. means Newnham College, Cambridge University.

50. On 14 April [1953], H.D. writes: "I did a last section of *Helen in Egypt*. It is to wind up that series — so *Choragus*, as impersonal leader-of-chorus, indicates that the sails are set, and she, Helen, now, can have a new life — with all Greek mythology before us. I don't know that I shall do any more, but the door is open! 'Helen, the sails are set.'" In this letter, H.D. also mentions that Sylvia Beach is arranging for the translation of H.D.'s "The White Rose and the Red" into French and that a German publisher is interested in a translation of *By Avon River*.

51. H.D. refers to surgery for an intestinal occlusion.

52. Euripides' *Andromache* opens in front of the temple of Thetis in Thessaly. Andromache, who was Hector's wife, is presently a slave to Achilles' son and has had a son by him. Andromache is threatened in the play and she takes refuge in the shrine of Thetis, who enters as a deus ex machina at the end.

53. In Euripides' play (trans. Edward P. Coleridge), Thetis mentions that Peleus shall live with her in the halls of Nereus, and see Achilles, "our dear son, settled in his island-home by the strand of Leuce, that is girdled by the Euxine Sea."

54. George Santayana (1863–1952) wrote a three-volume autobiography/memoir titled *Persons and Places*, published in 1944, 1945, and 1953. H.D. refers here to the third volume, *My Host the World*.

55. In 1951–52 Williams suffered strokes that left him partially paralyzed.

56. Mary Butts (1890–1937), British novelist, author of *Armed with Madness* (1928) and *The Death of Felicity Taverner* (1932). A friend of Bryher and H.D. in the 1920s, she was interested in magic and the occult.

57. Edward Alexander (Aleister) Crowley (1875–1947), Scottish poet and practitioner of black magic, wrote and edited books on magic and the occult.

58. On 22 July 1953 Pearson responds: "Ezra was sweet to have sent the CALLIMAQUE. He always yearns for news of you, and I suspect I must have told him that you were going back for the final curetage. Friends mean an immense deal to him. I was quite won over a year or so back when it was reported to me by an acquaintance that, as this man left, he said: 'And tell Pearson to write. I cannot carry on alone!'"

59. Pound wrote to H.D., "pearson sends an s.o.s. that I shd / send yu a Valentine NOW instead of waiting." He includes a poem with the lines "Hang on and come up with the spring, / of course you did wrong to / go reading other languages when you had a start / on a good one / get a KALLIMAXOS / ever bathe in ole KAL? If not sufficiently soaked, and if you haven't got a / cawpy, I will try to get one fer yu" (February 1953, unpublished letter, BL).

60. On 22 July 1953 Pearson wrote that Farrar, Strauss, and Young has agreed to publish H.D.'s memoir of Freud and that he will meet with them to discuss publication details.

61. On 31 July 1953 Pearson responds that he is interested in Heydt's comment about Pound's letter. He resents Pound's asking him to write angry letters to the press on his behalf, but forgives this side of him because of his excellence as a poet. He writes: "Yet when I read the *Cantos* I know what a poet he is: those lyric passages which are beyond anything that Tom has done, or most of them. And the consistency of the Pisan group, with their personal element revived out of history and in history. All history in his mind, and the Italian landscape to look out on through the stockade: la pastorella glimpsed like a Circe or Penelope or Helen."

62. On 2 September 1953, H.D. writes to Bryher: "This Leuké story (Achilles, not Paris) is authentic myth, Euripides refers to it etc. Anyhow, this gets away from war and I make *Leuké* a sort of Earthly Paradise."

63. The 1953 meeting of the English Institute examined *The Cantos* of Ezra Pound. Hugh Kenner, Guy Davenport, Wilbur Frohock, and Achilles Fang read papers. The first two were published in Lewis Leary, ed., *Motive and Method in the Cantos of Ezra Pound* (1954).

64. Omar Shakespear Pound (1926–), poet, translator, and editor, was born in Paris, lived

in England until 1980, and now lives with his family in Princeton, New Jersey. His works include translations of Arabic and Persian poetry, several editions of Pound's correspondence, and the book of poems *The Dying Sorcerer and Other Poems* (1985).

65. Antony Alpers, *KM: A Biography* (New York: Knopf, 1953).

66. H.D. probably refers to Donald Sutherland's *Gertrude Stein: A Biography of Her Work* (New Haven: Yale University Press, 1951).

67. Martin Buber's *For the Sake of Heaven*, trans. Ludwig Lewisohn, was published by the Jewish Publication Society in 1945 and by Harper's in 1953.

68. Pearson includes the first four sections of Blake's "Book of Thel" in his *Poets of the English Language*, vol. 4.

69. The anthology includes a "Calendar of British and American Poetry."

70. H.D. probably refers to *Twentieth-Century Poetry* (1929), coedited by William Rose Benét, John Drinkwater, and Henry Seidel Canby. It includes short biographical sketches of the authors.

71. On 18 October 1953, H.D. wrote to Richard Aldington of her Helen sequence: "I sometimes wonder if it makes sense, though Pearson seems to like it."

72. On 20 December Pearson responded: "I think of you often in your new room, looking out at the lake, the wind whistling, but the sense of comfort you must feel within. And if at moments I am a little jealous of the Papa, jr. [Erich Heydt], you must forgive me, and so must he."

73. Thornton Wilder, *The Long Christmas Dinner*, a one-act play published in 1931 in *The Long Christmas Dinner and Other Plays in One Act*. On 25 March 1954, Pearson mentions having sent her a copy.

74. She refers to the play as it appears in *The Poets of the English Language*, vol. 2. The text, taken from the Second Folio, is minimally altered.

75. On 20 December [1953] Pearson responds: "I am happy with the two new installments of poems. *Ca va*; *es geht*. One needs now the whole of this second section, in order to feel the parts of a whole. But I am confident of it."

76. Pearson offered to send H.D. a copy of Pound's *Selected Essays* (1954), introduced by T. S. Eliot. On 19 February, H.D. responded that she was glad of Eliot's imprimatur but that she didn't want the book.

77. On the back of the sheet, in H.D.'s handwriting, is the list: "V Helen-Helen; VI Achilles, the man hero; VII Thus Thus Thus; VIII Isis, yes Cypris."

78. The selection from Milton in volume 3 of *Poets of the English Language* includes: "On the Morning of Christ's Nativity," "At a Solemn Musick," "On the Late Massacre in Piedmont," "On His Blindness," "On His Late Wife," "The Fifth Ode of Horace," "Lycidas," selections from "Comus" and *Paradise Lost*, and *Samson Agonistes*. In the introduction, Auden and Pearson state that they are trying to maintain the "contemporary appearance of the texts of the poems" (xxvii).

79. Hugo von Hofmannsthal, the opera librettist, wrote a version of Euripides' *Alcestis*, titled *Alkestis, ein Traverspiel nach Euripides* (Weisbaden: Insel Verlag, 1911). It was also published "with music by Egon Wellesz, Op. 35" in New York by Universal editions in 1923.

80. Dan Pinck, "A Visit with Ezra Pound," *Reporter* 10, no. 3 (2 February 1954): 40–43. The piece is largely uncomplimentary, stressing Pound's paranoia and his motley crew of disciples at St. Elizabeths.

81. Eliot's *The Confidential Clerk* was published in 1954 in London and New York.

82. "Sophocles. *Women of Trachis*, A Version by Ezra Pound," *Hudson Review* 6, no. 4 (Winter 1953/54): 487–523.

83. H.D. refers to the "biographical booklet" accompanying Pearson's anthology.

84. On 4 February 1954, H.D. wrote to Bryher that she had finished *Leuké*, "and if I manage a third section it will be what Norman asked for."

85. When she was a child, Bryher visited Egypt with her parents. She is en route to Pakistan with Kenneth Macpherson and Islay Lyons.

86. Pearson enclosed postcards, one of which showed a picture of St. Gorgon.

87. Bryher's novel *Roman Wall* (New York: Pantheon, 1954) is dedicated to "N. P.," Norman Pearson. It is a historical novel, set in the period when Rome was overrun by barbarians. The main character, Valerius, feels torn between duty and his desire for "Fabula," the embodiment of a dream.

88. Pearson delivered the talk "Is Shakespeare Necessary?" on the program *Yale Interprets the News*, on 28 February 1954.

89. From mid-May to mid-June 1954, there were almost daily reports of finds in the archaeological dig at the Great Pyramid of Giza. A ship was uncovered that was apparently outfitted to take the soul of King Cheops to heaven.

90. H.D. refers to a checklist of her writings.

91. On 7 June 1954, Pearson wrote: "I am in no hurry for the final *Helen*, only anxious that she continues to roam your mind. She should not be rushed, this last section I mean. Possibly you take notes, sketch it out, make some trial runs during the Lugano time; then next winter one firms it up, possibly even knowing then how it comes out one goes back here and there in the earlier sections to scatter clues, invitations to the ending, and the like. This possibility of bringing finally together into a cumulative mystery with a full-bodied ending was what has kept me from pushing publication of the first two sections before. One has not been, so to speak, committed. Egypt? Greece? Switzerland and you and I, with Helen before us? England? Pennsylvania? What I mean is, directly or indirectly, the absorption into yourself, ourselves. With a landscape. A pastoral, a variety of the rod's flowering, the sense of Helen embodied, the reason for the image floating now for us, and the tendrils clasping."

92. H.D. refers to a musical version of the Helen story that Pearson described seeing in New York in his letter of 5 June.

93. Kurt Wolff (1887–1963), German-born publisher, produced works of great literary quality by new authors at his Kurt Wolff Verlag. Fleeing the Nazis, he emigrated to the United States before World War II. There he helped manage Pantheon Books and, with his wife, founded Helen and Kurt Wolff Books.

94. 14 June 1954, pp. 20–23.

95. Unidentified.

96. H.D. refers to Paul Milano, ed., *The Portable Dante* (Viking, 1947). It includes *The Divine Comedy*, trans. Laurence Binyon, with notes by C. H. Grandgent.

97. Neame, Alan, "*The Pisan Cantos* II. Considerations in Criticism," *European* 10 (December, 1953): 13–26.

98. H.D. refers to Pearson's letter of 21 July 1954, in which he mentioned a letter from Pound, with the following cryptic message: "Ric / St. Victor / Stanislas asked to translate. (Yanowski not Joyce, Stan)."

99. On 29 July 1954, Pearson described a trip he took to Ephrata, a religious commune founded by Conrad Beissel, which was committed to mysticism, ascetic communism, and celibacy. He wrote: "But oh Kat, our Helen would never have joined with Beissel and his 'sisters' in their white robes. Gnaddenhutten perhaps; that would have been a Troy!"

100. *The Classic Anthology Defined by Confucius* (1954), intro. by Achilles Fang.

101. On [24 September 1954], H.D. added, "The whole winter, since Xmas to spring, till I came here, end June, was so tangled with poor Bear's problems — but I am glad now, I was there and it left Br[yher] free, really, for Pakistan. So much comes back, as I had 1936 and 1937 sessions in London and Bear stood by during bad Blitz days."

102. On 14 October [1954], H.D. responds: "Your comments on the *Helen* script are wonderfully helpful and I want to read it ALL, as a whole, as you say, and re-arrange perhaps, or/and take or make a few notes. But I need psychic elbow-room. But really, I am so very happy about it. And have you, you, you to thank for spurring me on to the final *Eidolon* section — and I think *Eidolon* such a good sub-title, or title for III, too."

103. Pearson proposed meeting H.D. and Bryher in Rome at the end of October. In her letter of 14 October, however, H.D. writes that Bryher doesn't want to go and she herself is too tired. She proposes that they meet in Küsnacht. In his reply on 20 October, Pearson assures her that she is the main reason for the trip and that he wants to go over *Helen* with her.

CHAPTER FOUR

"Are You and Erich Perhaps the *Dioscuri*?"

1955-1956

In this interval H.D. documented her relationship with Erich Heydt, who had become linked with Pound and Pearson in her imagination. In the journal "Compassionate Friendship" (1955), she describes him as the inheritor of seven earlier male "initiators," beginning with Pound.[1] To the extent that Heydt reminded her of Pound, his attentiveness and interest in her work, along with problematic aspects of his background, revived the psychological tensions that were the source of her inspiration. For besides being infatuated with Heydt, H.D. was suspicious of his political affiliation during the war. She knew that he had grown up in Germany and wondered if he had been able to escape Nazi conditioning.[2] In her journal she conveyed the atmosphere of mistrust and suspicion that pervaded the postwar milieu in the sanatorium by recording conflicting gossip about Heydt's alleged half-Jewish background.[3]

Further, in H.D.'s imagination, Heydt, like Pearson, was a type of chevalier. She associated him with the "rosenkavalier" of Richard Strauss's opera.[4]

In "Magic Mirror" (1956), the unpublished novel derived from this journal, in which Heydt is fictionalized as Dr. Erich Heller, another facet of his function is revealed. Heller enables the heroine to relive in memory the loss of her first child; that is, she remembers "the deepest depth of desolation" at the core of the illumination she achieved in her occult historical romances. In fact, the letters, the journal, and the novel all reveal that H.D. had paired Heydt with Pearson during the composition of *Helen in Egypt*. As she put it, "I think the *Helen* has two god-fathers";[5] Heydt enabled her to recover previously inaccessible parts of her inner life, and Pearson linked her to her homeland, to the outside world, and to the literary tradition.

To complicate matters further, H.D.'s infatuation with Heydt coincided with a period of mild rivalry between H.D. and Bryher for Pearson's attention. (It is noteworthy that H.D. regarded her friendship with E. M. Butler, whose work had been a major influence on *Helen in Egypt*, as a supplement to Bryher's at this time.)[6] For although Pearson had been unsuccessful in arranging the publication of H.D.'s fiction, he had helped Bryher to publish several historical novels,[7] and he wrote to her and saw her more frequently than he did H.D. Although H.D. was pleased with Bryher's literary success and did not admit any jealousy to Pearson, his awareness of H.D.'s disappointments contributed to his determination to bring about the publication of her *Selected Poems* (1956). It may also have given impetus to the exhibition of her work that he arranged at Yale in 1956 in honor of her seventieth birthday.

Certainly Heydt became more entrenched in H.D.'s circle of intimates after Pearson's visit at the end of 1954. At the beginning of 1955, he became Pearson's ally in encouraging H.D. to record part of *Helen in Egypt*. H.D.'s pleasure at these recording sessions resulted in her decision to write introductory prose captions to the poems' lyrics, a choice that Pearson supported. On 11 January 1955, he described the effect as "bardic, rather Greek in an odd way, as though some court-bard were telling the myths." In the following exchange, he and H.D. discuss both the recording sessions and the prose captions.

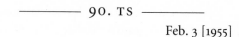

90. TS

Feb. 3 [1955]

Dear Norman,

Thank you for your letter and the beautiful carnation card. I am so happy about the disk-work [*sic*], went in yesterday by car and E[rich] came along and helped me. I did just 21 minutes this time, some of the first section with captions. It came up quite well — the first set, of Jan. 26, sent surface, is really the second disk, in time. The first one I did is more lyrical and has sections from Eidolon; this one of Feb. 2 has Egypt and some Leuké; one side of disk is Achilles, the other, Paris. It is difficult editing the sections but it has given me the idea of making some captions or short descriptive paragraphs, as introductions to cantos, not to all of them, but from time to time; they should be printed not as notes at end or beginning, but along with the poem, as I did the ION notes. This will require a good deal of thought, as I will bring in the mythology, explain certain references and some of the philosophy. I don't want to hurry this and it might make the book too long. But I hope to go over the whole, reading it aloud and changing a word or phrase from time to time. Look at the *Viking Portable Dante*, in the library, and you will see what I mean. I would want the notes in italics, not so many of course, as in the Laurence Binyon translation, but done creatively. I felt the captions that I did for the disk selections did help — you will see what I mean, when you run them off. I have ordered three of each of the disks for myself, but later, I might want more and would ask you to have them done for me — not now. We had Mr. von der M[uhll] send this (Feb. 2) set to you, air-mail, not so terribly expensive, about 8 francs, he said. I hope there is no special duty. He did not think there would be. I would like you to tell me what you would like, in case I do some from early poems. I thought the *Delphic charioteer* [8] would read well, fast — and it goes with the spirit of the epic *Helen* sections. I can not yet see any of the other poems, but I am going over them, as soon as I get the rather hypnotic rhythm of the *Helen* out of my head. I could not sleep last night — I was so excited. I have never felt so happy about my work, before. It is due to you — and I must say that E is very, very good, seemed impressed and wants me to go on. He really is a sensitive critic. Fido is due here toward the end of Feb.; I will be glad to see her but am also glad that she is not coming just yet, as once I break the disk sequence, I may find it difficult to return. There is a wonderful Etruscan exhibition here — E wanted me to run up to it with him, after our cup of coffee in a modest little cafe, the *Corso*, where I could SEE you — you were with me, I am sure in the "reading." Forgive all this about myself, but it is a sort of resurrection for me and the "reading" has fired the poems, given them new fire. I do, do long to know what you will think. I got the voice better yesterday and the disk on the radio-gram, of the first seemed to tone down what I felt was somewhat theatrical shouting. Yes — it shouts itself. Don't let it deafen you — and I think two sides of disk is best, as ten minutes is enough at a time. But you would do that anyway, I am sure. It is cold and damp now, but yesterday, it breathed of spring. Everyone was so kind when I had five teeth out — I was afraid it would interfere with the reading but the dentist here made me a miraculous little bridge, temporary; I must have some final work done, end March. So you see that I have been very involved but so grateful as I think those bad roots were poisoning me. I will stay on here, as I must have work finished at dentist and want to keep the mood of the readings. Or writing and correction or revising, as inspired by the reading. Fido is looking at flats in Lugano — but I do not want to move entirely, yet. And somehow, though winter is pretty severe here, there is so much to do. *Romeo and J[uliet]* is here, we saw it, in Italian in Rome and I want to go again — and there is a *Henry IV*, that E talks of, and really amazing concerts. I love Lugano for some months, but we will see about all that when Fido comes. O — Norman — how can I thank you?

Ever, dear C —

H.

————— 91. TS —————

17 February 1955

Dearest Hilda:

I have been listening this afternoon to the first recording from "Helen." But, my darling, you are absolutely professional! Actually better than any professional I know of. Even the man who runs the audio-visual center here, and who told me how many revolutions per second were best, was immensely impressed. I am quite serious. They have a wonderful studio where I had it played, and I could [have] wept with excitement when your voice came out with all its true tones and rich texture. Because, you know, I have never heard you read before. I came just after The reading in London; there never was another with you in it. So I was not quite sure what to expect, though your alarums did not worry me. But it was beautiful, very beautiful indeed — both from the sheer harmony of your voice, and for the interpretation which your phrasing gave. Your idea of the brief introductions was brilliant; I think something rather like this might be worked into the manuscript itself. But just now I am filled with what is to me an exciting idea. That would be, with your blessing, to approach one of the record companies and see if they would be interested in releasing it as a regular recording.[9] This would be rather fun, — and revolutionary. The first appearance of the poem, plus the first recording by you. No one has ever done this before; and I always think of you as being a first in things. It would not of course have anything to do with the publication of the poem itself. As a matter of fact I rather think it would serve to create interest in the book of Helen when it appears.

[. . .]

[unsigned]

In March and April, H.D. and Pearson discuss the recently published German translation of *Avon*,[10] as well as the possibility of German translations of "What Do I Love?" and *Trilogy*, war poems that Heydt thinks would interest Germans who had suffered the bombings of Dresden and Berlin. H.D. also describes her reactions to particular books. Of Harry T. Moore's biography of D. H. Lawrence,[11] at first she writes that "the general atmosphere has given [her] the creeps" and that she dislikes Moore's account of Amy Lowell's relationship to the Lawrences (15 March 1955). However, in later letters she reports enjoying the book because it supplies dates she had forgotten: "I had forgotten that Amy took R[ichard] and me to that cottage in Chesham in Buckinghamshire, before she left, August 1914, it must have been" (25 March 1955). On 4 April H.D. mentions having been "stunned" by G. Wilson Knight's book on Shakespeare's sonnets, which she has just read.[12]

The letters between them are sparser than usual throughout the summer of 1955. In June Pearson mentions having applied for a second Guggenheim Fellowship, again for work on his edition of Hawthorne's letters. Also he writes that he has sent H.D. a biography of Greta Garbo[13] and that the letters of W. C. Williams are being edited. They include a letter about Williams's first meeting with H.D., which Pearson offers to send. In July H.D. reports having had a terrible time trying to help Heydt with the treatment of Joan Waluga, in whom she has taken a special interest.[14] She also mentions Heydt himself having had an attack of mania that surprised her. Pearson responds that Bryher has written him of her reservations about Heydt.[15]

On 1 August Pearson continues to respond to H.D.'s concern about the mental health of Erich Heydt, whom Pearson thinks has "a basic fear of the future, post-Küsnacht, which haunts him and causes him to cast around for moorings." In this letter he continues: "These Germans of this generation have nothing to go back to; they were so to speak spawned in mid-air between invisible layers of generations." H.D. writes that she has been unable to work on the captions of *Helen* because of the excessive heat and the problems with Joan and Erich. She hopes to return to them in the fall and urges Pearson to keep writing to her. He responds with the latest news about Pound and a description of the funeral of Wallace Stevens.

H.D.'s letters in September and October mention a visit from Bryher and Perdita and express the hope of getting back to the *Helen* notes. She feels "lazy and guilty and behindhand that [she] did so little work" (4 October 1955), but she explains that she got caught with a "fistula" and fears another operation. Pearson responds with accounts of his weekly activities at Yale, which included entertaining Elizabeth Bowen and Robert Penn Warren in addition to his teaching duties. He looks forward to Bryher's arrival in November and wishes that H.D. could come too. H.D. replies that she is writing again, and in the following letter she expresses satisfaction at having finished the prose captions to *Helen in Egypt*.

———— 92. TS ————

Hotel Bristol
LUGANO
Nov. 26 [1955]

Dearest Norman,

Thank you for the two sets of delightful cards — and all news. I had Fido-version, as well and Perdita writes, so I feel right in the innermost circle with you all. I am in no hurry about the Freud — Fido speaks of the "letters," are you including them, after all? [16] I think the *Helen* should come out separately — I really want it all on its own, to hug to me'bosom. I am willing and ready to help with official expenses. I want a good edition. I don't especially want publicity — we can go into all that, later. I have the captions, the captions for the recording gave me this idea — and I think you will find that this whole set (no repeats from recording-captions) does hold the poems together, explain the at-times difficult "philosophy" and put some of the mythological matter on the map. I am sure that you will like the set. I have asked Miss Woolford to leave broad white space between each numbered caption, so that the pages can be cut and each caption mounted B E F O R E the poem, on a page facing the same, as for later printer. But I will write all this again. I warm my hands and heart at the glow of the *Helen*, and it is you and Fido who gave me the courage to go on with it. It is really so exoteric (difficult word — all war-problems) as well as being strictly I N N E R and esoteric and personal. I must blow my little tin-horn about this, as I never was know[n] really to blow any horn, I think, about H.D.; you and Fido chiefly did that for me — and Ezra of course, in the beginning, and the early R[ichard] A[ldington]; I have finally really written to E and told him you had asked me to do some home-work on the canto questions, that I had a long, long *Helen* sequence on hand, so could not write properly — you see, more trumpets! I feel the last days, that I am in Athens, the hills are miraculously "violet-crowned." There is much more to say and I will write again. Ever and ever gratefully, dear C

H.

On 28 November 1955, H.D. encloses a letter from her girlhood friend Margaret Sniveley Pratt, whose brother De Forrest introduced her to Ezra Pound when they were adolescents. She also comments that she received a card from Pound recently and plans to "go into 'home-work' on cantos as Prof. P[earson] has suggested," now that she has finished her *Helen*. In addition to the usual Christmas greetings, H.D.'s letters in December express some concern about where to spend the winter; she doesn't want to return to Küsnacht and has found a hotel near Zurich. She is working on corrections to her *Helen* and is very happy with the poem. On 24 December she writes that these are "the only poems I ever wrote that I memorized in part, and say over and over." She is also very excited about Pearson's plan to have an H.D. exhibition at Yale in honor of her seventieth birthday. In his replies Pearson praises her *Helen* notes, reports on the production details of her Freud memoir, and describes his plans for the H.D. exhibition.

On 17 January [1956], H.D. mentions that she is "re-working the ideas of Küsnacht that [she] roughed out" in anticipation of a move from there. She will later title this manuscript "Magic Mirror." In addition to expressing interest in this manuscript, in his reply Pearson describes the rapidly declining health of his father and its effect on his mother. He is looking forward to a leave of absence, when he will have more time to go over H.D.'s work, particularly "The Mystery," "which almost came to be my mystery too as we held hands and burned the candles" (28 January 1955).

At the end of February, Pearson sends H.D. news about an editorial, in *Life* magazine (6 February 1956), calling for Pound's release from St. Elizabeths Hospital. Also, he asks about a title for *Helen* and reports publication details of her book on Freud, assuring her that he is working on permission to include Freud's letters to her. He suggests *Tribute to Freud* or *Homage to Freud* as the book's title (instead of *Writing on the Wall*) so that they can keep "blameless physician" as a dedication. On 7 March, H.D. responds to his requests for the titles of both works: she agrees on *Tribute to Freud* but is uncertain about a title for *Helen* — "*Helen Sequence? Helen In Egypt?*" In this letter, she also mentions making progress on her manuscript about Küsnacht and asks Pearson to suggest a surname for the fictionalized version of Erich Heydt.

On 10 March, Pearson responds to H.D.'s query about a name for Heydt with the suggestions "*Kriegskind*," or "if you wish, for his sake, to give it a slightly more innate, quasi-faunlike character: *Waldkind*." He comments that both names convey "unrootedness, the uncertain nature, the aspect of unfound normatives." In the following letters, H.D. announces her own name for Heydt [Heller]. They also continue to discuss possible titles for *Helen* and names for other people and places in the fictionalized version of her Küsnacht notes.

March 15 [1956]

Dear Norman,

The two copies of the *Leuké* have come. I do thank you. It all looks won-
derful and I will have great pleasure in going over it, I hope, very soon. Thank
you for your letter, so quick an answer to my last one. What is the last date
possible for the photographs? Please let me know. Simply, I do not feel at
home with those pictures you speak of.[17] I am sorry. I realize they are well
done. I wrote of this before. I do not want them used — and is it necessary to
have one on jacket? It is embarrassing and you know how I like to be "incog";
after all, that was always *H.D.* — wasn't it? Erich wants me to go to a special
place in Zurich — but I am not going back immediately — but could the pho-
tograph wait? Please, please let me know. I want what I WANT — and I have
not got it — I will write you again. Please do not push out anything without
my knowing about it. What is time-limit?

I had not seen Erich for six months; he was here just for the day yesterday.
I found his name and he seems to like it — thank you for your own sugges-
tions. He will be Eric Heller — a simple enough name but he says not really
common-place and he likes the idea of the Heller, light — and relationship
with the Hellen [*sic*] — and he did help with those recordings etc.[18] I am get-
ting a few more names fitted in and will try to have a few chapters typed to
send later. So sorry about the theft[19] — it is a shock, it happened to me very
early, in War I, and then later once; it isn't only the loss of belongings, it's a
sort of personal affront. So glad that the flower-show was such a success —
what pleasure and reward for Susan — my congratulations! Remember me to
Ezra when you write. It is all heart-breaking! And I continue to grieve for the
Gardner sorrow.

Bryher is due now, in less than a week, on the 20th. We have both had those
giant post-cards from Perdita and from John — they seem very happy. I hurry
to get this off and to say that I am getting on to the poems — yes, I suppose
Helen is sufficient, but *Helen in Egypt* might be more explicit for the whole
theme — "Egypt" being a symbol for the mystery altogether. When must all
this finally be decided?[20] I feel sort of over-whelmed by it all — and just realize
that this is the year of Freud's 100th birthday — am I right? He was 30 years
older than I, 77 to my 47 (as I remember) at the time in Vienna — is anything
special planned? Is that why you wanted the *Tribute* for this year? I am sure
that I will remember something very special after I post this — but I do want

to get it out at once — with all thoughts to you and yours and special grati-
tude to C

from *H.*

March 28 [1956]

Dear Norman,

Eidolon has come and I do thank you and am very excited about it. I will
first however, send the few *Leuké* corrections; Page 79, I liked beginning the
caption with "That is — " but if it is confusing, change it. Page 87, read "or,"
not "of." Page 102, read "the bliss of" not "to rest in." Page 114, Helen is
recalled by Thetis with her own words, "Achilles waits," so if we take quotes
for the words and omit italics, I think it is clear. On Page 121, there is a whole
sentence omitted from the caption. I have indicated this and the other changes
clearly, I think, on the returned MS. On page 124, it is "wings," not "things."
I leave you to deal with the commas as queried — and have indicated a few
other punctuation marks, in margins. I think it is all in order. I do, do thank
you for going over it so carefully. Thank you for the enclosed notice of little
Susan's "Wedding in April," she looks a charming girl and Bryher says she is
most attractive. Thank you for cards, too. Bryher and I have had very un-even
Easter weather but we get out for walks and one day, had a beautiful trip on
the lake; the boats start again, some of the *Giro* trips but not yet summer
schedule. I feel rather guilty staying on here but really with weather conditions
and heavy grippe in Zurich, it does seem better to stay [in Lugano]. Bryher
goes, I think, about April 3rd, then I will seriously begin plans. Erich takes his
spring-holiday, a whole month this year, April 18th. I may wait just till he gets
off as confusion of his last days there may be a bit trying. I am so very glad
that you are in no special hurry for the photographs. I will really do something
about it, soon after my return. Do you think we could call part one, of the
Helen, just *Egypt*? After all, we have *Leuké*, the second place-name and the
Eidolon concerns the whole sequence. Then we could call the book *Helen in
Egypt.*[21] Of course, I will write more of all this. I want this to get to you at
once. We talk constantly of you and your mother and think of you, in a special
way, as you must know.

I work off and on, at the five chapters of the Küsnacht prose. Now, I am
stuck for names of the houses — what could we call *Geduld*? No mercy-pity-
healing sort of name seems to fit at all. I call *Am Strand*, *Waldhaus*, and *Va-*

rena, the *Rosiers*, as it is in or on the edge of the rose-garden; I call the central house, the *House*, would *Heimat* be better? I have no name for *Seehof*, perhaps I can leave that and the *Chalet*. It is *Geduld* that worries me. Well, this is pick-up work and fun but I do not take it too seriously. Bryher has brought me freesias and tulips, the room is paradise . . . I have run through *Eidolon*, but am now going over it very carefully and will soon post it back to you.

We found Aldous Huxley['s] "Heaven and Hell"[22] fascinating. Br keeps me well supplied with books and papers. This must, must go now. And thank you again and again, with all greetings and hopes for you and Susan, as to the "wedding" and a blessed *primavera*,

> ever, dear C
> H.

In the spring and early summer H.D. continues to report the progress of her novel about Küsnacht and Pearson to describe his efforts on her behalf. In April she begins to call the novel "Magic Mirror," after the nickname "Magic Mountain," used by Walter Schmide-berg (5 April 1956). Pearson describes difficulties he is having with the Freud family in getting permission to include in her *Tribute* Freud's letters to H.D., some of which they find too personal. However, by the end of the month, he encloses his jacket copy for the book, to which she responds with pleasure. In mid-June Pearson congratulates H.D. on the birth of Perdita's third child, Elizabeth Bryher, her first girl. On 26 June H.D. responds to this event happily, commenting, "It opens up new vistas, new vibrations and is super-imposed on the old." In this letter she also writes that she looks forward to continuing with her Küsnacht novel: "I did notes in winter 1955 — but began again, in Lugano and it was all a 'read.' If I get some chapters shaped, I will send them to you, later."

During July and August, Pearson and H.D. exchange letters about the difficulty he has had obtaining the rights to her *Selected Poems* from Liveright. Now that he has at last obtained the rights and a new publisher (Grove), he plans to check the selections he and Horace Liveright have made with H.D. when she arrives in September. In mid-August, H.D. expresses anxiety at the approaching trip to America, suggesting that it has revived old conflicts around motherhood and authorship. On 10 August she reports having discussed "psychosomatic" headaches with Erich Heydt. Speculating about their cause, she writes that she "felt the pre-arrival of E[lizabeth] B[ryher] very much and worried then — and so on. . . . My children and grand-children are in a special way, the MSS that you have accumulated there — and I feel guilty to make them all-important, but they are — and you have housed them, given them a home." In mid-August, Pearson discusses final plans for the H.D. exhibition at Yale, and H.D. goes to Zurich to get her visa. In the following exchange Pearson, encouraging her to make the journey, hopes to present *Selected Poems* to her as a birthday gift in person when he sees her in September. She responds enthusiastically to the publication of *Tribute to Freud* and to his new plans.

———— 95. TS ————

233 HGS
Yale University
New Haven, Conn.
23 August 1956

Dearest Hilda:

I have not been forgetting you — could not, in fact, with your several letters to delight me — and the photographs to fill me with Kennst du das land — and because, most of all, I have really not been anywhere but with you ever since last Wednesday when Horace and I were together in New York and made out a tentative list of choices for THE SELECTED POEMS OF H.D. Since then I have again been reading and re-reading in the harvest, making little changes, new suggestions for us to go over next week when I see Horace again, *and* typing out, line by line, as they will appear on the page, the poems which we want to go in it. For I want to put these pages in your hands, as of the 10th, as a birthday gift from Horace and myself. A gift back to you of yourself. Is it a gift? Not the poems, certainly; they were yours to begin with. But the selection, the table-of-contents, the epitome: this is the gift. I shall not tell you what we have chosen, but wait for you to see it. Not perhaps what you would have chosen: how is Cornelia to select among her jewels! So there it is, sweet Ha-de.[23]

And I have been otherwise with you. Letters back and forth with Merrill Moore ("Give her my love when you write"). His birthday comes on the 11th. Plans for reviews; I lunched yesterday with a John Dollard who will review it for the *Herald Tribune*.[24] I like him most because he wanted to read the poems first, so I lent them to him. A good one, and his analyst was Turtle [Hans Sachs]. The circle closes.

All love,
Yr C.

Verena

August 31 [1956]

Dear Norman,

The *Freud* just came two days ago. I am over-joyed with the print, the margins, all, all, all. I am only sorry that the others have not arrived as I wanted to send them out, as per your suggestion. I however, did write to M[errill] M[oore] to thank him again for the really exciting introduction. I must thank you immeasurably — and too, the translator of the letters. I can hardly believe that I actually wrote that *Freudbuch*. ('Calcomanias' troubled me, only, and in the proofs. Page 77. We used this word for what later, Fido called "transfers"; I find at last in my French dictionary, *decalquer*, to counter-draw, *calquer*, to draw, to trace, to copy, so this must at long last, be the word. I could never find it!) Thank you for your wonderful letter — the idea of leaving the crew worried me, and Fido too, it seems. She said she was writing you. I don't think they would be long there at the Club, but I leave it to you and Fido to arrange. It is difficult for me to write — this all seems such a fantasy, but I am going ahead with my plans. I had some old photographs copied, probably too late for the show, but I will bring them. I do not know if you have any family pictures — I don't mind any but one of my father that Harold had, my mother disliked it very much but somehow, it was never destroyed. It would shock me to see it. I have two small pictures, copied, one middle-age, the other at 17 in his uniform. I don't know if you want these or my mother's picture as a girl? Anyway, I will make up an envelope and you can keep some and let me have some back that I could later, have copied. We are in constant touch with Perdita — Br will arrange all that, too. She is due here on Tues. and Doris two days later. How wonderful of you to do the poems for me but I do not like to think of you typing away at this script! Please thank Horace, too. To-morrow week — I can't believe it and am trying to imagine just the usual 4 hour trip to the Tessin. Really, I am sure it will be easy enough — At least, I am praying for strength, I don't want to be completely wilted — but I won't talk of all this. Obrecht has done a huge, but H U G E enlargement of the Beethoven. I had to go to his studio to see it and he asked me to sign it in white chalk-ink, all amazing, and to see this looking out at me from the wall as I entered the studio. Obrecht seems very proud of it. I took him my German *Avon*. I told him you liked the pictures. I am glad to hear of John Dollard, too. Fido knew of him. Yes — I really do feel now (and thanks to you) that the symbolic ser-

pent has bitten his own tail. As you say, "the circle closes." Thank you —
thank you — thank you and D[eo] V[olente],

> a bientot,
> dear C
> *H.*

In the letter that follows, written in New York after the exhibition at Yale, H.D. describes
the relationship between Pearson and Heydt in her imaginative life.

————— 97. MS —————

> Beekman Tower Hotel
> 3 Mitchell Place
> New York 17, NY
> Sept. 15 [1956]

Dear Norman,

Are you & Erich perhaps the *Dioscuri*? It comes to me this morning — that
curious double "rescue," he the old Europe, or the new-old, and you the old-
new, "looking into the future." But it was not so much the "old," finding the
4-leaf clover & the cornel tree again, as the eternal — & there H.D. was di-
rected, I think, by the very-olds, to put her symbols into Greek or into Hellas.
I am happy writing Margaret Snively [*sic*] Pratt, this morning, of Watch Hill &
your house & their (our) *Blythebourne* — also, I remember it was she who,
not so very long ago, sent me some old photographs, "H.D. taking her first
fence" was among them & Margaret must have "snapped" it.

I am reading Havelock Ellis' (Chiron) *Marlowe*,[25] in my room, after break-
fast, at the counter (bar?) above, as Br[yher] went with Doris, as D. was a little
nervous, Br said. I was desolate, at first, to be away from "home" — the exhi-
bition & you & Susan & the sea-lavender. Now, I feel happier as we look
forward to E[lizabeth] B[ryher] on Monday, & V[alentine] — I will not try to
thank you & Susan. I will just scribble a line now & again, & will try to do as
you ask, re D[elia] Alton, though I forget what it was.

> Ever, dear C.- *H.*

In later letters in September, Pearson encloses a copy of the interview with H.D. that ap-
peared in the *New Haven Register*, and makes plans to take her to Bethlehem and Lancaster,
Pennsylvania. H.D. reports on the movies she has seen in New York, and on her visits with
Dr. Prutting (whom she says has given her a clean bill of health),[26] with her friends (includ-

ing Marianne Moore) and with her grandchildren. Pearson describes various people's reactions to *Tribute to Freud*, including that of Dr. Winfred Overholser,[27] Pound's chief psychiatrist at St. Elizabeths Hospital, who comments on the "mystical quality" of the book, with "its wide-ranging fantasy, its communion of spirit between the great teacher and his devoted pupil."[28] In the following letter, after a trip to Bethlehem with Norman and Susan, H.D. expresses her deep pleasure and gratitude at this return to her roots.

─────── 98. MS ───────

St. Venzel?
Beekman Tower Hotel
3 Mitchell Place (at 49th St)
New York 17, NY
Sept. 28 [1956]

Dearest Norman,

I am deeply touched with the Peter Wolle music. I thought it was a collection, & it is just our own great-great etc. (in the best Lancaster tradition) *Für mich* (für uns) *O Herr*. You seem to have given them to me, "Dad" & all — & "the curb-stone as it makes a generous curve" — only, in the reality-pictures, we seem to be facing the church, but still there again, we three made "a group, a constellation."

I enclose my last letter from George [Plank] (do not return) as you see it reflects my happiness & things I could never seem to be able to say to you & Susan. What *fun* we had! I am rather abashed, as after long check-ups & analysis, there is *nothing* wrong, Dr. Prutting said this morning — only, I am to watch my nerves, which he said really had given me my inspiration & my life. I have so *much* to say & I "see" the Uncle Fred story — he left all his folios etc. to Lehigh. Next time, we must go there, too.

Infinite gratitude to "the dear Pearsons"

from *H.*

In October H.D. continues to report on the friends she has seen in New York, including Marya Zaturenska and Horace Gregory. On 2 October Pearson asks about the specific wording of the dedication for the *Selected Poems*. Should it list the names of each child or read "To my grandchildren" or both? In the following letter H.D. encloses a newspaper clipping that refers to colonial history she shares with Pearson, and she comments on the "home" motif in the Theseus sections of "Leuké."

St. Amalie
Beekman Tower Hotel
3 Mitchell Place (at 49th St.)
New York 17, NY
Oct. 6 [1956]

Dear N.,

I enclose, as for us both — I believe the ab-original, Ur-vater and co. came on the *Speedwell*, but the two ships started out together; *Speed* was delayed — Holland? [29]

I find the "home" motive stressed in Leuké — Theseus sections, 4-4 especially, perhaps there is a better "come home" stanza there.

I got the *Minotaur* being "a dream" — a "gentle . . . beast," really, I think from André Gide's "Theseus." [30] I feel now that I like the Theseus motif, more than ever — I don't really see changes in it — a matter of taste — this part just did not appeal to H[orace] but I am so very glad of his reaction. [31] If only we had time to go over this!

Br[yher] only criticized the *Leuké* 5–6 list of names section — but I felt & feel it belongs . . .

We did have fun yesterday.

a bientot.
H.

Br found the Pilgrim church . . .

In mid-October, they exchange brief letters about details regarding the titles of some of H.D.'s *Selected Poems* ("Georgius Sanctus" and "Laïs"). H.D. is genuinely reluctant to leave America and plans to return soon. On 11 October she mentions that Bryher thinks that she might continue to work on "the notes and/or novel, *Magic Mirror*" back in Lugano. On 16 October Pearson mentions having received an indecipherable card from Pound, that he hopes H.D. can help him decode. Pound has mentioned "'DIonYsaurs,'" and that he's on "the home stretch of the Rock," the last section of his cantos. In the following letter, back in Switzerland, H.D. reports on her attempts to readjust.

St. Ewald
Villa Verena
October 23 [1956]

[no salutation]

Thank you, dear Norman, for your letter. Dr. Rudolf [Brunner] tells me that it took him two weeks to get his balance, after his return from N.Y.; he jumped into it all, when he arrived in USA, as I did. After all, he is Swiss, so I don't think my rather idle week can be held against me — but I wanted to write sooner. Not altogether inactive, indeed one series of alarms and shocks after the other — Joan of course; now her mother is here and that takes up time — such a saga with poor Erich in and out and telephone calls from English ladies, taken in by Joan's "I am leaving," "where are you going?" "I don't know" etc. etc. Rather funny in a way, pretty exhausting. Something will be settled perhaps — when Ethel[32] leaves — will Ethel leave? Perhaps she will be a fixture here too. . . . I come back from the extremes of excitement, I feel, from N.Y. and the peace and Haven (New and old) to *this*.

Now, I hear from Elizabeth S[chnack], says she is doing translation of the *Flowering of the Rod*. Wishes to place it with *Bibliothek Suhrkamp*, "which appears every spring with six volumes." Suggests if arranged with Suhrkamp, that Professor Pearson might "write a short introduction." I will tell her, as book dedicated to you, it may not be indicated — anyway, you may not want to do it. I will put off seeing her for a little while — I do so want to get at my books and papers —

I don't know what E[zra] meant about the blue dinosaur; he wrote me "and as to struggles with foto-plates, overegg-sposures to record yr / adolescent grace adequately at the start of the century. . . . all goes to show working of justice . . . wonder did they git a platinum or a blue-print." I must have written him on one of the cards, I did, that an old print of his was shown in one of the birthday cases. This was the letter you forwarded — thank you.

E. M. Butler has dedicated her new *Byron and Goethe* to *H.D.* (She also sends me her *Heine*.) She writes that "only one other person has read it yet and as he always likes what I write, he has uplifted me very much. Otherwise, dead silence (as usual) from everyone!" I will ask her to send you the two books — you may not have time for them but they are exciting, I find, reference and library books. I don't understand her "dead silence (as usual)." All this is a problem. I caught fire from her *Fortunes of Faust* that I read in Lugano, summer 1952 — then, started the *Helen* — all rather odd, so I feel that I owe her a good deal. Also the *Silver Wings* made me feel that she had shared an experience with me though she rejected the idea.[33] I can't concentrate at the moment — enough — but have read the *Byron and Goethe*. Do the people at Yale, I wonder — she is "Professor Emeritus of German in the University of Cambridge" — know her work?

I am so happy to think of you and Susan on that trip [to New Orleans]. Now, I can really share it with you. I won't write more now, probably you will [have] received several of my letters all at once, on your return. All, all thanks again and to Susan always,

from

H.

On 6 November Pearson hears from Bryher that H.D. has broken her hip, having slipped on a rug on the polished floor outside of the office at Klinik Brunner (6 November 1956). Despite his grief at the death of his father, which occurred shortly after H.D.'s accident, Pearson responds with comforting cards and letters, concerned more about her state of mind than his own grief. Indeed, Bryher's report, that Hilda feels that her fall and subsequent confinement are punishment for having enjoyed the trip to America, elicits a rare allusion from Pearson to his own physical suffering. In the following exchange, in an effort to change her perspective, he confides the spiritual benefit of having been wrapped in a cast earlier in his life. H.D.'s response reflects a degree of restored optimism that carries over into her letters for the rest of the year, during which she works with Elizabeth Schnack on a German translation of the *Rod* (which was not published) and with Pearson on the galleys of *Selected Poems*.

———— 101. TS ————

233 HGS
Yale University
New Haven, Conn.
21 November 1956

Dearest Hilda:

Your post card, as of yesterday evening's mail, brought us a special kind of Thanksgiving: — to see your hand, and to know of your good spirit. "That's my cat!" God knows I know what it is to lie abed this way. There were times when I was wrapped in plaster down to the ankle of one leg and the knee of the other, and up to my armpits, so that it took two people to turn me from flat on my back to flat on my face. And indeed it is tedious, save for the view of one's self when one's eyeballs float up to hang from the ceiling like flies, and I could look down on myself abed and helpless, and laugh at the vanity of the flesh. I presume that Catholics have something like this aesthetic distance when the spirit soars during a retreat. Anyhow, I know in retrospect that I have every reason to be grateful for such intervals. Perhaps in your case all this is a sort of strong caesura in the line of your life, and comes between adventures.

All love

Yr C.

———— 102. MS ————

Dec. 4 [1956]

[no salutation]

Thank you for beautiful, comforting letters & cards. I have been working on El[izabeth] Schnack *Rod* translation. She said Suhrkamp wrote of "Selected Poems" but I told her I knew nothing of any arrangement, & I thought it more suitable to have the short booklets brought out. She says she wants to do "What Do I Love" next. I have a feeling that *Rod* would be exquisite (your book) with double-pages, English & German & will ask her of this. I would be glad to contribute toward this but don't know about exchange. It might be done in Zurich — Do *we* pay Sch. for trans[lation]? I don't know how to approach her, but you might. I told her that I left it all in your hands. She has not been very well, I think she is working too hard on *Rod*. She is sending me last section, at end of week I will come in again, later. She has sent me or brought me so many flowers. I think she is happy at the contact. She seems in a way, a person of some independent means, but I don't know, she may depend on trans[lation] fees. The *Rod* gives me peace & hope — her German is so much more *me*, *moi-meme*, than Urzidil, though I realize his distinction. El. Schnack is *Beustweg 3 Zurich*, but you must have her address, anyway; she said she was writing you. I had a note from Ezra,[34] I will get Br[yher] to send you letters, when she comes over again. I believe I am here till well over Xmas but I am happier & really grateful that the 70 year old bone is knitted together so nicely — the last x-ray is most satisfactory, they say. I have another in about 2 weeks, then will sit up & *ride a bicycle* & hop about on sticks. I don't know *why* it happened but I have found peace — and as you say, renewed love & friendship, as *toward the future.*

Love to Susan. I will write again.

ever with infinite gratitude,
dear C
from
H.

1. On 9 April 1955, H.D. wrote: "Erich absorbs back into himself attributes of what I have referred to as seven brothers or minor initiators. Ezra was the first of these" ("Compassionate Friendship," MS, BL).

2. Heydt asked Pearson to sponsor his immigration to the United States, and he described his youthful political affiliations in a letter. He belonged to the Hitlerjugend (1933–38) and from 1939 was a member of the NS Studentenbund. He was never a member of the NSDAP party. He describes the effect upon him of his growing awareness of Nazi crimes as follows: "Throughout these last years [1940–41], my friends and I led the often described double existence: behind formal cooperation trying to save our integrity. . . . Since, many years have passed. But I have never regained an undisturbed feeling towards Germany" (Erich Heydt to Norman Holmes Pearson, 4 August 1957, unpublished letter).

3. On 18 February 1955, she wrote: "'He [Heydt] must have been a Nazi,' was remarked. Did I say it or did Bryher? She said, 'well, he wouldn't have survived if he hadn't been.' 'No, no he is not a German,' said Sister Grütli, 'he told one of the patients who told one of the Sisters who told *me* that he was a half-Jew.' 'Well,' said Bryher, 'he would have to say that anyway, to get out of Germany'" ("Compassionate Friendship," MS, BL).

4. On 26 March 1954, H.D. reported a fantasy of Heydt wearing a rose-velvet dinner jacket, a "*Rosenkavalier* coat" ("Compassionate Friendship," MS, BL).

5. 21 February 1955, "Compassionate Friendship," MS, BL.

6. In "Compassionate Friendship," H.D. calls Butler "the Astarte" of that poem.

7. *The Fourteenth of October* (1952); *The Player's Boy* (1953); *Roman Wall* (1954).

8. "Charioteer," from *Heliodora* (1924).

9. Recordings of H.D.'s *Helen in Egypt*, based on tapes made in Switzerland, were produced by Spoken Arts and Watershed.

10. *Avon*, in Johannes Urzidil's translation, was published by Suhrkamp Verlag.

11. *The Intelligent Heart: The Story of D. H. Lawrence* (1954).

12. G. Wilson Knight, *The Mutual Flame, on Shakespeare's Sonnets and The Phoenix and The Turtle* (London: Methuen, 1955).

13. John Bainbridge, *Garbo* (1955).

14. Joan Waluga was a niece of Bryher's friend Doris Banfield Long.

15. In a letter to Pearson, dated 10 July 1955, Bryher expressed concern that Heydt might be trying to take financial advantage of Hilda "by trying to have romantic scenes with her." She continued: "Now don't mistake me: Hilda has a fund of good American sense, she has told Heydt not to make a mother symbol out of her, I do not think she would be betrayed by any too obvious romance making. But knowing Hilda's love of antiquity there was apparently a constant pressure that she would take him to Egypt, or worse still to Arabia, for the winter, naturally paying all expenses."

16. H.D. refers to Freud's letters to her, which were included in the volume.

17. H.D. refers to old photos of herself to be included in *Tribute to Freud*.

18. On 20 March 1956, Pearson responds to this name: "It is excellent and perceptive. He does have that quality."

19. On 10 March Pearson reported the robbery of Susan's flat in New York.

20. On 20 March 1956 Pearson responds: "We can wait a little for the title to the Helen sequence. I am not sure what I think or suggest at the moment. Helen in Egypt is lovely, but then should we change the title of the first book, so as to make the title include the whole trilogy rather than seem to follow the common practice of titling from a single poem in a collection?"

21. On 2 April 1956, Pearson responds: "I do like Helen in Egypt for the whole. We must put our hearts together for a title for the last section."

22. Aldous Huxley, "Heaven and Hell: Visionary Experience, Visionary Art, and the Other World," *Tomorrow* 3, no. 4 (Summer 1955): 5–35, is a sequel to his *Doors of Perception* (1954).

23. Obrecht's pronunciation of "Hilda."

24. John Dollard, "H.D. to Freud with Love," *New York Herald Tribune Weekly Book Review*, 9 September 1956, p. 7.

25. *Christopher Marlowe: Five Plays* (1956), ed. Havelock Ellis, with intro. by John Addington Symonds.

26. In September 1956, Bryher wrote to Pearson that Dr. Prutting found H.D. fragile, especially psychologically.

27. Winfred Overholser (1892–1964), psychiatrist, specialized in the mental health of soldiers and criminals. He served as medical superintendent of St. Elizabeths Hospital in Washington from 1936 until his retirement in 1962.

28. Overholser to Pearson, 19 September 1956, unpublished letter.

29. H.D. refers to a newspaper clipping from London, 5 October, which reports the reopening of the newly restored Pilgrim Fathers Memorial Church in Southwark, a historic quarter of London. The oldest Congregational church in Britain, it was where the Pilgrim Fathers prayed before sailing to America.

30. André Gide's *Theseus* (1946) was first published in French and then translated into English by John Russell the same year.

31. On 4 June 1956, Pearson quoted from Horace Gregory's response to *Helen in Egypt*. Gregory called the poem as a whole "'one of the very, very few superlative long poems of the 20th century.'" However, he found the beginning of the Theseus section less successful. He wrote: "'The poem, marvelously sustained as it is, sags only in the group of stanzas introducing Theseus; Hilda has a little trouble here that she should work out herself.'"

32. Another patient at the Klinik Brunner.

33. On 23 February 1953 Butler wrote that she is more skeptical about magic than H.D., and that "there is no *personal* emotional experience behind *Silver Wings*" (unpublished letter).

34. On 29 November 1956, Pound wrote: "I am sorry yu bust yr / bone and thankful you bust it in a more moderate place than is fashionable for those seeking affliction. I trust the mending will procede and that you will keep off soAP and other treacherous substances, cineri doloso (yes, that's o.k. as the -o applies to the igne)" (unpublished letter).

CHAPTER FIVE

"'Another Canyon ... Bridged'"

1957-1959

In these years H.D.'s incomplete recovery from her fall and consequent relative confinement acquired symbolic significance. She was bedridden during the composition of "Vale Ave" (5 April 1957–13 May 1957) and much of "Sagesse" (9 June 1957–January 1958) and unable to walk without "sticks" until October 1958, well after the composition of *End to Torment* (7 March 1958–13 July 1958). Always somewhat shy and intensely introspective, she found that her physical disability increased these tendencies. As in the years of privation in London during the Blitz, she turned for fortification and meaning to spiritual exercise. Again she took up ideas about reincarnation associated with Lord Dowding's lectures on spiritualism and, drawing on a long-standing interest in angelology, she practiced rituals of invocation inspired by Robert Ambelain's *La Kabbale Practique* (1951), which she kept by her bedside. In the

"Hirslanden Notebook" (1957–59), a dream book begun when she started to walk again, she focused upon integrating her most recent collapse with those that had preceded it, creating out of the series of "confinements" a personal myth of compensatory spiritual wisdom and heightened creativity. Significantly, H.D. assigned Pearson the attribute of an enabling angel in her psychological firmament; he is one "qui donne la sagesse" (25 June [1957]).

A mood of anamnesis and reprise governs H.D.'s poetry and correspondence in this period, in her letters to other friends as well as to Pearson. To Bryher's chagrin, H.D. wrote frequently to her former husband, Richard Aldington, who was himself ill and alone, having remained in France with his daughter, Catherine, after his wife, Netta, returned permanently to England. (H.D. and Bryher also became attached to Catherine, whose education they helped to fund.) In addition to keeping each other apprised of current work, friendships, and health problems, H.D. and Aldington often alluded in their letters to mutual acquaintances from their World War I days in London. By 1959 H.D. was so concerned about Aldington's health that she invited him to visit her and have a medical examination at Dr. Brunner's Nervenklinik. Indeed, although Bryher is the "Amico" to whom "Vale Ave" is dedicated, and the air marshal (Dowding) figures prominently in the poem, Bryher felt that Aldington was the source of the interrupted erotic affinity that H.D. mythologized.[1]

With the exception of her letters to Bryher, the mutual acquaintance who dominated H.D.'s correspondence was Ezra Pound, with whom both Aldington and Pearson were also in touch. Aldington had been unsympathetic to Pound in his earlier letters to H.D.: he deplored Pound's fascism and anti-Semitism, diagnosed him as a paranoiac, and advised her to avoid the controversy around him.[2] By 1957, however, Aldington thought Pound was being unjustly scapegoated by the international press, and he supported his release from St. Elizabeths Hospital. In 1958 Aldington sent H.D. the interview "A Weekend with Ezra Pound," by David Rattray,[3] commenting, "It is such a welcome change to have him reported as a human being, and not as a journalist's abstraction or political cause."[4] H.D. quoted from Aldington's letter and drew upon Rattray's interview in her memoir of Pound, *End to Torment*; they set her thoughts in motion, allowing her to explore her own profound ambivalence about Pound.

Pearson was even more instrumental in the composition of H.D.'s memoir of Pound than Aldington was. As he had from the beginning of Pound's incarceration at St. Elizabeths, Pearson continued to inform H.D. of Pound's activities there and of the efforts to obtain his release, about which Pearson was elated. Recognizing that H.D.'s relationship with Pound was charged with unresolved conflicts both recent and remote, Pearson thought that writing the memoir would be therapeutic. The letters show that he urged her to complete it despite Bryher's forceful objections. In fact, H.D. dedicated *End to Torment* to Pearson and referred to his letters in it twenty-two times. Most significantly, she concluded the work with a long quotation from a letter from him, an aesthetic decision that foregrounded his mediation and, at the same time, allowed her to maintain a critical distance.[5] Reconciliation, in a more mythologized form, did not occur until the writing of "Winter Love" (3 January– 3 April 1959).

Indeed, by this time Pearson was closer to Pound and his circle than H.D. was. Despite his objections to Pound's fascism and anti-Semitism, he continued to admire and teach Pound's poetry, praising the "epic" scope of *The Cantos* and its metamorphic design and sending recent interpretations of the poem to H.D. Having lent his name and prestige to the editorial board of the Square Dollar pamphlets, a series of essays masterminded by Pound, Pearson did not withdraw from this enterprise despite his repugnance at the racist activities of John Kasper, the series' young coeditor. Apparently Pearson's loyal support of Pound was also rooted in the new political tensions of the "Cold War" with Russia. His letters to Bryher suggest that he saw Pound's prolonged imprisonment as symbolic of the threat to artistic freedom represented by Soviet-style totalitarianism.[6]

Pearson also carried on a vigorous correspondence with Sheri Martinelli,[7] a young painter and Pound acolyte who also admired H.D. and considered her a role model. Martinelli was distraught at Pound's rejection of her after his release, a situation with which H.D. sympathized and found evocative of her own past. At H.D.'s request, Pearson forwarded Martinelli's letters and served as a conduit between the two women. After Pound returned to Italy, Pearson and H.D. exchanged news about the entire Pound ménage — Martinelli, Dorothy Pound, Olga Rudge, Marcella Spann,[8] and Mary de Rachewiltz. H.D. incorporated references to several of these women from these letters into *End to Torment*.

Throughout her confinement, H.D. relied upon the company of Erich Heydt, to whom she continues to refer. Heydt visited her several times a week at the Hirslanden Klinik and continued his visits afterward when she returned to Villa Verena. Apparently, she was concerned about how long his attention would last, however. In 1957 Bryher reported Heydt's fear that H.D. might have another emotional breakdown; she felt neglected by everyone and withdrew into herself.[9] H.D. alluded to this concern in her poem "Sagesse," in which Heydt becomes "Germain," or "german, a near-relation" who fears the speaker's "abstraction."[10] According to the poem his fears are mistaken, however; for the speaker is inspired not by his presence but by his absence, absence based in biographical fact. Heydt visited America in 1957, married in 1958, and then visited again, planning to emigrate. Somewhat resentfully, Bryher wrote to Pearson that she thought Hilda's obsession with Heydt's "'leaving' relate[d] both to Ezra having left her and then to Aldington" (22 November 1958). Upon returning to Zurich from New York after Heydt's wedding, Bryher added, "I have stuck by Hilda now for forty years but it is as if I were nothing to her and believe me, it is not gay to come back here. She said she was glad to see me so that she could talk to me about Heydt" (19 December 1958). Indeed, Heydt's stimulus was also crucial to the composition of *End to Torment*, where he is represented as both a goad and a support. He reinjects H.D. with a Pound "virus or antivirus," insists that she is hiding "pathological" details of their early unconsummated romance, and, finally, helps her to voice deep, painful feelings of rejection and loss, the expression of which brings relief.

Although she remained a faithful friend, writing almost daily, sending books, and visiting the Hirslanden Klinik, Bryher deplored H.D.'s reconnection with Pound, and H.D. was careful not to discuss him with her. Other strains in their relationship were heightened by H.D.'s physical disablement and immobility. Possibly fearing the eventual burden of H.D.'s care, Bryher began planning to sell Kenwin, the home in Switzerland that had once served as a base for them both. Also, H.D. longed to visit America again, even though her injury made travel very difficult. Responding to H.D.'s homesickness and isolation, Bryher tried to arrange for her to return to America permanently, involving Pearson in this plan. (She also feared continuing political instability in Europe as a result of the Hungarian revolution and the Suez Crisis in 1956.) At Bryher's urging, Pearson traveled to Switzerland in 1958 to help H.D. regain American citizenship, a symbolic homecoming that she found comforting. In contrast, Bryher could travel easily and did, sometimes in the company of Pearson. Not only did she go to America and England regularly, she and Pearson journeyed to the Arctic twice in this period: to northern Canada in 1957 and to Greenland in 1958. They were planning a third trip in 1959, when Pearson was hospitalized with a severe ulcer condition.

Aided by Pearson's efforts on her behalf, in this interval H.D. was awarded the first two of several American prizes: the Harriet Monroe Memorial Prize from *Poetry* in 1958, and the Brandeis University Creative Arts Award for Poetry in 1959.[11] She also attracted a following among younger American poets, whose contact with her was enabled by Pearson. The most prominent among these was Robert Duncan,[12] whose name begins to appear frequently in the letters during 1959. H.D. read Duncan's work with interest, sent him the manuscript of "Vale Ave," and was pleased to be connected, through him, with members of the "Beat" generation, whom she recognized as members of the new American vanguard.

In the first two letters that follow, still relatively soon after her accident, H.D. describes her shattered state of mind. She also mentions the beginning of a "dream sequence" that is the "Hirslanden Notebooks." Pearson's responses, not included here, are particularly comforting in their assurance of her recovery, based on his own experience of similar suffering. Most important, he carries on with details of the publication and promotion of *Selected Poems* as if he expects her work to continue, and he reports good reviews of her memoir of Freud.

---

103. MS

Jan. 14 [1957]

Dear Norman,

Thank you for letter & check.[13] I am sending it to Br[yher] who arranges with Mr. Beney.[14] Forgive my not writing. It seems more & more difficult, as I am inwardly so rebellious; now that I can move a bit, I want to push ahead & get about. As far as externals are concerned, however, it is perfect, my big window looks out on country-scene, we are half-way to Dolder; the Hirslanden front is just outer-town, I see it when I go down the hall. I can't make any decisions now — I beg & beg Br not to force me.[15] I can not think ahead. It was such a shock; in ten seconds, my world was, or seemed to be, shattered. It is ten weeks to-day since I came here. I don't know what, psychologically, will happen when I get out. I never thanked you properly for the Count Zin[zendorf].[16] How many associations. . . . I have shown the Bethlehem pictures. George Plank was so interested. Gulls swoop past the window, though we are forbidden to feed them — the balcony sometimes is like a little ship-deck. I have an azalea from K[enneth] & I[slay], pots of primroses from Sister Gertrude and a pot of one blue and one white hyacinth from Madame Sch[?] — I must see her again — but later. I am sorry to be so very dull.

Bally and Boss,[17] "the popes" as E[rich] calls them of ps-a here, were given the Freud[18] for Xmas, by E. He said they were both impressed. E. ordered the books, by way of the shop, I told you of. I have tried to get the Freud, and it never comes, from *Pantheon*. Br. always says it takes a long time, but 2 copies were ordered long, long ago. Could *you* see to it? I have only my one copy — could the 2 go to Verena? *Please*. Boss said he was astonished at the "between-the-lines," another (German) word, *musé*. Bally wrote and spoke of the humanitarian quality, devotion etc. — so E. reports. And by the way, he was so annoyed as Lüdeke[19] rang me from Küsnacht, but it was getting late & I was so tired. He said he had a car & would come over again. I was surprised when he said he was American, he spoke of you, of course.

I had asked Mr. L. on telephone, if he were Swiss was he originally German or what? *Please tell me*. I will try, later, to see him. I was happier in my "frame" to-day, as they let me go with just one sister. Two of them made me feel rather too guarded & dependent. The doctor says I have made great progress. I should never grumble . . . but you know . . . sometimes . . . I do, do thank you again & again for everything — & thank Susan, too for me. Blessings, dear C,

from *H*.

———— 104. MS ————

Jan. 29 [1957]

Dear N.,

Thank you for two long letters.[20] As to first, Jan. 23, I was *eight* years old when I left (in the middle of a term) the "old school." I am sure divorce was 1938 though actual *decree nisi* may have been a very little later — *1938*, I am sure, however. I never saw the Ezra quote; thank him sometime.[21] He writes asking what (so to speak, "the Hell!") "have you been reading the last 30 years." I can not answer. I believe he is worried, as he wrote [Viola] Jordan and M[argaret] Pratt that I had slipped on soap. Always in his letters is a jibe at the "stews of Vienna" or such. Send him a card, as from me. And thank you for the article in Enc[yclopedia] Am[ericana]; it is excellent!

Letter Jan. 26 — Thanks *Tribune* offer,[22] later some copies perhaps, when I have time to go over books etc. at Verena. I will certainly autograph sheets — but all, all later — and I will talk over recordings with Erich.[23] I am very, very happy as I began some dream-sequence as for Jan. 10–29 (so far) — I had strange nightmares the first evenings after my first walks.[24] I have followed this up with associations & it has released tensions, given me back my old dream & day-dream dimension. I had an amazing letter from Dr. Max Schur,[25] 875 Park Ave. He is the "distinguished specialist" of page 13 of the *Freud* — also, heard from Marie B[onaparte], "our Princess."[26]

I asked Dr. Schur about J. J. van der L[eeuw]'s books.[27] I knew nothing of this. I heard, long after the analysis & the *Freudbuch* that he was half-English & in the R.A.F. — I also wrote E.M. Butler of him but have not heard. How old was he? And any other details . . . astonishing get-together now, with Dr. S. & the Princess!

I am sure that I have missed points in both your letters — but there is Sister Otilia always on the prowl & now waiting to get me out in the hall, "boulavarde des Invalides," they call it. I am *so* much better. Please thank the Grove again for the two beautiful books — Mr. R[ossett] sent Jap[anese] Lit[erature] & the Greg[ories] the Henry James — [28]

O — thank you *all*, and bless the coming spring — & S[usan] & the orchids — dear C

from *H.*

Br[yher], George [Plank] are due in tomorrow. . . .

During the first half of February, H.D. is increasingly anxious about her prolonged convalescence, sending Pearson progress reports but often appearing hesitant and indecisive in matters relating to her work as well as her health. Their ongoing conversation about J. J. van der Leeuw, whose sessions with Freud preceded H.D.'s in the 1930s, provide a distraction. Pearson views H.D.'s affinity with van der Leeuw as a continuation of the mysterious web, both personal and literary, that undergirds her life and work. On 22 February, H.D. responds positively to Pearson's gift of one of van der Leeuw's books, as well as to his suggestion that she write a foreword to her story "The Death of Martin Presser," which he is planning to have privately published as a book design project by the Yale graphic arts class.

On 28 February [1957], H.D. writes that she is sad about newspaper attacks on Pound that accuse him of having influenced the racist activities of John Kasper. These newspaper articles were sent by Richard Aldington, who deplored the "'baiting of poor old Ez'" and feared the worsening of Pound's situation (2 February 1957).[29] In the letter that follows, Pearson clarifies the controversy around Pound, and in March the two continue to discuss his situation.

233 HGS
Yale University
New Haven, Conn.
10 March 1957

Dearest Hilda:

[. . .]

Sad about Wyndham Lewis's death.[30] Did you know him well? I only met him once, and that was unsatisfactory. But I did respect.

You ask about the *Herald Tribune* articles on Ezra. Alas! It was all apropos of his protégé, John Kasper, one of the original editors of the Square Dollar series, and the one who suddenly appeared in Clinton, Tennessee, to stir up the riots about admitting Negroes to mixed schools, as by the Supreme Court order. Kasper comes from New Jersey, but organized a white supremacy group, calling Supreme Court Judges criminals. Is now on bond awaiting trial. Meanwhile has shifted his ground to Florida where he is giving violently anti-Negro and anti-Semitic speeches. His bookshop in Washington is now called the Ezra Pound Bookshop. I am sick about it. Ezra sent me a copy of his newspaper with some semi-flattering remarks about Kasper, and hopes I can help keep Kasper's press going. Poor Ezra is so hungry for attention and the sense of *being in* things, that anything goes apparently. He makes all efforts to get him out of St. Elizabeth's [*sic*] hopeless, now that this new angle can be brought up; and what *would* he be up to, if free. I was going to get Mrs. Luce[31] interested, but I cannot now. The *H-T* articles, about Kasper, were all head-lined with Ezra's name. Damn it!

All love,
Yr C.

March 13 [1957]

[no salutation]

So very sorry, dear C, that you have been groggy, as you say. Thanks for clarifying the *H[erald] T[ribune]* situation. I am writing R[ichard] of it and of the mention of Sophocles by you,[32] to E[zra] — thank you. E. does not want records.[33] I gave his last to me, to B[ryn] M[awr], for you. You may have had it. I did not know of W[yndham] L[ewis]'s death. He was about blind, as you know, or blind. Can you give me any details, though no doubt, I will see account in some mag[azine].

K[enneth] and Is[lay] came to tea at Küsnacht, yesterday. K. said they had had 24 flights — he counted them. Is. did not. Is. was in his element, I gathered, but K. was glad to get back — loved our garden, "look — snow-drops" — I ambled with him, feeling happy that he was content to amble, middle-age-ed-ly with me, while Br[yher] & Is. darted ahead.

We did see W. L. in the very early days — he used to come in at breakfast and borrow R.'s razor, much to R.'s disgust. The Ford-Fords made a good deal of him & he painted an inset over mantel-piece—considered daring, at time, especially in a Pre-raf house, with Burne-Jones cartoons, right, left, center — or on stairs — & Ford himself with an apple, painted by Ford Madox Brown, no less.

Thanks van der L[eeuw], to come. Amazing that that Theosophist stream-of-consciousness flows into the couch memories & sessions. Would it have helped, if I had realized it, at the time? But I think not — it all comes back now. I can not get *over* it & the fact that it was E. who first brought the Yogi etc. to me. I carry the little first book in my hand-bag & read from time to time. I am over-whelmed by the *H-T*[ribune] & poor, poor Ezra. Thank you for clearing it all up — I was a little puzzled.

Yes — P[erdita] wrote me too, of the party. How happy they are & we owe much to you, dear C, for helping lure her from London. I must get out in the *sun*. I can't walk very far — or could, but it tires me. I am content in garden & Erich gets the local car & we go to *Ermitage* quite often. Br was wonderful, I had 3 tea-sessions with her and she says she is coming at Easter. So much love to S[usan] — and always gratitude.

from H.

———— 107. TS ————

233 HGS
Yale University
New Haven, Conn.
31 March 1957

Dearest Hilda:

[...]

Yes, R[ichard]'s book on Mistral[34] seems to be going down well, which pleases me. As to efforts to release Ezra, it seems to be this way. Friends, wealthy or not, cannot get him into a private clinic so long as he is under indictment for treason (as he still is). Unless this indictment is quashed (that is withdrawn by the government for lack of evidence or unwillingness to prosecute — by no means a simple step), he must first be declared able to stand trial, then tried, and whatever judgement or sentence is given be declared. Until then he is under arrest and in the custody of the government, and by law could not be released into private custody. Ezra would not mind the trial, for he looks at it as the chance to vindicate himself and his beliefs, and in doing so to alert the country to present dangers. This would be acceptable to some but not to all, and would not endear him to judge or jury. The only step seems to be to try to have the indictment quashed. It is at this point that the association of Ezra with young Kasper is difficult, for Kasper regards Ezra as *cher maître* (and, to a real degree, vice versa). Kasper as you know has been sentenced for inciting riot etc. in connection with Negro desegregation, and is out on bail while this is being appealed. Meanwhile he has made an oratorical tour of Florida under the auspices of the Ku Klux Klan, combining his attacks on Negroes with outspoken anti-semitism. A week ago he returned to Clinton, Tennessee, and was again arrested for inciting riot. Because his present Washington bookshop is called the Ezra Pound Bookshop, and because every article links him to Pound, this has called attention to Ezra as an active force; and there is some feeling that if he was released he would take it as justification and issue statements. In any event, there would be opposition in the press for his release because of the revival of anti-semitism activity. Not that this is in itself actionable except for defamation, but that the concentration camps are still recalled. My hunch is that no one wants to do anything at this moment, not out of fear but because a defeat might postpone it inevitably. You must remember that even if Ezra were released, there is no guarantee that he would be given a passport, and Dorothy is reported as saying that is a sine qua non, which I understand. I feel wretched about the whole thing, but part of the wretchedness comes from Ezra's continued backing of Kasper.

Tell R[ichard] what you think best, but ask him not to quote me publicly.

All love from yr

C.

In April and May, H.D. complains of the necessity of continuing bed rest, mentions a visit from Eric Walter White, and, prompted by Aldington, continues to ask about details of the problems around Pound's release. Pearson mentions his research on Hawthorne and his future trip to the Arctic with Bryher. In June, H.D.'s excitement at receiving the first, unbound copy of *Selected Poems* prompts her to mention her recently completed poem, "Vale Ave," in the following letters.

June 4 [1957]

[no salutation]

I am *so* happy with the paper-book & will be sending list. I rather want to send out just this one. It is so nice to hold & I *love* being an *Evergreen*[35] — & I am happy you remembered the inspiration of your "rock-bound coast" — all my surge-of-the-sea effects really came from that — I am glad you asked me & I told you. Br[yher] will *scream* about *New Yorker*.[36] Was *Scribe* ever published? I was keeping my new series *Vale Ave* very dark — now, I want you to have it — trouble is getting typed. I will ask Fido. I call it my Merrill Moore 1000 sonnets. It can go on forever but I stopped at LXXIV. They are fairly regular & roughly average sonnet-length & some are independent, more or less, of the sequence.[37] I wrote them April 5–May 13, roughly — was so desperate — now I am happy & hopeful — I go for x-ray to-morrow — & Br brought over all my books from Verena & I will have much to go over, when she leaves Friday. I think.

───────

Fido just in — said she was writing later — had been to Z[urich] — I had good letter and Longfellow[38] & "Edith with golden hair" yesterday — so all is in order & I will write — & you will write? Really, I was *sunk* (you will see) in the *Vale Ave* sequence, but it did, all the same (to mix metaphors) keep my head above water.

I am so glad to have the 3 grand-children in on this.[39] Please thank Grove again & H[orace] and M[arya] — I could not be happier. Really, I am more elated about my "Evergreen" than I have ever been about an opus — & this is real *morçeaux choisis* (you used the phrase ironically once, to the Dame — remember?)[40]

I must rush this out with so much gratitude & it was just as well to be so "alone and apart" while I was doing *Vale Ave*. You note I have reversed the usual *Ave atque Vale*.[41]

Erich has been very kind & said he had been writing you.

So much gratitude & love to Susan's flowers — exotics & sea-lavender & sea-rose.

> Love, dear C,
> from
> *H.*

I loved your folksy Maine gossip![42]

June 25 [1957]

Dear Norman,

Your letter has made me very happy — & the really enchanting *Evergreen*. Could I suggest they send out to the more-or-less Freud group & the usual "family?" I was so deep in *Vale Ave* that I did not get list done. But do not bother or hurry. Br[yher] can help me, later.

I am not concerned about the Moravian story — would *really* rather hold it over. I was going to write you, actually, but did not quite know arrangement.

I enclose 4 more corrections for V[ale] A[ve] — (page 3 — over.) [43]

I am grieved that you have been so tired — & hot — but soon . . . yes . . . I do tease Fido, but I am deeply involved emotionally with the adventure. [44]

I was happy & am, with the Angels & degrees — was lifted out of my *De Profundis*!

Your attribute name is *nom de Dieu Orsy, suivant la langue des Mages*. It is: *Dieu qui donne la sagesse*. The angel is *Charcumis*.

This relates too, to the *Tribute to the Angels*, written at the time of the *Vale Ave* London scenes.

I am glad that [section] LI got across to you — & I pray that the *Lucifer* motif does not cause offense. It "brightens" the whole sequence for me!

Do take care of yourself & don't work too hard on the [Hawthorne] notes. I am getting this out, at once — I am *so very grateful*. I have been cheated of my morning (set apart for you) by Masseur & Hieronymous, as we call Dr. Bosch, the original Hirs[landen] surgeon.

So bless you & bless you —

from *H.*

233 HGS
Yale University
New Haven, Conn.
2 July 1957

Dearest Hilda:

Your letter of the 25th delighted me, and I am happy to find the *C* carrying over into Charcumis, for like all good letters in the alphabet it has its various personae, its shifting blossoms, all without losing the identity of the stem.

V & A I have read again, as of course I shall keep re-reading it, and my pleasure and admiration increases. As to the Lucifer episode, — no, certainly I am not offended; it has beauty and strength. The truth is you have too much held in your own passionate vitality, denied the robes of Cos, deprived us: the C at your feet, and the C whose wings hover at your shoulder.

The corrigenda are all entered. But perhaps you will find more as time goes on, and while we wait for HELEN to appear.

At the moment, because they stand alone, so to speak, I rather think there are four which I will send out. Will you forgive me for putting on titles — knighting them for their appearance in court? But correct the titles of course, for I will not send out until you approve their names. #IV: SOMETIMES AND AFTER; #XVIII: LUCIFER; #XXXVII: IN TIME OF GOLD; #XL: AMENTI.??[45]

> All love
> from
> yr
> C

In July, H.D. and Pearson bask in the glow of *Selected Poems*. They also anticipate Pearson's and Bryher's Arctic adventure, which has been delayed. On 4 August [1957] H.D. is able, finally, to bid them a wistful farewell: "I hope this reaches Amico I and Amico II, for *bon-voyage* again." Rather defensively, she then turns to the ongoing melodrama at the clinic around Erich Heydt's departure for the United States. One of the younger women patients (Joan Waluga) has become distraught, and H.D. herself is anxious about Heydt's future plans to emigrate.

Back in New Haven, in September and October Pearson sends reviews of H.D.'s work, places new poems, and anticipates Heydt's visit. Their letters in November discuss her new "Owl sequence," which she is hesitant about at first.

———————— 111. TS ————————

Nov. 21 [1957]

Dear Norman,

I hardly think this *Owl Sequence* is suitable. I am sorry it is so badly typed. If you have copy made, perhaps you could send me a carbon — as with this, it is so VERY easy to make funny mistakes. You will see from IX what Erich thought.[46] You might be able to use X and possibly II. I will just leave this, as Joan is due in and I want this to get to you at once.

Thank you for letters and for getting the poems out.[47] Will you please keep any amounts that may come in, for the moment. It is cold and foggy, though

I have been out with Erich, about four times, the run into Z[urich]; and Fido and Joan and I went out, my first trips for some three or four months.

It was a bad period with Erich away — as I had Joan very much on my hands, but it was all an experience. He spoke of his charming visit with you, but said he had been unable to write any thank-you letters to USA. He passed his English exam. I really don't know what the future holds. I am trying to concentrate on papers etc.; I don't think I can get to Lugano.

I must write Dr. Jones.[48] Dr. Schur says he is ill. I never thanked him for the notice of the Freudbook. The last Vol. of the Jones' Freud[49] is magnificent and heart-breaking, the long martyrdom — the more than 30 operations.

Maybe later, I can type better. I had not touched the machine for months.

Thanks for everything again, and love to S[usan] & C.

from H.

———— 112. MS ————

Nov. 26 [1957]

Dear N.,

Read for Germain[e] & Germaine, in last poems, Germain — VIII & IX. Actually, the vibration goes on, as from gardenias, "the flowers he left," VII — also note Germain for Germaine in VII — rather symbolical, this insistence on the f[eminine] gender. The Professor said mine was "mother fixation," so prob[ably], I went on to f[eminine] gender Germaine transference — such a lovely name. I shall poss[ibly] continue Owl Sequence,[50] on some return to the first, the only original gardenias of the Freud-book — by way of Dr. Max Schur — & my desire to get to N.Y. for my next birthday. Dr. Schur writes, & I have finally written E[rnest] Jones.

Thank you for Atlantic — I shall so enjoy it.

I am afraid Br[yher] will be disappointed with me — I can not see Lugano! Erich goes away over Xmas to Stutt[gart], back a few days, then St. Moritz with (or for) Melitta — he will be gone then 10 days plus 10 days — but my own objective is to get more "mobile" & I walk on my carpet, back & forth, as to or toward America. That is my one problem.

Forgive swift script or scrawl — I am sure you understand — & don't take the Owl or Germaine poems too seriously!

Ever
dear C,
& with love to S[usan]
H.

Dec. 1 [1957]

Dearest Norman,

Your letter has made me supremely happy.[51] I will get Joan to air-mail you the pages, so beautifully typed. Actually, there are few corrections, the *Germain*, without the feminine "*e*," three times; one comma in VI, second to last line, after "the outcast." Then, I was concerned about V. I had *pelicans*, at first, not *penguins*. Read the line, number 9. "not crumbed it for the pelicans — birds too?" Leave out "are they." I felt *pelicans* wouldn't eat crumbs but neither would *penguins*, probably, but the child wouldn't know that, & anyway, she regrets the "piece of bun." *Pelican* is significant too, as it was one of the old sigils or symbols of the Christ, the mother-bird feeding the young in the nest, from its own flesh fragments. The last line should be separated by white space, and three dots . . . , not question-mark, I think now, as it leaves the "mystery" as it were, to go on . . . the line following the last line is unexpressed . . . *Pelicans* is better for the rhythm, too . . . funny, all this, it means so very much to me. Thanksgiving, yes and now Christmas and already today, they light the first red candle, one a week, as they do for each Sunday in Advent. *Sagesse* is a wonderful title & may take us far. The "caller before noon" in IV was Madame Herf. I am trying to get another copy of the Owl picture. I dare not let my little *Listener* one go — I fear it might be lost, even if it could be sent to be photographed. It would make a magnificent jacket design — you see I am thinking ahead.[52] Thank you for the *Essence* write-up. Please thank J.P.B.[53] if you know him — what beautiful print and satisfactory & sustaining, to read new poems.

It would be wonderful if "Grove" liked *Sagesse*.

Your letter meant so much to me. How can I thank you?

> Love always,
> & to S[usan]
> from
> H.

Later

My candles are white — 4 in a wreath of evergreen. I lighted the first & gave Madame Herf, who brought my Advent, a glass of sherry. I said that I had been writing you of her — didn't say what — she sent you her special love.

Dec. 10 [1957]

Dearest Norman,

Enclosed is the *Owl* — *do not loose* [*sic*] *him*, though I have two other prints.[54] Also, here are 4 more *Sagesse* poems. No need to send doubles; if typed, send me carbon & I will let you know of any corrections. I have not put Angel names in italics, as there are so many others, the French & Germain's German! Don't bother with these, just clip them with the others, as for sequence. "Angels & Ministers of Grace (?) defend us." Can you get that quote right — Sh[akespeare]? & where? It would be impressive on introductory page of *Sagesse*, if ever a book!

Fido is due tomorrow from Denmark.

Infinite gratitude for & from the *Owl*.

And love, dear C.

from

H.

H.D. and Pearson continue to discuss H.D.'s "Owl Sequence" throughout the Christmas season: H.D. reports that Heydt is thrilled with it and has encouraged her do more sections, and Pearson writes that the *Evergreen Review* will publish the first ten. H.D. also writes that she and Bryher are immersed in Isak Dinesen's *Tales*, which they are appreciating anew after Bryher's recent trip to Denmark. On 14 January [1958], H.D. encloses new sections of her "Owl Sequence," with the following comment: "In the margin of XX I have indicated 4 lines. It made me very sad to type these, but I think that is how it goes — if I don't let it take its own way, it stops altogether, and we have got back to *Grande Mer*, in the end.[55] This is the end of a phase. I could go on forever, and I may be prompted to continue but I know that I will neither stop nor go on, until I get this off to you." In the letter that follows, she discusses a possible title for the poem, and mentions a new report about Pound's life at St. Elizabeths that she finds amusing.

Feb. 6 [1958]

Dearest Norman,

Your letter card and fresh typed poems, come JUST as I have opened my type-writer. How can I ever thank you? I have lived for and by the duckie sequence[56] — do you think we might call it Heures Sacrea — you see how hard it is for me to write *HEURES SACRES*? That brings in the Owl and all the rest — Ezra?[57] I was happy for the first time about him as R[ichard]

A[ldington] sent me an article[58] — I must try to get it back — anyhow, Ezra served tea in a JAM JAR and I laughed and laughed and George was here and we howled and Br[yher] said that he could have a most exquisite porcelain one from one of his Chinese fans or Dorothy could get him an old-time common-or-garden brown one supposed to make the best tea. But no . . . he handed out extras from the St. E. canteen to some of his visitors, "here's your rations." It all sounded exactly like Kensington or the Paris studio. Anyhow, we go on and on from the OWL — and I say the names, as in the last three sections, to myself — this WILL work a miracle, I say and really think — especially the LAST one.

Now, I talked to E[rich] about the little girl.[59] He is truly sympathetic and says that he would help, if he could at any time. Do tell Susan again, just how I feel about it. I have been meaning to write but waited for Br and G[eorge] to go — such a good visit — so that I could type the LAST poems. Tell me if there are too many Angels and decants [sic] etc? Anyhow, Joan is taking this now, and I will really write again. I am sorry to make so many mistakes. I have used the machine only for the last poems. Yes — spring will come and we must laugh, laugh . . .

Ever

H.

Thank you so much for the Deford [sic] Jap[anese] book[60] — it has set me to reading Wallace Stevens . . . again . . . among other things . . .

In March they return to a discussion of Pound, whom Pearson is preparing to visit. On 18 March he writes that he will convey H.D.'s "affection," adding, "Don't say no to that; it will be too late to object." In H.D.'s response, on 21 March, she thanks him for conveying greetings to Pound and mentions going over an English/German edition of Pound's poetry and discussing "*Canto* problems" with Erich. In the following letters they continue to discuss Pound and his circle.

———— 116. MS ————

March 23 [1958]

Dear C.

I have been feverishly reading *Motive & Method*[61] that you sent me, though I had read it superficially before. You once asked me to check up on some *Canto* references. I had not the time or the inclination then, but now, due to Erich's interest & contributions, I am really pro tem, at any rate, involved.

"'Another Canyon . . . Bridged,'" 1957–1959

Now, will you *please* tell me if you could get or lend me another of *Canto* articles — but *no*, I look now & see that "E[zra] P[ound] & the Metamorphic Tradition" is really an earlier version of "The Metamorphosis of E[zra] P[ound]" — by Sister Bernetta Quinn,[62] O.S.F. What I want to know is: What is O.S.F.? (Joan just found it for me in Chambers.) Do you know [her]? Does she *teach*? She can't go around begging — Claribel? Is she related to U[niversity] of P[ennsylvania] Quinn whom E[zra] knew? I was started on all this by the "Weekend" article & Erich's interest & I have been reading the Eva Hesse German with Joan.[63] Erich said it was so very "de-ear" of you to send him the Litt. folder.

Would you rather Grove had the Yale birthday "Looking into the future?"[64] or another by Obrecht. I am waiting to hear of your visit to St. E[lizabeths] — And tell me of Dorothy, too.

I have found all I need know of Frobenius in the "M. & M." article.[65]

This is just to thank you again, dear C —

H.

———— 117. TS ————

231 HGS
Yale University
New Haven, Conn.
30 March 1958

Dearest Hilda,

I wanted to write you at once after my return (I hope the card from the National Gallery reached you), but it has been a week for making out impossible reports for the university of plans of needs for the next ten years. I should live so long!

But what I much more wanted, of course, was to tell you about Ezra and my visits to him. I had suggested several alternatives; his answer was to command them all. So at nine o'clock on Saturday morning I was driven by one of his followers to St. Elizabeth's [*sic*] where he met us in the main office, got into the car and drove to a point of land within the grounds from which one could look out over the Potomac and see the Lincoln Memorial, the Capitol, and all of the symbols of his chief present concern. Our companion was Horton, of the Square Dollar Series, and the morning was spent chiefly (it seemed to me) in their conversation about politics, economics, and the injustice of Ezra's incarceration. There was much talk of kikes and kikeressas [*sic*], although not vicious; but it was a little difficult for me to join enthusiastically. We left at 11:30, his luncheon time, and drove to Dorothy's little apartment in the basement of a lower-middle-class frame house about three miles away. She cooks her breakfast and suppers there, and eats out each noon at the Hong Kong Restaurant which is en route to the Hospital. Perhaps she receives a few people there, but if so they are chiefly Ezra's "students" toward whom she is in something of the role of a headmistress, lending them books, giving them little scoldings, and holding aloof from the naughtiest of them until they come to heel. She looked amazingly well, and we were most friendly; talked about Ezra and the hopes for his release, which she now feels she anticipate[s] enough to plan where they will go "first," and then afterwards. But what a life it is for her! We were back at the hospital, she and Horton and I, at 1:30 and found Ezra again at the point of land (when there one is quite out of "it" in spirit), this time with a young lady school teacher of 27, Marcella, who came from Texas to Washington, to study under him, and supports herself mean-while by work at a school. It is she with whom he is planning an anthology.[66] Into our car they piled, Ezra with several pamphlets for me, and a vast array of foodstuffs: chocolate brownies cooked for him by Horton's wife; a jar of peaches, two kinds of bread, cheese, breakfast cake, etc, all given him by the kitchen workers at the hospital ("otherwise it would go to the pigs in Vir-ginia") out of the left-overs, at which he munched, we munched, and the rest Dorothy took home with her ("I needed some bread."). The afternoon's con-versation was more literary, Ezra read some poetry, we told jokes and laughed. And the afternoon was soon over. Sunday morning I was met again, and taken out to the hospital. This time there was a message that we were to go to his ward where he had things to show me. We climbed up the stairs, rang the bell (which chimed like a glockenspiel), and entered the iron door after the key turned to admit us.

The last time, you may recall, was a Saturday afternoon and there had been a football game on television: turned up to the maximum roar of static and cheerleaders, so that to walk down the hallway between the patients was like a procession in Hades, the descent to Tiresius. This time it was quieter and better: the patients lay stretched out upon the benches, their heads bandaged, or walked slowly up and down carrying what seemed like pillows on their heads (perhaps only two did, in fact, but the sight of them was overpowering.) But there was Ezra like a monument of sanity, running down to greet us with three great folio volumes of Coke in his hands at which I must look and marvel, for Coke is the latest addition to the paideuma and the rocks upon which the city of Dioce is to be built. Then he took me to his room, which he has to himself, and which I was delighted to see. It was like a boy's room in school, or the rooms of an old bachelor. Books were on the floor, under the bed, piled high on dresser and stands. Papers were in boxes, like a helter-skelter muniment room of a man who never throws anything away. On the walls were paintings and drawings, chiefly by his protégé La Martinelli (Mrs. Pound: "I do not see her, I do not know her address, there are things it is better to keep away from"), who does paint very well indeed, and perhaps you know her work from the little Vanni Scheiwiller volume for which Ezra wrote an introduction.

Have you this? You'd better. And this? He filled two string bags with documents of one sort or another; or little booklets I might not have seen; or letters from various people which he wanted to read to me; and an agenda which he had carefully prepared. Half running, half skipping, like a twenty-year old, full of vigor and good humor, he led us down the corridor and out the door and to the car. The temperature had risen, it was nearly sixty and springlike, and he was in top form. We followed the agenda carefully, things were planned for decades to come, enemies were scouted, friends were embraced, in the almost ceaseless conversation. He lay back in the seat and relaxed. I think I'll have a cigarette. I only smoke three a month. I think I'll have another. Stories of the past, of Idaho and Wyncotte, of London and Rapallo, of Eliot and Williams and you. He was at complete ease, and when I left he could hardly say good-bye. He looks exceptionally well, his beard jaunty, his skin as fresh as a baby's. He tires easily, Dorothy says, and forgets things a little now, but the writing goes on, and he seems to touch life even at his distance. There does seem to be an increasing hope that he might be released, and at least the outlook is not cloudy. I lunched with Dorothy Pound again at her Chinese restaurant, and packed the messages of love to you from her and Ezra, and caught my train back to New Haven.

One thing I wonder if Joan or unser E[rich] could get for me. Eva Hesse's *Wort und Weiss* has been put out by the Arche Verlag of Zurich and is filled with some interesting photographs of Ezra.[67] Look at first before sending it on.

Yr

C.

231 HGS
Yale University
New Haven, Conn.
2 April 1958

Dearest Hilda:

The enclosed clipping from this morning *Times* makes very exciting news indeed, and it looks more and more possible that the day of liberation may finally come.[68] That earlier notice in the Washington *Star*, just before my trip, which was interpreted as a trial balloon, gives what is likely to be the pitch; for in it Overholser was quoted as saying that many people who were unable to stand trial were still perfectly safe to move freely in society. I know from other sources too, and not via the Pounds, that Overholser has no objections to freeing him. In fact he has been moving, himself, to help in this direction. The quashing of the indictment is what we have all been working for. In this way Ezra will not lose his passport, not being guilty of an offense against the state, and so can go back to Italy.

You will probably see him again yourself. I spoke to Dorothy about the possibility of your coming down, if you came over this summer; and she was delighted at the possibility. "If Ezra goes back to Italy," she said, "he always intended to go to see her!" I think I told you how pleased she was to have your card, and hoped that you liked the woodcut she sent you of Ezra Wyncote home. (By the way, he gave me one too, so no need to send yours along, if you want to keep it *comme souvenir*.)

All love to the various Brunner Easter bunnies!

Yr

C.

April 3 [1958]

Dear Norman,

Thank you so much for the 2 *Atlantic* copies. Now, your letter comes, following your welcome card. Can you tell me if I could or should send a cheque to Dorothy? Let me know — or should it come, through you? I have been infinitely distressed, & only now, after 12 years, have been able to face the *Pisan* legend. I have made a few *very simple* notes on my reactions.[69] It is Erich's interest & concern that are responsible. He always said, "You are hiding something." It seems, yes, my deepest depth did hide the real Ezra relationship cum family — you know! Then so much, so much after! Well, I waited in such trepidation for your letter. A question — *how* can E. get "out?" Thanks all news of Sister B[ernetta] — it is hard for me to write, but I will keep it in mind & thanks for seeing to Anth[ology] poems[70] — & photograph. Erich did ask me if I wanted the book you speak of. Now he has gone to Venice for about 10 days — I will get Joan to have the vol. sent you — but shops now, over Easter, prob[ably] closed. So *much* to say, but this in a rush, for late Easter blessings to you & Susan, Val[entine] II[71] & all! Br[yher] is here. I am so very happy about her new book & "Gate" pictures.[72] She seems pleased (so modestly) too.

I will selfishly wait more news — as to *where* the two Pounds would or could live, outside St. E[lizabeths] — Also, money . . . I mean, I could make over to *you*, to hand out — don't like all the hangers-on — but what a wealth of devotion.

I can't write more, as Fido is due in & Sy[lvia] Beach, after lunch. I wish I could *talk* to you. D[orothy] P[ound] sent me a wood-cut of a little house, I suppose the one she lives in now — but she said "do you recognize it" . . . & said one must study it "in reverse" — very puzzling.

I can't even read this over: you will understand *how* much I value all you have done — & now EP & DP help to add . . .

dear C
from
H.

——— 120. TS ———

231 HGS
Yale University
New Haven, Conn.
7 April 1958

Dearest Hilda,

[. . .]

Part of your question about how Ezra will get "out" will have been answered in a later letter from me. This morning's radio announced that the lawyers were filing the appeal for his release, and "that it was not expected that the Attorney General's Office would make any objections." Even the tabloid *New York Daily News* had an editorial saying "so what! Why not get him off the government's expense account." This afternoon I had a telephone call from Washington to say that a Representative Sellers had raised an objection, and asked if I would write the Attorney General. I could say I already had. La Drière,[73] who called, said that Dorothy was naturally quite nervous about the whole thing, but that it ought to move more swiftly. Apparently it was planned to happen while Congress was having its Easter holiday, in order to keep the publicity down. So there we are. It is all quite incredible and swift-moving once the ball has begun to roll.

Now as to the funds. It is hard to say what to do. La Drière, whom I had several years ago comforted by saying that if Dorothy were ill I would see that there were funds to take care of, wanted me to give them their tickets to Italy, but one must at least wait. If Ezra is released, they will be all right for funds at the moment, I think; there has been a fund which has taken royalties, *and* (altho this is a secret, I gather, and Ezra has said nothing to me), I know that the lawyers of his father's estate have tried to get us to persuade him to take the money so that they could close it out. But so long as he was a ward of the state, it would only have meant giving over the custody of the money to the government. So they could turn to that. Finally I had seen that (thanks to Fido) Mary had enough money to come to Washington this winter or spring, with the grandchildren so that Ezra could see them. Her delay undoubtedly has been because of the growing possibility of his release. I shall write Mary to turn the money over to Dorothy and Ezra, since the same reunion would be accomplished. So you do not need to worry, although I shall keep your generosity in mind, and we can instruct Harold if necessary. How amazingly the cloth of your memory becomes rewoven. The Mystery, our mystery of coming together and drawing your past in with it. Nothing is hidden, really; it simply becomes visible with the passage of time. How much we will have to talk about when we are together again.

[. . .]

> All love,
>
> Yr
>
> C.

[Margin note]: The woodcut which Dorothy sent was of [?] Pound's home at Wyncote.

231 HGS
Yale University
New Haven, Conn.
8 April 1958

Dearest Hilda,

This morning's mail brought a most distressed letter from Fido, vis-à-vis Ezra and the letters about my visit to him that I wrote you and asked to be shown to her. "I truly am most morally shocked at your attitude about Ezra," she says; and that I should suggest his seeing you, or Dorothy's seeing you; and that I should have driven out with some one from the Square Dollar Group.[74] My only reason for writing you about it, is that you will not, perhaps, say much in the future about my letters to you about Ezra, lest it disturb her further. I am not angry, certainly, only troubled that she should be troubled especially now when Elsie's[75] problems are so much on her mind, and when the possibility of Ezra's release should be an added faggot to her burden of cares.

I think you yourself do understand the various reasons for my helping Pound. I should not try to put a priority to any one of them. There was, first of all, your friendship for Pound and your natural worry about him; and there has always been this sort of triangle between him and yourself and me. Secondly, there was the human response to his agonized appeal: "Tell Pearson I can't go it alone!" And then, of course, although Bryher feels that Ezra's *Cantos* are the product of a diseased mind, and that the best lines are translations from other poets, I don't feel this way about them; they are an ambitious poem and a great poem, and the problems he presents (even when I don't agree with the solutions) are the problems of our age. I do not approve, as you know, of what Ezra says about the Jews (he would say "some Jews" not all Jews; but I still disapprove). But I think I know perhaps even better than Pound does what he is really talking about, and I have no problem in teaching *The Cantos* to Jews, when they understand him through me. As to the Square Dollar Series, this is composed of books of excerpts from Confucius, Fenellosa, Benton, Agassiz and Coke. I see nothing treacherous in this, I'm afraid. I think Ezra did and has done wrong things, but God knows he has been punished, and if he can return to Italy for his last years then I should wish him to do so. As to his seeing you, I quoted that only to show his continuing affection for you; one would see him or not see him for other reasons, and I suspect that he will be too tired to want to make any trip of this sort; the affectionate thought behind it, as desire, is another matter. Only let's not trouble Bryher about these matters. I am so fond of her that I cannot bear that she is distressed. I shall simply write to tell her why I continue to be interested in Ezra, and then drop the matter.

> All love, as always.
> Yr
> C.

Don't mention to Fido that I have written you about this.

—————— 122. MS ——————

April 11 [1958]

Norman dear,

Thank you for your letter. Now, *that* is clear! I had a terrible evening with Fido and [Sylvia] Beach,[76] who both turned violently on me about poor Ezra. I did not speak again of him — nor will I. Fido read your letter — refused to read the news-item. The only thing is, it has given me back the early American scene, when almost everyone I knew in Philadelphia was against him, after that Wabash College *débacle*. Erich always said I was "hiding something." It was all *that*, my deep love for Ezra, complicated by family (& friends) lack of sympathy — my *inner* schism — outwardly, I went on, after E (1908) went to Venice. I have been writing of this & Erich has been helping me — & maybe, Fido felt my *inner* soul was not with her — not with them, she & Beach. I *did* have a life in US, before Fido — & I feel so violently American, in the pro-Ezra sense, though it has gone so badly with him. I bless you for your loyalty & Erich comes back today. Joan has been wonderful, I can talk to her about it. She ordered the new E[va] Hesse for you & I have a copy. I have been *shattered* over Easter, but kept up. Joan found Fido very "mysterious & fascinating." A new turn — & was interested in poor Beach & her war experiences! I have E. P. books piled up on my table. I had to try to hide them — & talk of everything but of what most deeply concerned me. I think our last letters crossed. This is just with infinite gratitude — & for your help in bringing E. & Dorothy, too, nearer. This is in such a hurry. I have been so *happy* writing the E. P. "story" — it must not be taken away from me. I can't re-read your letter, nor mine, lest this is delayed — poor, poor Ezra. Only now, with the hope of his release, dare I go back & on. "It is so long ago," I say to Erich. "No," he says, "it is existentialist," (his word) "eternal."

You will be with us here, when I talk of this, at last, with Erich.

So much, much love & gratitude,

from

H.

──────── 123. TS ────────

231 HGS

Yale University

New Haven, Conn.

19 April 1958

Dearest Hilda:

As you will have known from the radio, Ezra is free! I should have cabled you, but I hadn't known until this morning's paper came, and then it was too late. I have been waiting all week for the chance to write you this. It is satisfying. Ezra committed treason of course, though not in his mind; the point is that whatever the penalty should be, he has more than paid it.

> If the hoar frost grip thy tent
>
> Thou wilt give thanks when night is spent. [Canto LXXXIV]

The whole thing has been a kind of birthday week present for me. I enclose the clippings, and will let you know what Ezra's plans are when he or Dorothy writes. I suspect they will be too excited and busy for a bit, but perhaps some one else will communicate. I am still not sure, of course, that he will get his passport and be allowed to return to Italy. MacLeish,[77] with whom I spoke earlier in the week, seemed convinced that the government would still not go that far. I am not so sure, and I certainly hope they do. He will have the passage money for himself and Dorothy to go back, and I understand that Laughlin (of New Directions) will guarantee him $3000 a year from his royalties, if Eliot will have Faber come in on the guarantee. Possum played cozy about this, but I think it will work out.

Your letter about Ezra and yourself warmed my heart. I knew it already of course. Or what good is a "C?" But there has always been this little veil between the admission of it to yourself, which has been there even in the difficult psychoanalysis days. I think somehow of the exhibition at Yale as having restored you to your father so that he became no longer the "professor" but Daddy ("did I call him Daddy?" you asked Harold). And now another canyon has been bridged by Ezra's end to torment; perhaps even Bryher's fury (which may have a little jealousy in it) may have helped. And these things are a birthday present to me too. I am glad you are writing it down, and *unser* knows how important it is for yourself that you should write it down. I hope you will let me see it, and I can have my good and careful secretary copy it for you if you want. It is so good not to be hiding, something — anything from those you love and who love you.

C.

———— 124. MS ————

April 25 [1958]

[no salutation]

Thank you, dear C., for letter of April 19 & the cuttings.[78] I seemed to have waited so long — but I did know that you yourself, wanted to send me the very final bulletin. Br[yher] wrote me that she heard in morning (15th) that it was about to be "quashed," then I heard, evening of 18th, that it *was* "quashed." I was glad Br wrote first & I sent her one of your cuttings, just to keep in touch with the "man in the news." Of course, she doesn't know what I know. It was *piano* last visit, she did pronounce, it was because of Kasper etc., she said, that she felt as she did. But we don't *know* fully about that. Only, I didn't argue. I was under a terrible strain. I am sure we all were. I will try later, myself, to type the new E[zra] P[ound] notes — thank you for offering to help. Erich has been very good, of course, & eager, too, for all news. Your letter of 7th reached me after letter of 8th — about possible funds. But you write now of the N[ew] D[irections] $3000 etc. It looks good, but just in case of need, you will remember that I want to help. You speak of money for fares — was that an outside gift or just part of general fund? Dorothy stands out like the *Bona Dea* of classic integrity. I would so love to see them, but that must wait! I do pray the passport goes through. You will let me know? I haven't written them. If you do, send messages for me. How wonderful the world will look to them — to us, too, through their eyes.

This is to thank you. For all the special understanding. I can't write of that now — but you must surely *feel* it.

Love,
dear C
from
H.

April 30 [1958]

Dear Norman,

Thank you for news. Joan found me a copy of the little Martinelli booklet, in an off-street.[79] "O, Ezra Pound," they said & led her to a shelf, exultant. *Did* you ever get the Consulate paper? It seems to worry Joan. We have a rough copy, in case you never had it.

I really wanted the *Owl* for the Grove magazine, but you will know best. About the picture for *book*, may I write later.[80] Will they *please* credit B[ernhard] Obrecht, Zurich, in any case. It seemed to mean so much to him to have American connection, as he has a sister in Chicago & wants to go there. Yes — I am mystified & charmed by the Arabic![81] Let me know if I can do anything for Martinelli. What will you give her, as from Ezra? I have not written them. There seemed too much to say. *Please* send the Martinelli letter. I will go over it with *unser*. Fido has "warned" me against the Cal[ifornia] group, but I take it in my stride, as Duncan whose review you liked is one of them — & Erich seemed happy there[82] — & with a cousin of Wilder. They sounded gay & Martinelli-ish. Joan takes La M. much to heart, "but what will she do? Ezra used to feed her from the canteen." We got our information (not very flattering, re M.) from David Rattray, *Weekend with Ezra Pound*, Nation, Nov. 16, that Richard sent me. Do you know Rattray? This article is what started me on the "E.P. Notes" — but I am stuck, as I too *feel* the Olga, Mary, Schloss Brunnenberg in the middle distance. I hardly knew Olga, but have had some letters from Mary de R[achewiltz] — & I identify myself with the whole lot — & just am puzzled. Dorothy, in a way, saved his life, his sanity — don't you think? But . . . I can't write of it, but will go on later, & *unser* is amazingly perceptive! I must get this off.

That same *Nation* has a poem by Ramon Guthrie[83] — do you know him? — *E.P. in Paris & Elsewhere.*

Thank you — thank you for writing, dear, dear C

H.

How dreadful about Schnack.[84] I haven't seen her for such a long time. Her interest in Am[erican] Lit[erature] seems just off my beat. . . .

233 HGS
Yale University
New Haven, Conn.
4 May 1958

Dearest Hilda,

[. . .]

Not a word yet out of Ezra, who is I gather still at St. Elizabeth's [*sic*] and I presume busy with preparing to leave. He has given one interview, echoes of which I saw in a brief release in the New Haven newspapers, and the whole account of which (or at least a much longer one) I saw in copies of the two Washington newspapers who had reporters there.[85] As his friend Horton[86] remarked (he is the Square Dollar man who took me to the hospital in Washington), "one or two more interviews like that and the government will shanghai him out of the country." It was really dreadful: Roosevelt as a damned fool, St. Elizabeth's [*sic*] as a hell-hole, all the clichés he said to me that first uncomfortable morning. And when they asked him about Frost who had made two special trips to the Attorney General, all Ezra could say was: "He sure took his time about it!" It is all understandable of course; the excitement of saying things to a new audience was an irresistible occasion, and I daresay he regards his release as a vindication. But he forgets that saying things to cronies who came to St. Lizzie's is one thing (they will not repeat), saying them all around is another. He took Cournos to task for something years ago, bringing in the kikery again, although protesting as always that he is not anti-semitic. However all this will pass, and if he can get back to Italy the situation will be much better. Poor Dorothy must be shivering, however, meanwhile.[87]

Yr

C.

233 HGS
Yale University
New Haven, Conn.
10 May 1958

Dearest Hilda,

No — there is no reason why you should [write] Ezra directly. When your letter came asking me to pass on your happiness at the outcome, I wrote him so, quoting. But I have not heard a word from him since the moment of the court decision. He is apparently still staying on at St. Elizabeth's [*sic*], but can leave the grounds at will — to judge from the interview he gave at Congressman Burdick's home. I think they may feel it is better for him to break gradually from his hospitalized routine rather than rush into the world, and Dorothy may feel that Ezra at breakfast is a little more than she can take all of a sudden. Bryher wrote that Horace had written her that Ezra would leave D[orothy] and go back to Olga. I hope not, and in any event this would hardly be easy. For after all E is released into Dorothy's *custody*.

Do keep on with private EPistles to yourself. This is the moment on paper for a kind of catharsis, the ordering and getting it down which will free you. It is the ordering, not the data which is important, and I hold your hand while *unser* guides your pen. The ink is from your heart.

The Martinelli continues to write in a weird, appealing fashion; and has sent me a self-photograph in bikini, with the banner very much at half-mast. I will send along the letters, but wait for one or two more which will round out the story. But they must be kept *zwischen uns*, though perhaps one might permit *zwischen unser* too. The Martinelli "says" she is sending me a group of her drawings, paintings, and ceramics which I am to store for her while she goes with her Chinese lover to Mexico to live in a palace (loaned) while she seeks for an Aztec temple whose interior she can paint. I advised her that she could make an Aztec temple by painting the interior of anything. I really only gave her fifty dollars, but I gather she needs money desperately. Sometime if you like, I could take whatever you say from the royalty account and buy you something from what she sends. But perhaps you should wait until you read her. She does have talent as a painter as well as a flair for language, and Susan finds her letters as amusing as I do. I think she is not quite D[orothy] P[ound]'s cup of tea, anymore than she would be Fido's.

Yr

C.

In mid-May, H.D. sends a check for Sheri Martinelli, to be bestowed through Pearson, and asks him to forward Martinelli's letters. Pearson's response, on 25 May, explains that he thought it best to send the check to Martinelli as a "tribute" directly from H.D. He encloses an adulatory letter from Martinelli to H.D., in which Martinelli addresses H.D. as "the real 'Isis'."[88] H.D.'s response to this letter follows, as does more discussion of the resonance that Martinelli's story has for H.D. In July, her memories are brought into focus by Pearson's account of Pound's departure for Italy.

———— 128. MS ————

May 28 [1958]

Dearest C.

Your letter of May 25 arrived yesterday, very quickly, but the letters, "her letters to me . . . en route since Monday" have not come. I am rather shattered by La M[artinelli] letter — it needs a lot of translating, as you suggest . . . "especially of my race."[89] What is "my race?"[90] The whole content is exciting & overstimulating. If you write, tell her — as I am diffident, as you know, about writing & am *driving* myself to type the E[zra] P[ound] notes. What name does one use? She gives herself another, now. When does she leave for Mexico? Does she still see Ezra? I did not know that Olga had been over. How well La M. writes. She should write all this up or down. My own notes are pianissimo *piano-piano* but I mean them to be, & Erich says "the simplicity is wonderful in face of the confusion." You made the E P legend live & I felt lost with no new news, for some weeks. La M. fills the dim, uncanny "St. Liz" canvas with flame. I am so sorry you have been so over-worked. Fido has worried, but I wrote her that I had heard, about "Grantor" & Grove, & was keeping the letter to answer.[91] There is a notice that BBC talks on *HD* (with others) Fri., 10.10.

The La M. photographs are fascinating.[92] Thank her. I will re-read your letter — & hers. They go together. I was a little upset that you *told* her about the *tributissimo*, but I am glad too, as her letter is so rewarding & inspiring. More of all this, later — & grateful thanks — we are at-one with all this enthralling saga!

Dear C.

from your ancient May Day,

C.

———— 129. MS ————

June 3 [1958]

Dearest C,

Thank you for the La M[artinelli] letters — & with (& apart from), the perfectly enchanting Vol. II.[93] I will keep the Vol. II pictures to show Fido & perhaps I may keep two or three of them. I will return the La M. pictures & letters later. I hope you don't mind, but Joan said she would type them out for me. La M. does get in-under & *what* a father fixation. I read bits to *unser*; he felt she was intrinsically *lonely* — why? I want to work this out as it touches (very distantly) my own shock at Ezra leaving for Europe — 1908? I am intensely curious about La M. & so is Joan. It is good for her, Joan, to be jolted out of herself — & she is doggedly (English) discreet. I found her picture, late, it was with some E[zra] P[ound] that I had duplicates of — anyhow, it escaped me. But surely La M. is very attractive? Joan thought so. I sent her a letter to the old address, before I had the La M. letters from you. I don't suppose she will get it. The letters are hair-raising. Could she be persuaded to *write a book*? It is so much more rewarding than D.H. Lawrence. Tell me what you think — & let me have any news. I have not heard from any of the Ezra group — not E. or D[orothy] — or Mary. I can't thank you enough for the La M. letters & the connection, as brought about by our Norman. I *do* hope it's all right to have the copies? Only as for self, Joan & *unser*.

Grateful,
Grateful
thanks, dear C.

from
H.

I am sorry that we can't share this with Fido . . .

———————— 130. TS ————————

June 26 [1958]

Dear Norman,

I would like to brood over this letter for an hour or more, but must just dash it off. Thank you for writing of La M[artinelli]; I find I write "Martin" in my notes, it is good for her, a boy name and here in Europe, a sort of swallow — also in USA? I had a premonition always that Mexico spelt disaster[94] — I may be quite wrong. I did not, of course, write her of it, but spoke to Erich — maybe that put me off the Aztec poem?[95] Anyhow, there was the D.H. L[awrence] illness at the end, the usual — and Erich wanted an opinion on the Kerouac (spelling) *Road*,[96] so I glanced over the end Mexican chapters. There was also my own *Yucatan* motif in the last London "last attachment" period. I would do anything for Martin — Joan even said "she might come here." "But what could she do?" "She could sit in the garden and draw — you — like she did the others in St. Elizabeth[s]." If I could travel, I would even want to take her to Venice. But you know that I can't get about. Erich seems to think it pretty serious, "The Undine type can't usually find their way back to life." He was intrigued by the idea of "full flesh for me as in New York."[97] But I don't quite get it — nude, or what? Anyhow, interesting. No, *unser* is not "Victorian." I would like ANY letters or pictures to show him — I am, of course, more discreet with Joan. I have never known her to "open up" to anyone or anything as she has to the La M. letters (what I read of them) and the pictures. From my letter, "This is WAR. The male just can't go about like that ditching a spirit love." She blames chiefly Marcella with her "hoop-skirt tactics," flattering the Maestro etc.[98] Thank you for sending off my letter with yours. I will probably write her again. I leave the matters of the pictures to you. This is very, very tragic and the Amaral accident carries out my "feel-ing," but perhaps this is the "sacrifice," and not the Martin herself. We must do what we can. Would it be better if she stayed in USA? This must go and thank you for everything — and give the Martin suitable messages if you write again.

And send me anything & as for *unser* that you can temporarily spare — *but if you feel it is better not, OK, I will understand.*

Bless you again and again. What a strange get-together this is — we two, E P and the Undine.

> Grateful love
> dear C.
> from *H.*

———— 131. TS ————

> 233 HGS
> Yale University
> New Haven, Conn.
> 8 July 1958

Dearest Hilda,

[. . .]

All last week, after Tuesday, I wanted to write you; but instead had to keep my nose on the keyboard while I finished the first two of the three articles on Hawthorne which have been so long overdue, and for which they are holding up the magazine. I shipped these two off yesterday afternoon, but before I start the third I must write you first. Tuesday was an event! I went to New York to see Ezra and Dorothy off on the Cristofor[o] Columbo for Italy. He had written and asked me to go. I could not refuse. What a day. It was over 90 and humid. I did errands for myself in the morning, before lunching with the

Wolves (of Pantheon),[99] and every hour had to retreat to douse my head with water. I got to the pier at 2:30 and after a little false search found my way to cabin 128, tucked away in a corner of first-class at the end of a corridor. The door was closed, but a young man opened it and greeted me: "*You* are the one we *want* to see. Come in!" The door closed behind me. There on one bunk lay Ezra, stripped to the waist, his torso rather proudly sunburned and the white hairs on his chest dancing by the breeze from the fan. At his knees on the bunk sat Marcella, shoeless. On the other side of the cabin was Dorothy, smiling and looking very well. She rose and kissed me, to my surprise; and I gave her a single yellow rose. "H.D. wanted me to give you this," I said. Will you forgive me? I told her you knew she was going but not when. "You were commanded, then!" Dorothy said, and she was really touched. "Yes," I answered, for the spirits had told me you did command. She had a few other flowers, but yours she put in a vase on the dresser. The other flowers she gave away; yours she saved. "One flower is just right," she said. Horton and his wife (of the Square Dollar Series) were there, and later the editor of New Directions came in.[100] Eventually I discovered that the young man who had let me in was Omar. He was guard against the press who kept coming for photographs and interviews, neither of which was permitted. It was hot but cozy. Ezra was no different from ever. For a half hour he lectured me on college entrance examinations, and his anthology, and what I must do about it. He gave a dissertation on the Constitution, being corrected by Horton who gave article and section and paragraph as authority for each of Ezra's opinion[s]. Ezra showed me his press card, proudly. He had gotten it from a Richmond, Virginia, paper. He showed me Canto 99 which had just appeared in the *Virginia Quarterly*. I will get a copy for you eventually. And so it went. Then the whistle blew at 3:30 and we all bade farewell. Ezra took both hands and pressed them warmly; Dorothy gave three affectionate kisses to me, and an invitation to Brunnenburg. "Don't look so sad," Ezra said.

And so that is ended, and I wonder if I shall ever see either of them again. Marcella goes with them for a year or two. What a strange ménage it will be at Mary's. I had a drink with Omar and the New Directions man afterwards, and discovered what had happened after Ezra's release. But this I will write you about later. It was not extraordinary, but interesting. And in any event your rose was with them. It is for the Paradiso, I said at the end.

Yr

C.

July 12 [1958]

Dearest C,

Bless you for the miracle of the rose [Letter 131] — my letter to them, via N[orman] P[earson],[101] was late, but it would not contradict, "I told her you knew she was going but not when." You say, "Tuesday was an event." Is that July 1? It must be, but confirm for my "notes." How *happy* your letter made me — makes me. Thank you for *Evergreen*,[102] I will give it to Fido for *July 17* — the Day she comes to celebrate, as we met in Cornwall, July 17 — 1918 — can you beat it? *40 years ago? Unser* is all over the place with *Germain* & found some misprints, but it doesn't matter. He said, they should have a note in next number, as per Guggenheim, page 160. But as *Evergreen* is a quarterly, I can do this later, if you think indicated. *Unser* has the California number, but wants the others. What do you think? "But this is No. 5," he said, "we ought to have the others." It is, of course, a joke to see old classic on-the-shelf *HD* in that *galere*[103] — *I am* amused, really — but what will Fido say? Myself, it gives me a new perspective & I do, do thank you. I wish they could bring out the XXVI *Sagesse* — maybe, a book later. We will talk of this. I sent back Martin letters, surface. See that your secretary does not send them back to Denmark — & some old note-books, *Owl* & *Vale Ave*, that I will get Fido to post, must wait your return.

Yes — I knew Gaudier,[104] in the old days, slightly. I still don't "see" La M[artinelli] here. *Can't you keep the picture at the shore?*[105] And I really think "Magic Head"[106] should stay with you. I only read the letters once — frankly, since the *ungluck*, I am a little frightened.

Perhaps, they better send the whole set of old *Evergreens* — could you arrange — or not? Shall I send you or they, check? I must send Obrecht & Schnack — & I am sure *unser* could do with another copy of 5.

You *know* I would like to help Martin, if I could. You must keep me informed.

But bless you for the letter. I am re-reading it now. Love to Susan — I feel *Leucothe* belongs to the shore & to her.

I will wait to learn what happened "after Ezra's release." . . . . Repeat: I had 3 *Owl*, & asked you to have *3 or 4* more sent — so perhaps just the *4 old Evergreens* will do. But I leave it to you — dear C —

H.

July 17 [1958]

Dearest C,

Will you be there? We huddle over the radio. Br[yher] says she will take Joan, in any case, to Denmark. I have just numbered my E[zra] P[ound] pages to send to Miss Coigny to type & I will have them for you. I finish on the *Rosenkavaller* [*sic*] motif from your letter — what happiness it brought me to feel that you were there — and I, with you. So indeed, it is a sort of *finis*, & what now will come seems remote, another chapter, another world. We will follow from a distance, but we know that our concern, our real affection must have helped, at the end. Erich said even, that my notes (some of which I read to him) "helped get him out." Well, they helped get me *out* of some sub-merged anxiety, which had to be battened-down & suppressed during the 12 dreadful years and before.

─────

I just receive *Evergreen No. 4*, complimentary copy. 12 seems a lot of No. 5, but I can post from here to Ezra & the others. We will talk of this. I can't give Joan a copy, because of *Unser* poem — a pity — she resents & rages against him, but sticks on, a terrible conflict. He has check-mated her by saying that he won't take her, unless she has a job. She is a fascinating problem. Erich says you will be good for her, "he is very intelligent & as shrewd as she is." I do hope it all works out & you have a wonderful *Abenteuer*.

I am glad you came out with *Omar*.[107] I have always been very careful. I spoke to Br superficially of La M[artinelli] & Mexico, as I thought picture (if there — & I hope not) would have to be explained. She brushed it all aside, "not up her street," as you had said — but I felt it better to say something — but I won't bring it up again.

A thousand thanks for everything, & love

> dear C
> from *H.*

[A postscript contains the following note by Bryher: We arrive *SAS* Sunday night — no Swissair available.]

The few letters exchanged throughout the remainder of the summer refer to Pearson's trip to Greenland and Denmark with Bryher and his prospective birthday visit with H.D. in Zurich at the beginning of September. During that visit Pearson sets in motion H.D.'s application for renewed American citizenship, for which she is grateful, and he reads her "Pound Notes," which they decide not to show Pound. (Pearson's letter of 15 September implies that he decided against showing them to Pound because of the latter's recent praise of Oswald Moseley, the British fascist.) Later in September, he sends news that she has won the Harriet Monroe Memorial Prize from *Poetry*, an honor she associates with her recent symbolic return home. On 26 September she writes: "I am deeply touched and it *is* an 'omen and blessing.' It all comes with the birthday visit and the USA 'return,' on 12th. Thank you so *very* much for following up passport — and how good *they* are. I do feel that I am wanted, somehow! The *Poetry* recognition adds fresh light and life to *Vale Ave* and I have been re-reading it again."

In the autumn, H.D. and Pearson continue to discuss Sheri Martinelli's distraught reaction to her rejection by Pound, a subject that H.D. keeps from Bryher, whom H.D. finds increasingly restless and demanding. They also discuss Erich Heydt's forthcoming marriage to a colleague, Dori Gutscher. Perhaps because she depends so much on Heydt for company, H.D. is obsessed by this news, commenting on it in a number of letters with an embarrassing intensity. In particular, she is struck by the fact that Heydt's fiancée was also his analyst. On 5 November [1958] she writes, "I have been in an agony of suppressed mirth — hysteria? — *why* is it funny? I see it in New Yorker psychoanalytic joke terms. *Why?*" And, in response, she wants to "assert [herself] with a *book* in the best Bryher manner."

However, as Heydt reassures her of his constancy, H.D. comes to accept his marriage with more poise. On 15 November she focuses upon his past helpfulness: "Of course, he absolutely *dragged* Ezra out of me, & sustained me, at a distance, in the *Helen* sequence, though it was you who stabilized or recognized or *legalized* the *Heldgeburt* — a word the Professor used about something, about myself!" In the following letter, H.D. dedicates her poem "Sagesse" to Heydt and his new wife.

——————— 134. MS ———————

Dec. 7 [1958]

Dearest Norman,

Enclosed letter — *if* you write and send a poem from *Sagesse* or *Vale*, will you explain that I leave all such decisions with you.[108] I have dedicated *Sagesse*, with line from XIII, thus:

> *Venus, Venus, Mercury, be near . . .*
>
> for
>
> Dori
>
> and
>
> Erich.

My chief concern now, is the getting to Lugano, early Jan. By some miracle, I may, with Br[yher] to help me pack. *Sagesse* grows on me. You are its *god-father*, you named it. Wouldn't a *book* be wonderful — even, if indicated, with the *Beethoven*, which somehow goes with the *Owl*? Would an introduction be "useful" to explain the zodiac-clock? [109] I feel that it might be a center & stimulus, as for or/and toward Lugano.

Dec. 8. I am stuck, as I rather expected a letter, as in answer to the yellow envelope that Fido brought you. Meanwhile, R[ichard] A[ldington] writes: "Will you tell Pearson that from a fan letter in to-day I think I have got hold of an unpublished R[obert] L[ouis] S[tevenson] letter. If it is of any interest to Yale, I will try to get them a copy. R.S.V.P."

———

I really am worried as you said you had grippe or flu, but Fido writes she is seeing you again, so I expect all is well.

Thank you always — & love to S[usan] & Val[entine] II.

ever

H.

In December, H.D. turns again to America and Pound. She thanks Pearson for arranging her American passport, the anticipation of which she describes as "a wedding-day for me" (16 December). She also mentions having met with Dr. Lüdeke, with whom she discussed Pound's poetry. On 26 December Pearson responds with comments about a book of drawings he has received as a Christmas gift from Sheri Martinelli. It contains, among others, a number of "superb drawings of Ezra," prompting Pearson to relay to H.D. Martinelli's description of her relationship with Pound. [110] He then expresses interest in H.D.'s view of Pound's "Canto C," along with the private sentiment that he hopes Pound won't continue the *Cantos* much longer. In the following letters, from the beginning of 1959, H.D. continues to allude to Pound, and to a new series of poems, based on the emotional residue of *End to Torment*, which she thinks of as "Helen-Odysseus." She also sends Pearson her novel "Magic Mirror," based on her relationship with Heydt, cautioning him to keep it between themselves. In his replies Pearson responds to her comments about these manuscripts.

——— 135. MS ———

Jan. 6 [1959]

Dear Norman,

I will return La M[artinelli] surface, [111] later, & a Bryn Mawr folder. Possibly, your secretary could write on back of 1909–1959 "information for profiles" page, a partial list of H.D. books. I will keep their addressed envelope, just in case, I write — but really, really, it is beyond me now. A letter from Ezra, asking for name of a boy whose mother we knew, "I don't want to chuck all labour on N.H.P." I wrote E. & asked him if he would care to read *End*. We have had a *terribly* hectic time. Fido must have written you. As George [Plank] can't get out & Elsie [Volkart] is ill, we have decided to wait a little longer here, & perhaps it is as well to see *Unser* a few times. He came yesterday unexpectedly, & perhaps will come to-day. Fido was here & talked chiefly of all the events here, which I *wanted to ignore*, so it was hardly an *Unser* contact for me. I want to talk of Ezra & advisability of seeing him at Lugano — & I can't discuss E. with Fido — also my new poems are "too long" or unlike "early H.D." or something — though Fido otherwise has been a *miracle* of comfort & strength. I think as *toward a Helen, Odysseus* sequence[112] — could follow on the three "Canto" *Helen, Achilles* series. It would be *End* findings, in a way. I feel near to you, La M. & Ezra when I read the letter. There is so *much* to say but I am over-charged, sur-charged still with Xmas & New Year *débacle*. Yes — it is dramatic but I want to get back to pre-Troy & an early *Helen*. John S[chaffner] sent me Kazantzakis[113] & I think that helps.

Could you return the R[ichard] A[ldington] letters I sent? I think one was about *End* & I wanted it for reference.

Forgive rather scrappy letter. There is snow & much yet to do with stacking & packing — may as well wait a bit.

I do bless you & ask your advice, re Ezra. I will have to wait anyhow, till Fido leaves Lugano, about Jan. 27th.

All, all love to Susan & to C

ever

from
H.

Did I thank your secretary for beautiful copy of *Sagesse*. What can I do for her — please. . . .

———— 136. MS ————

Jan. 7 [1959]

Dearest C,

I wrote yesterday, but want your help. I wrote Ezra, asking him if he would like to see my *End*, written for & dedicated to Norman. He says "the efforts . . . of N.H.P. have been considerable," then adds, "I don't know 'Norman' (or did I meet him?) & can't judge his stance." I am rather frightened, feel the pages may be misjudged or get into wrong hands, as R[ichard] A[ldington] wrote some time back, of a private reference in a letter, misrepresented by one of the news-hounds. I am rather sad about this, but won't send the pages till I hear from you.[114] He says . . . "the efforts of Drew Pearson[115] & other non-relatives of N.H.P. have been considerable." What does that mean? I am shattered & will keep the pages. I have written Ezra, saying I am writing you. And I have embarked & hope to go on with *Helen & Odysseus.*[116]

I had a very happy contact with *Unser* yesterday, his old self & more!

I send now surface, the letters I wrote of.

. *Much* love & to Susan, please,

from
H.

———— 137. MS ————

Jan. 16 [1959]

Dearest *C*,

I have three letters from La M[artinelli] & I can not read them. I will post surface to you, later. I suppose I should send you the copy of *End* with R[ichard] A[ldington] corrections[117] — & on page *30*, I have added a note, re Sylvia Beach.[118] I *felt* it necessary. The whole was written for *Norman* absolutely — you must do what seems indicated. I will not send it to Ezra — I am *afraid* of his *not understanding it.*[119] You might return me your copy of *End* when you get this one, surface, both. There is no hurry! I will then make corrections, as from my corrected copy. *Unser* was glad that *you* were glad to hear.[120] I am still shattered by repercussions here. I don't think I'll get off to Lugano yet. *For you alone, Unser* said to me, "I am as much married to you, as I am to Dori." But there was confusion, the last few visits, but he comes to-day. Then Fido on Sat. & we can talk over Lugano. I am sure Dori is "his salvation," as Rudolf said — & I will write more of it all.

It is the *outside pressure* that threatens my inner peace & security. But I trust you to advise me! I suppose the shock of "Norman" too, upset me. Your explanation is rational — but *what* a strange breach in consciousness, somehow.

I must hurry! I will try to keep the *Unser, Norman* contact in a cabalistic [△] too,[121] for you *both* sustained & inspired the *End* notes.

Love & in haste — & love to Susan —

ever, dear C.
H.

Mr. Nelson[122] rang & sent me pre-final passport.

paper and number: 225801

Jan. 13, 1959

Jan. 12, 1961

H[ilda] A[ldington] is "the bearer of the following passport." I wrote &
thanked him & *thank* you . . . I am proud & happy!

———

I am sending the *End* now, surface.

———— 138. MS ————

Dearest Norman,

Did I thank you for the poem? [123] *Gymnosophes, Philosophes* should be in ital-
ics, but it doesn't really matter. I like the title, too. And I never told you how I
enjoyed the photographs — I am there with you & Fido. No, don't send La
M[artinelli] book now.[124] Her last letters are very odd, though *one* of them is
quite different & beautiful. I am sending them. I don't want them back. Now, I
had Chapter 1 & 2 sent surface yesterday, & 3 of *Magic Mirror* will go registered
to-day. There are 6 sections. Don't hurry to read them & you will consider as
personal & confidential, as I work in, a symbolic sort of motive or *motif* about
an imaginary group or "circle" in Z[urich]. I call the Erich, Eric Heller — & self
Rica — or sort of Erica — or better still *Am-Erica*. This name centered & sus-
tained me, the bitter cold Lugano winter, 1956, where I wrote these chapters.
Don't take the slightly sinister connotations of the imaginary "group" in Z. too
seriously — but, in any case, the story is for ourselves now — & I am sure, you
will understand — also, the weaving in of fantasy, another Eric Heller manifes-
tation or mystery.[125] He has not seen the story & does not know of my feeling
about a problematical "group" — & my imaginative apprehension — but in
that respect, he is "safe," we may conclude, now. The "group" or/and "circle"
phobia was very real to me at one time, but added to the fascination of the Eric
Heller contact. You *do* understand that I never spoke of this to him & it is
"imaginary" and *between ourselves*! I will send the other chapters — it is really
simply another record or "recording" that kept me *en rapport* with it all here &
with Dr. Heller, during that long Lugano winter.

> Grateful
> blessings
> dear C
> from
> *H.*

So glad to hear good news of Lizzie [126] — tell Susan, with love . . . .

In early February 1959, Pearson suffers a couple of setbacks. First, his plan to travel with
Bryher to Greenland is canceled because the Denmark-Greenland boat that would have

carried them is sunk by an iceberg.[127] Then he is hospitalized with a stomach ulcer. During his hospitalization he reads H.D.'s novel "Magic Mirror" and "revel[s] in it" (10 February 1959). Responding with gratitude to his attention, on 11 February H.D. sends him the remaining sections of part 2 of the novel and mentions that she has "some pages of dated record entrances," titled "Compassionate Friendship," that she will explain later. In the same letter, she also mentions having read a new book on Havelock Ellis, sent by Bryher, that brings back early memories.[128] On 18 February, still in the hospital, Pearson congratulates her upon winning the Poetry Medal from Brandeis University[129] and offers to represent her at the award ceremony.

On 20 February H.D. describes "Compassionate Friendship," the notes on which she based "Magic Mirror." She reports that she wrote them in 1955 but did not have them with her when she wrote the novel the following year. "The 'Notes' are simply direct record of books, past memories, life at *Heimat*, actual names & dates." On 22 February she continues: "I wrote around and about *Unser*, but I would not have the urge or desire to keep the notes, & have them properly typed, but for N[orman]. It was odd how *Unser* kept me interested in the old books & MSS — asking of them. If there were a [O] beyond, I felt he was prompted in this & hence the [O], whatever it was, kept me in touch with my Daemon: Demon or Inspiration."

At the end of February H.D. mentions the difficulty she has had with part 3 of "Magic Mirror." On 27 February she writes: "It is neither the novel nor the notes. I was really putting down some *depth* findings — but I am going over it and may get copy made." On 25 March she sends Pearson a copy of "Compassionate Friendship," commenting that the notes "are a part of the weaving-in of past and (then) present, and no doubt [it] was good for my unc[onscious] to do it," but she suggests that he file them away unread.[130] Also in March, they exchange news about the ongoing difficulties of Pound and his ménage,[131] and they discuss arrangements for the reception of the gold medal from Brandeis. Since the award ceremony is to be on 7 April in New York City, Pearson assumes he will be well enough to attend, but he encourages H.D. to come and receive the medal in person.[132] She demurs and offers the medal to him as a fiftieth birthday gift. In the following letter, H.D. comments on the award certificate and reports progress on her new poem sequence.

——————— 139. MS ———————

April 21 [1959]

Dear Norman,

Thank you for the beautiful folder — my "certificate" or diploma. I am deeply touched — did "they" give the leather envelope or frame — or you? Such a beautiful blue — I will write more of this. I am deep in *Espérance*, a short sequence — I connect the title with your *Sagesse* choice. This is helping me, & the lovely tribute is part of it. The enclosed place-card & the S[usan] II & V[alentine] II is part of *Espérance*, & short runs that *Unser* has taken me lately in "Dori's little *folkswagon* [*sic*]." I told him you had the flowers & he said you must not trouble to write, as he knows how busy you are. It was wonderful to get your letter. Perdita also wrote. I was so proud to have you represent me & P. said you were so gracious & charming & looked so well.

Thank you for C[harles] Norman — no, don't "write his book for him," nor will I.[133] T.S.E[liot] is "embarrassingly" something . . . it is really for him or anybody, such *bad poetry!* [134] I have written R[ichard] A[ldington] about Ezra books & mags. — there had been some trouble which this Mr. Harald [135] will straighten out, about cheques not being properly presented — R. writes they must present cheques to E. in *lire* from "European" with whom Mr. H. was connected, "it has now stopped publication." I heard from Mary [de Rachewiltz] some weeks ago, "I'd like to meet you & have a long talk for I am pretty down-hearted." This is *entre nous* of course, but I wonder what?

This is to thank you & "them" — I am really deeply, deeply moved & glad Ezra is mentioned [136] — but I don't know why W.C.W[illiams] — however . . . I am proud & happy & hurry this off, with love & infinite thanks

> from
>
> *H.*

At the end of April and early May, H.D. and Pearson discuss the plight of Mary de Rachewiltz, who has turned to H.D. as a confidante. Mary feels let down since her father's departure and, to help meet the expenses of the *Schloss*, is looking for possible tenants. On 3 May H.D. mentions having started to type her new poem sequence, which she now calls "Winter Love," and comments, "Some of the poems are done in a strangely familiar, Swinburnian metre — I can't think that I *must* be Pound-Eliot. I just wonder what Ezra would say: *What song is left to sing? all song is sung* . . . I can't rip out lines like this." In the following letters, she continues to discuss this poem and "Magic Mirror," and they exchange more news about Pound and his household.

─────── 140. MS ───────

> May 17 [1959]
>
> *Pfingsten* [Whitsuntide]

Dear Norman,

I am sending you *Magic Mirror*, Part III — 5 chapters. It is scattered — hardly "belongs" — turns from "her" (Erica) to "I" (the author) — explains the "story," what is real, what imagined in Chapter I, & so on. The chief motive that seems to belong to the "Notes," is the connecting links between the *Viking Ship* & the news broken, about *Lusitania*, in 1915, that caused the tragic event of the still-born child. I would not like R[ichard] A[ldington] to see this, though I have tried to modify it, as possible fantasy. The amazing thing is that *Unser* got this right in the open for me, though I had not wholly "forgotten" it. Please do not hurry to read this & no comment is necessary — it can stay with the rest of *M. M.* & someday, one might recast it as for "Notes" — but please do not worry with it. It was marking-time, before 70th birthday trip. And I feel for myself & "the few," the *Totenschiff* connection is very important — *Lusitania* shock compensated for or balanced by *Viking Ship* —

May 18

Mr. Rogers[137] sent me a letter, thanking me for two packages of books — & with it, the Pound pro & con.[138] But I will be glad for another copy for R[ichard] A[ldington] or E[rich] H[eydt].

We have been *very* happy here over Whitsun.

I sent 22 pages, XXVIII sections of poem to be typed but it will be late, as Miss Woolford was going away for Whit[sun] — I call it *Winter Love*

(*Espérance*)

& it is the first (conscious) poem I ever wrote E[zra] P[ound], Odysseus here. It serves as a trailer to the *Helen* or *Helen & Achilles*. The motive is desertion, but *actually* there is *no* desertion. I worked out a Paris-Oenone theme — but that, too, is pure symbolism. *You will understand!*

Poetry came. *Unser* was enraptured with the printed *Regents* — and the note on p. 135 is very satisfactory.[139] You wrote it? I have an odd folder from "Lee, Calif." & am *deeply* touched to read N.H.P. on Leda-Helen and *H.D.* I could weep. . . .

I worked on & off at *Winter Love* from Jan. 3 to April 5. It was oddly a *great comfort* to me!

Perdita seems to absorb the atmosphere & is such fun here. Fido has been *infinitely* helpful . . .

Thanks — & S[usan] sent me the lovely Durer "Violets" & thank *her* & love from a grateful

H.

9 June 1959

Dearest Hilda:

I rejoice in the fact that I can write you a third letter now without having one from you to reply to. Not that I deserve any advantage after so shocking a period of silence. . . . *But*, come to think of it as I do or as I can in this 90° heat I realize that all I have said is rot. For Part III of the *M.M.* has come, and *Espérance* as well. And what more I could want in the way of communication I cannot imagine. I have really been delighted with both. *Espérance* so much so that when Horace Gregory called me on the phone this morning, I exclaimed about it to him and he so deviled me that I send it on to him by mail today. It gives a new strange richness to the Helen poems, unexpectedly catches the series up in its arms, says: see, feel, what myth really is, mon semblable, mon frère.

And the M[agic] M[irror] unravelled, or wove together — both of these paradoxicals at the same moment. I am anxious this summer, when all of the pages are together to begin this again from the beginning.

I still have had no answer from the Grove Press about either *Helen* or *Madrigal*. They are desperately slow, after all these months, still to be silent. It is *Lady Chatterley*[140] of course, now that Rosset has published Rico's original study of class warfare. It has been said before, but it struck me so forcibly in looking at it again: how much anger and resentment there was between the classes, how the gardener in a sense was revenging himself on the upper classes — how he *had* to be a gardener and her husband a knight — this really more than any phallic thrust. In this kind of class warfare the penis mightier than the sword. Otherwise why not the struggle within one class, within Rico's own miners. How he must have suffered! How the younger British (from the masses) *hate* class. The Colin Wilsons,[141] the younger writers generally. I think you and I as Americans can see this; I am not sure that Fido can, for she is one of the fortunate ones a little outside of this from the beginning, not in *or* out. How Rico must have hated Bloomsbury. Or didn't he? I mean, deep down, underneath. You would have seen it better than the others could, because you were an American, your breast was classless, therefore classical.

Susan joins in love.

Norman

June 19 [1959]

Dear C. & Horace,

Will this do for page 17 (line 9): "the legend lives in re-awakened ecstacy" —
Page 1, 5 from end *is*, not in.

14, 8 *comma* after *reality*.

14, 7 from end, *stone* (singular).

15, line 8, comma after *Phoenix-nest*.

16, 9 — quotes before "*Helen* . . .

    5 from end, quotes after *laughter*."

    4 *" "*, comma after *whispering*.

    9 *" "*, end line, semi-colon.

This excites me so much & I will go through the whole sequence, as soon as I
finish *End* copy for Mary de R[achewiltz]. She sent photographs, some years
ago, of 3 children. I must try to find them. She said she had adopted Gabrille
(?) from a home, as *she herself had been a foundling*.[142] I don't know if the little
Italian girl is still with them. Maybe, Mary was upset by some of "the precious
M S" [*End To Torment*]; her last letter said, "I suppose it's useless going on
writing — I don't know why I felt so sure that you would tell me *more*." I
have written, asking her to ask me questions. Mary says, "'End to Torment'
— whose?" R[ichard] A[ldington] wrote (did I tell you?) that his friend,
M[ichael] Harald had seen E[zra] at Rapallo — & while there, a check arrived
from Hemingway for $1000. E. showed this. I could contribute, *sub rosa*, via
some "Pearson" channel, if indicated. What do you think? I love the Arabic
trans[lation] & show it, "here is a poem of mine," a thing I have never done
before. Thank you again! I read and re-read the *Checkbook*.[143] Mary wrote of
it, "those cruel professors — as if father was dead." R. A. seemed to conclude
from items from broadcasts, that E. really had been insane, at some times. He
said, now more than ever, one should not publish *End*, but I think, anyway,
we had decided against it. Yes, it was strange how the *Winter Love* came into
the sequence & it explained so much to me & was (& is) a comfort.[144] I don't
really think it echoes Kazantzakis' "Odyssey," though the quotation sort of
fired my own, "it is more, more than ten years." The quotation is Book III,
line 1076.[145] It might be a tribute to Kaz. to have the original *modern* Greek
line by Kimon Friar. How could it be found — or Kimon?

———

June 20   E. B.'s Day

Now R. A. writes he has had "an embarrassing friendly letter," from E. asking him for re-prints, anthologies, names of editors & so on & so on. "This is a bit much for 'old Aldington' (cf. casebook, p. 107)." R. A. feels that "a more humane & realistic attitude toward poor old E. would be reached if only these fans of his would realize that he *is* crackers." This is of course *entre nous* as most of E. & *Schloss* gossip is. I do, do hope x-ray turned out well & dentist ordeal is over! So much love to you all & thank Horace again,

from

H.

I could go on & on writing of my gratitude to you & H. for the *Helen*. Yes, Kaz. & Kimon must have helped. John S[chaffner] sent me the huge vol. for Xmas — but I had not heard of Kaz. & Kimon, when I began the *Helen*.

At the end of June and the beginning of July, Pearson and H.D. discuss details of the publication of "Winter Love," which Grove Press has agreed to add to *Helen in Egypt*. On 24 June, Pearson, who considers the new poem "Part IV" of the larger poem, suggests that H.D. omit its epigraph, the following line from Kazantzakis's *Odyssey*: "And dull life burst with stars, and turned to fabled myth." He thinks that including it "may divert attention from the poem as a whole by seeming to break it up." He also encourages her support of Mary de Rachewiltz, and introduces a new admirer, the "semi-beatnik" poet Robert Duncan.[146] H.D. agrees to omit the quotation from Kazantzakis but is reluctant to rush either poem into print (28 June 1959). She also invites correspondence from Duncan, whose review of *Trilogy* impressed her, and she continues to report Mary de Rachewiltz's hurt at Pound's attentions to Marcella Spann. At the beginning of July, having had two disjointed, bad-tempered letters from Pound, she decides not to send him a copy of "the so-called 'coda'" (7 July 1959). On 14 July, H.D. reports having heard from Robert Duncan and that she and Erich Heydt have been amused by Robert Lipton's account of the Beats' "case-histories" in his book *The Holy Barbarians* (1959). In the following letters, she elaborates upon her contact with Duncan.

——————— 143. M S ———————

July 25 [1959]

Dearest C,

I am so glad to hear & to know that your mother is so peaceful.[147] You should not worry. It is wonderful for her to be in her *own* surroundings. I am so glad that you are not too far away. I had a little village booklet from you —

saw-mill etc. made me most nostalgic! I hear from Duncan, Stimson Beach, he writes if "Erich Heydt & his Dori" do come "as far as San F[rancisco]" they must visit "our village," & "the house we have here." Who is "we?" Anyhow, it is a pleasant, friendly, coast-to-coast contact.[148]

I have just written Perdita & Fido about a *March* event.[149] Yes — "a little Hilda, which *is* her name." I have asked Perdita to change Hilda to Helen. I feel not a little shattered — not scattered — there is concentration; as Perdita writes, "there it is, with some sort of psychic determination to be." This now repeats my 1918–1919 condition — & the last stanzas of the so-called *Coda*. Yes, it is very strange. I could write so much, so much, but you will understand this. I am glad Ezra wrote — he never thanked me for parting with *my* precious, inscribed E. P. script.[150] But I am glad, glad he was happy.

I must send this — & now — now — bless you, dearest C. — is this 4, four, IV really true — a new canto — with "psychic determination to be."

Love to you all there,

from

H.

(Hilda? Helen?)

Bless you for books[151] . . .

Unser was very kind & made suitable funny-faces . . . and as-if-speechless gestures . . .

————— 144. MS —————

Aug. 10 [1959]

Dear C,

Can I keep the interesting new occult book,[152] read, & give over to Br[yher], as for 2nd? Will you *pay* yourself back. This does sound unappreciative — it is anything *but*. I will tell Br that you choose [*sic*] the book, but that I *gave* it. It will help, as I don't know if or if-not the Grove present will come in time.

Thank you for the *Owl* & for cutting about D H L[awrence].[153]

I have just sent off the old, untidy, first Coigny script of *Vale Ave* to R[obert] Duncan, as I have now the fresh copies, in slightly larger type. I have his typescript of *The Field*, and the book, *Letters*.[154] I must read through carefully, not just hop-skip-and-jump. I feel he deserves our attention. As usual, I fall back on you. He writes me of the Zohar, Yoga etc., very Californienne. But it draws me — don't worry, if we go "incog," we go together. Poor Fido. I did give her a turn. "You think Heydt will be there." Indeed, she was wrong —

for once! Heydts are in the Wolff flat from Aug. 7–22. Then from 22 Aug.–
1 Sept. in Cal[ifornia] — Miss Raber gave this last address, *entre nous* — can
you beat it?

> Motel Capri
> 2015 Greenwichstreet
> (as written)
> San Francisco 23, Cal.

They get back about Sept. 14. *Unser* did give me the Wolff address, if you want
to get in touch.

Fido should be here, 13th & Joan the 16th.

Thanks again, again. I wonder if you are well — I mean, Viola writes of
excessive heat & exhaustion, "Hilda, sometimes I can't believe it's me, shuf-
fling from one room to this — "

I have so much *more* to say — again, all felicitations to S[usan] & S II on
future event![155]

> Ever *H.*

In the remainder of August, the two continue to discuss Duncan's poetry, Pearson's visits
with Heydt and his wife, and Pound's ill health and depression, of which Pearson is in-
formed by Dorothy Pound and Marcella Spann. Pearson is particularly interested in
H.D.'s comments on Duncan's *The Field*; he thinks "parts of it very striking" but is con-
fused about "the overall structure, which [Duncan] calls something in the order of a be-
coming" (11 August), continuing that Duncan "has the real drive of a poet" (15 August).
H.D.'s reply (19 August) is hesitant but positive: she has "not been able to give [her] whole
self to 'The Field,' but [she] did find lyric passages, and later, may get the form and drive
of his philosophy. Yes, there is intensity." In this letter she also mentions having received a
long, fascinating letter from Duncan about his childhood[156] and that she is engrossed in
Kazantzakis's *The Greek Passion*. On 8 September, after Heydt's visit to Duncan in Califor-
nia, H.D. comments excitedly on a new letter from Duncan, in which he enclosed his
poems "'for H.D.'s birthday.'" In the following exchange, Pearson and H.D. discuss the
publication of H.D.'s novel *Bid Me to Live*, which H.D. wants to publish under the nom de
plume Delia Alton.

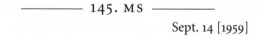

——————— 145. MS ———————

> Sept. 14 [1959]

Dear, dear C,

I have two copies of *Madrigal* — do you want another? I can make *no* dras-
tic changes. I will leave matter of punctuation to you.[157] I worked off & on at

M. for many years, rough sketch was really begun *in situ*, Cornwall, 1918. Just before I made plans to return to London for War II, summer 1939, at Kenwin, this version "wrote itself." Of course, all earlier version[s] were destroyed, they were "forced" & without the center — I did write the last part, the letter to Rico, in Lausanne, about 1947 or 1948 — as the end as was, trailed away — & I pointedly made the *book*, the *child*. How can I "work over" this? It is a mood, a poem, & I will not worry if *Grove* does not want it.[158] *Unser* blew in, full of news of you & La M[artinelli], of Duncan and the Schaff[ner] *famille*, or the two of them. Excuse hurried note. I was going to wire, but Fido said, air would be indicated, she felt. I presume the book is by *Delia Alton*. I, as H.D., could never have done it or the other later ones. How I bless & thank you. *Unser* seemed *begeistert* by La M[artinelli] and Dori seemed helpful. If I can do anything at all, please, please let me know.

Grateful

thanks &

all, all

blessings,

blessed C,

from

H.

──────── 146. TS ────────

231 HGS

Yale University

New Haven, Conn.

18 September 1959

Dearest Hilda,

[. . .]

You mention the question of the book as "by Delia Alton." It is quite understandably by her, as you needed, had to have, a persona in order to get the aesthetic distance in the actual writing of the manuscript. A curious progression of personae in which H.D. is one remove from Hilda Doolittle, and Delia Alton a further remove from H.D. and Hilda Doolittle Aldington. So I shall always be grateful to Delia Alton for the gift of this and the other later books. But I had not mentioned this to Grove who of course have been thinking of it as an H.D. listing on their books. In fact one wonders whether, people being what they are, and since it will be evident enough that it was written actually by you, it will not be misinterpreted as coy if it were to be published as anything but by H.D. I rather feel that Grove would have this reaction, and might indeed blame me for not telling them that it must appear otherwise than they would interpret. I repeat, I think the important thing about Delia Alton is that she enabled you to write this book, and now gives it back to H.D.[159]

Yr

C.

————— 147. MS —————

Sept. 26 [1959]

Dearest Norman,

I am sending you the Ethel Christian book folio of *Madrigal*, in a few days. I have another numbered the same & I can write you. I read, page 188, "*But I will find a new name. I will be someone.*" Maybe, I am a little un-nerved by several incidents here or/and the visit of Catha, R[ichard] A[ldington]'s 21 year old daughter.[160] Fido must have written you that she arranged for Catha to have a vocational test in Z[urich]. The girl is bi-lingual & has had offer to work on a mag[azine] in Paris — but R. seems concerned about her future, & Fido suggested this test.

Thank you for all letters, the last enclosed your charming "venerable."[161] I have a few lines to change in *Espérance*. I will write later, am now literally swamped with 3 copies of *Madrigal*, on my bed. Thank you for checks & looking after all the odds & ends. I must indeed "contemplate" the "little lama." There is *something*, I can't quite get what it is, stirred up — I am sure Fido will have a clue, perhaps, *the* clue, but you must beg *Grove* to be patient — & I am grateful for their appreciation of *M*. —

From what I gather, La M[artinelli] spoke with dignity and warmth of "Professor Pearson," but, as you infer, the talk veered to the old times. I have not heard from Duncan, since the last long letter, after the visit. Dori had taken a coloured photograph for me & actually Duncan looked rather mild, a la Wm. Morris with moderate beard. He was sitting on a sort of carpenter's "horse" that they had found washed up on the beach, & marked on the wood, with initials — H.D., I ask you! Erich said that he (Duncan) was very annoyed with the picture they put in "Barbarians," without his permission. E. said he had the impression that Duncan had changed radically, for some reason, in recent years. If you write, say that I have seen his Wm. Morris picture & am waiting to hear from him. Stinson Beach is a village, rather

Maine islands, or familiar New England, from a second photograph with blue sea in distance.

Again thanks to you & Susan for the exquisite *Hours*. And I pray you, *wait just a little, re M.* Love

H.

Throughout the end of September and October, H.D. and Pearson continue to discuss the publication of *Bid Me to Live*. On 28 October, Pearson, who has enlisted Bryher's support, gently cajoles H.D. to drop the "nom de paix" Delia Alton. Perhaps stimulated by the thought of publication, H.D. also reports that she is "involved with the *Gift* notes" (7 October) and that she wishes him to destroy earlier versions of the Madrigal material. On 14 October [1959] she singles out *Her* and *Asphodel* as examples, asking Pearson to destroy the carbons. She explains, "These were written in London, 1926–1927. It is the old *Madrigal* & *Gift* material without the daemonic drive or the *daemon* that (or who) was released by ps-a, I suppose, & the second War. The 'story' without the daemon makes pleasant reading, at the moment. Strange, that *Madrigal* only 'came true' on the verge of War II, though no doubt, it Phoenixed out of *Asphodel* that was put far away & deliberately 'forgotten.' The *Asphodel* 'nest' should, in the traditional manner, be burnt. Untraditionally, I am picking it apart to see how it was put together." Further, on 22 October, in response to Pearson's having asked if she wants to insert a dedication, perhaps to Lawrence, who dominates the final chapter, she replies, "Dedication — Isn't it already 'To Anthea,' that is to the spirit of the whole, shot to bits, even as in Herrick's day. I agree, that Rico centralizes & enflames the story, but the others have almost as much importance in the processus or 'process,' as Ezra seems to call it. But we can see."

In November and December, H.D. and Pearson discuss the deteriorating health of both Pound and Aldington. Mary de Rachewiltz has written H.D. that Pound, who is depressed, refuses to see doctors, and Mary has asked H.D. to write to him and show him *End to Torment*. H.D. has agreed. On 9 November [1959] she writes to Pearson: "I told Mary she could show him the *End* — she suggested it — & I sent the *Coda*, as I wrote him, to scratch up (& return to me) as a *divertissement*. But of course, now, he can't really change the writing." At Bryher's suggestion, H.D. has invited Aldington, whose physical health is failing, to visit her and consult her doctors. As his visit approaches, however, she becomes anxious, especially since Pound has suggested visiting her too. In the following letters, H.D. describes the problems this would create. However, Aldington's visit proves rejuvenating and she ends the year happily, anticipating the appearance of *Bid Me to Live*.

Nov. 17 [1959]

Dearest C,

Arrangement is made for R[ichard] A[ldington] as for 24, for long, 2 hour session with a Dr. Blickensdorfer. Then report on Dec. 1 — & I must arrange oculist. Br[yher] is Sesame Club, due back here about 24 Nov. — I suppose it is fun, but *Unser*, though helpful, criticizes my state of nerves etc.[162] "Who suggested A. coming — & why?" It was Fido, of course. I suppose that I should not have written Ezra (*Unser* implied) as Ezra was for coming at once & seeing R. with me. I only hinted at this to Br, as Mary wrote he wanted to talk to me about *End*. Fido had a fit — she would leave pronto for USA, if Ezra ever, ever emerged. I have written R. A. that I want to talk about Ezra, but not in Bryher's presence, & Catha must not be mentioned if Joan is around. Now, Ezra writes that N.H.P. will "deduce that I am a fair swine . . . the Martin as Ariadne." I wrote that on the contrary, you had vastly enjoyed her letters etc. etc. — & we both made allowances for her "disturbed" condition. I meant *tea* though I did not say so.

Ezra now wants the "Helen-Achilles," as he called it, or I, writing in *End*. He says "Torment title excellent, but optimistic." I asked if he wanted title changed. I am going over *Helen* scripts, some are fragmentary — but I won't send yet. I was surprised that Ezra was so interested in *End* & the *Winter* Coda. He sent me the paperbook *Odes*, though I had had your first copy. Yes, you are here with us, & I treasure your great goodness & greatness. I don't feel that there is room in me for it; "make room for me," you say.[163]

I could say so much more.

Sympathy & constant thought & love to Susan,

& gallant C

from

H.

Nov. 21 [1959]

Dear N.H.P. (as Ezra says),

Before things get too out of hand, may I ask a correction in *Winter*: — XVIII *Antistrophe* — page 13 — last 3 lines,

the Paradise,

the ring.

Pass — not —

change to:

> reality of the white sand,
> the meadow . . .
> *Parthenos*

the 2nd is Greek — the first, Siegfried or Hobbit! [164]

I sent Ezra, the *Helen* yesterday. Long letter about "the mermaid." He *wants* it cleared up with you.[165] I can only later send the letters. It was the "'horse' (if you know that term,)" "marijuana party in the village" on proceeds of "hocked" typewriter, some trial re dope, & La M[artinelli]'s friends tried to get her into St. Liz to save her from a tough Virginia asylum . . . "leave Theseus some shred of decency." I just tell him to write me these "notes" & I will see that they are safe with you. I can't myself re-write *End*, thankful that I did it then. "I am beaten down low as a louse egg." I must try to make Fido see how important this is to me. Apparently, the Dame in London spoke admiration of the *poet*, E.P. — Br[yher] actually wrote this — Br is a bit on the edge, re E. P. — not easy for me, but there is a "miracle" somewhere; as Mary wrote of Marcella's going. If only I could *believe* in my strength, I would go to Lugano & meet them there. Perhaps R[ichard] A[ldington] can help, as Ezra wanted to see him. I must do my best. I need *Unser* just now, but oddly, he has been taking days off, last Fri. & yesterday when I needed to see him. Herf thinks he looks ill. Fido, you know, is a *miraculous* mainstay, but it's just a little overwhelming, at the moment. She *asks* R.A. here & I am sure she will see that through — but in a strange way, Ezra wants to be *in* this — well — all that —

Please — did I thank you for the *Greek* Mermaid? A lovely, lovely book —

> Ever & ever
> gratefully,
> & with tender messages to
> Susan
> from
> H.

My *Silver Wings*, E. M. Butler died Nov. 13.

──────── 150. MS ────────

Dec. 10 [1959]

Dear N — Dear C. —

This will be two vibrations — two letters — *one* — to thank you for the presents to come. Yes — I will keep them with Fido's & we will open them together, Dec. 25, & talk of you & Susan & our visits. I don't like *mixing* this but you will understand — *two* — thank you for your *Madrigal* effort. Marya wrote, saying Grove had seen the H.D. picture she had, & wanted it. I said that you & I had thought (had we?) that another photograph of the same period would be better & I sent her a larger print of the little picture I sent you. But in the mad-Madrigal wood, I said that I wanted the title back. (I had not then, had your letter, re same.) After I sent out Marya's letter, *yours* came, so mad-Madrigal I was, & wrote Horace, asking if Grove could do another title-page — well, *why* couldn't they? But do not *you* bother, I told Horace that I had nagged you enough.[166] I said that I would *pay* for new title-page — I don't think they'll do it, & hope if they do, I won't be let in for too much. I felt denuded, naked, my original name, Delia Alton gone, my title gone. Now this — can they leave me a shred of protection on the blurb? Could it start in large letters or coloured letters (or red-lights on Broadway) — "MADRIGAL, the original title of this book etc. etc." Macmillan sent me the dust-jacket of *Avon*, before publication — could Grove send me *Madrigal*? I am sorry for this "Howl" — but things were so odd & real, R[ichard] A[ldington] simply stepped out of the book & we went on, calmly, where we left off. Apropos "Howl" — one remove. R[obert] Duncan never had *Helen*. He wrote that he had photostat of the *Coda* sent him. I sent him $30 for "stamps" or/and Christmas, & asked him to send *Vale-Ave* & *Sagesse* MSS to you. I am pleased that he will be seeing you.

I had extraordinary letters — from George Plank & Cole (Henderson) as if it was their "story" and apparently the legend does go on or "belong" in some strange way. Fido will have told you of Marya's letter. I made no mention of the re-marriage myth in writing her. [Note in margin: She said Covici of Viking had heard from someone — who? — that R.A. & H.D. were to "re-marry" —][167] Please forgive this untidy page — I write in early morning after breakfast — with *infinite* gratitude for *Madrigal*, however it turns out.[168] All love to S[usan] & C & you

from

H.

1. On 8 June 1957 Bryher wrote to Pearson: "[Aldington] treated Hilda shamefully, but if this reflurry of emotion helps her, fine. I turn into Amico in the poems. A half name for Fido."

2. Richard Aldington to H.D., 16 December 1950, 17 January 1953, unpublished letters. See also 20 December 1953 in Zilboorg's edition.

3. David Rattray (1935–), American poet and translator of French literature, who interviewed Pound at St. Elizabeths Hospital.

4. Richard Aldington to H.D., 7 March 1958, unpublished letter.

5. In the last entry, H.D. quotes from Pearson's letter of 8 July 1958, in which he describes the Pounds' departure on the *Cristoforo Colombo* and his own presentation of a yellow rose in H.D.'s name to Dorothy Pound. Cf. *End to Torment: A Memoir of Ezra Pound* (New York: New Directions, 1979), 62.

6. On 15 April 1958, Pearson defends his support of Pound against Bryher's aggrieved accusations. Although he joins her in deploring Pound's fascism and anti-Semitism, Pearson downplays these aspects of his work, placing them in the context of a struggle against communism. He writes: "Pound was never a Hitler man; he was only violently anti-Communist." Also, he disagrees with her about the value of Pound's poetry, calling the *Cantos* a "major achievement" and "the most ambitious poem of this century."

7. Sheri Martinelli (1918–1996), artist, began to visit St. Elizabeths regularly in 1952. She became devoted to Pound, sketched him, and was a mistress/muse. Pound wrote an introduction to a pamphlet containing reproductions of her work titled *La Martinelli* (Milan: Vanni Schiewiller, 1956).

8. Marcella Spann Booth (1932–), a young admirer from Texas, discovered Pound's poetry in college and came to visit him at St. Elizabeths Hospital. In 1957 she moved to Washington to become a regular member of the Pound circle, competing with Sheri Martinelli for Pound's attention. Miss Spann accompanied Pound and his wife, Dorothy, to Italy in 1958, staying until Dorothy Pound's annoyance compelled her to return to the United States.

9. Bryher to Pearson, 12 December 1957.

10. *Sagesse*, in *Hermetic Definition* (New York: New Directions, 1974), 74, 69.

11. H.D.'s earlier ineligibility for prizes in America played a part in Pearson's effort to help her regain American citizenship.

12. Robert Duncan (1919–1988), American poet associated with the Beats and the Black Mountain School, helped make San Francisco a poetry center. He described the influence of H.D.'s poetry and its relation to modernism in his *H.D. Book*, and he wrote a sequence of poems for H.D.'s birthday.

13. In his letter of 9 January 1957, Pearson enclosed a royalty check from RCA Victor to H.D. for a poem read on one of their records.

14. Bryher's banker in England.

15. Urged by Bryher, on 9 January 1957, Pearson suggested that H.D. reclaim American citizenship before the publication of *Selected Poems* so that she would be eligible for prizes.

16. H.D. probably refers to a Christmas gift from Pearson.

17. Prominent psychiatrists in Switzerland.

18. H.D.'s *Tribute to Freud*.

19. Henry Lüdeke (1889–1962), a friend of Pearson's, was a scholar who wrote critical books on Chaucer, Shakespeare, and topics in American literature.

20. H.D. refers to unselected letters dated 23 and 26 January. In the first, Pearson asked her to verify a few dates in connection with a biographical sketch to be published in *Encyclopedia Americana*.

21. In his biographical sketch of H.D., Pearson included the following quotation from Pound about H.D.'s early poetry: "This is the sort of American stuff that I can show here and in Paris without its being ridiculed. . . . Objective — no slither; direct — no excessive use of adjectives, no metaphors that won't permit examination. It's straight talk, straight as the Greek! And it was only by persistence that I got to see it at all."

22. Pearson offered to send extra copies of *Tribute to the Angels*, which he bought from Oxford University Press.

23. Pearson asked H.D. for fifty autographed copies of *Selected Poems* and about the possibility of recording a group of them.

24. H.D. describes dreaming that her mother is about to be raped in the first entry (12 January 1957) of her "Hirslanden Notebooks" (unpublished M S, BL).

25. Max Schur (1897–1969), received his M.D. from the University of Vienna in 1921; a member of the American Psychoanalytic Association, he was also on the faculty of Downstate Medical Center, SUNY.

26. Maria Bonaparte (1882–1962), Princess Marie of Greece and Denmark, was analyzed by Freud in Vienna between 1925 and 1929. Later she became an analyst and was active in the Paris Psychoanalytic Society.

27. J. J. van der Leeuw (1893–1932), whom H.D. refers to as "the Flying Dutchman" in *Tribute to Freud*, wrote several books about theosophy: *The Fire of Creation* (1926), *Gods in Exile* (1926), and *Conquest of Illusion* (1928), all three of which Pearson eventually sent to H.D. In an unselected letter, dated 10 February 1957, he mentions that H.D.'s inquiry to Dr. Schur about van der Leeuw set up a chain of correspondence.

28. On 4 January [1957], H.D. mentions to Pearson that Horace Gregory sent her a book by or about Henry James. She writes, "[A]nd I will travel back to Europe with some of the Florence associations."

29. In this letter Aldington also wrote: "Have you seen the *Paris Tribune* for today the 2nd Feb? It contains a front-page sensational attack on Ezra who is alleged to have influenced a certain John Kasper to anti-negro racist efforts in the South. The article is raucous and American-philistine-yahoo, and seems designed to get E[zra] deprived of the privileges and amenities he enjoys."

30. Wyndham Lewis (1882–1957), English painter, novelist, and critic. Like H.D. and Aldington, he was part of the circle around Ford Madox Ford and Violet Hunt in his early days and he coedited *Blast: Review of the Great English Vortex* with Pound in 1914–15. Later his polemical writing style and attraction to fascism made him a controversial figure.

31. Clare Booth Luce (1903–1987), playwright, editor, and war correspondent, during World War II, for *Life*, *Time*, and *Fortune*, magazines owned by her husband, Henry

Luce. She also served in various charitable and diplomatic offices; she was the American ambassador to Italy in the 1950s.

32. H.D. refers to Pearson's having assured Pound that both she and Aldington received copies of his translation of Sophocles' *Women of Trachis*.

33. H.D. refers to the recording of *Helen*.

34. On 20 March [1957], H.D. wrote that Aldington's new book, *Introduction to Mistral* (London: Heinemann, 1956), was well received. She continued that he, too, worried about Pound and hoped he could be put in a private clinic.

35. *Selected Poems* was part of the Grove Evergreen series.

36. On 1 June 1957, Pearson wrote that the *New Yorker* would publish H.D.'s poem "The Moon."

37. On 21 June 1957, Pearson responded: "*Vale Ave* has just arrived and I have read it through once with great pleasure. The metrics are wonderfully exciting and just enough off-beat to be truly fresh. Surely this is a truly personal poem and a private one in the sense that it communicates most to those who know why the air marshal and the time in bed have meaning in the structure. I was particularly struck by 18, 35, 51 and 66 on the first reading; but of course a first reading only spins the kaleidoscope. . . . Amico [Bryher] will be most proud."

38. H.D. refers to a card Pearson sent from a visit to Longfellow's house.

39. H.D. dedicated *Selected Poems* to her grandchildren.

40. H.D. probably refers to Dame Edith Sitwell.

41. Cf. Catullus's "Atque in perpetuum, frater, ave atque vale," from *Carmina*, 29.l.10.

42. On 30 May Pearson mentioned meeting some of Hawthorne's friends' descendants in Maine.

43. H.D. encloses four small corrections to the typescript at the beginning of the M S, p. 3.

44. H.D. refers to the trip to the Arctic planned by Pearson and Bryher.

45. On 5 July [1957] H.D. responds: "[G]ood of C & C to approve V[ale] & A[ve]. Title for IV is well named. I do not know about XVIII — I think the number is a mistake, for this Hugh who drags her 'through the hedge' is in a sense, an antidote or contrast to 'Lucifer,' as per your title. . . . XXXVII title is suggestive & poetic, & alleviates the 'I am old, old, old . . .' XL — *Amenti* seems inevitable — but isn't the poem too *personal*?"

46. In section IX of *Sagesse*, the speaker quotes Germain's criticism of the poem: "'isn't it over-weighted? / can you have so many angels' names, // a list of dates, months, days, / a prose in-set? or is it poetry? Egypt, // hieratic rhythm, then the most ordinary association'" (66).

47. Pearson sent parts of "Vale Ave" to *Poetry* and to the *Atlantic Monthly*.

48. Ernest Jones (1879–1958), British psychoanalyst and biographer of Freud. In his review of H.D.'s *Tribute to Freud*, he wrote: "[It is] surely the most delightful and precious appreciation of Freud's personality that is ever likely to be written. Only a fine creative artist could have written it" (*International Journal of Psychoanalysis* 38 [March–April 1957]: 126).

49. Ernest Jones, *The Life and Work of Sigmund Freud*, vol. 3, *The Last Phase, 1919–1939* (New York: Basic Books, 1957).

50. On 27 November 1959, Pearson responds: "I DO LIKE IT VERY MUCH" and suggests

publishing the whole sequence in the *Evergreen Review*. He also proposes the title "Sagesse" to indicate a "wider implication of response."

51. See note above.

52. *Sagesse* was inspired by a photo of an owl that appeared in *The Listener*. This photo was included when the first ten sections were published in the *Evergreen Review* 2, no. 5 (Summer 1958): 27–36.

53. Joseph Payne Brennan reviewed *Selected Poems* in *Essence* 16 (Winter 1957): 12. An acquaintance of Pearson's, he worked in the technical services department of the Yale libraries.

54. On 13 December 1957, Pearson responds: "You warn me not to 'loose him.' Nor will I, either that or lose him, for his eyes are keyholes. I was deeply moved by the last poem, to Germain, which makes one's heart skip a beat."

55. H.D. refers to section 23, line 9 of *Sagesse*.

56. H.D. refers to sections 20 and 21 of *Sagesse*.

57. On 18 January 1958, Pearson speculated that Pound would like the last sections of *Sagesse* because of the way H.D. "keeps the rhythm of speech."

58. David Rattray, "Weekend with Ezra Pound," *Nation* 135 (16 November 1957): 343–45.

59. Pearson wrote about the emotional problems of his youngest stepdaughter.

60. Sara De Ford, *Lectures on Modern American Poetry* (Tokyo: Hokuseido Press, 1957).

61. Lewis Leary, ed., *Motive and Method in the Cantos of Ezra Pound* (New York: Columbia University Press, 1954), contained essays from the English Institute of 1953, among them "The Metamorphosis of Ezra Pound," by Sister Bernetta Quinn.

62. Sister Mary Bernetta Quinn (1915–), entered the Order of Saint Francis in 1934 and became a professor of English specializing in American poetry. Her publications include *The Metamorphic Tradition in Modern Poetry: Essays on the Work of Ezra Pound, Wallace Stevens, T. S. Eliot, Hart Crane, Randall Jarrell, and William Butler Yeats* (1955) and *Ezra Pound: An Introduction to the Poetry* (1972).

63. Probably *Fisch und Schatten und andere Dichtungen* (Zurich: Im Verlag der Arche, 1954).

64. H.D. refers to a photo of herself that was in the Yale exhibition.

65. Leary, *Motive and Method*, includes an essay by Guy Davenport titled "Pound and Frobenius."

66. Ezra Pound and Marcella Spann, eds., *Confucius to Cummings: An Anthology of Poetry* (New York: New Directions, 1964). Pound nicknamed the book, which was for use in the schools, the "Spannthology."

67. Eva Hesse's *Wort und Weise* includes photo portraits of Pound dated 1908 and 1923, a photo of him with Ford Madox Ford dated 1932, and a later photo of Pound with two American government officials after World War II. The last is captioned "Der gefesselte Dichter."

68. "Ezra Pound May Escape Trial and Be Allowed to Go to Italy," the *New York Times*, Wednesday, 2 April 1958.

69. H.D. refers to the beginning of *End to Torment*.

70. In an unselected part of his letter of 30 March, Pearson mentioned giving permission to publish H.D.'s poem "Orchard" in an anthology.

71. Pearson's grandson.

72. Bryher's historical novel *Gate to the Sea* (New York: Pantheon, 1958) contains photographs of present-day Paestum by Islay de Courcy Lyons.

73. Craig La Drière, a professor at Catholic University, one of Pound's circle at St. Elizabeths.

74. In this letter, dated 5 April 1958, Bryher condemned Pound's fascism and his literary reputation. She wrote: "And why this worship of Ezra's poetry? His best lines are translations from other poets. Most of it is the outpouring of a diseased mind; even before the *Cantos* anyone with remote psychological training could see that the person who wrote the poems was insane or on the borderline. . . . What you all like in Ezra is that he has skimmed the cream from a great number of poets representing all stages in European culture that most of you are too lazy to read."

75. Elsie Volkart, Bryher's housekeeper.

76. Sylvia Beach (1887–1962), American-born publisher, writer, and bookseller. Her bookstore, Shakespeare & Co., became a social and literary mecca in Paris. A friend of Bryher and H.D., she was interned for anti-fascist activities during World War II.

77. Archibald MacLeish (1892–1982), Pulitzer Prize–winning poet, playwright, statesman; appointed librarian of Congress in 1939, assistant secretary of state in 1944; spoke out politically even after he left public politics to become Boylston Professor at Harvard University in 1949.

78. "U.S. Asked to End Pound Indictment," the *New York Times*, 15 April 1958.

79. On 27 April 1958, Pearson mentions having had a letter from Sheri Martinelli, "whose work [H.D.] may have seen in the little Vanni Schiewiller booklet devoted to her work, with an introductory note by the maestro himself."

80. Grove Press used a photo of H.D. by Bernhard Obrecht on the cover of its reprint of her *Selected Poems*.

81. Two of H.D.'s poems, "Fragment" and "Oread," were translated into Arabic.

82. Erich Heydt visited Robert Duncan in San Francisco on his trip to America.

83. Ramon Guthrie (1896–1973), American poet, novelist, and professor of French literature. In his poem "Ezra Pound in Paris and Elsewhere," in the *Nation*, 16 November 1957, 345, Guthrie remembers Pound's charisma and craftsmanship in his early days in Paris and asserts his continuing superiority to his attackers.

84. On 27 April 1958, Pearson mentioned that Elizabeth Schnack had taken hours of his time with questions about her translations of Faulkner.

85. Mary McGrory, "Ezra Pound Still Sees Mad World Out of Step," the *Washington Star*, 30 April 1958. McGrory reports Pound's visit to Rep. Eugene Burdick, to whom he continued to express the "virulent views" that got him indicted.

86. David Horton, coeditor with Kasper of the Square Dollar series.

87. In her response to this letter, dated 6 May [1958], H.D. wrote: "I don't seem to be able to write [Pound] — if & when you do, tell him . . . what? No words for the relief of UNK — some block, some black out, re it all."

88. Sheri Martinelli to Pearson, 20 May 1958, unpublished letter. Martinelli's tribute to H.D. begins: "Most high, most beautiful, most tragic, noblest and best of my sisters."

89. Martinelli to Pearson, 20 May 1958, unpublished letter. The part to H.D. continues: "[I]t made me so sad . . . that I was the one to be saved of all the poor peoples of this world and especially of my race."

90. On 1 June 1958 Pearson responds: "'Her race': Italian, obviously, 'human race,' perhaps — but she seems unworldly in a worldly way."

91. H.D. refers to a copyright matter and to an assurance from Grove Press that credit would be given to Obrecht for his photo of H.D. in *Selected Poems*.

92. On 25 May 1958 Pearson referred to photos of Martinelli and her husband, Gilbert Li.

93. H.D. refers to the new edition of *Selected Poems*.

94. On 23 June 1958, Pearson wrote that Martinelli's friend José Amaral was in a car accident en route to Mexico, where he was taking her work for a show.

95. In letters dated 6 and 13 June 1958, Pearson sent a request from a Miss Ashton, asking that H.D. write a poem inspired by pre-Columbian art.

96. Jack Kerouac, *On the Road* (New York: Viking, 1957).

97. On 13 June 1958, Pearson wrote that Martinelli offered him a picture of herself in a scanty bikini.

98. On 9 June 1958, Martinelli wrote: "Part of Marcella's hoop-skirt tactics were to pump up poor maestro's vanity." Later in the letter she implied that Marcella had used sex to lure Pound away, calling her "the Court-whore."

99. Kurt and Helen Wolff.

100. James Laughlin (1914–), American poet, founded New Directions when Pound advised him to take up publishing.

101. On 11 July 1958, Pearson wrote that he would forward her letter to Ezra and Dorothy to Castle Brunnenberg.

102. *Evergreen Review* 2, no. 5 (Summer 1958) contains part of *Sagesse*.

103. The issue of *Evergreen Review* with part of H.D.'s *Sagesse* had a photo of James Dean on the cover and included work by Samuel Beckett, Robert Creeley, Charles Olson, Denise Levertov, Jack Kerouac, Edward Dorn, and Kenneth Kotch.

104. In an unselected portion of his letter of 8 July, Pearson compared the "line" of Martinelli's drawings and paintings with that of Gaudier-Brzeska, the sculptor who helped Pound define the goals of the Vorticist movement.

105. H.D. refers to a five-foot nude, painted by Martinelli, that Pearson is housing temporarily in his office.

106. In an unselected portion of his letter of 8 July, Pearson has described this as a "mystical painting of Leucothe, on wood," intended as a gift for H.D.

107. On 11 July 1958, Pearson mentioned rumors about the parentage of Omar Pound.

108. H.D. refers to a letter from Bryn Mawr forwarded to her by Pearson in his letter of 22 November. Bryn Mawr would like to include one of her poems in a publication being prepared for the fiftieth reunion of her class.

109. On 13 December 1958, Pearson replies: "Why not try your introduction to *Sagesse*. I do think some sorts of semi-identification or comment would be helpful."

110. In this letter, Pearson quotes Sheri Martinelli as follows: "'Pearson mah man / grampa paid the rent and clothed and fed me for 4 years — one was his "paper daughter" at the office . . . so one could help out and give D[orothy] P[ound] a rest . . . by taking grampa out on the lawn / I loved him dearly as the only man who could stand up to my mind — and the terror of the last 4 years . . . was a love for him that he wanted to be physical — and I could not for anything in the world lie to him — not from pity or compassion . . . I loved him too much / indeed it was I who paid him the compliment of continuing to adore him when he physically frightened me.'"

111. H.D. refers to letters forwarded to her by Pearson.

112. H.D. refers to what will become her poem "Winter Love." In his reply, dated 10 January 1959, Pearson writes: "I was much intrigued by the suggestion that you might go on to another half of *Sagesse*. It sounds like an exciting possibility, but you will have to see how the muse strums on your soul."

113. Nikos Kazantzakis, *The Odyssey: A Modern Sequel*, trans. Kimon Friar (New York: Simon and Schuster, 1958), is a book-length poem that takes up the story of Odysseus where Homer left off and recounts the hero's search for God.

114. In his reply of 12 January 1959, Pearson mentions two possible reasons for Pound's not knowing him: "One is that he has never called me Norman, or referred to me as such — you have not called me that to him, but referred to me as Pearson . . . he thinks that there may be another Norman in your life. . . . The second might be quite truthfully that he does not 'know' Norman, in the sense of putting quotation marks around the cognition, and therefore would not know my 'stance.'" Also, in this letter, he suggests that the book needs "no dedication at all, except to Ezra."

115. Pound refers to Andrew Russell Pearson (1897–1969), the influential newspaperman, whose syndicated column was very widely read.

116. On 6 February [1959], H.D. described the new poem as "a sequence, though hardly a *Canto* or 'big poem.' It keeps the connection with the original and the 'early H.D.,' too."

117. On 13 November [1958], H.D. wrote that she sent "*End* to R.A. to get 'outside opinion.'"

118. H.D. added a sentence to the manuscript in which she acknowledged the hardships of Sylvia Beach's confinement in a detention camp.

119. On 24 January 1959, Pearson responds: "And I agree too that Ezra would not be likely to understand *End*; indeed, why should he really. He can [think] back to Dryad, but not to what happened afterwards: what it is that has its 'End.' I think you know what I mean."

120. On 12 January, Pearson mentioned having had a letter from Heydt, who is pleased with his new apartment, away from troublesome patients in the clinic.

121. On 12 January, Pearson described a triangle comprising himself, Pound, and H.D. as a "magic," "cabalistic" mystery.

122. On 13 December 1958, Pearson wrote that Lloyd Nelson, a vice consul at the State Department, would send H.D.'s passport.

123. On 18 January 1959, Pearson wrote that he sent out "The Shell," a portion of *Sagesse*. He asks for instruction about quotation marks.

124. On 18 January 1959, Pearson mentioned Martinelli's recent drawings of herself and Pound, which she plans to send to H.D.

125. On 24 January 1959, Pearson responds: "I am very excited and eager to see 'Magic Mirror,' which will be entre nous. One can't really be German — 'zwischen uns' becomes too close to 'zwischen *unser*'; he can still be in the [△] but now it will be us looking at his [○]. Substantive or not, I can't help but believe that there was an [○] from which *you* saved him. It was you, you know, who really had unser on the couch (bench), whether he knows it or not."

126. H.D. refers to Pearson's having mentioned that his stepdaughter returned home from the hospital.

127. On 6 February 1959, H.D. writes that she is "very upset" about this occurrence: "My 'Viking Ship' comes back, with 'other phantom ships.'"

128. In 1959, Ellis's centennial, two books were published about him: John Stewart Collins, *Havelock Ellis: Artist of Life* (New York: W. Sloane Associates) and Arthur Calder-Marshall, *The Sage of Sex: A Life of Havelock Ellis* (New York: Putnam). Ellis traveled with H.D. and Bryher part of the way to Corfu in 1920.

129. H.D. was the third American poet to win the Brandeis Creative Arts Medal. The first two were William Carlos Williams and John Crowe Ransom. In 1959 the poetry jury included J. V. Cunningham (chair), Lloyd Frankenberg, Barbara Howes, Stanley Kunitz, and Henry Rago.

130. Pearson did read "Compassionate Friendship." On 5 April 1959, he wrote to H.D.: "It is really fine; you must not belittle it. I could only wish that you would take it up again as of Erik's resettlement. For me it has double value; it puts my hand in yours, or rather takes it in yours, and I am grateful to you for sharing the passion; and of course, like the Delia Alton notes, of which this is intermittently a continuation, I learn by just this sharing. . . . There is really very fine writing in these meditations — very straight, seismographic, evidential."

131. On 25 March, H.D. reports having received pictures of "the Schloss group" from Viola Jordan; on 25 March, Pearson writes that Pound and Dorothy have "returned to settle in Rapallo."

132. Pearson did attend the ceremony, which he described in his letter of 15 April 1959, noting especially the "long and fine tribute" made to H.D. by Stanley Kunitz, who presented the award.

133. Charles Norman, author of an early biography, *Ezra Pound* (1960), had queried H.D. in March about her early relationship with Pound. She passed the query on to Norman Holmes Pearson, who answered for her.

134. H.D. responds here to Pearson's reference, in his letter of 15 April, to Eliot's dedicatory poem in his new play, *The Elder Statesman* (1959). Pearson called the poem "embarrassingly porno."

135. Michael Harald was associated with the *European*. On 9 April 1959, H.D. wrote to Pearson that Aldington told her Harald was in touch with Pound, who complained he wasn't getting books and magazines.

136. H.D. refers to the following line of explanation accompanying her medal: "Her literary ambitions were stimulated by her friendship with Ezra Pound and William Carlos Williams (winner of the 1957 Brandeis Creative Arts Award)."

137. William D. Rogers, the American lawyer who arranged H.D.'s passport, did not charge for his services. In appreciation she sent him autographed copies of some of her books.

138. H.D. refers to William Van O'Connor and Edward Stone, eds., *A Casebook on Ezra Pound* (1959). Pearson mentioned the book in his letter of 2 May 1959 and asked if she wanted a copy to send to Aldington.

139. H.D. refers to *Poetry* 94 (May 1959), in which, as part of the note on contributors, Pearson wrote: "H.D. was given the Gold Medal for Poetry last month in the Brandeis University Creative Arts Award, and *Poetry*'s Harriet Monroe Memorial Prize last November. She lives outside Zurich but has recently repatriated herself as an American citizen. (By a ruling which has been amended since that time, she had automatically

lost her citizenship at the time of her marriage.) Grove published her *Selected Poems* in an Evergreen paperback a few years ago."

140. Grove Press published the first unexpurgated text of Lawrence's novel in May 1959, but it was banned as obscene by the postmaster of New York City, who stopped its distribution through the U.S. mail. Grove then brought suit, claiming that the novel should have the protection of the First Amendment. The case was decided in favor of the novel's literary merit in July 1959.

141. Colin Wilson (1931–), prolific British writer of nonfiction, novels, biographies, plays. His first book was *The Outsider* (1956).

142. H.D. responds to a query from Pearson, on 16 June 1959, about whether Mary de Rachewiltz adopted a little girl.

143. H.D. means *A Casebook on Ezra Pound*.

144. On 16 June Pearson commented on the mysterious way in which "Winter Love" seemed a sequel or coda to *Helen in Egypt*. He wrote: "[I]t ["Winter Love"] was not overtly written as such, could not have been planned, simply worked itself out through the subconscious, given an unexpected occasion in history. I keep calling things your Cantos. This Winter Love section is really like the Pisan section, calling up what goes before — as in a moment of stasis which is climactic. I liked *Helen* before; I like it twice as much with the *bon chance* of Winter Love."

145. Kimon Friar translates book 3, lines 1073–76, of Kazantzakis's poem as follows: "Perhaps a lightning moment passed, perhaps ten years, / Those ten years that had flashed to take those toppling towers; / All things now turned to stone and in the heart lay still, / And dull life burst with stars, and turned to fabled myth."

146. On 24 June 1959, Pearson wrote that Duncan asked for H.D.'s address in order to send her a copy of *The Opening of the Field*.

147. Pearson has described the failing health of his mother.

148. On 1 August 1959 Pearson responds: "I should think Unser might well like to visit Robert Duncan in his 'pad,' and would find him cool, man, cool. Have you managed to converse with Unser in all this jargon of theirs? I find it fascinating, even though a bit altmodish. I am curious about your final reactions to the book [*The Holy Barbarians*], after the case histories . . . were cleared away and one got into the 'argument' or 'rationale.'"

149. H.D. refers to the prospective birth of Perdita's fourth child.

150. H.D. refers to the script of Pearson's TV broadcast on Pound that she forwarded to Pound.

151. On 14 July 1959, Pearson mentions that he has sent "two novels by Kazantzakis which may interest you because of the *Helen*." Later letters reveal that they were *Zorba the Greek* and *The Greek Passion*.

152. John Senior, *The Way Down and Out: The Occult in Symbolist Literature* (Ithaca: Cornell University Press, 1959).

153. On 21 July 1959, Pearson mentions having sent two clippings: one about the "owl cult" that Robert Duncan had written her of and the other about the outcome of the lawsuit involving Lawrence's *Lady Chatterley*.

154. *Letters* (1955).

155. H.D. refers to the pregnancy of Pearson's stepdaughter Susan.

156. Duncan's letter, dated 15 August 1959, appears in Robert J. Bertholf, ed., *A Great Admiration: H.D./Robert Duncan, Correspondence 1950–1961* (Venice: Lapis Press, 1992), 12–13.

157. On 9 September 1959, Pearson asked if she had a copy of the novel to work on should she want to make changes in punctuation.

158. On 17 September [1959], H.D. continues to express anxiety about publication: "[F]orgive *Madrigal* hysteria of my last letter. I am *afraid* to be published, but feel the mss are sprouting wings and want to get *out*."

159. On 24 September [1959], H.D. responds: "I am just stuck, I can not say *yes* to *Madrigal*, without its wind-screen or very obvious protective coloration of D[elia] A[lton] — but Br[yher] comes Monday & I will go into this. . . . I guess reading the *Gift*, with its long *Appendix* has unsettled me a little."

160. On 5 October 1959, Bryher writes to Pearson about Hilda's anxiety around the visit of Catha Aldington: "Hilda seemed very nervous this last time but that was perhaps natural; she equated Catherine with the baby she had with Aldington that died at birth."

161. In his letter of 2 September 1959, Pearson enclosed a clipping about a visiting Buddhist monk he had hosted in the summer.

162. Aldington's actual visit proved to be less troubling to H.D. than the anticipation of it. On 27 November she wrote to Pearson that he is "mature, worldly, amusing and paid *no* attention to Joan who seems to have fallen for him." And on November 30 she reported that even Bryher enjoyed talking politics and literature with him.

163. On 12 November 1959 Pearson commented on the "mystery" of Aldington's reappearance in H.D.'s life just as *Bid Me to Live* is about to appear. He wrote: "I feel, a little, within your skin; you must forgive me and make room for me."

164. Both H.D. and Bryher admired J. R. R. Tolkien's *The Lord of the Rings* (1955).

165. H.D. refers to speculation about Sheri Martinelli's use of drugs.

166. On 30 November [1959], emboldened by Aldington, H.D. asked Pearson if they could "retrieve" the *Madrigal* title.

167. On 15 December 1959, Pearson responds to H.D.'s query: "I can only presume that Covici's romantic mind must have picked up some false clue from Richard's letters to him — he is, I think, Richard's editor at Viking — and thought he was again in pursuit of your heart instead of his own gallbladder. And maybe he was. Who knows!"

168. On 6 January [1960], H.D. writes happily that Horace Gregory suggested the title *Bid Me to Live (A Madrigal)*, which solves the problem.

CHAPTER SIX

"Grove of Academe"

1960-1961

Publication of *Tribute to Freud* and *Selected Poems*, accolades from *Poetry* and Brandeis University, American citizenship regained: these events led to the culminating moment of H.D.'s last years, her reception, in person, of the award in poetry from the American Academy of Arts and Letters, its first to a woman. After years of critical neglect, such recognition by her peers must have seemed a manifestation of her vision on Corfu, forty years earlier, of being welcomed into the sun disk. For H.D. incorporated it into the central section of her last poem, *Hermetic Definition*, written during this period. Titled "Grove of Academe," this section alludes not only to specifics of the above event — particularly a gallant gesture by St.-John Perse,[1] whose poetry she quotes and responds to; it also acknowledges, more tacitly, her gratitude at having been nurtured and sustained by her "chevalier" at Yale, Norman Holmes Pearson. In fact, as these letters reveal, H.D. proposed dedicating the poem to him.

Plans to attend the award ceremony in New York, in May 1960, began in Küsnacht in February. They intersected with the publication of *Bid Me to Live (A Madrigal)*, which appeared in March of that year, bringing with it H.D.'s last romantic attachment. When Lionel Durand,[2] the Haitian-born chief of the Paris bureau of *Newsweek*, came to Zurich to interview H.D. about the book, she was smitten. In letters to Pearson she comments on his dignified bearing, his personal charm, and, several times, the implications of his color and racial background. Later, they also speculate about Durand's possible mixed allegiance during the war in Algeria, which H.D. follows closely through his reportage. Indeed, H.D.'s strong feelings about Durand generated the first section of *Hermetic Definition*, "Red Rose and a Beggar," the content and intensity of which embarrassed her. She did not show the poem to Pearson until its completion after Durand's death, which she saw as a harbinger of her own.[3]

H.D. and Pearson also continue to exchange news about Erich Heydt, Richard Aldington, and Ezra Pound in this interval. H.D. reports further on the psychological repercussions of Heydt's marriage, which she also documents in the journal "Bosquet (Thorn Thicket)," composed in 1960. She describes Aldington's reactions to *Bid Me to Live*, mentions Bryher's more generous attitude toward him since his recent visit, and responds to news of Pound's difficulties and depression. Repeating his encouragement during the composition of *End to Torment*, Pearson supports H.D.'s wish to meet Ezra and Dorothy Pound in Venice despite Bryher's anticipated disapproval. They also discuss new interpretations of the work of Pound and herself, with Pearson conveying reports about the progress of poets Robert Duncan, Denise Levertov,[4] and Thomas Burnett Swann,[5] whose interest in H.D. Pearson encouraged. He thought especially highly of Duncan's response to H.D.'s late poetry, commissioning him to write a book for her birthday that became *The H.D. Book*.

In the following letters, H.D. responds to Pearson's announcement of the academy's award with a mixture of anxiety, pleasure, and excitement.

231 HGS
Yale University
New Haven, Conn.
10 February 1960

Dearest Hilda,

[. . .]

This afternoon I was called by the Secretary of the American Academy of Arts and Letters in New York, to say that the Academy by mail ballot of all the Academicians had voted to award you their Special Award of Merit at their annual convocation on May 26th in New York City. This is given only every five years for poetry, and consists of a gold medal and $1,000. (Naturally I want the gold medal to take the place of the one I lost for you last year.) It has only been awarded three times: to W.H. Auden, to St. John Perse, and to Jorge Dias.[6] You are the first woman ever to be given this. One does not have to be an academician to win it — in fact one is supposed not to — but one does have to be in America to receive it, and they could not hold another election now that everyone has made up his mind that it should go to you. Perhaps I am a little responsible, because I said something casually to Louise Bogan[7] early last fall, that I hoped you would be over in the spring for a brief visit. [MS: Naturally I knew nothing of the award.]

Will you come and not disappoint them? I know you would not come for the honor, although it is the biggest honor they give, but you really must save my reputation.

I know all this will come like a bombshell, and seem impossible at first. And that you will want to talk it over with Unser perhaps, and Fido certainly. You can show Unser this letter, but so Fido will understand I am sending a carbon of it directly to her when I go to the post-office now to get it in the mail as quickly as possible. The Academy says it can wait for a couple of weeks for your answer. Of course I think it simply wonderful that they have chosen you for the honor of being the first woman to receive the Award. But I am selfish, and what I like best is the chance that it will give us to see you. Susan will feel as excited as I do when I tell her tonight. (I had to stay down for a Fellows' meeting at the college.)

Somehow, and I don't know why, I can't help feeling all this working out as it has is a part of the Mystery in which you have let me share. That it is somehow a means for bringing us together again just now, of letting you have a glimpse of the children, of being here just after the publication of *Madrigal*, though not having to partake in all the publication cocktail parties, of (and you will know how pleased Grove will be to have the prize so soon after the novel is published) speeding up almost certainly the publication of *Helen*, and, in so many ways, being a part of the cycle and circle. When it is the Mystery one follows it.

> With excited love,
> Yr
> C.

---------- 152. MS ----------

Yes! Dear C.,

I come to you like the very dear & charming little Christmas child, with a lot of "too tight" string to unfasten. *Yes!* I am proud & very happy about the new Award & I will come & fetch the gold medal, if only for the pleasure of handing it on to you. I think that I had a leaflet sent me of the A[cademy] of A[rts] and L[etters] — description of a huge banquet. Is this it? I don't think I could face such a thing. I might *try*. I will talk it all over with Fido, who is due now, after tea. I have been a bit nagged & harassed by *Unser*, & his ideas of what I should do — slightly sadistic of late. But I did have a quarrel last time & have had time to re-adjust a bit, as they both have had grippe. He may be different when he gets out again. He will be *stunned* by the news — & I can go on from there. No *Madrigal* folder has come, I long for it — probably it will arrive tomorrow, this is Sunday. No, I would not consider Joan.[8] She is interesting & fascinating, but I wouldn't have time for her "too tight" string. Anyway, she is taking her holiday in Aug., when *Unser* is presumably away. Fido has been very persistent, for some time, "now, you *must* arrange for someone to be with you." This will work out in time, I *know*. I don't want to be *forced* into some artificial, frustrating, daily, hourly contact. I know the snags too damn well. But I am keeping "companion secretary" idea in mind & will write you for advice, either as from this or your end.

Who is Jorge Dias or Dian? *Please.*

264   "Grove of Academe," 1960–1961

Feb. 15

There is so very, very much to say, but I want Fido to take this out now.

I owe it *all to you.*

I will write soon again.

   Terribly

   excited,

with much love to S[usan] who has helped you help me — and on her own, sustains us.

Ever & ever,

H.

N.B. I have the [word?] *Longview* list.[9] I will study it and return. But *where* is *Madrigal* folder?[10]

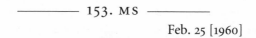 153. MS

Feb. 25 [1960]

Dear Norman,

Thank you for two letters & the MacLeish pages.[11] This is a great help to me. It is just as well that I asked you about Guillen.[12] Is there no Auden[13] speech? And tell me the exact dates of the 3, though I could work that out. I have "practiced" extemp[oraneous] speeches to myself but they are all bright and facetious (?) & not in line with St. Leger etc. Could you not sketch out a speech for me, as Churchill is supposed to have done for "Prince Edward?"[14] No. I won't tell Swann.[15] I think I will consult Fido & keep quiet generally. I am relieved that there is no banquet. *I do congratulate you both on the Anniversary.* I am glad you understand about the Valentine that E[rich] & D[ori] wept over.[16] I have a new rapport with *Unser,* as he very occasionally gives a sort of cat-hiss & bats the air with a paw. This happened yesterday. I said, "how wonderful . . . I remember the first time you did that, making a bandage for me, in the dispensary . . . I was pseudo-modest . . . & you did that cat or jaguar." *Unser* said, "Dori *hates* it." So we will keep our early rapport. Poor Dori — one often wonders. I begged them not to send me award-flowers, so they had an enlargement made & beautifully mounted of a sort of visionary N[ew] Y[ork], seen from Park, across trees, that Dori took — very mirage-like and Arabian Nights. By the way, did you ever get a letter from me, with a note in pen or pencil at end-page by *Unser*? We were out for coffee & I asked him to post the letter. He said he could never be trusted to post his own or other people's letters. . . .

There is so much more to say — all blessings to S[usan] & S[usan] II, we are all waiting together.

I will see Fido, D[eo] V[olente], about March 4 & we will go into "award" & *Madrigal* details —

> Gratefully, dear C,
>
> *H.*

At the end of February, Perdita's fourth child, Timothy, is born, adding to H.D.'s excitement about the publication of *Madrigal* [17] and her coming trip to New York. In March, she and Pearson discuss further details of the trip, particularly who will accompany her. H.D. doesn't want Heydt, with whom she has been quarreling, and she suggests that even Richard Aldington "would be better" (6 March). It is noteworthy that Bryher is not mentioned in this regard, although the following letters suggest that H.D. assumed her presence in New York as late as the end of March. [18] Also, H.D. is pleased to hear from Bryn Mawr that she is to have a "citation" at the seventy-fifth convocation of the university. [19] The most important event in March, however, is a telegram from Pearson, alerting H.D. to the desire of *Newsweek* in Paris to interview her in connection with their review of her new novel. The following letters document both her ambivalence about this news and then her strong response to the interview with Lionel Durand.

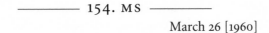

154. MS

March 26 [1960]

Dear Norman,

I have a very nice letter from *Newsweek*, Lionel Durand, chief, Paris Bureau. He says that he wants to come between April 3 — 10. Now, Catha will be here April 4–7 — And R[ichard] A[ldington] will be here for a few days, before going on to Kenwin for a little visit. We had lunch with R.A. & his Australian friends, the Duttons. He is at present (G. Dutton) [20] a prof. Litt. at Leeds. We had a very gay time. I want to fit in Mr. Durand. Fido & I will talk it over this week-end. He must not take pictures of me, like the funnies of Ezra in a recent *Newsweek* issue. Could I get glossies made by Obrecht from the 1956 set? I could get *Unser* to ring him. I do not yet know if or/and when I could see Mr. Durand, but I will write, in any case. You see, I did not speak to R. A. of this yesterday but he wrote & wired that I must not see *Newsweek*. This is very, very un-nerving.

Erich Walter White (the Arts Council of Great Britain, 4 St. James Square, London S.W. 1) is here. We had coffee with him & *Unser* after the Dutton party — it was almost too much. I gave E. W. W. address again, as he is very keen on getting the *Freud* & the *Madrigal* placed in England. He is about the only person in England who cares, really, for my work. I told him that *everything* was in your hands, but I knew that you would be open to suggestions. He will be coming later to USA (autumn, I think) and you & Susan must see him. You will really like him. He liked the *Newsweek* letter & was most sympathetic about the R. A. letters & telegram — & general conflict.

Thank you for March 20 letter & this morning's N. Y. *Times* with Islay's picture. I like your choice of it — thank you again. I can't plan N. Y. theatres — but thank you. My very best to Susans II, III, IV & little Justus.[21] I will write again. *Unser* no doubt will help on Mon[day] & we see E. W. White tomorrow again.

All, all thanks & love from

H.

Fido has *tentatively* booked me, Swissair, *May 13*, arriving *14th* with a Schwester. *Not final.*

———— 155. MS ————

March 31 [1960]

Dear Norman,

The A[merican] A[cademy] of A[rts] and L[etters] asks for the names of "not more than five friends" for the Ceremonial. I am sending you & Susan, Perdita & John & Fido. I hope that this is all right.

I had your March 27 letter yesterday. I spoke to E[ric] W[alter] White about the R[ichard] A[ldington] wire, he just laughed. He read the letter from Lionel Durand of *Newsweek* & thought it tactful & dignified. Now, I have written Mr. Durand to come April 3 or 4 or 8, 9, 10. He said that he might come between 3 & 10. I said that the idea of interview embarrassed me, because of my fracture, difficulty of meeting here etc., but I wanted to make the effort as Prof. Pearson had suggested it. I have not yet heard from Mr. D. but I will write you. I will do *anything*, radio, television, *if I can*. I have not been away for over 3 years. Thanks for Limited "legwork." [22] I am under impression Pearson was in list — if not, please keep extra — or send Fido. Thank you for F[rancis] Wolle. I thought he was on my list, but I can't find his name. No. [Dorothy] Cole is *not* in *Madrigal* except at parties — I read & re-read the blurb — *and* the book. I am apprehensive about next week, 5, 6, 7 April, as Fido asked Catha here for a sort of check-up with Dr. Dori. To my surprise, Mr. A. is coming, too. I think this will negate our influence with Catha. Mr. A. was in terrific form last Friday, when we had lunch with him & his Australian friends, the Duttons. He will go from here with Catha to Kenwin, for a few days. I can not take this in *at all* & *Unser*, though professionally discreet, seems also flabbergasted but non-commital. It seems *too much* on top of everything — & I am dragging out the end of a sort of suppressed (by inoculation) grippe.

Thanks *very* much for van der Leeuw suggestion.[23] I think that I have the book, Fido stacked small books behind big books, I am in that state just now. I have touched on him in these new notes, Jan. 1, Feb. 29, 1960 — & one extra for March 23, "The child & the book are adequately synchronized."[24]

Thank you for all the "little checks" & all that great work.

I am feverish when I think of this change — even if I don't come, my whole metab(?)ism is changed. Possibly my companion would be Sister Regina, a very pretty & tactful young German girl. We will see —

ever with love to all,

H.

Birthday thoughts, *all the time!*

——————— 156. M S ———————

[April 5, 1960]

Dearest N.,

"Mine eyes have seen the glory of the coming of the Lord" — for which, grateful thanks! Fido thinks he must be Martinique. I didn't dare ask him. He is Lionel Durand, Chief, Paris Bureau, *Newsweek*. He is tall; standing against the window in the hall, I just saw the impressive statue, stature, strong, graceful, he comes forward to greet me!! He is half something, Spanish? "I am French," he tells me, when I ask how people pronounce his name. It was the rugged, graceful strength . . . he wrote on his knee, everything I said & I said nothing of importance. *Unser* was shocked, "didn't you even talk about Kazan[tzakis] & Perse?" No, I just drifted along & trust I was not too indiscreet. It didn't matter; anyhow, one meets such a *chef* once in a lifetime. Suavity, charm, simplicity, kindness — not too young, shade of della Fountaine (spelling), I imagine. He had not had *Madrigal* & I lent him my copy, but I had to write his name in it, so I have only my No. 1 Limited, which I will give Fido for Easter, unless her copy went out. Can you get another copy for me? I had my first letter, ordinary *Mad*[rigal] list, from Swann, so American copies are getting around now. Mr. or M. Durand had not had a copy, he was reading the one I gave him (he said, he would send me his, when it came) on train to Geneva. He took the early 1917 study & Obrecht's front-face, which you had not used, looking out — & the Beethoven. I told him you wanted to reserve the Beethoven, but he said, it wouldn't break across, as the reproduction would not be very large. He wanted to take pictures, but seemed to like the 3 I gave him. He said he would return them.

I am 2 weeks on with grippe-cold — but nothing matters. I can dream through Aldingtons' visit with Martinique — & dear Fido is here. *Unser* seemed very impressed with my *chef* connection — again, thank you.

I like the way you produced the Yale picture, Sylvia B[each] sent it.

Love to S[usan] & S[usan] & S[usan] & C.

from

H.

──────── 157. MS ────────

April 14 [1960]

Dearest Norman,

A Happy Easter to you all! It is 4 weeks to-day to Thurs. May 12, when I Swissair, *if* I Swissair. Most important, please note: Lionel Durand.

c/o Foreign Department,

Newsweek, 444 Madison Ave., N.Y.C.

He will be in N.Y. between April 15 & May 15. I don't know if I could or should see him, but if I write to that effect, I will say that I am leaving it to Prof. Pearson, as I don't know what he has planned for me. He says, "I will probably speak with Professor Pearson," so I gather he wants to see you. He wrote me of *Madrigal* & the meeting here, "Both are the sort of 'white stones' which, as the French say, should mark one's path in life." I have had amazing, not to say hair-raising letters, La M[artinelli], George Plank, this call from McDougall that Fido told you of — & so on. Probably Fido wrote of plan to take Blanche Brunner, Dr. Rudolf Brunner's 21 year old daughter, as "secretary." She was at St. Moritz as laboratory assistant & now is getting married in fall, so I judge she is giving up her job. It was Frau Dr. B[runner] who suggested this & it is splendid, as they have near friends in N.Y. & the girl can be much on her own. On the other hand, she is intelligent & attractive & could be with us, anywhere. But I told them & everyone, that I am *not sure* about May 12–13. I must have a loop-hole or a mouse-hole emergency exit, as I tell Fido.

Thank you for all anthology arrangements — you are much too good!

Tell me, if you can, why Durand speaks & writes such perfect English? He tells me he will send me another *Madrigal*, but tell him, if it comes up, not to. But I will try to write him.

Thank you for *all* — & blessings for S[usan] & S[usan] & S[usan] & V[alentine] & C always

from

H.

————— 158. TS —————

231 HGS
Yale University
New Haven, Conn.
April 24, 1960

Dearest Hilda,

[...]

No word from Durand, but I presume all is well in that bureau. One guesses he must be creole, which is an exciting combination. I will drop him a note, but better *after* whatever appears in *Newsweek*. One does not want to seem to press. I am amused at your various echo-notes from *Madrigal*. You will naturally want to keep, but do bring them along when you come so that we can giggle together about them, over a bottle of wine. (Shall I have Chianti in store for you, or some vin rouge?)

Blanche seems sweet, and by her name suitable for a role in the Helen cycle. I shall pray she likes me.

However I did have the chance to meet your Duncan who proved to be very attractive indeed, exceptionally well-read and well-housebroken, and with an uncanny understanding of what you are after. It is a little frightening to find him with all the right props. He came in the morning of Wednesday, and was nicely self-sufficient during my absence to address the Kiwanis Club and teach my graduate seminar. We had a few people out to dinner to meet him, and then I introduced him for his reading in the evening. He did an excellent job of it, has splendid enunciation, and makes remarks of the right sort in between his selections. He read the birthday sequence in your honor, and I realized how much of an offering it was, stripping himself open as it were for your praise. He is doing several readings, and his book *The Field* is now to be brought out in the fall by Grove rather than by Macmillan. He has real integrity, and I think you would like him.

[...]

All love,
Yr C.

April 30 [1960]

Dearest N.,

Thank you for all arrangements. I have just written John S[chaffner] to confirm later — & *not* to break across *your* good ideas, *but* I would rather have one small room on the quiet side than the royal suite on traffic; but perhaps rooms would be high up & out of it. And Blanch[e] not *too* near & not, not too far. We have our blue bags & tickets & a chair, alas, is to wheel me out & perhaps, in, & J[ohn] & P[erdita] will *meet* me, so it would really be more fun to see you & S[usan] later. I have the Harry T. Moore review — I see Madrigal is a problem quiz, a "fun the reader has." [25] I was at first shocked, then emerged undaunted. I suggested John see that I have a screw of tea & perhaps Nescafe, but this can come later & I only wrote to get the *feel* of things & I said that it was *all* in N[orman]'s hands. I have had wonderful letters about the book & I keep blessing you for it — & Horace too & Mr. Rosset. [26] R[ichard] A[ldington] writes about poss[ible] later translations, Fr[ench], Germ[an], Italian — but surely, that can wait.

Yes, we can talk of the Ceremonial lunch later. I don't think we *can* go — but more of this, later.

It is a comfort to me to feel that Robert D[uncan] is there. Thank him (& you) for his Bonnard card. Will I see him? We must work that all out. M. Durand said he was leaving 15 May, I think. I said that I would love to see him, if he had a minute to spare — but Norman Pearson might have arranged something for me. *Would* he come around? I just wondered — does *Creole* matter? [27] No one would know he was French — I have not yet had *Newsweek*.

Fido waits for this — forgive — I am happy & exhausted & apprehensive.
Love to S[usan] S. S. & C.

from
H.

May 4 [1960]

Dear N.,

Thanks 2 letters or envelopes with press. Harry T. Moore is un-perceptive & very, very nose-y. I have sent my extra copy to R[ichard] A[ldington], who will have something to say. Fido found *Newsweek* on the way home to Kenwin on Mon., & posted me from station, only 2 on the news-stand. I had just had your copy. I *study* every *word* of "Life in a Hothouse." [28] Was it? Perhaps it was.

What gets me is that M. Durand, if it *was* him, quotes things I wouldn't have said, notably the "Boring Images."[29] I never mentioned the "Angry" either, but did speak of beatniks. The "Hothouse" makes me think & pleases me.

I think M. Durand will be there for a day or two, when I arrive. But it might spoil the effect of "swans weaving their way,"[30] to see him in confusion & a crowd. I wrote him that I would like to see him, but that I must consult Prof. Pearson who may have made plans for me. I have not heard since writing him that I was sending you his address. Did you see Ezra in March 21 *Newsweek*? Very revealing, "homesick poet."[31] I sent my copy to R. A., but perhaps you saw the March 21, with funny photographs.

What M. Durand (or whoever) says of *my* saying *Bid Me* was started as a tribute to DHL is in a way *very* true, but how come he wrote of it, when we had not spoken of it? Anyway, thank you for sending him. And for everything — & more later — & all love to every S[usan] & to C.

from

H.

The important thing. I get awake at 5 or 4.30 every morning, in order to write my "merit" speech. I can not get it on paper. If the worst comes to the worst, will you ghost for me? Not to exceed 2 minutes, to be sent at least 10 days before May 25 — But I will *try* to write . . .

———— 161. MS ————

May 7 [1960]

Dearest C,

Thanks for all. But no *chianti*, it is too much part of this & I want a *change*, *Dubonnet*, if it is, as you say, N[ew] Y[ork]erish. I suppose someone will provide corkscrew. I am getting clutch-y & would prefer Blanche *near*. But we will see, I can't make & re-make plans. No, don't let Duncan *ring*, I can't really make contact & he will write when he gets back to his pad. You did not tell me what you thought of M. Durand's *Hothouse*. Please do! John sent me *N. Y. Times*, May 1 adv[ertisement],

Congratulations

to

H. D. —

rather impressive.

No — I don't think I can do with T.V. to start, maybe radio later. I am *weak* with the wedding.[32] I will be glad to have Br[yher] here. She heard from

London, a few days ago, "the Wedding gets more & more scandalous & extraordinary."

O — the Swann! He brought *Newsweek* — the Obrecht picture is "like Hestia, the sacred flame." Can you beat it?

Could you post me a *paper-back* Huck. Finn? I want to read it, after some 50 years, & I think Blanche should.

I don't know Sara Teasdale[33] of whom Swann writes. Should I?

I don't think I'll have the strength for M. Durand — but thank you "rather smart" assurance.

And thank you for everything, and do *not* go out your way, nor S[usan] — but Susan can tell me where to find a hat — or the hat.

Love again,

H.

——————— 162. MS ———————

The Stanhope

5th Ave. at 81st Street

N.Y. 28

May 15 [1960]

Dearest C.,

B[lanche] typed this [her acceptance speech]. Can you have it sent to the Arts Merit people. They wanted a copy 10 days before the event. This may be a little late. I have come to *love* your version & I do thank you for help & inspiration.

M. Durand came in, he was *not* as dark as I had visualized. He said he was just back from Washington & appreciated your writing him. We have just come from the *famille* Schaffner & B was so good with them. I can't write more — but bless & thank you.

Ever

with love

& to S[usan] & S[usan] &

S[usan]

H.

I carry your Greek bag . . .

B sends greetings . . . & had learnt by heart a whole Sunday paper . . .

The Stanhope
5th Ave. at 81st Street
N.Y. 28
June 8 [1960]

Dearest C,

Just to thank you for *Ruan*.[34] I had not seen it & now, I *know* it. I have written Fido to Sesame, to say how pleased & happy I am. I have written to Mr. Davidson.[35] Does he begin to realize these "angels" — 72, as I note in *Sagesse*, XIX. I rather "fancy" now an introduction. And I don't want to dedicate it to E[rich] and D[ori] — that was a sort of private wedding-present, but the series was written before all that & it must be kept abstract & clear of all those repercussions. It is *your* Sagesse really.

What fun we had! Bl[anche] is so *happy* with her books and enters into La M[artinelli] & everything.

Ever & ever & ever
H.

After her return to Küsnacht, H.D. continues to bask in the glow of her trip to New York. In the following letters her thoughts return repeatedly to Durand, even as she reports rumors at the clinic about the earlier marriages of Erich Heydt's wife or answers Pearson's questions about the background of an old manuscript he has discovered.

July 4 [1960]

Dear Norman,

I think of you all to-day! I hope that the enclosed letter will do. Yes — things quiet down a bit & I get down to tea on the terrace, & called on Joan at *Seehof* yesterday. Belinda is in Z[urich] for a few weeks & came to see me, with more lurid details, some of which I had already collected from Blanche, "did you know her first husband killed himself?[36] I don't like it at all." How & what effect would this have on her — on him — well, I tell you everything as it comes — forgive me. I have ordered the *Kabbale Pratique* [*sic*] of R[obert] Ambelain for you. I have not been able to get to it, am trying to be *pratique* in other dimensions. No word from Durand. He doesn't smoke, he doesn't drink, he refused our nuts that short call on Sun., May 15, "I can't eat salt."

What is wrong with him? I must write Fido now, Sesame. I sent you the Bryn Mawr photographs that Mary Herr inscribed for me & a copy of *Two Cities*[37] that M. Temple sent me. Please give 4 July greetings to S[usan] & all. Forgive rather dull script. I see *Unser*, I believe tomorrow, but *thanks to you*, I see the "archetypal" formula — sliced. Infinite gratitude.

H.

——————— 165. MS ———————

July 15 [1960]

Dear N.,

It is uncanny seeing this.[38] I have no copy, had "forgotten" it, must have destroyed "the novel." A memory came back, at the time we discussed the *Hilda Book*, as this Karen is Frances Josepha Gregg Wilkinson, the boy is Oliver Wilkinson, who might have found the book. I tried to get in touch with him when I heard of his mother's death, but I had no success nor did his godfather Andrew Gibson. This was written around the Kenneth period, late 20s I suppose; Frances sent him ("Adrian") to me, in the first place. "The Usual Star" touches on this. I sent you the letter from Mr. Clodd,[39] via the Fido "bag." I think he spoke of a poem in a novel — but I do not find it here. I wrote a story [I have no copy] by "Rhoda Peter" for a west, mid-west (?) mag[azine].[40] It might turn up, about Fido & me in Corfu, rather artificial. No — you do not "pry." I am touched by your interest. That Karen-Adrian period is hard to re-assemble. It was before my ps-a & I think *Madrigal* & the new notes are infinitely more *real*. By the way, Dori's 2nd husband was with her for 14 days, then fled. Why? I got this from Blanche & perhaps it explains much, as No. 1 committed suicide. Why? again. Don't think me inhuman to mention this. *Unser* was in a state as I had "allowed Belinda to talk." How could I stop her? "He has raised his fees — did you know her first husband killed himself?" I did not then know of No. 2 & would not have told her anyway. *Unser* said that Belinda said "horrible things" to him & blamed me, but I went for him. I hadn't half remembered what I said but feared that I might have quoted Blanche — but Blanche said that "everyone knew anyway" — Anyhow, *Unser* & I have gone for little runs & he seems more himself, after my howl — "I do not need you now. *I have America.*" You did not tell me what ails Durand, no drinks, no smokes, no *salt*. I do not hear from him. Do comment on this! Fido is due tomorrow for tea. I am glad about the furniture and hope the weather improves, & all the S[usan] S[usan] & V[alentine] II are happy with you. Do keep well. This won't go till tomorrow, but I had to write you at once, over my dinner-tray.

All love to Susan & C.

from

H.

———— 166. MS ————

July 30 [1960]

Dearest N,

Two letters. I must just rush out my thanks for all the *bricks* in the *bridge* that they give me.[41] Fido & I feared you were ill — now I rejoice! Thanks for comment on M. Durand.[42] He asked me for my news of "American enterprise" & I told him of the 3000 & the gallant Léger Léger's gesture, as I staggered — no swayed gracefully — from the reader's desk. Then, I felt when he did not write, that I had been too sky-rocket-y & wild, too, with Blanche — when he called, so late, that Sun[day], before leaving for Paris. He said he was coming at 12, & it was 12.45 when he did turn up. He was so prompt here — anyhow, I do not think he is at all well. I am really amused about Stephen.[43] In a way, I found him very helpful & a good *brick* in that London N.Y. bridge. Ask if he has any papers of mine. We might retrieve something.

———

[in Bryher's handwriting]

So sorry ulcers troublesome — here for a brief weekend — back to Kenwin Monday and will write you from there, Love

Bryher

———

No. Mr. A[ldington] didn't select the *Helen* scraps.[44] I did. He does not refer to any later work of mine, but has been very interested in *Bid Me* reactions. He writes of a poss[ible] interview as from *Sun[day] Exp[ress]* in London. I have not contacted this, but it seems indicated, in a way. I must wait & see. It is wonderful to have Fido here, now at *Kunstube*. Tomorrow is Sun[day], then Mon[day] is *Swissday* & all closed down, I haste to get this off at once. Blanche has gone off to St. M[oritz], but she talked much of N.Y. It was a rare escapade for her & for us to have her there. Please greet S[usan] & V[alentine] II & S[usan] again. I wait to hear more of the Hon. Stephen. Blanche liked him & he did help with the Gregories. His idea about Huxley & his Indian circle was interesting but I don't just *see* it. But do tell him to write me & get hold of the incriminating pages if you can. He was at one time, rather on the *Herf* level — seemed very normal when I saw him. There is a Swiss conversation going on between F. and [Benedetti?] — hard to concentrate, but I *had* to write. We were really worried. Do, do keep well,

ever & ever gratefully

H.

——— 167. MS ———

Dearest N.,

I wrote you this morning but now I find: — *Daughters and Rebels*, Jessica Mitford, Houghton Mifflin ($4).[45] I think Fido would like this story of the 6 rebels — as she liked the U-game of Nancy Mitford, when she & Doris first discovered it. It is easier to ask you to order it, if you don't mind, saving me the trouble. I am happy to find something — & want to read it, anyway — so will you send it here to me? I have dug out Ambelain *Adam Dieu Rouge*, thinking I might send it to Mr. Dav[idson] but I am deep in it, not having read it — for years, & I will keep it. The books, it seems, are many of them, [*epmise?*] and difficult to come by. I have 4 of about 20, your *Kabbale, Adam, Dans l'Ombre des Cathédrales, Le Martinism*[46] (I think it is, but that vol. is chez Fido). I am tempted to contact the Paris publisher — a pity that this does not appeal to Fido, as there is such a treasure for my "graduate studies." It is good to be reading French too, as the mixed Germans got me down until I had my N.Y. visit. I don't care now, one way or another, about the chatter.

The sun has half come out, but it is really cold.

Thanks always for everything, dear C.

H.

In August, Pearson reports more news about Stephen Hayden-Guest and also about Sheri Martinelli, who still bemoans the loss of Ezra Pound. H.D.'s replies contain fragments that she will incorporate into her poem *Hermetic Definition*.

——— 168. MS ———

Dearest N.,

I have just addressed envelopes to Duncan & Swann to whom I have not written since my return — is it 8 weeks ago? But of course, I must write you, instead. R[ichard] A[ldington] sent me a note he had just had from E[zra]. It began, *"What have I done with my life?"* [47] He spoke of H[ilda]'s re*mark*able book, or *RE*-markable — anyhow. I never heard from Mary about it. I asked R. to tell E about Viola. It is so difficult for me to write into the void. Fido got off, in great style. She is due back, Wed., Aug. 31 for a few days — then, about 5 days around 10th. I dared to dream of getting away, as to Venice, over that time, but Br[yher] rather broke my nerve about it. Joan goes down Sept. 8 to meet her mother for Hellenic cruise. I even thought that Mary or D[orothy] or even E. might come up & visit me in Venice, but Br seemed so upset that I dropped the subject. I do *not* want to come [to America] in Oct. with Fido & Helen. Perhaps, I could get to Venice, then; it is only 2 hours, good connection, Milan change.

I am really very, very sorry about Lizzie. [48] For her, of course, but particularly for S[usan] — & for your sorrow about it all.

I will send you my long La M[artinelli] letter, later — yes, she wrote me & Lee (Li?) would be the chauffeur, "as pretty as a Chinese prince." [49]

We have had a *little* sun, lately.

All, all love and sympathy to S[usan] & gratitude always, to C.

from

H.

La Schnack comes tomorrow . . . [50]

——————— 169. MS ———————

Aug. 27 [1960]

Dearest N.,

Three books have come for Fido, & a letter from you to greet her return, next Wed. — I have my "Rebels" too, & have ordered a Nelson & book on Arab Kings from London, & am trying to find a book here on old German *mills* — so as Mr. A[ldington] will be sending book (I believe), we have a gala birthday pyramid!

I have not yet written Swann nor Duncan — I will tell Swann, I think, to *return Rose* (if he has not already done so) to Prof. Pearson.

I am near nervous prostration, like Dame Edith, as I refused absolutely Express interview, & last wire from R[ichard] says that *Br[yher] promised* Express interview, so I wired R. that I must wait Br's return. This anxiety has been accumulating since before Aug. 1. It is really not funny, but Fido is soon back and will help me.

I am happy reading about *Decathlon* Star, Rafer Johnson, *Time* Aug. 29 and *Newsweek*.[51] If you see anything special about him, will you send it.

All blessings to you and S[usan] — I seem to write everyday.

> Ever,
>
> H.

Is Stephen now Lord H-G-? Let me have news of meeting —

——————— 170. MS ———————

Sept. 10 [1960]

Dearest N.,

Before I open my stack of Sept. 10 cards, I want to thank you & Susan for the wire. I will see Fido now, for lunch. I am *deeply grateful* to you for your clairvoyance (again);[52] my poems which I was & am ashamed to show you, deal with Durand, the two visits, then his complete "withdrawal" *and* I bring in Rafer Johnson as a re-emergence of my poems & *Red Roses for Bronze*, in general / . . . "but I must finish what I have begun, / the tall god standing / where the race is run./"[53] I do not mention Rafer by name nor say he is bronze.[54] I have waited for news — so he *did* win? Thanks for news re Stephen.[55] London paper that Fido sent cites the Hon. S[tephen] G[uest] as "heir to the peerage." Is he trying to keep it dark in U.S.? He gave me name of hotel-club sort of thing. I can't find it — perhaps you would ask again. No — *not* Blanche, even if she could come & not Silvia D[obson], but there are many to choose from & I am not coming yet. Yes, the Hon. or his Lordship would be good company. I have had 2 copies of the E[zra] P[ound] — you sent one; I think Lüdeke [prodded?] de Nagy to send the other.[56] I think that I wrote you. I will try to go over some Mr. A[ldington] letters — perhaps they are not so remarkable but Fido always screams. Lorca doesn't matter.[57] I am so very deep in my own MSS. — I have a long Duncan paper, "Towards a study of H.D."[58] I don't think the *Rose* book for him. *Ought* he to see *Helen*? I can't take it myself now (what with Rafer & Lionel). I am opening the two books later with Fido. I do, do bless & thank you. I did "ask" for Rafer to win . . . Thank you Schnack & Schmidt to come. It will work out in time. *Unser* is very affable, now that he knows of Rafer-Lionel, though of course I would not divulge my secret to him. I guess Lionel (as he signed his last letter to me) is *not well*. Anyhow, you understand all this. Bless & thank you & love (special) to Susan.

> from
>
> H.

"Grove of Academe," 1960–1961

In September the two exchange reports on the visit of Christoph de Nagy, a Pound scholar whom H.D. interviews for Pearson in connection with an academic post at the University of Toronto. In his letter of September 25, Pearson mentions reading Charles Norman's biography of Ezra Pound,[59] which he will send to H.D. He asks H.D. about the overall title of her *Helen* manuscript, envisioning a book with four parts, the fourth being "Winter Love (Espérance)" and the first "Helen in Egypt." He also asks if there is a dedication. The two discuss the structure and publication of the book-length poem in the following letters as well as H.D.'s new poem, *Hermetic Definition*.

─────── 171. MS ───────

Oct. 1 [1960]

Dear Norman,

How many copies of *End To Torment* have you? I must get a fresh copy, but it would be simpler to correct an old one. De Nagy took the re-numbered Miss Coigny script. He may return it, in which case, I will get *that* copied by a London typist that Fido has found. But let me know what you have there.

I must take time to work out my *Helen*. I think *Helen In Egypt* is best title. I feel so much might be clarified — should *I* do a foreword? I don't feel Helen in public — maybe, if I go over script carefully, I will find the way. Thank you for C[harles] Norman to come. I don't somehow feel akin to it — de Nagy seems to have put me on such a direct path & I feel it helps, considering E[zra] pre-Cantos. The next book of de N[agy] is the "Imagist Phase" — he is now about to burrow in at British Museum — but I told you? . . . . But I get back the de N[agy] *End* just now, so you need not send copy, but let me know what you have. Please anyhow, correct the note, of p. 30, on S[ylvia] Beach — please cross out *"concentration"* & write *"prison camp"*.

Fido is due back to-day. It will be good to hear her on telephone again. I have been living hectically with news. I think half the point of T.V. is getting *out* of my room — and I wouldn't want to listen to the German alone. I only stay an hour, then get up by 9 to get the A[rmed] F[orces] N[etwork]. But thanks for your thoughtful idea.[60] What a *picture* of the children you gave! Love to S[usan] & C.

from

H.

Oct. 10 [1960]

Dearest Norman,

I wrote you Oct. 8. This is just to say that I have worked out *Helen In Egypt* idea.[61] The point is, I was blocked by the *Coda*. We must omit it. Later, it could be brought out, perhaps with some additions, as *Helen After*. The whole atmosphere of the *Coda* somehow contradicts the real psychic or spiritual achievement of the *Helen In Egypt*. The first book, by the way, can be called *Pallinode*, as I think you once suggested. But don't commit me entirely yet, to *Grove*. I have *Ruan* & am very happy about it, & Fido is due here to-morrow. I have a letter from La M[artinelli] who says she is getting out an H.D. number & what can I suggest? If she writes you, will you deal wisely. I have no idea & I fear, no contribution. I feel rather mean, as I "warned" de Nagy, as I thought he might be going to Cal[ifornia]. Joan & I get in a huddle & talk about "Xmas with Pounds in Venice." I have written Mary — but Fido won't approve.[62] Did I thank you for the Dec. 27 list of fascinating talks[63] & for an earlier Yale magazine *and* the enchanting V[alentine] II pictures which I am sharing — first, will show Fido here. I don't know about *H[elen] in E[gypt]* dedication. I am reading it now, again. I am pleased by "At Baia" and thank you always.[64] La M. encloses a clamped-shut note for "beautiful Eric H[eydt]." I will write again, but things pile up when Fido is here. All love to S[usan] & to C. all gratitude as ever & ever

from

H.

You won't mention my Venice fantasy to Fido?

If I send R[ichard] A[ldington] letters, they need not come back at once. . . . but thank you. I sent the *Grove* trans[lation] list & he wrote sympathetically of it.[65] I will send letter.

Oct. 16, 1960

Dearest Hilda,

[. . .]

Thanks for your letter of the 10th. Yes, "Pallinode" will be excellent for Part One, and we can call the whole "Helen In Egypt." As you will with the coda; it doesn't matter one way or the other so long as you are happy. Horace and I simply had the feeling that this was an unusual and vivid twist of the fabric, suddenly taking it straight to the heart of the poet and today, a metaphor of the Mystery by which the past comes down and then out into ourselves. No one has so boldly done this before you did it, with the courage that the Martinellis and Duncans and Levertovs admire. I don't think though it would do to insert the coda later; it either goes now or I think not at all. But you understand, this is only the way Horace and I saw it and understood it: why one thinks about Helen. The story simply in itself is a beautiful work of art, by which I mean the first three books only. There is no hurry with the ms., we can go over it when you come over.

All love from yr C.

––––––––– 174. MS –––––––––

Oct. 28 [1960]

Dearest N.

Thank you & S[usan] for lovely card of the Great Spirit or the "Indian ghost" as Herf called it — she was so pleased to have your foot-note! Now, I am in rather a "state" about *The Unicorn, Wm. Butler Yeats' Search for Reality* — by Virginia Moore, the MacMillan Co., NY, 1954.[66] *Can you order a copy to be sent to Robert Duncan for me?* This is his copy & I must have it on hand. Don't speak to Fido of this, as I will hope to give her this or another new copy, as for Xmas. — I like the Dec. 27 "papers"[67] — it would be fun to be there. Thank you for Doolittle's *Concord & Lexington*.[68] I really feel that I belong, almost as much as you and Paul Revere. I see a good write-up of the Norman P[ound] in *Newsweek*. I don't think that I can get to Venice. I don't see *how*. It made Joan happy to talk about it — & I will discuss possible plans later, with Fido. Duncan said he had ordered the book, but if you have had it sent, all the better, as he can return his copy to his friend's shop, where he gets a reduction. Please see that he doesn't starve — metaphorically! Thank you for all news. I have been re-living the Award & remembering. *How* kind everyone was. They took a picture of me & Van Doren.[69] Could I ever see it? *No* — I have said *no* to new photographs. And I have *not said yes* to *Helen* publication. Thank you for all home-news. What a lot you have been doing! Now bless S[usan] & our own C

H.

Oct. 25 letter has just come.[70] Please fill out *Who's Who* folder as you think best — & thank you.

Thank you, as for Duncan — *please draw on my reserve*. His work is, as you say, uneven, but he has a rare perception.

Thank you for account of visit. Fido did love it all

Ever,

H.

Nov. 12 [1960]

Dear Norman,

Thank you all for cards — & *Ruan* excellent write-ups. I had wire that Fido was in London yesterday. I had photographs from La M[artinelli] that I will send in next envelope, with another R[ichard] A[ldington] Jap[anese] folder.[71] He had had the Ch[arles] Norman book & actually seemed to like it — & sent it on for possible notice to some London "colleagues." Was the book sent me? I have thought about *Helen* & re-read it, & I like the *Coda*, but if published (or not) I now agree that there should be some captions. I will maybe see to this, later.[72] I am surprised that Mary wrote you of Venice — it was & is a dream — & I am sure Fido will squeal. Anyhow, I have not heard from E[zra] P[ound] nor D[orothy] P[ound] — Venice is part of the new poem sequence that I am writing: *Hermetic Definition*. I am pretty sure that you would not care for it — but I am getting Coigny to type some of it. Fido will be a tonic — now, I can't seem to externalize or make travel plans — but I have been busy on "Definition." Weather has just been continual blanket of fog — so forgive my dim note — & thanks again, again for everything — & with love to S[usan] & C

from

H.

Nov. 19 [1960]
Enclosed Die Tat [Swiss
paper]

Dearest Norman,

Fido is here, much for me to hear about you — & the N.Y. family. I have torn myself away from Ch[arles] Norman — I am very pleased & happy with the book. It is by far the best, all-round E[zra] P[ound] — It gives me the sense of *continuity & finality*.[73] I will have to write Mary that winter-Venice will be *too much*. I don't know how Joan will take it. I have been upset by a review of *Bid (Madrigal)*. I will try to send you a copy — it has been all over the place here & dear Fido only thinks it's funny. *Perhaps it is*. I have written R[ichard] A[ldington] & must write Schnack for she must have lent her copy. The review is by H.W. Hausermann & I think he must be the Eng[lish] prof[essor] at Geneva that Sch[nack] said she had lent book to. The review is fairly interesting, but in par[agraph] 3, Hilda Doolittle writes to clarify her position, after R. A. in an open autobiography talk about the women etc. At the end, after her separation & the death of the hero, she (H.D.? Hilda Doolittle? Julia?) *Verliert sie jeden Halt* and (in R. A. English): "She travelled a good deal, always with a pretty large brandy-flask, & had more lovers than was good for her — or for them." The review is in *Die Tat*, Nov. 12. — Surely it is "defamation of character" — but I will wait for R. A. letter.

I feel that I could fight *legally* for Julia, but don't suppose I will go so far. To me, *Madrigal* & the *Helen in Egypt* are sacrosanct! The *Coda* is too earthbound, I could not *fight* for it — that is why I didn't want to *mix* the dimensions.

Fido will be a great help, but I do feel the *Die Tat* review must not set a standard for poss[ible] later write-ups. Do you agree?[74]

Love to S[usan] & C

from

H.

In the following letters, Pearson's comments about H.D.'s manuscripts and literary circle are interrupted by news of Lionel Durand's activities in Algeria, where he is reporting on the war. They then discuss the news of Durand's death, to which H.D. will allude in *Hermetic Definition*.

——— 177. TS ———

Dec. 17, 1960

Dearest Hilda,

[. . .]

All this is fine,[75] but the event of the week of course has been the arrival of your *Thorn Thicket*.[76] I agree with Fido: this was very much worth doing both as exercise and in terms of the result. It is excellent reporting. And done with your sure touch. I felt it again, through no power of empathy on my part but rather your power of exciting my share in the mystery. I think Fido and you both have it strongly, this power of ubiquitous metamorphosis. I have perhaps a little of it, enough to let me tag along as the outer edge of your cosmos. In terms of characterization you get wonderfully Unser's hesitation, eagerness, insecurity in terms of his own identity or role. And one feels Dori a little like a witch drawing small lads into her hut. There is at any rate a thorn thicket. If I felt a section capable of possible later expansion it would have been the New York period, with a little more slowness of pace as Unser came back on the scene in order to be exorcised.[77] I mean the gradual revelation of his association with The Snow Maiden (Blanche) and the talks with Melitta. The latter especially would make a contrapuntal effect with your early mentions of the Unser-in-Amerika passages. Visiting you, I felt the growing knowledge and understanding on our part; you make it come almost too fast. It does not matter of course, only the whole is already so near a chapter in reconstruction. Having the chance to read it is a wonderful Christmas present.

All love,

from yr

C.

─────── 178. MS ───────

Jan. 6 [1961] *Trois Rois*

Dearest N.,

Mary de R[achewiltz] writes, "I am very worried that Prof[essor] Pearson does not answer my letter or send back the proofs. I am sorry actually I bothered him for I know he has so much work. It was kind of Pearson to send you Boris' book[78] & I am glad you like it." She says that "father" doesn't seem to mind the cold as much as he used to. "He is a bit more cheerful these days. We are having pleasant company, especially the presence of a beautiful Chinese lady has drawn him out of his abuleia (?) — he sat up until 2 o'clock on New Year and had champagne and [panett?] at midnight. He has even read some Chinese Odes (& Pao Veneziani has read the Chinese text)."

Mary wanted to get "father" to Rome, but the friend there is very ill & Mary didn't want "father" to go about alone, as "he is sometimes very weak."

Thank you for your Philadelphia news. You did *too much* there![79] Yes, I did myself write to Horace, simply saying that I hoped possibly to see him in March & speaking of our last meetings, his books — especially the Ovid[80] — that I have here.

Yes, I agree, I don't know in how many directions Durand is torn.[81] He got into the casbah (?), native quarters, not encouraged but permitted by paratroop guard — French against French, Moslems against Jews, sacred texts from Synagogues shredded on the pavement, unveiled women clawing their faces, someone says "you can write special article — how I kill 12 Frenchmen," & so on. Nothing more from or about him, since this, 3 *Newsweeks* ago.

This is just to give you the Brunn[enberg] news, with love to S[usan] & C

from

H.

——— 179. TS ———

Jan. 15, 1961

Dearest Hilda,

[...]

This is rather sad as a missive, unless you already know what Susan found in this morning's *New York Times* and immediately called to my attention.[82] It is rather curious, this being the son of an ambassador to France. Your instincts were correct on every score. And from his letter to me I had very much the feeling that there was a response to you which was exceptionally meaningful. It does all rather fit into the mystery, if you sense what I mean. It is a resurging of the Achilles figure, I feel. But there is nothing really I can say to you, except to have you sense the touch of my hand when you wish it.

Yr.

C.

——— 180. MS ———

Jan. 20 [1961]

Dear Norman,

I heard from Ch[arles] Norman. I sent MS of E[zra] P[ound] to him. He apparently received it early in Dec. — He writes now that he has moved & married. (I suppose a 2nd, as I think he dedicated the Cummings to his daughter.) He says he will write, now that he is getting back to work — but I think that I will ask him to return the MS to you. It was sent on an impulse, as I got so deeply involved in his own E. P. findings. His address is: 12 E. 11th St., New York 3. He is probably tired of the E. P. material by now.

Thanks for the Durand. I had not heard. He never wrote me after my return here — the casbah etc. Algerian details I wrote you, were from one of his mid-Dec. *Newsweek* articles.[83] Then, no word for 3–4 numbers & I had a very real impression of Azrael, the Angel of Death — & I did some of this poem-sequence. It *may* be fair — anyhow, now I must re-work it, in recognition. He *did* something here, filled this room & the downstairs hall where we had coffee, with a sort of *Presence*. I am glad to know of his background. I will write again. It was so good to hear from *you*, it was after coffee & the room was warm & full of carnations & a funny sort of Xmas begonia like a tiny tree. It is perhaps as well that Fido comes this week-end. Thank Susan for finding the notice — wordless blessings

from
H.

I have written Ch Norman.

———— 181. TS ————

Feb. 12, 1961

Dearest Hilda,

[...]

I was afraid you might not have heard about Durand, and am glad I sent the clipping even if it was sad news. Fido tells me you are distressed that I never mentioned Durand or the poetry? But I did write about Durand when I sent the clipping, and referred to the mystery and the like. And I did talk about your Küsnacht Heydt-Durand prose notes ["Thorn Thicket"] when you sent them to me. I have not been sent any of the poetry you have been working on since you went back last early summer. You have only told me about them, and as of your letter said you must rework them. But as for Durand and his "connection," I do of course feel it very strongly, epecially as it came at shall we say with Thoreau "in the very nick of time and at the right place." One does, as he did, emerge from the shadow, step through the door, appear and then fade back into the shadow again leaving the memory and a rose. I spoke of him before as part of the "Mystery," and continue to think of him so.

I have to go off to Northampton tonight so that I can talk on Pound to some of the undergraduates tomorrow morning. I regret the time. Denise Levertov spent Wednesday night with us, and gave a reading of her poems to the university that afternoon. She read very well indeed, and both Susan and I liked her immensely. She is deeply devoted to you. After dinner we had a party for my graduate seminar, and she was superb with them: like a great hostess, talking easily with everyone. We spoke much of Duncan and of you, naturally.

Susan joins in love. Write soon, or as you can.

Yr.
C.

Feb. 17 [1961]

Dearest Norman,

Thank you for the lovely Valentine! I was about to write again & now your Feb. 12 letter comes. I am happy about the flower on your desk — but I re-read your letter *twice* & find no mention of a flower — this sort of "thing" never happened to me before. I read the letter once — then, started this, then looked up reference to "flower on my desk." This comes with & through the Durand. I am sorry Fido wrote. You sent Durand to me. It was just *nine months* between his stepping through the door &, as you say, "into the shadow again." I was a little disturbed by what I began writing, last August. Then when he went in Jan[uary], I found the 3rd section, *Star of Day*. I feel a little "shocked" by the intensity of the first part, *Red Rose & a Beggar* — the second part, sustained by my reading St. Léger Léger & to balance intellectually the emotional *Red Rose*, I call (cliché, but it can't matter) *Grove of Academe*. All this is involved with Ambelain & my reading of *Dans l'Ombre des Cathédrales*. Well, I am getting Coigny to type & I have not finished *Star of Day* — that is, the death is a sort of Christmas "birth" — but please understand, I have been myself a little abashed, & possibly, I didn't want to "involve" you.

Fido is due in a week. I have perhaps been too immersed in Brontë find-ings[84] — & now Fido sends me *Wuthering Heights*, which I am sure I have not read for 50 years.

No, I am not sorry that Fido wrote about Durand. It was thoughtful of you to send the press-notice — of course, *Newsweek* had a write-up — it came a few days later and Joan brought me Paris *Herald Tribune* — D[urand] was twice imprisoned by Germans. I will write again — & love to the S[usan] & S II — we are having sequence of Days,[85] too. Dear C, thanks infinite

from

H.

March 8 [1961]

Dear Norman,

Thank you for the Freud. Yes — I think that you & I have done our home-work there. I will hope to send you *Hermetic Definition*, when I get big enve-lope. The second part really is your doing — for the matter of fact, the whole is. Part II is addressed to a Presence, Poet, not named but quoted, St. Léger Léger. It is an odd set of poems but it took me round the corner — & certainly "there is always an end." Now, there is fresh hysteria as Miss Raber reports Hollywood wants to film the place, as they are doing *Tender is the Night* & this is the place described.[86] Did you know that? I don't care anyhow — but Dr. Brunner is in Egypt & will be until about March 20, when some sort of decision will be taken[87] — & Fido is due about 18th. Gertrude is in a state as she is trying to arrange for Lady Wms. & others whom Brunner wants to send to Kilchberg across the lake — of which Joan has heard no special good. Fido will help with the rescue work. I am pretty fed up & don't particularly want to *see* you here — but could I get to Venice?[88] And when approx[imately] would you be able to get there? I would have to write Ezra. Now, Mr. A[ldington] talks of Venice, but I can make absolutely no plans. I had a really *enchanting* letter from Ch[arles] Norman, said he was sending you the MS. I think, yes, Duncan might have it, if not too much trouble for you to send. I must write Denise L[evertov] who was full of your & Susan's kindness, hospitality & charm. De Nagy wants to call, around 25th on his return from London, en route to Canada. I don't think I can arrange somehow . . . I mean, inwardly. I will write again, I hope the desk flower is flourishing. *N.B.* Ezra asks me to *edit* "some 40 pages by Ariga . . . if I don't get time to do it" — do you understand, apropos Fenollosa? La M[artinelli] sends me a B[lessed] V[irgin] medal, rather my *Notre Dame* vibration in the new poems. I have so much more to say — forgive this — Love to S[usan] and C.

from

H.

——————— 184. MS ———————

March 13 [1961]

Dear Norman,

Will you, if it comes your way, thank the Academy for the Proceedings. I am happy & secure in the beautiful Presentation & "our" Acceptance. I will never forget how you helped me & you will find yourself in Part II of Hermetic, though truly, the *escape* from Part I came through some tough homework with St. Léger Léger. You will understand — & if I find a suitable line, I would, with your permission, dedicate the Hermetic Definition to you.[89] I had a very perceptive letter from Duncan, who said he had typed out the E[zra] P[ound] for himself, so as to return your copy. I will try to send him the Hermetic Definition rough type script, of which I have a carbon, & tell him he can keep it *unless* N[orman] P[earson] wants it, as he sometimes likes the early rough copy. There will be no hurry, anyway. I am really deeply grieved

about the Ch[arles] Norman book.⁹⁰ I have written Ezra, not mentioning of
course, & asked R[ichard] A[ldington] to write or send card; of course R. A.
would not speak of the Ch. N. but I am sure it will distress him. He is on his
way to Venice. De Nagy comes back to Basel in a few days, but I gather he will
be in Italy for some weeks in the summer, "before leaving Europe in July," so
I really don't feel that I can see him here just now, I will suggest a Venice-
mirage. He wants to meet Ezra so much & if I can't manage, maybe you can.
I have already written E., I will try to write again, either to him or Mary, about
de N. —

Thanks all about Helen. I leave it to you. I can't think where I am. But will
you note this name: — Christof Wegelin (*The Image of Europe in Henry
James*). He is on U. of Oregon faculty, taught at Johns Hopkins & Princeton.
The point is, his *sister* is a secretary here & goes out to USA in Aug., wants to
stay in East for about 6 months, before going to her brother — she is very
language-proficient — a very large spinster-matron type. I said I would write
you, re poss[ible] job — but just as gesture of friendliness. I have *so much more
to say* but end now with endless love to S[usan] and C.

from

H.

——————— 185. MS ———————

Easter Sat., April 1 [1961]

Dear Norman,

May we call the new poem series *Notre-Dame d'Amour*, with the sub-title
Hermetic Definition? Will you note, Part I — XIV — p. 11, 4 or 3 lines before
end . . . last April / and last May — It wasn't *before* — or perhaps it *was*. Will
you advise?

Part II — I — line 1. I think we better make it clearer that Part II is ad-
dressed to someone else — *so you (this other) are the Presence* — Just insert
this other in brackets, don't you think so? I did mention last line of III – VIII
— *Night brings the Day*.⁹¹ It was strange how St. J[ohn] Perse filled in & fol-
lowed on from my Ambelain "studies." Strange how I put him aside just be-
fore I heard of Durand. The poems have held me together, during this time.
I had you[r] card & S[usan] greeting from S[outh] Carolina, suggesting my
Part II, *indigo petal-drift*.

This is to welcome you home, with much un-said — only, to start the new
month, after my rather isolated Good Friday, March 31, morning, waiting as
I always do, for Perdita to arrive, about lunch time — 42 years ago! Now, I

feel happy again. I trust the Durand birth-death symbol doesn't seem too exaggerated — well, it was *like* that.

Forgive this, all about *Notre-Dame d'Amour*, with love to you & S[usan]

from

H.

I have had two letters from Dorothy [Pound]. She says she has written de N[agy]. I told her again about your seeing Omar.

——— 186. MS ———

April 21 [1961]

Dearest Norman,

Bless you for the "Final Proof" poem, for the pack of 9 numbered cards.[92] I have read & re-read the captions. I have been making a study of *The Brewton Corner*[93] & *Unser* exclaimed yesterday "enchanting." I take the *Corner* to Fido, tomorrow. We both feel displaced persons, though I don't know why we should. Well, we will cling to the *Corner*. I am overwhelmed with Mr. Laughlin's letter[94] & feel the *Notes* will draw me back to them & will fill my new room or rooms with their vibration. I hardly dare touch them now — but perhaps the "story" should be published.[95] Odd, how it worked out from *outside* really, the events in sequence to which Mr. L[aughlin] refers, "she has given the things real form as a story." You know I never worked over it, but jotted the notes down, as dated — of course, your letters helped & *Unser's* pronouncements. Enough . . . dear, dear Norman. Don't you think *Star of Day* is really the title of the Hermetic sequence? It is more convincing than the French *Notre Dame* title. I am deeply touched with your idea of Christmas card — & already?[96] It works in with the candles of Part III. And please send "little Denise" any of the sequence that seems suitable.[97]

Yes, *Star of Day (Hermetic Definition)* needed a real birthday, *your* birthday.[98] I have read and re-read *Star* — nothing I ever wrote became such *incantation* such *prière*.

Such a lot in your letter, to solace me for this difficult change.[99] I am so happy, by the way, about Horace — really pleased.[100] I will write again. I feel now *Star* is a shared experience. You projected it — remember?

With love to S[usan] & all gratitude from

H.

Despite the attempts by Bryher and Erich Heydt to make her comfortable, H.D. did not survive the move to the Hotel Sonnenberg in April; the loss of her haven at Küsnacht proved overwhelming. When Pearson wrote that he planned to visit her at the end of June, she reported a severe cold and a collapse, commenting, "I only hope that I will be more alert and alive by June 25" (14 May). She did recover enough to take pleasure in a sample page from *Helen in Egypt* sent by Pearson, writing that she hoped he would bring the page proofs with him (1 June). However, their plans to go over the proofs together in Zurich were not realized. On 6 June Bryher wrote to Pearson that Hilda had suffered a stroke and was unable to speak or move her right arm or leg. After that, H.D.'s decline was rapid, and Bryher and Pearson discussed the possibility of bringing her back to the United States.[101] Instead, H.D. spent her last days at Hirslanden Klinik with Erich Heydt in attendance. Before her death, on 27 September 1961, he read to her from her publisher's copy of *Helen in Egypt*.[102]

Pearson's efforts on H.D.'s behalf did not end with her death, however. In his position as literary executor, he continued to handle permissions for the publication of her work, to write introductory material, and to encourage the critical endeavors of others. His correspondence with James Laughlin of New Directions and with Donald Hutter of Scribner's shows his unabated enthusiasm for H.D.'s work, his desire to protect and enhance her reputation, and his sensitivity to her wishes. For example, Laughlin was interested in publishing *End to Torment* as early as 1961, but both he and Pearson feared "a sensational type of promotion" that could be unpleasant.[103] In accord with H.D.'s wishes, Pearson was particularly concerned that her late poetry receive fresh critical attention. In 1966 he exchanged several letters with Donald Hutter of Scribner's about publishing a new collection of H.D.'s poems, but Pearson's insistence upon an edition that consisted solely of her late work ended these negotiations. On 9 July 1966, Pearson wrote to Hutter: "Perhaps it is the sense of a pledge to H.D. herself that makes me still want to stick to my former conviction that I ought first to bring out *Last Poems*, follow this with the charming autobiographical account of her relationship with Pound . . . and then have a substantial *Collected Poems*." Despite his queries to other presses as well, such an edition was not published.[104]

Similarly, Pearson's responses to the letters of poets and critics reflected his determination to give H.D.'s late poetry and unpublished prose a full hearing so that the old "Imagist" tag, and H.D.'s status as a minor poet, would be reconsidered. In a letter to Peter Quartermain,[105] who suggested small-press editions of "Winter Love" and *Hermetic Definition*, both of which were circulating underground, Pearson insisted that "it must be all or nothing, and at the moment I think we need a commercial press in order to get the widest possible distribution."[106] Certainly this impulse governed the special issue of *Contemporary Literature* (1969) that was devoted to a reevaluation of H.D.'s work. In addition to several critical essays on her later work, it contained previously unpublished excerpts from her poetry, a chapter of *The Gift*, a selection of letters from the Imagist period, a preliminary bibliography, and an interview with Pearson. As the editor, L. S. Dembo,[107] pointed out, drawing upon Pearson's views in the introduction, H.D.'s work needed to be "compre-hended in terms of its psychological and metaphysical context."[108]

After the success of this special issue, Pearson contacted New Directions again about the publication of H.D.'s manuscripts. This time he stressed that the younger poets (Robert Duncan, Denise Levertov, Robert Kelly)[109] wanted the "war trilogy"[110] reprinted, as well as the late poems that were to comprise *Hermetic Definition*, and that he preferred to wait until Pound's death before publishing *End to Torment*.[111] Pearson died in 1975, having writ-ten to Laughlin that he was "very much convinced" that H.D. "is the finest woman poet in America since Emily Dickinson."[112] His long-standing commitment to her work ensured that H.D. would take her place as one of the major poets of our century.

1. St.-John Perse, nom de plume of Alexis Saint Léger Léger (1887–1972), West Indies–born French poet and diplomat, winner of the Nobel Prize in 1960. Throughout his distinguished diplomatic career he wrote poetry in secret. During World War II he opposed the Vichy government's policies, was stripped of French citizenship and forced to flee France in 1940. In the United States he served as consultant on French poetry at the Library of Congress from 1941 to 1945. He regained French citizenship in 1945, and after returning to France in the 1950s, spent time in both countries. H.D. was reading his poetry in 1959. She wrote to Bryher on 5 August 1959: "I am reading St. J. Perse with a new grasp. He wrote *Vents* from one of the Maine islands, 1945 — and *Exil* from Long Beach, New Jersey, 1941. This brings the Islands, his and mine and yours into a new perspective."

2. Lionel Durand (1921–1961), Haitian-born French journalist, Paris correspondent for *Newsweek*; joined the French Resistance after the fall of France; came to the United States in 1943 as head of the French arm of Voice of America in New York; returned to France and *Newsweek* in 1956.

3. On 22 January 1961, Bryher informed Pearson that Hilda was depressed by Durand's death: she "said that the 'dark angel of death' was summoning her."

4. Denise Levertov (1923–), British-born American poet, associated with the Black Mountain School after she moved to the United States in the 1950s; introduced to H.D.'s late work by Robert Duncan. Levertov corresponded with H.D. in the late fifties and met her in New York in 1960.

5. Thomas Burnett Swann (1928–1976), American poet and professor of English, wrote a critical study of H.D.'s poetry, *The Classical World of H.D.* (1962).

6. The third recipient was Jorge Guillen. Pearson is mistaken here.

7. Louise Bogan (1897–1960), American poet and essayist, associated with the *New Yorker* magazine; elected to the Academy of Arts and Letters in 1959.

8. Pearson suggested that H.D. bring Joan to New York as a helper.

9. H.D. probably refers to a list of previous winners of the Longview Award, which she also received in this year.

10. On 18 February [1960], H.D. acknowledged receipt of this folder, with the following remarks: "I especially want you to thank the writer of the jacket introduction (and I think *you*) for the precise presentation of the theme. . . . I like the orange letters and the seascape (?) and feel now, glad of the title as it stands. . . . No book I have ever *done* has given me such pleasure, as *Bid Me To Live* and I feel the 'hypnotic spell' drawing me back to it."

11. Pearson sent H.D. Archibald MacLeish's translation of the acceptance speech by St.-John Perse, a previous winner of the American Academy award.

12. Jorge Guillen (1893–1984), poet, was born in Spain and came to the United States in 1938, where he taught at Wellesley College from 1940 to 1957. His works include *Guillen on Guillen: Poetry and the Poet* (1979).

13. Wystan Hugh Auden (1907–1973), British-born poet, deeply concerned with political and social matters in the thirties; settled in the United States in 1939; winner of the National Book Award for *The Shield of Achilles* (1955).

14. On 5 March 1960, Pearson responded: "The thing for you to do is to write it in your own way, with perhaps a generalization or two about poetry or being in like nightingales' tongues; then send it to me if you want, and we can sling it back and forth across the seas until it becomes a little poem, or one of your beautifully evocative paragraphs of 'prose.'"

15. On 21 February 1960, Pearson mentions having received a grateful letter from Thomas Burnett Swann, who has queried him about the classical sources of some of H.D.'s early poems. Pearson says, however, that he daren't tell Swann of H.D.'s coming arrival, lest he come to New York.

16. H.D. refers to having given Erich Heydt a valentine sent to her by Pearson.

17. On 6 March [1960], H.D. writes: "I am very happy with the book — and Timothy arrives with it."

18. Bryher wished H.D. to have some other person in attendance on her trip to New York as a secretary/companion. Although she did not attend the award ceremony, she kept in close touch with H.D. from her club in London, even setting her clock to New York time.

19. On 16 March [1960], H.D. wrote: "Now, Bryn Mawr writes that I am one of 75 alumnae at 75th anniversary year to have 'a citation at the convocation.' Sounds like Rome."

20. Geoffrey (Piers Henry) Dutton (1922–), Australian writer; works include *Findings and Keepings: Selected Poems, 1940–1970* (1970).

21. Pearson's grandson.

22. On 27 March 1960, Pearson mentioned giving Grove Press a list of people who were to receive copies of the limited edition of *Bid Me to Live*.

23. On 27 March 1960, Pearson asked if he sent van der Leeuw's *Gods in Exile*.

24. H.D. refers here to her unpublished journal "Bosquet (Thorn Thicket)."

25. Harry T. Moore, "The Faces Are Familiar," *New York Times Book Review*, 1 May 1960, p. 4.

26. Barney Rossett, director of Grove Press.

27. On 3 May 1960, Pearson responds: "No one does not mind Creole. It is rather smart, and the Stanhope is a place for diplomats, in that way an upgraded Beekman, but rather less expensive."

28. *Newsweek*, 2 May 1960, p. 92.

29. H.D. refers to a subheading, "Boring Image," in the *Newsweek* column. She is quoted as having said she "became bored with that image" [of D. H. Lawrence] as a cult figure who was considered perfect.

30. H.D. quotes a phrase from the *Newsweek* review describing Küsnacht on the Zurichsee.

31. On 21 March *Newsweek* published an interview with Pound in Italy titled "The Homesick Poet." Pound is quoted as feeling a "hunger to go home again" (130).

32. H.D. probably refers to the controversial marriage of Princess Margaret to Antony Armstrong-Jones, a commoner. They were married on 6 May 1960.

33. Sara Teasdale (1884–1933), American poet, awarded a Pulitzer Prize for *Love Songs* (1917).

34. Bryher, *Ruan* (Pantheon, 1960).

35. Gustav Davidson (1895–1971), poet, editor, and secretary of the Poetry Society of

America. He and H.D. shared an interest in angelology; his books include *A Dictionary of Angels, Including the Fallen Angels* (1967) and *Moment of Visitation* (1950). He met with H.D. in New York.

36. H.D. reports rumors about Erich's wife, Dori, who was married twice before.

37. Three short segments from H.D.'s *Helen in Egypt* were published in *Two Cities* 4 (15 May 1960): 33–34.

38. On 12 July 1960, Pearson asked H.D. about a fragment of a novel titled "Tatter" that appeared in *The European Caravan* (New York: Brewer, Warren, and Putnam, 1931).

39. Alan Clodd, publisher at Enitharmon Press in London, was compiling a bibliography of H.D.'s works.

40. "Pontikonisi (Mouse Island)," *Pagany* 3, no. 3 (July–September 1932): 1–9.

41. On 24 July [1960], H.D. complained that she had not yet been able to bridge the gap between New York and Küsnacht. She requested that Pearson send Sara Teasdale's *Collected Poems*, hoping to find a kindred spirit.

42. On 26 July 1960, Pearson explained Durand's silence as follows: "As to his not writing, I suspect this is because of the pressure of affairs: the Congo, with its connection with Belgium etc., all of America's international fumbling, the reactions to the American political convention — all these must be overwhelming. And I daresay he must be physically careful."

43. On 26 and 27 July 1960, Pearson refers to Stephen Hayden-Guest, an old friend of H.D.'s from London whom she met again in New York. Hayden-Guest discussed the Huntington Hartford Colony with Pearson and also Aldous Huxley's involvement with occult circles.

44. Pearson thought that Aldington selected the poems for *Two Cities*.

45. *Daughters and Rebels: The Autobiography of Jessica Mitford* (1960).

46. H.D. refers to the following books by Robert Ambelain: *La Kabbale Practique* (Paris: Editions Niclaus, 1951), *Adam, Dieu Rouge* (Paris: Editions Niclaus, 1941), *Dans L'Ombre des Cathédrales* (Paris: Editions Adyar, 1939), and *Le Martinisme* (Paris: Editions Niclaus, 1946).

47. H.D. quotes this question in *Hermetic Definition*, part 1, 15, 2.

48. Pearson has reported the intensifying emotional problems of his stepdaughter, Elizabeth.

49. On 20 August Pearson wrote that Martinelli wants to be a valet to a rich older woman. "Li" refers to her husband.

50. On 15 August Pearson wrote that Elizabeth Schnack had mentioned translating *Bid Me to Live* into German.

51. On 29 August 1960, *Time* featured a picture of Rafer Johnson on the cover. Inside he is portrayed as seeing himself as a goodwill representative for the U.S. State Department and is quoted as saying: "I like people. I want to do all I can to help them in whatever little way I can." H.D. incorporates these words into *Hermetic Definition*, part 1, 13, 13–15.

52. On 7 September 1960, Pearson wrote: "All America is grateful to you for putting your touch on Rafer Johnson. You must have touched hard after his poor start, for to what else could we lay his recovery and victory in the Olympics. I suspect there will be much on them, and I will send accounts and pin-ups as they appear. He is certainly a handsome devil, a little I should think like a black-coffee Durand."

53. *Hermetic Definition*, part 1, 12, 1–3.

54. On 15 September 1960, Pearson responds to this comment: "I like very much the idea of the Durand decathlon image — a kind of dark Achilles, as there was a black Helen (wasn't there?)."

55. Pearson sent a clipping about the death of Lord Leslie Hayden-Guest, Stephen's father.

56. On 6 September [1960], H.D. wrote that she enjoyed Christoph de Nagy's book, *The Poetry of Ezra Pound: The Pre-Imagist Stage* (1960), "especially Yeats' contribution with his symbols and masks, re *Personae*." The book was one of the Cooper Monographs founded by Henry Lüdeke.

57. On 3 August 1960, H.D. asked Pearson to send "a Lorca translation," apparently for Bryher's birthday. She has a Penguin edition, translated by G. L. Gili, but the print is very small.

58. H.D. refers to a draft of Duncan's *HD Book*. In a note to his "Outline and Chronology," Duncan writes that a "first draft of the Book was done in 1961. . . . It had been commissioned by Norman Holmes Pearson as a Book for H.D.'s Birthday" (*Ironwood* 22 11, no. 2 [Fall 1983]: 65).

59. Charles Norman, *Ezra Pound* (New York: Macmillan, 1960).

60. On 24 September 1960, Pearson suggested that H.D. get a small TV for her room. He also vividly described a recent visit with H.D.'s grandchildren.

61. On 4 October 1960, Pearson agreed that *Helen in Egypt* was a good title. He also suggested that an introductory paragraph was needed to part 4 ("Winter Love") to make it like the other three sections.

62. On 7 October [1960], H.D. also mentioned this plan to meet the Pounds in Venice, despite Bryher's disapproval: "I won't tell Fido but Joan is mad about Venice and I said what fun if we could meet Ezra (and — whoever) there *for Xmas*. If you mention this, do it sub rosa, on a separate page, as Fido and I usually share letters from N[orman]."

63. In his letter of 30 September, Pearson enclosed a list of the talks he chose for a proposed MLA panel.

64. On 4 October 1960, Pearson mentions a letter from the South African Broadcasting Corporation asking permission to broadcast "At Baia."

65. H.D. refers to Elizabeth Schnack's German translation of *Bid Me to Live*. Aldington has helped with questions about foreign rights.

66. On 7 October [1960], H.D. also mentions having read *Yeats's Iconography* (London: Gollancz, 1960) by F. A. C. Wilson, the second of two books by Wilson sent by Bryher. The other was *W. B. Yeats and Tradition* (New York: Macmillan, 1958).

67. H.D. refers to interviews with Bryher that appeared in American newspapers.

68. Amos Doolittle, *Four Drawings of the Engagement at Lexington and Concord, April 19, 1775*, reprinted from Doolittle's original copperplate engravings with explanatory text by Rev. Edward G. Porter (Boston, 1883; reprint, 1903).

69. Mark Van Doren (1894–1972), American poet, awarded the Pulitzer Prize for *Collected Poems, 1922–1928* (1939); he was the master of ceremonies at the American Academy award ceremony.

70. On 25 October, Pearson described Bryher's recent visit with him. He also offered to fill out the questionnaire from *Who's Who* and assured H.D. he would take care of sending books to Duncan.

71. H.D. may refer to a Japanese translation of an article by Aldington on Lawrence of Arabia, with a reference to H.D.

72. On 15 November [1960], in response to Pearson's having written that he already signed a contract for *Helen* but could still negate it, H.D. wrote that she wanted to publish the poem without the Coda: "*Helen* but *not* Coda."

73. On 4 December [1960], H.D. continues to praise Charles Norman's book about Pound and asks Pearson to send Norman a copy of her *End to Torment*. She writes: "I think Ch[arles] N[orman] really cares. No — to me, it helped, opening up those decades — and he maintained strict censure, re Ez[ra's] anti-sem[itism], prob[ably] Mary hardly knew what was going on, so that part of the book might shock her."

74. On 25 November 1960, Pearson expresses his annoyance at the review but does not think it will influence anyone.

75. Pearson has recounted requests for permissions and so forth.

76. On 15 November [1960], H.D. wrote that she sent the "*Bosquet* — Thorn Thicket" pages for the archive.

77. On 22 December [1960], H.D. responds: "I could have written 5 or 10 or 20 times as much about the N.Y. visit. But I wanted to resolve or solve the *unser* story. I didn't want to be nasty about Dori — it was just shock on shock, the repercussions of all here."

78. Probably Boris de Rachewiltz, *Incontro con L'arte Africana* (Milan: A. Martello, 1959).

79. On 31 December 1960, Pearson described his activities at an MLA meeting.

80. Ovid, *Metamorphoses, A Complete New Version*, ed. Horace Gregory (1958).

81. On 28 December [1960] H.D. wrote that she carried Durand's reports from Algeria in her handbag. She quoted one in which he was said to be "'recovering from the effects of tear-gassing.'" On 31 December 1960, Pearson replied, "Poor Durand, what hell he must be going through with French Algeria. And shall we surmise that he may be pulled in several directions? I should think this was altogether likely. You caught him so well in the allusions in *Thorn*."

82. Pearson refers to Durand's death, from a heart attack, reported by the *New York Times* on 15 January 1961. The obituary mentions that Durand, a member of the French Resistance, was twice arrested by the Gestapo and twice escaped.

83. On 19 December 1960, *Newsweek* ran a firsthand account of fighting in the streets of Algiers, by Lionel Durand, titled, "Into the Eye of the Storm." It vividly described mob violence in the Casbah between Europeans and Moslems.

84. On 10 February [1960], H.D. mentions having read Daphne du Maurier's *The Infernal World of Branwell Brontë* (1961). She comments that she "seemed to find some resemblance to my own divided personality — or world."

85. H.D. refers to Pearson's having been marooned for a few days by a snowstorm.

86. H.D. refers to Dr. Brunner's Nervenklinik.

87. On 1 March [1961], H.D. reports the proposed sale of the Brunner clinic to a commune, which is causing hysteria among the patients. They have until December to relocate.

88. On 5 March 1961, Pearson mentioned that H.D. might meet him in Venice and that they might also see Ezra Pound. He plans a trip to Munich in June.

89. On 23 March 1961, Pearson responded: "To have a part of the series dedicated to me would make me very proud."

90. On 11 March 1961, Pearson mentioned Omar Pound's attempt to stop Charles Norman from publishing his book on Ezra Pound's trial for treason, *The Case of Ezra Pound* (1968).

91. On 27 March [1961], H.D. asked Pearson to change the last line to "*Night brings the Day.*" She continued: "I felt *dawn* toned it down, but the section is *Star of Day*, anyhow."

92. H.D. refers to "Final Proof," a poem by A. Rutledge on one of nine numbered postcards Pearson sent from Charleston, South Carolina, where he and Susan were vacationing.

93. On Easter Sunday, 1961, Pearson enclosed a description and map of the Brewton Corner in Charleston, South Carolina, a cluster of historic buildings and charming shops, with the comment that H.D. might enjoy staying at the Brewton Inn on her next visit to the United States.

94. Pearson sent H.D. a copy of a letter (13 April 1961) from James Laughlin praising her *End to Torment* as follows: "What a touching human document! And yet, she is such an artist, to the core, that consciously or not, she has given the thing real form as a story. I think this certainly should be published some day, and I hope you will keep in mind that we would be very keen to do it."

95. H.D. is changing her mind here. In her letter of 27 March 1961, she wished not to publish her memoir of Pound, after having seen a news clipping showing Pound meeting with the British fascist Oswald Mosley in Rome. She wrote: "It made me feel quite ill . . . *Mosley* smug and patronizing and E[zra] 'magrissimo,' the text said, and looking humiliatingly grateful for the pat on the head and the old chewed bone! *I felt I couldn't have the notes published after that.*"

96. On 15 April 1961, Pearson asked if he could send out lines from the new poem as a Christmas greeting.

97. On 15 April 1961, Pearson mentions a letter from Denise Levertov asking for a poem by H.D. for the *Nation*, where she is to be guest editor.

98. On 29 April [1961], H.D. commented again on the relation to historical reality of both *End to Torment* and *Hermetic Definition*: "But I do think, through you & Fido (who has not read the pages) that my E[zra] P[ound] & the later Durand sequence, do keep 'in time' and 'out of time' together. I didn't want to *escape* today. Today gave me the magic & mystery."

99. H.D. refers to her move to the Hotel Sonnenberg in Zurich.

100. On 15 April 1961, Pearson thanks her for permitting Horace Gregory to write the introduction for *Helen in Egypt*.

101. In a letter to Bryher on 5 August 1961, Pearson offered to shoulder the responsibility of H.D.'s care if she were brought to America: "I know now that my life will find what expression it has out of helping others who are more gifted and in a position to be more dedicated directly to art and its making. When she comes she will depend entirely on me, and there will be no other on whom she can or should depend."

102. On 27 September 1961, Bryher wrote to Pearson that Hilda was tremendously pleased with "the Helen," and that Heydt read it to her daily.

103. James Laughlin to Pearson, 20 April 1961, unpublished letter, BL.

104. In a letter to Peter Quartermain, dated 24 June 1968, Pearson mentions having negotiated with Alfred A. Knopf.

105. Peter Quartermain (1934–), English-born Canadian critic and professor at the University of British Columbia; founder of Slug Press, dedicated to producing limited editions of the works of contemporary writers.

106. Pearson to Peter Quartermain, 14 June 1968, unpublished letter, BL. The poems were published by New Directions in 1972, with an introduction by Pearson.

107. Lawrence Sanford Dembo (1929–), professor at the University of Wisconsin; works include *Conceptions of Reality in Modern American Poetry* (1966).

108. *Contemporary Literature* 10, no. 4 (Autumn 1969): 433.

109. Robert Kelly (1935–), American poet in the tradition of Pound and H.D. His poetry includes *A Joining: A Sequence for H.D.* (1967).

110. On 22 January 1973, to James Laughlin, Pearson commented on the title of *Trilogy*: "This gives me an occasion to ask what your reaction would be to calling the book for next November by the title of *War Trilogy*. Hilda herself never gave it a title except when she seemed to have used 'The Flowering of the Rod' as a group title for the trilogy as well as a single title for the last poem. It seems to me that this is not half as significant as *War Trilogy* would be. Moreover it has somehow adopted this title for itself, and is always referred to in that way. I think I started it but cannot be sure, since Hilda referred to it for convenience with the same phrase."

111. Pearson to J. Laughlin, 20 April 1971. The book was published in 1979.

112. Pearson to James Laughlin, 11 October 1971.

INDEX

The initials NHP are used for Norman Holmes Pearson in subentries and are alphabetized as Pearson. The initials H.D. are used for Hilda Doolittle in main entries and subentries and are alphabetized as H.D.

Doolittle, Helen Eugenia Wolle (H.D.'s mother), 5, 13(n30)

Doolittle, Hilda. *See* H.D.

Douglas, Norman, 43, 64(n73), 121

Dowding, Hugh, 22, 75, 79, 80, 81, 94, 104, 108, 113(nn45–47, 50), 196, 197

Duncan, Robert, 200, 242, 243, 244, 246, 250, 251(n12), 259(n148), 262, 270, 271, 277, 282, 283, 289, 293

Durand, Lionel, 262, 266, 267, 268–270, 271, 272, 273, 274–278, 279, 284, 287, 288, 291, 298(nn82, 83)

Dutton, Geoffrey (Piers Henry), 266, 268, 295(n20)

Dryden, John, 52

Edward the Martyr (king of England), 15(n52)

Edward II (king of England), 15(n52)

Egoist, The, 86

Eisenhower, Dwight David, 71

"Electra-Orestes" (H.D.), 97

Eliot, T. S., 22, 35, 42, 45, 61(n21), 65(n79), 74, 86, 153, 168(n21), 170(n43), 238, 258(n134)

Ellerman, Winifred. *See* Bryher

Ellis, Havelock, 237, 258(n128)

End to Torment: A Memoir of Ezra Pound (H.D.), 4, 12(n20), 169(n32), 196, 197–198, 233, 235, 241, 247, 249, 280, 291, 292, 293, 299(n94); dedicated to NHP, 198

English Institute, 70

escapism, 10, 19

Espérance (H.D.), 237–238, 239, 240, 280

etymology, 33, 45, 63(nn49, 50), 150

Euripides, 127, 128, 138, 140

Evergreen Review, 211, 256(n103)

Farrar, Strauss, and Young (publisher), 171(n60)

Faulkner, William, 124

Fido. *See* Bryher

Fields of Asphodel. See Asphodel

"Fire, Flood and Olive Tree." *See* "Body and Soul"

Fletcher, John Gould, 42, 58, 64(n66), 94

Flowering of the Rod, The (H.D.), 22, 46, 56–57, 64(n71), 87; dedicated to NHP, 55; translation, 191, 192

Ford, Ford Madox, 48, 112(n25), 204

Fourteenth of October, The (Bryher), 96

"Fragment Thirty-Six." *See* "Sapphic Fragments 36, 113"

"Fragment 113." *See* "Sapphic Fragments 36, 113"

Freud, Sigmund, 2, 3, 13(nn25, 29), 22, 47, 52, 81, 202. *See also* H.D.

Friar, Kimon, 141, 259(n145)

Frost, Robert, 25, 62(n36), 170(n43)

Garbo, Greta, 179

"Garden" (H.D.), 14(n50)

Gate to the Sea (Bryher), 217, 255(n72)

George VI (king of England), 121–122

"Georgius" (H.D.), 97

Gide, André, 189

Gift, The (H.D.), 3, 13(n29), 21, 26, 27, 29, 69, 71, 87, 92, 93, 105, 292

Giza (Egypt) archaeology, 157

Good Frend (H.D.), 46, 68, 156

Gray, Cecil (1895–1951), 3, 13(n24), 15(n53)

Greece, 10

Gregg, Frances (1885–1941), 5, 13(n31), 130

Gregory, Horace (1898–1982), 1, 11(n3), 59, 64(n65), 75, 76, 138, 184, 185, 186, 188, 189, 195(n31), 206, 240, 250, 281, 285, 291, 299(n100)

Gregory, Marya Zaturenska, 41, 64(n65), 125, 170(n43), 188, 206, 250

Grove Press, 184, 206, 223, 240, 242, 250, 253(n35), 255(n80), 264

Guest, Barbara, 18

"Guest, The" (H.D.), 68, 72, 75

Guthrie, Ramon, 223, 255(n83)

Harald, Michael, 241

Hathaway, Katharine, 7

Hausermann, H. W., 284

Hawthorne, Nathaniel, 74, 89, 95, 120, 179

Hayden-Guest, Stephen, 276, 277, 296(n43)

H.D. (Hilda Doolittle) (1886–1961): accent, 2; admirers of poetry and writing, 27, 40, 41–42, 71, 198, 200, 225–226, 291; American passport (1959), 233, 235–236; on American writing, 2, 69, 70, 73, 120; appearance, 1–2; astrology interest, 65(n81); "Autobiographical Notes," 4, 15(n62); awards, 4, 13(n27), 200, 232, 237, 238, 251(n11), 258(n139), 259, 261, 262–265, 266, 267, 294(n9); broken hip, 191, 192, 196; brothers and half-brothers, 5, 13(n30), 76; and Bryher, 1, 2, 11(n1), 17, 18, 20, 21, 22–23, 27, 28–29, 38, 44, 45, 49, 51, 58, 59, 65(n78), 71, 77, 86, 91, 97, 114(n58), 125, 142, 146, 147, 160, 165, 168–169(n28), 176, 179, 207, 232, 266, 269, 272, 277, 282–283 (See also Bryher); and Bryher correspondence at the Beinecke Library, 65(n78); on Bryher's writing, 96, 176, 281, 284; Bryn Mawr lecture preparation, 48–49, 53, 54; and cats, 39–40, 41, 93, 106, 107; childhood, 45; children, 5, 11(n1), 13(n24), 260(n160) (See also Schaffner, Perdita Macpherson); citizenship, 13(n27), 48, 50, 199, 200, 231, 233, 251(n11); in Cornwall, 36, 37–41; cousin (See Wolle, Francis); dream book (See "Hirslanden Notebook"); emotional breakdown and recovery, 3, 54–55, 56, 58, 67, 102; engagement, 5; on England, 17, 18; and English literary tradition, 67–68, 74; as expatriate, 70; family roots, 2, 11–12(n8), 13(n29), 68, 188; on Freud, 19, 45, 81, 89, 91, 150, 180, 182 (See also Tribute to Freud); friendships, 1, 4, 5, 11(n11), 12(nn12, 20), 13(nn23, 26), 18, 19, 23, 31, 60(nn5, 11), 68, 110(n2), 109, 176, 181, 262, 276; health, 187, 188, 195(n26), 291–292; on history, 120; homesickness, 31, 47–48, 59, 70, 199; husband (See Aldington, Richard); journal (See Bosquet [Thorn Thicket]; "Compassionate Friendship"); journal-essay (See H.D. by Delia Alton); literary

liaison officer, 25; lovers, 11(n1), 12(n12), 15(n53); malnutrition, 54; and music, 90–91; on Nazism, 2–3; neuralgia, 18; New York visits (1911, 1951, 1956), 1, 101–102, 187–188; noms de plume, 76, 77, 81, 115(n71), 121, 244, 250; novels, 1, 13(nn21, 32), 22, 25, 68, 116(n76), 176, 275; parents, 2, 4, 5, 13(nn29, 30), 186; and NHP (See H.D. and NHP); personality, 196; photographs of, 78, 102, 187, 223, 273, 282; poetry, 2, 4, 5, 7–8, 10, 12(n11), 14(n50), 25, 42, 62(n35), 68, 88, 96, 97, 98, 136–137, 138, 139, 140, 261; on poetry, 8–11, 26, 31, 32–33, 43, 49, 119, 127, 261–262, 292; as "Poets' Reading" participant (1943), 22, 61(n21); problems with publishers, 2, 12(n11), 47, 52, 104, 121, 142; psychiatrist, 46, 65(n81); psychoanalysis with Freud, 2, 3, 13(n25), 22; psychoanalysis with Schmideberg, 3, 13(n25), 55; reading, 40, 46, 47, 58, 66(n102), 70, 72–74, 75, 81, 92, 93, 95, 111(n13), 136–137, 138, 139, 140, 179, 184, 187, 209, 211, 212, 214, 243, 244, 250, 255(n80), 273, 282, 288, 298(n84); residences, 1, 3, 17, 22; roman à clef (See Bid Me to Live [A Madrigal]); romantic thralldom to male mentors, 3, 121, 167(n10), 175, 262; and Shakespeare, 19, 45–46, 55, 68, 74; short stories, 18, 25, 85, 87, 88; and spiritualism, 22, 68, 196; surgeries and recovery, 13(n26), 121, 136, 139, 141–142; and television, 280; translation, 161; typists, 79, 95; verse play (See "Hippolytus Temporizes"); war, effect on, 4, 5, 17–18, 20, 22, 34, 35–36, 40, 46, 47–48, 54, 55, 87; war trilogy poems, 22, 34, 42, 43, 45, 161, 292 (See also Trilogy); in Who's Who, 282, 297(n73); on writing, 31–32, 68, 83, 87; writings, 1, 3, 4, 11(n3), 13(n29), 18–19, 22, 24–25, 68, 69, 75, 76–77, 79, 82, 85, 87, 88, 89, 94, 95, 115(n71), 176, 196, 198, 261, 262, 275, 296(nn37–40); Yale archive, 4, 69, 85, 87, 89, 102, 103, 156. See also Pound, Ezra

H.D. and NHP: accepts Brandeis award for, 238; as Cavalier, 68; as Chevalier, 3–4, 96–97, 100, 104, 262; common experiences, 2, 3, 21, 25, 68, 176, 188; emotional ties, 3, 4, 6, 7–11, 31, 57–58, 68, 104, 119–120, 125, 137, 175, 262; first meeting, 1; on H.D.'s place as poet, 293; as literary executor, 75, 112(n35); as Lowndes Square group member, 20; number of letters exchanged, 4, 93; poems dedicated to, 22, 43, 55, 56, 64(n71); on poetry and prose copyright and contracts, 23–24, 45, 48, 75, 77, 78, 123, 131–132, 137–138, 155, 161, 184, 292; poetry books of H.D., 52; poetry list for, 51–52, 53; poetry manuscript of *The Gift*, 26, 27, 29; professional/creativity relationships, 3–4, 13(n27), 21–22, 34, 36, 42, 44, 45, 48, 49, 53, 56, 59, 68, 69, 71, 75, 78, 82, 83–84, 85, 86, 87–88, 89–90, 91, 94, 96, 97, 101, 104, 105–106, 107–108, 114(n62), 115(n69), 121, 124, 128, 130, 140, 142, 148–149, 155–156, 160–161, 163, 171(n60), 178–179, 181, 197, 233, 240, 242, 244–246, 247, 253(n37), 253–254(n50), 281–282, 284; "Puritan element," 17, 30, 38, 50, 55; reviews, 46; visit (1949), 292–293

H.D. Book, The (Duncan), 262, 279, 297(n58)

H.D. by Delia Alton (H.D.), 4, 5, 68, 69, 76, 100, 102, 104, 112–113(n37), 120, 125

Hedgehog, The (H.D.), 24, 104

Hedylus (H.D.), 25, 62(n33)

"Helen" (H.D.), 9, 14(n50)

Helen in Egypt (H.D.), 4, 11(n3), 119, 121, 126–130, 136, 138, 140, 146, 151, 152–153, 154, 155–156, 157, 158, 159, 160–161, 176, 180, 183, 189, 242, 281, 283, 292; Horace Gregory response to, 189, 195(n31); introduction by Horace Gregory, 291, 299(n100); introductory prose captions, 176, 177, 179; parts, 120, 121, 128, 136, 139–140, 143–144, 148–149, 161, 163, 164, 165–167, 242, 275, 280, 296(n37);

quoted, 126, 127; recorded by H.D., 176, 177, 178–179; title, 182, 183, 195(nn20, 21), 280, 281

Helforth, John, 29

Heliodora (H.D.), 12(n11), 24

Henderson, Dorothy Cole, 20, 81, 250, 267

Her (H.D.), 247

Hermetic Definition (H.D.), 261, 262, 277, 283, 288, 290, 291, 292, 293, 296(n51); dedicated to NHP, 289

HERmione (H.D.), 13(n32)

Herr, Mary, 19, 60(n11), 157, 275

Herrick, Robert, 52, 53

Herring, Robert, 20, 23, 43, 45, 54, 61(n25), 63(n59), 77, 79, 80, 81, 138

"Hesperia" (H.D.), 87

Hesse, Herman (1877–1962), 70, 91, 105, 106, 111(nn12, 13)

Heydt, Erich (*Unser*), 3, 13(n26), 121, 141, 142, 143, 152, 154, 155, 157, 160, 163, 165, 175, 177, 179, 182, 183, 187, 190, 198–199, 204, 206, 208, 209, 212, 216, 220, 231, 233, 237, 239, 243–244, 249, 263, 264, 266, 274, 279, 292; as literary character, 176, 181, 182, 285; marriage/wife (Dori), 232, 262, 265, 274, 275; visit with Robert Duncan, 244, 245

Hilda's Book (Pound), 130, 169(n32)

"Hippolytus Temporizes" (H.D.), 9–10, 14(n50), 24

"Hirslanden Notebook" (H.D.), 197, 200, 201, 252(n24)

history, mythopoeic view, 120

Hitler, Adolf, 2

Hogarth Press, 138

Holmes, Oliver Wendell, 35, 63(n54)

Hopkins, Gerard Manley, 96

Horton, David, 224, 229

Houghton Mifflin (publisher), 26

Howell. *See* Dowding, Hugh

Hudson Review, 153

Hudson River school, 137

Hughes, Randolph, 124, 168(n21)

Hulme, T. E. (1883–1917), 24, 62(n31)

Hunt, Isobel Violet, 73, 112(n25)

Pearson, Norman Holmes (*continued*)
297(n70) (*See also* Bryher); career
decision, 7, 19–20; characterized by
H.D., 7; childhood, 5–6; co-editor
of *Oxford Anthology of American
Literature*, 2, 11(n5), 12(n14); education,
2; on England, 21; in Europe (1930s), 2;
godfather to Valentine Schaffner, 101;
grandson, 217, 254(n71); Guggenheim
Fellowship, 76, 113(n38); on history, 120,
167(nn2, 3); illness, 5–6, 55, 56, 199; as
letter writer, 41, 50, 51, 70; literary
interests, 2, 19, 21, 22, 118(n113), 120, 136,
155, 170(nn45, 46), 179; in London
(WWII), 3, 19, 20, 30, 36; on male poets,
21; marriage (1941), 19, 20, 60–61(n17);
Mexican trip (1946), 50–51, 55, 56; in
New York (1945), 47, 48; at OSS, 19, 21,
55; OSS code name, 17; outlook on life,
6–7; parents, 5, 6, 191; and Perdita
Schaffner, 28, 62(n38), 101; Ph.D. (1941),
19; physical disability, 5–6, 19; poetry, 2;
and *Poetry*, 113(n40); on poetry, 52, 57;
and Pound, 89–90, 94, 98–99, 111(n11),
130, 131, 132–135, 145, 152, 167(n8),
169(nn32, 33), 171(nn58, 59), 197–198,
213–215, 218, 224–225, 228, 229,
257(n114), 287; sister, 6; son, 42;
stepdaughters, 20, 60–61(n17), 136,
183, 257(n126), 278; ulcer, 237; at
University of Colorado, 19; wartime
service awards, 55; wife (*See* Pearson,
Susan Silliman Bennett); writings, 82,
87, 89, 94, 96, 108, 114(n60), 118(n114),
124; at Yale University, 1, 3, 7, 12(n10),
19, 52, 68, 69, 110(n1), 180. *See also* H.D.
and NHP
Pearson, Susan Silliman Bennett (NHP's
wife), 47, 55, 59, 60–61(n17), 65(n83),
66(n102), 105, 106, 108
Perrault, Charles, 41, 64(n64)
Perse, St.-John (Alexis Saint Léger Léger),
261, 262, 288, 290, 294(n1)
Peter Pan (Barrie), 98, 117(n97)
Pisan Cantos, The (Pound), 42, 64(n68),

70, 100, 115(n72), 121, 133, 134, 145,
158–159, 168(n21), 199, 233
Plank, George, 20, 30, 31, 62(n41), 150, 154,
188, 200, 234, 269
Poe, Edgar Allan, 74, 136, 137
Poetry: A Magazine of Verse (1912),
15(n54), 72, 96, 97, 113(n40), 200, 232,
239, 258–259(n139)
Poet's Club (1908), 62(n31)
Poets of the English Language, The (Pearson
and Auden), 96 120, 146–147, 150, 154
"Poets' Reading, The" (1943), 22, 61(n21)
Pool (publisher), 62(n39)
"Pool, The" (H.D.), 10, 14(n50)
Pound, Ezra (1885–1972), 2, 3, 4, 40, 95,
108–109, 116(n74), 125, 131, 170(n42), 181,
189, 195(n34), 198, 204–205, 233, 238,
251(n8), 255(n83), 256(n104), 258(n133),
278; biography, 280, 283, 298(n73);
Bollingen Prize, 93, 111(n11), 115(n72);
daughter (*See* Rachewiltz, Mary de);
engagement to H.D., 5, 12(n20); H.D.
on, 8, 90, 93–94, 100, 102, 114(n64), 121,
142, 155, 156–157, 159, 169–170(nn40,
43), 175, 180–181, 190, 192, 197, 201, 202,
203, 204, 211–212, 213, 216, 217, 219–220,
221, 231–232, 233, 234–235, 238, 241, 242,
243, 248, 249, 272, 283, 286, 289, 290 (*See
also End to Torment: A Memoir of Ezra
Pound*); on H.D.'s poetry, 98, 248,
252(n21), 254(n57); health, 247, 262;
photographs, 215, 254(n67); release
and return to Italy (1958), 221, 228; son
(*See* Pound, Omar Shakespear); at
St. Elizabeths hospital, 98–100,
117(nn98, 101), 121, 132–135, 136, 153, 197,
225; translation, 153–154, 173(n82); wife
(Dorothy), 135, 198, 217, 225, 229, 291;
and World War II, 64(n61), 69–70;
writings, 90, 130, 163, 169(n32) (*See also
Pisan Cantos*). *See also* Bryher; Pearson,
Norman Holmes
Pound, Omar Shakespear, 145, 146,
171–172(n64), 229, 231, 356(n107),
291, 299(n90)

Pratt, Margaret Sniveley, 181, 187
Pre-Raphaelite circle, 4, 68, 69, 74–75, 76, 112(n25)
"Priest" (H.D.), 97
Proctor, Katherine, 90
psychoanalysis, 120. *See also* H.D.

Quartermain, Peter, 292, 300(n105)

Rachewiltz, Mary de, 136, 170(n44), 198, 238, 241, 242, 247, 285
Rattray, David, 197, 223
Red Roses for Bronze (H.D.), 24, 88
remembering, 105, 118(nn109, 110), 121, 239
"Responsibilities" (H.D.), 98
rivers, 9, 33
"rosenkavalier," 176
Rossetti, Dante Gabriel, 77, 82, 83
Rossetti, Elizabeth Siddal, 4, 69, 76, 82, 83, 84
Ruan (Bryher), 274, 281; reviews, 283
Rudge, Olga, 136, 170(nn42, 44), 198
Rummel, Walter Morse, 90, 116(n76)
"Running" (Schaffner), 21
Russell, Alys, 96, 117(n91)
Russell, Peter, 130

Sackville-West, Vita, 61(n21)
"Sagesse" (H.D.), 196, 199, 208, 210, 211, 253–254(n50), 254(n52), 256(n103), 257(n123); dedication, 232, 274
Santayana, George, 140–141, 171(n54)
"Sapphic Fragments 36, 113" (H.D.), 8, 9, 14(n50)
Sarah Lawrence College, 50
Sarton, May, 71, 111(n17)
Schaffner, John, 94, 234
Schaffner, Perdita Macpherson (1919–), 5, 11(n1), 13(n24), 18, 20, 27, 35, 38, 47, 50, 53, 58, 60(n16), 71, 77, 91, 93, 105, 179, 238; children, 100, 102, 105, 117(nn100, 102, 104), 125, 136, 168(n26), 184, 266; marriage (1950), 94, 95; in OSS office, 28, 41, 62(n38); in U.S., 58, 69, 85; visits

to H.D., 125, 164, 165, 239; writings, 21, 61(n21)
Schelling, Felix Emmanuel, 86, 115(n65)
Schmideberg, Walter, 3, 13(n25), 53–54, 55, 58, 66(n97), 141, 152, 154, 155, 157, 160, 161–162, 163–164, 184
Schnack, Elizabeth, 191, 192, 223, 255(n84), 278, 284
Schur, Max, 202, 209, 252(n25)
Scribner's (publisher), 292
Sea Garden (H.D.), 24
"Sea Gods" (H.D.), 10, 14(n50)
Second American Caravan, The, 25, 62(n34)
Selected Poems (H.D.), 123, 176, 184, 185, 191, 200, 205, 206, 208, 253(n35), 261; dedication, 188, 253(n39); reviews, 254(n53)
Shakespeare, William, 19, 45, 51, 72, 74, 137, 155, 179: *See also Good Frend*
Shaw, George Bernard, 90
Shelley, Percy Bysshe, 21
Shepard, William Pierce, 90, 116(n74)
Sherwood, Robert E., 110(n2)
Siddal, Elizabeth. *See* Rossetti, Elizabeth Siddal
"Sigil" (H.D.), 97
Silver Wings (Butler), 138–139, 141, 191, 195(n33)
Sinclair, May, 73, 112(n26)
Sitwell, Edith (1887–1964), 20, 22, 23, 29, 34, 48, 49, 50, 59, 61(nn21, 26), 71, 84, 85, 103
Sitwell, Osbert (1892–1969), 20, 23, 25, 32, 43, 44, 48, 49, 59, 61(nn21, 26), 64–65(n74), 84, 86, 103
Sitwell, Sacheverell (1897–1987), 23, 61(n26), 62(n43); wife, 50, 65(n92)
Smith, Logan Pearsall, 49, 69(n91), 96
"Song" (H.D.), 8, 14(n50)
Spann, Marcella, 198, 242
Spenser, Edmund, 51
Square Dollar series, 108, 109, 118(n113), 134, 198, 219
St. Dunstan (London church), 28
Stein, Gertrude, 137

Stevens, Wallace, 179, 212
Stevenson, Robert Louis, 212, 233
Stone, Faith (Mrs. Compton Mackenzie), 22, 61(n20)
Stratford-upon-Avon (England), 45, 46, 47
stream of consciousness narrative technique, 112(n26), 204
Swann, Thomas Burnett, 262, 265, 273, 277, 294(n5), 295(n15)
Swinburne, Algernon Charles, 124, 125, 168(n21)
Switzerland, 55, 70. *See also* Vaud; Vevey
Sword Went Out to Sea, The (H.D.), 22, 68, 69, 76, 79, 88, 89, 94, 95, 96, 102, 104–105, 113(nn45, 46, 48), 121, 128, 139, 155, 157; characters, 81, 104; NHP as literary character, 75, 81, 112(n35)
Synthesis of a Dream (H.D.), 87

"Tatter" (H.D.), 296(n38)
Taylor, Rachel Annand, 109, 118(n116)
Teasdale, Sara, 273, 295(n33)
Tenney, Calvin, 59, 66(n104)
tin mines, 11
Trenoweth (Cornwall flower farm), 61(n29)
Trevelyan, Humphrey, 30, 62(n42)
Tribute and Circe, The (H.D.), 24
Tribute to Freud (H.D.), 13(n29), 47, 52, 68, 139, 142, 143, 156, 171(n60), 181, 184, 185, 202, 207, 252(n27), 261; acceptance, 188; introduction, 186; NHP's jacket copy, 184; reviews, 185, 195(n24), 200, 253(n48)
Tribute to the Angels (H.D.), 22, 36, 37, 43, 52, 63(n58), 201; review by NHP, 46
Trilogy (H.D.), 3, 19, 43, 45, 71, 88, 111(n19), 138, 179; reviews, 45, 242
Turner, W. J., 61(n21)
Two Cities (journal), 275

University of Colorado, 19, 111(n21)
Unser. See Heydt, Erich
Untermayer, Jean Starr, 103, 118(n108)
Unwin (publisher), 47
Usual Star, The (H.D.), 24

"Vale Ave" (H.D.), 196, 197, 200, 205, 206, 207, 243, 250
van der Leeuw, J. J., 202, 252(n27), 268
Van Doren, Mark, 282, 297(n69)
Vaud (Switzerland), 9, 10, 87
Venice (Italy), 283, 289
Vevey (Switzerland), 1, 17, 67
Vienna (Austria), 2, 3
Viking (publisher), 80, 102

Wake (journal), 96
Waley, Arthur, 50, 61(n21), 65(n94)
Walls Do Not Fall, The (H.D.), 21–22, 31, 32–33, 34, 37, 42, 65(n79), 127; NHP's jacket copy and ad, 33, 42, 63(n53); reviews, 44, 64–65(n74), 72
Waluga, Joan, 179, 208, 209, 227, 264, 282
Warren, Robert Penn, 180
Wegelin, Christof, 290
Wells, Julia R., 91, 116(n79)
West, Rebecca, 93
"What Do I Love" (H.D.), 18–19, 97, 103, 118(n106), 179
White, Eric Walter, 205, 266–267
"White Rose and the Red, The" (H.D.), 4, 65(n80), 68, 69, 75–76, 77, 82–84, 85, 88, 89, 91, 92, 96, 128, 170(n50)
Whitman, Walt, 51
Wilder, Thornton, 22, 46, 65(n79), 75, 111(n2), 151
Williams, William Carlos (1883–1963), 2, 12(n14), 71, 86, 106–107, 109, 114(n64), 141, 179
Wilson, Colin, 240, 259(n141)
Windsor, Rita, 48, 50, 53
Winks, Robin, 19
"Winter Love" (H.D.), 198, 238–239, 241, 242, 248–249, 257(n112), 280, 292
Within the Walls (H.D.), 88
Wolffe, Kurt, 157, 162, 229
Wolle, Francis, 72, 111(n21), 267
Woolf, Leonard, 138
Woolford, Miss (typist), 79, 95, 180, 239
Wordsworth, William, 51
World War I (1914–1918), 4, 5, 18, 70
World War II (1939–1945), 3, 17, 18, 24,

35–36, 45, 61(n30); semireligious zeal, 21

Wormser, Rene, 79, 80

Writing on the Wall (H.D.), 22, 35, 53–54, 63(nn54, 55)

Yale French Studies, 136, 170(n47)

Yale Review, 96, 117(n92)

Yale University: American Studies program, 52, 66(n95); Collections of American Literature, 69; H.D. / Marianne Moore exhibition, 89; H.D. exhibition (1956), 176, 181 221; Sitwells visit, 84, 114(n57). *See also* H.D.; Pearson, Norman Holmes

Yank (newspaper), 42, 64(n69)

Yeats, William Butler, 48, 51, 90, 282; H.D.'s review of poetry, 98

Yucatan, 53